D0394453

HIGH-PROFILE CRIMES

HIGH-PROFILE CRIMES

When Legal Cases Become Social Causes   LYNN S. CHANCER

The University of Chicago Press, Chicago and London

Lynn S. Chancer is professor in the Department of
Sociology and Anthropology at Fordham University. She
is the author of two other books, *Reconcilable Differences* and
Sadomasochism in Everyday Life.

The University of Chicago Press, Chicago 60637
The University of Chicago Press, Ltd., London
© 2005 by The University of Chicago
All rights reserved. Published 2005
Printed in the United States of America
14 13 12 11 10 09 08 07 06 05   1 2 3 4 5
ISBN: 0-226-10112-6   (cloth)

Library of Congress Cataloging-in-Publication Data

Chancer, Lynn S., 1954–
    High-profile crimes : when legal cases become social
causes / Lynn S. Chancer.
        p.   cm.
    Includes bibliographical references and index.
    ISBN 0-226-10112-6 (cloth : alk. paper)
        1. Crime—Sociological aspects—United States. 2.
Crime—United States—Public opinion. 3. Trials—United
States—Public opinion. 4. Crime and the press—United
States. 5. Crime in mass media. 6. Mass media and public
opinion—United States. I. Title.

HV6789.C397 2005
364.1—dc22   2005009143

♾ The paper used in this publication meets the minimum
requirements of the American National Standard for
Information Sciences–Permanence of Paper for Printed
Library Materials, ANSI Z39.48-1992.

CONTENTS

The Larger Symbolism of Symbolic Cases

After nearly a decade spent working on this book, I view it as more than only an analysis of a brand of high-profile crime cases. My interest in the subject was initially sparked by the much publicized 1983 rape case in New Bedford, Massachusetts, on which the movie *The Accused* was based. This interest then led me to consider later cases that similarly grew in the 1980s through the mid-1990s to become symbols of racial and gender-based discrimination in the United States. However, as research continued and my own life unfolded alongside, the book gradually itself became for me symbolic of larger intellectual issues.

I am often reminded of the book's analytic framework at regular intervals when discussing, and sometimes becoming worked up about, news events that surface far from these crime cases' locales. For instance, immediately before the United States invaded Iraq in 2003, sparking demonstrations throughout the world, I was struck by the predominantly "pro" and "con" framework of debate that came to typify the media's and the public's discussion of the possibility of war; serious consideration of any "third" possibility receded into the background. Indeed, during the 2004 presidential campaign, which pitted positions on the Iraq War taken by John Kerry against those by incumbent President George W. Bush, I noticed high-level supporters of the latter (as well as the president himself) challenging Kerry as to whether his positions fit into a dualistic framework. Did Kerry support the war and vote for it, or did he not? In this context attempts at articulating more complex or "nuanced" positions arguably placed a politician at a disadvantage.

In much the same way, old antagonisms between Israelis and Palestinians have continued to escalate in a seemingly endless spiral of violence. A possible "third option" to resolving the conflict—one that is not simply "pro-Israel" or "pro-Palestinian"—is hard to recognize and sustain amidst primarily two-sided understandings of this conflict. Thus posing alternative formulations may be unsettling, and perhaps even threatening, in a world where one side "versus" the other formulations are more usual than exceptional.

Questioning engrained habits of thought is not new for me. My first book, *Sadomasochism in Everyday Life: Dynamics of Power and Powerlessness*, was inspired by debates in the early 1980s in which feminists took positions either for or against sadomasochism as a sexual practice—unwittingly, it seemed, since much of feminist theory has underscored gendered troubles wrought by overly simple and sometimes specious dichotomies (between, for instance, masculinities and femininities, emotionality and rationality, public versus private). In that work, I contended that sadomasochism itself needed to be redefined, and that sadomasochistic dynamics are commonly encountered within work, gender, and racial relations as well as in sexuality. Consequently an "either/or" framework failed to capture the complexity of this subject as well.

My second book, *Reconcilable Differences: Beauty, Pornography and the Future of Feminism*, focused on four additional contemporary debates: pornography, prostitution, beauty, and violence against women. Here again I found that bare "either/or" formulations proved overly rigid and resulted in dividing feminists, sometimes bitterly, from one another. In place of framing the debates only in terms of "pro" and "con," I suggested alternative approaches that could bypass the political and ideological stalemates on these issues.

The present book obviously relates to my prior work, but this study is also fresh for me in several respects. For one thing, *High-Profile Crimes*, relying on interview data and newspaper materials, is simultaneously an empirical and theoretical work; unlike my previous books, this one required investigating the social world through primary as well as secondary sources. As a result, I hope to show more concretely than elsewhere how structuring a debate merely in terms of "us" against "them" both straitjacketed and magnified debates in crimes that politically exploded, merging "legal cases" and "social causes." I hope this use of primary sources helps to enliven the broader points of my argument, especially in those chapters that both narrate and analyze the 1989–90 "Central Park jogger" and the "Bensonhurst" cases. My intention in these chapters, as in the book as a whole, is to illuminate patterns in American culture generally, certainly not to settle questions of guilt or innocence in particular criminal cases.

Significantly, though, the "Central Park jogger" case became news again in 2002, fourteen years after the initial crime, when a belated confession and new DNA evidence shed doubt on the convictions of already incarcerated youths—so much so that several convictions were overturned and it was questionable whether there had been a gang rape at all. In the face of this development, however, it turned out that surprisingly little of this book needed rewriting. The focus on cultural patterns of simplistic "either/or" debates and on the merging of legal cases and social causes in American culture still seemed pertinent. Indeed, I believe the book's basic framework of analysis provides some insight into how the original outcome of the "Central Park jogger" case was possible. For a rush to judgment and other problematic consequences can result when legal cases become enmeshed with controversial social causes. In some instances, as this book's conclusion suggests, the result may be detrimental to both adjudicating of individual legal cases and forwarding of broader social values and social movement claims.

High-Profile Crimes explores in more concrete detail than my previous works both the sources and consequences of cultural habits that have led to thinking and feeling in dualistic terms. To the question "From where do two-sided orientations emanate, and how are they reproduced?" I respond in chapter 1 that the media and law both have overlapping "institutional logics." Later chapters develop the argument that media and law, separately as well as jointly, reinforce this convention of using two-sided (and often antagonistic) frameworks of discussion. This is not to say that such two-sided parameters of debate are not sometimes valid. Such a conclusion would be simplistic itself. For example, whether someone did or did not commit a particular murder or rape is by its very character an "either/or" question. Likewise, certain pressing decisions by political leaders—say, whether to invade a foreign country—require making a choice that cannot be gotten around by appeals to sometimes nebulous "third way" alternatives.

Rather, my intention in this book is to argue that discerning when two-sided formulations are appropriate and when they limit our cultural imagination and sense of options matters. Otherwise our extraordinarily complicated universe may be conceived too starkly and simplistically in terms of "us versus them." Such conceptions can become self-fulfilling prophecies that bode serious consequences by leading to further situations that necessitate "either/or" decisions in turn. Moreover, the deep familiarity of dualistic frameworks noted here also fits with long-standing American beliefs in individualism and in using the legal system to resolve myriad social problems. Yet civil or criminal litigation usually only settles one case; litigiousness may therefore co-exist with the cultural propensity to individualize problems rather than address them structurally and systematically.

Nor do I mean to ignore, or to deny, that many people find dualistic frameworks satisfying and sometimes even pleasurable. Such frameworks allow us to "root" for one side or the other and to express frustrations and resentments that might otherwise have no clear outlets. This is appropriate in some situations like sports, where rules that produce clear-cut winners are easily justified and often bring enjoyment to participants and spectators. But in high-profile crime cases of the kind this book analyzes, another troubling consequence that arises from a dualistic framework of debate—regardless of whether some participants at some level find it satisfying—is that underlying social tensions may, through this framework, be rechanneled rather than eased. Once social problems are debated within a limited two-sided structure, "social-psychic dynamics" (as I refer to them in chapter 6) that recall Freudian concepts—though occurring at the level of groups or subgroups—are likely to ensue.

For example, rather than holding "society" accountable for discriminatory practices involving gender, race, and class that come to light in the course of a criminal case, angered energies may find substitutive—or, as Freud might say, displaced—outlets. Thus parties aligned on either "side" of a case may unduly blame victims, dismiss mistreatment in the press or criminal justice system of accused defendants, or, for that matter, accord to "the media" more culpability than may be reasonable.

Therefore, another concern of the book is the way conscious and unconscious social processes are constantly intertwined. This rich nexus also is limited rather than illuminated by the rote application of dualistic formulation. Are people really conscious of the ambivalent effects, or the sources, of the cultural phenomenon that I examine through the lens of high-profile criminal cases? I think it is more accurate to say that conscious and unconscious processes are in an ongoing process of intercourse with one another, just as our emotions and rationality are interwoven in complicated ways as we engage in social life. Sociologists are still learning how to depict and to theorize such interaction. If the present work manages to convey at least some sense of the simultaneously conscious-and-unconscious, emotional-and-rational, character of everyday social life as can be glimpsed through attention to high-profile crimes, I feel it will have made a contribution that is both different from and related to perspectives developed in my previous works.

But, in other respects, the book has a quite specific focus. For one, I do not consider criminal cases that do not meet the criteria of "provoking assaults" as defined in chapter 1. Thus I believe it accurate to say only that the book is suggestive about a particular kind of criminal case; I leave it to others to explore those cases that are overlooked in media coverage or that receive only moderate publicity. Moreover, I have focused in this volume only on high-profile crimes in the United States, bracketing the intriguing question of whether this book depicts what is a distinctively American cultural phenomenon. This, too, is a question that merits further research. For example, in the British context, a high-profile crime case that involved a racial bias crime—the murder of a boy named Stephen Laurence—came to media attention in 1993 and sparked protests against police mishandling of the case that eventually resulted in demands for policy changes.[1]

Finally, I have not devoted much attention to cases that foreground distinctions of class rather than discriminations based on gender and race. One reason for not delving into cases like the savings and loan scandals of the 1980s and 1990s that involved Michael Milken or Charles Keating—or, more recently, the Enron scandals of 2002—is that these cases did not provoke responses on the part of social and community activists in the same way as did the "Central Park," "Bensonhurst," "Rodney King," and "O.J. Simpson" cases. Yet, it would be productive to explore why cases that feature the element of class are less likely to anger us or receive as much media attention as those involving gender- and race-based violent crimes.

One might argue that the recent case involving Martha Stewart attracted sufficient public interest and media coverage to fit within the parameters of this book's subject. The famed home expert/decorator was convicted of lying to investigators about using insider information to sell off a portion of her financial investments. Perhaps owing to her status as a female celebrity (thereby giving the story a peg that tapped cultural interest in matters of gender), the "Stewart" case received far more "human interest" attention when it appeared in the news than surfaced, by comparison, in coverage of the Enron case. Nonetheless, by the definition set forth in chapter 1, the "Martha Stewart" case could not be said to be a provoking assault. Although the icon "Martha Stewart" came somewhat fuzzily to symbolize the problem of rich people assuming they can get away with breaking the law—thereafter receiving less punitive sentences than would be meted out to others—public reactions did not mushroom over symbolic sides in the way that occurred in other cases this book details. Given that class-related concerns seem generally less resonant than gender- or race-based ones in the U.S. context, hardly did social movement groups become involved or spring into existence around this case; nor did community figures, from politicians to religious figures, feel compelled to comment on the case's symbolic implications. Consequently the "Martha Stewart" case, too, confirms that the subject of how and why class-related crimes do not stimulate the kinds of politicized debate found in High-Profile Crimes also cries out for further exploration than is provided in the account that follows.

ACKNOWLEDGMENTS

Over the years spent researching and writing this book, I received more en-couragement and support from colleagues, students, close friends, and fam-ily members than can easily be acknowledged. In advance, therefore, I apol-ogize to anyone whose name—and support—I fail to mention.

Among my various colleagues over the years, Bob Alford immediately comes to mind. During the five years or more of our good friendship, many lovely evenings were spent talking about this project and his work as well (Bob was working on a project that drew on issues also raised in the book). I am deeply saddened that Bob died of cancer before he could see this book in print, but am grateful for all his help during my years at Barnard College and Columbia University; he was a wonderful scholar and editor as well as friend. I also appreciate the comments and thoughts of many other colleagues who, in various capacities, listened to presentations or read through drafts of the book's chapters. Among them are Gregg Barak, Susan Caringella MacDon-ald, Patricia Clough, Bill DiFazio, Susanna Danuta Walters, Cynthia Epstein, Mark Fishman, David Garland, Drew Humphries, Eugene McLaughlin, Kelly Moore, Francesca Polletta, Jonathan Rieder, Ruth Sidel, Susan Silbey, Cath-erine Silver, Susanna Danetta Walters, Loic Wacquant, Ellen Willis, Christine Williams, and Eviatar Zerubavel. Jon Rieder consistently believed in the value of my work and ideas: for his efforts on my behalf, I thank him sincerely. Among many other colleagues in the Sociology Department at Fordham Uni-versity, Doyle McCarthy was also wonderfully supportive, responding with great interest to this subject matter and my work as a whole. Without her support and that of Rosemary Cooney and Orlando Rodriguez, also at Fordham, this book might never have been completed. Isabel Pinedo, my friend and media expert colleague from Hunter College, has urged me for years to finish this book so she could use it in her classes, as has Susanna Danuta Walters, my funny and smart friend newly moved to Indiana. Ruth Sidel has provided ongoing inspiration through this and earlier books; she is a wonderful, supportive, and extremely special friend. I also wish to thank David Meyer, who read with great care chapters I presented at Chuck Tilly's "Contentious Politics" workshop at Columbia University and encouraged me to write this book—as in the end, I did—for myself.

Over the years, a number of student assistants helped me in a variety of ways. Beverly Watkins was a terrific early researcher, as was Isolde Brielmaier and Abhaya Kaufman (who later contributed editorial commentary, and enthusiasm, as well). Abhaya and Ayana Byrd accompanied me on research trips to Los Angeles while students at Barnard; I'm sure I learned from them as much as I hope they did from me. Thanks for research help is also deserved by then-graduate student, but now professor, Pamela Donovan. In addition to assisting with the journal I coedit, *Theoretical Criminology*, Amy Desautels at Fordham was also a fine reader of the finished manuscript and a great help in pulling everything together.

Among friends who are not also academics, I thank Karen Williams for voluntarily accompanying me on two occasions when I did research in Florida and Indiana. She, too, provided consistent encouragement. Fran Jacobs and the late Robert Peak loved the book's argument and listened for years to descriptions of its progress, as did other dear friends David Forbes, Woody Goldberg, Joseph Gubbay, Jessica Karmen, Andrew Karmen, Iris Lopez, Janet Poppendieck, and Leslie Salzman. I am also extremely grateful to Jackie Dryfoos for wanting me to complete this book and for her faith in me.

I deeply regret that my mother-in-law and father-in-law Phyllis and Julius Jacobson will not see this book in print. They were both always interested in my ideas and work, taking pride in any and all my accomplishments, and always treating me as a daughter. Blossom, too, provided loving support.

As in my two previous books, I cannot end these acknowledgments without expressing gratitude to two people whose place in my life is unique—however to their names, so very special to me, I now add a third. To Anna, thank you for always being there, even in the post-9/11 years that were so tragic for you. To Michael, words continue to pale at how much you mean, have meant, and will always mean to me. And, to Alexander, my sweet and intelligent five-year-old, thank you for putting up with your mommy during the first (stressful) months and years of your life. If anything I write contributes even a little to a better world for you, it will have been worth it.

PRESENTING PROVOKING ASSAULTS
From New York to Los Angeles

CHAPTER 1

When Cases Become Causes

ROY BLACK: When you defend a case like this [the William Lozano case, in which a police officer was convicted of killing a black motorcyclist on Martin Luther King's birthday in 1991, after which riots broke out in Miami], everyone all of a sudden forgets about everything except that if we can get this guy in jail that's going to remedy everything that's wrong with Miami. . . . Because we don't want to confront our racial problems. We don't want to really solve them, because we can't afford to solve them. We don't have the money or the time or the effort to put into solving the racial problems of Miami.

LYNN CHANCER: So cases like this one, a high-profile crime case . . .

RB: In the "Lozano" case, it's no longer William Lozano, it has an image above and beyond whomever he is as an individual. He becomes a symbol. If we convict this cop, it'll prove that blacks have a right to participate in government, that they are really not being oppressed, it shows that we can get fairness in the courts.[1]

AL SHARPTON: Lynn, that's your name, right? I'll guarantee you, the average white in this town doesn't realize that every day we sit here handling cases. Many never hit the papers. They think that I'm somewhere asleep until a big case happens (clap of hands) and we run out. What they don't understand is many of the cases, we made big. We made Bensonhurst big. With the marches. We made Howard Beach big.

LYNN CHANCER: So do you feel like these cases become important . . .

AS: Yeah, they are very important. And they are politics. They're important in a judicial sense, and they're important politically. I think Yusef Hawkins [young black man shot by a group of young whites in Bensonhurst, Brooklyn, in 1989] got David Dinkins elected mayor in New York City. . . . When people turned on the news, and started seeing nigger-calls, it energized the local black community to vote. And now Crown Heights may get him unelected. Yes, absolutely. These cases are very important.[2]

In 1998–99, two high-profile crimes—which would come to be known as the "Louima" and "Diallo" cases—took place in New York City, each involving allegations of police brutality. After the second incident, in which four members of the Police Department fired forty-one bullets and killed an unarmed Guinean man, Amadou Diallo, demonstrations against these and other incidents of police misconduct took place daily outside 1 Police Plaza. For the first time during his tenure in office, Mayor Rudolph Guiliani and his philosophy of crime control encountered visible opposition.

Ironically, Giuliani himself had been elected in 1993 in the wake of another high-profile criminal case that he had used effectively to criticize his opponent, then-Mayor David Dinkins. In the Crown Heights section of Brooklyn, rioting erupted after an African American child named Gavin Cato was run over by a Hasidic rabbi, who sped from the scene; that same evening, a group of African American youths, apparently motivated by revenge, stabbed a Jewish student named Yankel Rosenbaum to death. Giuliani contended that Dinkins had reacted belatedly, and inadequately, to each of these racially charged events.

Looking back even further, to 1989, one can see that Dinkins too had arguably been swept into office on the tide of other high-profile crime cases. Following the "Howard Beach" homicide and "Central Park jogger" rape cases, which generated broad discussions of both racial tensions and, in the latter crime, gender biases, the murder in Bensonhurst of a young black youth named Yusef Hawkins triggered demonstrations only days before a Democratic mayoral primary. As activist Al Sharpton noted at the time, and media commentators likewise observed, hardly did it seem coincidental that on the heels of these demontrations three-time Mayor Edward Koch was defeated and Dinkins became the city's first African American mayor.

Nor were connections between high-profile crime cases perceived on the East Coast alone. The 1991 case of Latasha Harlins, in which a female Korean grocery store owner was sentenced only to community service after shooting an unarmed black teenager to death, stoked racial tensions in Los Angeles while Mayor Tom Bradley was in office. This case slightly predated the beating of Rodney King in March 1991 by white police officers. In April 1992, when riots in Los Angeles erupted on the same day four officers were acquitted of attacking King, a white truck driver named Reginald Denny was assaulted by four black young men. As the racial focus of these highly profiled crime cases shifted from an act of whites-against-a-black to an act of blacks-against-a-white, Republican Richard Riordan beat Democratic candidate Michael Woo to become Los Angeles's mayor. This occurred in June 1993, several months before Republican Rudy Giuliani defeated David Dinkins, a Democrat, in the New York City mayoral race against an analogously shifting backdrop of concerns about racial reversals.[3]

Thus these high profile crimes were incidents with which local politics—in New York, in Los Angeles—were interwoven. Other highly profiled crime cases were equally controversial, though less closely associated with particular urban conflicts. Publicized crimes like those involving William Kennedy Smith, Mike Tyson, and O.J. Simpson also called forth passionate argumentation; like the "Central Park jogger" case, they highlighted controversies of gender and/or racial discrimination. In the 1991–92 "Smith" and "Tyson" cases, the form of violence against women at issue was rape; in the "Simpson" case it was domestic violence that may have led to murder. Issues of class inequities were also present in the "Smith," "Tyson," and "Simpson" cases, though not necessarily openly flagged as such in the discussions generated by these incidents.

But why consider these cases together—what do they have in common? This book contends that these and other locally and nationally known incidents became culturally resonant in the United States of the 1980s and 1990s as high-profile crimes, or "provoking assaults," became vehicles for crystallizing, debating, and attempting to resolve contemporary social problems. The intense debate surrounding these cases often entailed allegations of discrimination based on race or gender that became linked with incidents of assault, rape, or homicide. Likely it was not accidental that such criminal cases were able to gain prominence after the rise of the civil rights, black nationalist, feminist, and gay rights movements during the 1960s and 1970s, movements that catapulted "identity politics" into American consciousness. But the cases also surfaced during the Reagan–Bush years of the 1980s and early 1990s when many social movements were on the defensive. Indeed, as scholars in the "social problems" tradition have suggested, high-profile crimes of the 1980s and 1990s may have offered a way of calling attention to issues of discrimination that otherwise, at that time, might have been overlooked.[4]

Not all high-profile crimes qualify as provoking assaults. Nor do I suggest that famous criminal cases have failed to fascinate Americans in the past. My aims are more limited, involving several objectives. One is to present a genre of crime cases that I believe to be at once sociologically revealing and historically specific. Another is to assess the phenomenon to which this book accords "high-profile" attention itself. If indeed provoking assaults became a distinctive American form of politics during the 1980s and 1990s, did such crime cases help to produce a more equitable society? As the two interview excerpts at the beginning of this chapter indicate, the question can be answered in different ways. One is exemplified by defense lawyer Roy Black's remarks: the kind of crime cases analyzed here may serve to deflect attention from the resolution of deep structural issues American society cannot "afford," that "we don't want really" to solve. Another response comes from Al Sharpton. In his view, crime cases from "Bensonhurst" to "Louima" in New York (and we can add from "Rodney King" to "O.J." in Los Angeles) may produce important political outcomes; they may be eminently suitable as a form of protest in a post–civil rights, mass-mediated age. Remaining to be seen, though, is which opinion is best borne out by analyzing these cases in greater depth. Is one interpretation more valid than the other, or are aspects of both necessary to encompass this subject's complexity?

Initially, though, a provoking assault needs to be differentiated from other crimes that become well known through media coverage. To this end, in the section that follows I suggest four traits that together constitute criteria of provoking assaults as a subset of high-profile crime cases. These were developed in the course of a back-and-forth process of mutual adjustment between empirical data and theory, which evolved in close relationship with one another rather than in isolation.[5] Moreover I use "provoking assaults"—a term purposefully intended to have multiple associations—as a more precise name to identify this subset of crime cases. Indeed, the cases I studied were provocative in stimulating wide-ranging public debates into which several groups—the media, the law, diverse public participants—were drawn. Then, too, a recurrent topic of debate aroused by these cases was whether an accuser, not the accused, was actually to blame. Even in cases of grave injury or death, victims were sometimes perceived as having "provoked" their own victimization; not unusual, too, was for apparent perpetrators to be seen as victims. Finally, these cases were and remain provocative in the sense of calling forth indistinguishably emotional and logic-based responses; to fully understand these crimes requires more than a rational choice theorist's relatively one-dimensional calculus.

DEFINING A GENRE OF CRIME CASES

"Provoking assaults" are crime cases with the following characteristics. First, they are highly profiled incidents of violent crime that become symbolic of perceived social problems in a given time and place, engaging a broad range of participants. Second, as they become symbolic, these incidents frequently merge legal cases and social causes. They are processed by participants through a two-sided mode of argumentation I call "partialization," one that structures and limits debate around a framework of "sides." Third, as cases and causes become enmeshed, provoking assaults generate controversies about whether responsibility for a given crime rests with individuals or social forces, and whether apparent perpetrators were actually victimized, or apparent victims were culpable to some extent. Fourth, because only a single incident is decided by an "either/or" verdict (and then only for one side or the other), dissatisfactions tend to remain even after verdicts are handed down. In the wake of such disappointments, some people may become involved in thematically linked incidents; in this way, an ongoing symbolic politics may ensue from the character of these incidents themselves, capable of redressing only some of what they come to represent.

Before elaborating on these traits, it should be noted that I sometimes use quotation marks when talking about certain cases, using names often repeated in media and public discourse. This is to underscore my sense of provoking assaults as symbolic entities. Sometimes, as in the "Bensonhurst" case, the name itself can be understood to play a role in how the case was perceived. Brooklyn residents might have reacted differently to the case had it become known by the victim's name—that is, had it been referred to as the "Yusef Hawkins" case. Not wanting to lose the texture of how the cases were discussed in the media and in public, I use the quotation marks to stress the debated and debatable character not only of the cases but their "names."

Diverse Participation

Not all violent incidents become high-profile crimes via media attention; nor do all cases of high-profile crimes become provoking assaults. Rather, provoking assaults are a subset of high-profile criminal cases in which three groups of people become engaged as news stories mushroom. Members of the media, especially reporters and editors, play a key role; without their involvement, high-profile crimes would not exist as such. Then there are the myriad parties within the criminal justice system—from police and detectives to lawyers, jurors, and judges—who get involved each in their own way as they carry out their official functions. Finally, beyond those institutionally engaged—the media in search of stories, the criminal justice system because a crime was committed—a wider public, too, starts to participate and react. These responses often attract media coverage in turn.

This third group of players often includes such public participants as political figures (a mayoral candidate or incumbent who comments on the case), community and social-movement leaders, and members of organized or informal interest groups. Someone active in a neighborhood association may be prompted to intervene on the side of a victim; a well-known businessman may call for social policy changes because the crime was outrageous; and/or local religious leaders and community activists may criticize the media's coverage or the treatment of the defendant by the criminal justice system. These responses by members of the wider public can become a topic of daily conversation, as the cases are discussed avidly at family gatherings, among friends, or with co-workers.

These strikingly diverse public reactions—characterized in chapter 6 as official, protest, and conversational reactions, respectively—are what distinguish provoking assaults from the many other crimes, even those accorded some measure of media coverage, that move through the legal system with relatively little notice taken of them. Whether spurring "official" public figures to speak out, or prompting various parties to "protest" what happened on one or the other side, or fueling informal conversations about the case, provoking assaults are crime cases that stimulate discussion of simultaneously general and particular issues. They arouse debate about matters that include but also transcend individuals, potentially affecting large numbers of people. This is what lends provoking assaults symbolic stature.

For example, the murder of Yusef Hawkins in "Bensonhurst," the 1991

"Rodney King" case, and the 1999 cases involving "Louima" and "Diallo" did not compel public interest simply because they involved the killing and beatings of individuals. These cases were responded to as if they represented class actions. Each crime raised collective concerns about whether any minority male in the United States was safe from police brutality or victimization by "hate crimes." Similarly, regarding gender, the "Central Park jogger" case raised the question whether woman are free to go where they want and do what they choose without running the risk of attack. The "William Kennedy Smith" and "Mike Tyson" cases touched widespread fears women have about violence on dates. In this respect, provoking assaults are different, for example, from other high-profile cases involving a serial murderer or a psychopathic robber.

By the criteria set forth for provoking assaults, they obviously are not unique to the present time period. Crimes that become culturally and politically symbolic, prompting broad public commentary and protest, have long existed, from the "Dreyfus" case of late-nineteenth-century France to the cases of "Joe Hill," "Scottsboro," "Emmett Till," and others that took place in the United States during the twentieth century.[6] Such well-known crimes can be seen, in retrospect, to reveal much about a bygone era's anxieties and fears; they may manifest disparities between a period's idealized expectations and its troubling realities. Yet while provoking assaults have certainly surfaced at other times and in other places (and are therefore of broad social interest), they seem to have occurred particularly close together over the last several decades—media references regularly connecting them—as three historical factors converged in the 1980s and 1990s.

For one thing, opinion polls and surveys confirm that Americans' concerns about crime, especially violent interpersonal crime, were on the rise during the 1980s and 1990s. Whereas 2 percent of Americans in 1988 identified crime and violence as "the most important problem facing this country today," the figure jumped to 37 percent by 1994.[7] However, around the same time, reported violent crime rates had actually declined.[8] Nor did it seem to matter when criminologists like Stuart Hills noted in the late 1980s that more Americans were then dying from acts of "corporate violence"—ranging from occupational to environmental and consumer-related corporate crimes— than from interpersonal violence.[9] The public perceived matters differently: people were far more likely to be outraged by the 1989 rape of the Central Park jogger than by corporate crimes like the Charles Keating and Michael Milken savings and loan scandals that also garnered news attention through these years. Also, by the early 1990s, concerns about rampant violent crimes between individuals—that is, about assaults, rapes, homicides—had made their way into both politicians' speeches and emerging public policies. Mandatory sentencing and "three strikes and you're out" legislation were enacted in many states beginning in the late 1980s. In 1994, just as the "O.J. Simpson" case was hitting the news, the Omnibus Crime Bill called for hiring one hundred thousand more police nationally and using federal funds for new prison building; renewed calls for capital punishment to be reinstituted were slowly taking hold, too, in many states. Thus it was during these years that later "tough on crime" policies were incubating; indeed, these cases may have been one factor contributing to a resurgence of punitive public sentiments.[10]

Second, during these decades, high-profile crimes of the provoking assault variety came to symbolize not only problems of violence but stubborn biases of race, gender, and—though less recognized—class. Discussions about economic disparities took place, but class rarely was a direct focus of attention. Instead, reflecting the comparatively hidden character of economically based claims in American life (and their less legitimized fate relative to race-, gender-, and sexuality-centered issues), class was present but placed well in the background of the controversies these assaults typically provoked. Still, even the social movements born in the 1960s and 1970s out of the politics of race, gender, and sexuality were in a contradictory position several decades later.

On the one hand, these movements had succeeded in leaving an indelible mark on American culture. Social recognition of ongoing manifestations of racial discrimination, from hate crimes to police brutality, attested to the long-term influence of the civil rights and black nationalist movements. Likewise, American feminism had brought unprecedented recognition to issues of sexual violence—from rape to battering—affecting women. The gay rights movement had underscored not only heterosexist biases but the socially constructed character of sexuality itself.

Nevertheless, by the late 1980s and into the 1990s, these movements found themselves on the defensive as countermovements also began, in reaction, to appear. In 1991, journalist Susan Faludi depicted multileveled challenges that, taken together, comprised an antifeminist backlash against the gains women had made in the workplace, in the redefining of families and living options—indeed, in the general quality of their lives.[11] At about the same time, sociologist Stephen Steinberg documented retrenchment that was taking place as affirmative action programs and other measures aimed at combating the historical legacies of racism were "turned back."[12] Gay rights, like the issue of gay marriage, remained contentious, a subject of ongoing cultural negotiation. In this push/pull environment of social ambivalence, "hate related" crimes—acts of assault, homicide, or rape just about universally condemned—may have offered especially credible, and telling, illustrations of persistent discriminations.

A third historical explanation for provoking assaults' emergence in the 1980s and 1990s is that these symbolic violent crime cases coincided with—reinforcing and itself reinforced by—changes in the media. Competition within and between news media intensified throughout these decades.[13] This meant that, once a given crime case of the provoking assault variety evoked interest, it was likely to be picked up across a range of media; it could move faster than before through an expanding infrastructure of mass-mediated communication. In this way, a common vehicle—indeed, a distinctive forum—for "back and forth" cultural debate was facilitated by technological developments. For instance, in 1989, when the "Central Park jogger" and "Bensonhurst" cases exploded onto the news, not only were four daily newspapers competing for readership in New York City, but court television was emerging nationwide; later, Internet news services entered the mix as well.

Moreover, as economic pressures on journalists to capture and maintain readers thereby increased, so did lines between elite and more sensationalistic, between "high brow" and "low brow," approaches to news become blurred. The possibility for cases to become spectacles was brewing during these years, too, in step with increasing media competitiveness. Imagine, for instance, that one relatively sensationally oriented newspaper—in the New York City media market, say, the New York Post—became interested in a particular high profile crime. Thereafter, pressures on other relatively more "elite" newspapers like The New York Times or the Los Angeles Times also tended to grow. Likewise, once a given television station decided to undertake coverage or "scooped" a story, other small stations felt pressured to follow suit.

High-profile crimes that became provoking assaults were especially suited for the collapsing of the boundaries separating news and entertainment. As crimes that evoked debate over broad social issues for varied social participants, provoking assaults were serious and thus, at least to some extent, legitimate news. At the same time, each case was a story that promised interesting narratives. Determining whether a given individual did or did not commit a particular murder, rape, or assault is often highly suspenseful, and sometimes even titillating, thereby engaging both emotions and logic in more compelling ways than more abstract or "drier"—that is, less entertaining— crime reporting could accomplish. Also appealing, offering virtually literary potential for elaboration, were the various class, gender, racial or ethnic, or possibly celebrity backgrounds of accused parties in contrast with their accusers.

It is likely that the appeals of provoking assaults for journalists were furthered by another trait as well. As legal cases, they pitted one side against another in ways that had immediate cultural repercussions, but repercussions that also extended beyond the 1980s and 1990s. This two-sided structure of debate affected each of the three groups—parties in the media, the law, and various reacting members of the public—at once similarly and differently.

Confusing Cases and Causes

Provoking assaults are not only incidents that come to symbolize social problems and stimulate diverse reactions: as serious crimes, they are also bound to end up in courts of law. In this respect, a highly profiled incident like the 1999 school shooting in Littleton, Colorado was not a provoking assault; Eric Kliebold and Dylan Harris took their own lives after killing a number of fellow students. In contrast, provoking assaults routinely evolve from highly profiled initial incidents into highly profiled court trials; they are crime cases that continue to attract media attention while moving chronologically through punctuated stages.

In this light, provoking assaults have a dual character: they are at once legal cases and social causes. As legal cases, they are adjudicated in the context of an "either/or" framework, the function of which is to determine either the guilt or the innocence of the accused. But this framework is less well suited for the more complicated task of tracing the metamorphosis of a given incident from a social problem to a symbolic social cause. The legal system seeks to resolve once and for all the question of guilt or innocence, but the underlying social reasons for the incident in the first place—which may include such social factors as racism and gender biases and class inequities—are far too deeply rooted to go away once jurors reach their case-specific verdicts.

By merging cases and causes, provoking assaults produce another tricky effect as well: they are played out through a process of "partialization." By this I mean that because provoking assaults unfold through a two-sided legal framework aimed at producing decisive "either/or" verdicts, they require arguments to be marshaled loyally in the service of one side or the other. Thereafter certain interpretations start to repetitively characterize each side's arguments; many participants start to think and feel about an incident in ways "partial" to the side with which they are inclined to sympathize. But precisely because partializing tends to classify and assimilate most commentary to one or the other side, alternative perspectives may go unnoticed; third or fourth interpretations may be placed at a disadvantage, seemingly irrelevant or "unrealistic" if they do not conform to the dominant two-sided framework. In the end, more nuanced understandings of the social world may take a back seat to more simplistic ones.

Thus partialization tends to produce oversimplified frameworks for debating complex issues. Take, as an example, the "O.J. Simpson" case of 1995–96, which became a media spectacle indeed. Two contemporary social problems, gender inequities and racial injustices, were symbolized on either side of this now famous case: feminist concerns about domestic violence were aligned with the prosecution, while the specter of racism came to characterize the defense's position. Concerns about domestic violence raised by the case seemed justified considering O.J. Simpson's past record of abusive behavior, while the Los Angeles Police Department's unsavory history of racist brutality and misconduct made worries about racially motivated improprieties equally understandable. Moreover, the "Simpson" case also provoked questions about class inequities—namely, whether an individual facing similar charges who was unable to afford a "dream team" of lawyers could have obtained an acquittal.

Yet, on the day the jury's finding was announced, it did not appear possible to "root" for the recognition, the symbolic vindication, of both factors—let alone for class-related matters to be redressed besides. Instead millions of people gathered around television sets to hear the final verdict seemed as though constrained to take one side or the other through the partialized terms the case had encouraged. Perhaps if one did not "take a side," one would feel guilty, or face social recriminations from others who hotly disagreed or felt betrayed by such a refusal (or abstention). Partialization, then, can subtly inhibit public debate and, in so doing, sow social divisiveness. Following the "Simpson" case, for instance, some individuals who had previously been friendly across racial or gendered differences recounted feeling alienated from one another; the very "either/or" framework that demanded "sticking together" was obviously separating people as well. In a related way, partializing has potentially divisive consequences for social movements, as again is evident in the "Simpson" case, which came to symbolize the gendered issue of domestic violence on one side and the race-based issue of police misconduct on the other. As I have argued elsewhere, the result was to "play gender against race." [14]

This is not to overlook academic and political attempts in the 1990s to withstand partialization in general and the effects of "playing gender against race" in particular. For instance, in a volume about Clarence Thomas edited by well-known writer Toni Morrison, law professor Kimberle Crenshaw bemoaned the unavailability in common cultural discourse of "beyond either/or" language capable of depicting the complex character of gender- and race-based discrimination African Americans in the United States have experienced. [15] Then too, following Mike Tyson's 1995 release from prison after serving time for rape, activist Jill Nelson organized a vigil as part of the group African-Americans against Violence to protest violence against women. This group was both sensitive to the history of racism black men and women have suffered, and concerned about not "celebrating" Tyson's return such that the seriousness of violence against women seemed to be downplayed. [16]

But what I am suggesting is that such efforts may have encountered difficulties taking hold *en masse* precisely because the dominant framework of partialization is and was so strong. Why—where does partialization come from, and why does it seem to have so much power? Two-sided frameworks can operate in more or less the same way and yet have different social roots depending on different participants' vantage points. For those involved in civil and criminal case law, the legal system reasonably imposes a two-sided, "either/or" framework for adjudicating questions of innocence and guilt. Yet the press can also be a source for such frameworks even before criminal cases are tried in court. No doubt, to some extent, journalists themselves are apt to see matters in a two-sided fashion, in step with the broad cultural sway of legalistic thinking in American life. In addition, though, reporters and editors may perpetuate two-sidedness for their own institutionally based reasons: in the interests of objectivity, as traditionally conceived, journalists have long been taught that there are two sides, and often two opposed sides, to every story.

Partialization is reflected in still other aspects of American culture. As already noted, the broadly popular and greatly influential world of sports is also obviously structured in terms of sides. The rules of the game are meant to lead to a decisive outcome declaring who "wins" and who "loses." In turn, the language of sports is used metaphorically in the everyday language of the corporate world, where people may, or may not, be deemed "team players"; for that matter, "legal teams" in the courtroom are often said to be winning or losing. Given this pervasiveness of two-sided frameworks, it is not surprising that many people feel constrained to align themselves with one side or another when confronted with provoking assaults.

While the problems imposed by a number of conventionally accepted dualisms are by now well recognized—for instance, feminists have convincingly argued that supposedly "natural" dichotomies between masculinity and femininity are largely specious and socially constructed—less analyzed is how such dualisms have been sustained by other institutionalized and coinciding cultural logics as well. Thus provoking assaults help to explore where dualisms produce—as seen through high-profile cases—both advantageous and disadvantageous social effects.

Reversing Victims and Victimizers

We have seen how provoking assaults can confuse cases and causes, and how they unfold through the partialization of two-sided frameworks. A third typical trait of provoking assaults is that the issue of culpability becomes cloudy: many high-profile cases engender debate over whether alleged victims are as innocent as they appear and whether accused parties are as culpable as they seem (indeed, whether they may be innocent altogether). Simultaneously, the cases recycle questions about personal versus social responsibility; they offer a way for some people to express, and others to challenge, individualistic propensities in American culture.

Contention over issues of responsibility emerged in each of the cases to which I have alluded thus far. For example, common to the "Rodney King," the "Louima," and the "Diallo" cases, symbolizing police brutality in Los Angeles and New York City, was that some parties on the "side" of the police officers questioned whether apparent victims might have brought about their own victimization. Perhaps it wasn't the officers' fault but Rodney King himself who menaced the police and brought about his brutal beating, captured on videotape? Perhaps years later it was Abner Louima who picked a fight with officer Justin Volpe one evening, resulting in his serious abuse in a

Brooklyn police station? Perhaps Amadou Diallo was flashing something that he clutched in his hand in a threatening manner before he was shot to death in an apartment building entranceway? In each case, the defense suggested that to hold police officers fully responsible was itself unfair. But such rechanneling of blame away from the accused victimizers was at odds with group-based arguments made by the prosecution. Here, it was contended that King, Louima, and Diallo were attacked not as individuals but because they were members of minority groups; the crime would not have occurred, asserted the prosecution's side, if not for the police officers' racist views.

Even more familiar may be the "victim blaming" in gender-based incidents. Rape cases have long been notorious for subjecting women to questions about their past sexual histories, whether or not relevant to the case at hand. Although many feminists had already started to protest this practice, defense attorneys and parties sympathetic to defendants in highly profiled rape cases during the late 1980s and early 1990s managed sometimes to insinuate that the women had "provoked" their own victimization. For instance, in the "Central Park jogger" rape case, those aligned with the defense publicly wondered why a young woman jogger would run so late at night. In the "Mike Tyson" case, some local residents asked why young Desiree Washington would accompany the famous boxer to his Indianapolis hotel room unless looking for trouble, or hoping to procure a book contract. On the other hand, feminists who have monitored these cases do so because they link rape to group-based socialization about codes of masculinity that can result in violence against women. They have struggled to redefine rape as acts of violence, not sex, and feminist arguments about "victim blaming" have influenced the adoption of rape shield laws in many states.[17]

Victim blaming is not limited to cases of rape. This may be because rape cases themselves take place in the context of an individualistic culture that permits apparently clear-cut relations of dominance and subordination to be reversed with special ease. Moreover, this third trait of provoking assault relates to the second insofar as public reactions that accord culpability to apparent victims (while diminishing that of apparent victimizers) are also facilitated by the partializing framework. Thus even if some people are troubled by the social cause that is implicated in a particular case—perhaps they feel resentment toward the government or criminal justice system because of racial biases an incident evinces, or at the press because of what seems to be biased coverage—these sentiments may be "displaced" from abstract social entities like "society" or "the media" onto accused or accusing parties who offer more concrete objects of blame.

Provoking assaults have both advantages and disadvantages as a medium of politicized American debate. Certainly the cases provide opportunities for impassioned debate by concretizing social issues through single cases that permit emotions to be vented and reasoned arguments to be made. However, at times, these cases may also generate social-psychic dynamics that "defend" against what some people, consciously or not, may intuit to be a problem. For provoking assaults do not allow social forces to be indicted even if parties have cause to feel angered or resentful at the broader societal context and its representatives. In chapter 6, I call one of the defensive dynamics that can thereby arise "substituting" (or "blaming the victim") and a second dynamic "reversing" (or "defending the defendant(s)"), when referring to the somersaulting perceptions of responsibility borne by accused and the accusers that can emerge in such instances.

From One High-Profile Crime Case to Others

Dissatisfactions with such high-profile cases can stem from the repercussions of "either/or" verdicts themselves. While provoking assaults are likely to imbue both sides of a crime case with symbolic significance, only one side and its proponents can be vindicated at a trial's end. From this flows a fourth and last defining trait of provoking assaults: after the delivery of the verdict, one side's symbolic win becomes the other side's symbolic loss. Someone, or something, is bound to feel "let down."

Thus provoking assaults are crime cases with a proclivity to create left-over resentments and dissatisfactions. Disappointed parties are motivated to undo, often by appeals to the legal system, the wrong thought/felt to have been rendered. For instance, the loss for the prosecution of the "Rodney King" case in Simi Valley was followed by a win in federal court in downtown Los Angeles; the loss in downtown Los Angeles by the prosecution in the "O.J. Simpson" case became a win for that side on retrial in a Santa Monica civil court. Bracketing questions about whether such retrials may be merited by factors that can include how the judge conducted the case or perhaps by the emergence of new evidence, one ramification of this appeals process is that the case and its symbolic associations are maintained over time.

Indeed, a kind of "intertextuality" may emerge between provoking assaults not only through such thematic linkages, but by connections between "casts of characters" who reappear from one crime case to a next. Such reappearances happened among all three sets of social actors whose joint participation comprises these instances. For example, among social movement activists, new crimes that manifest biases also present ongoing opportunities for political consciousness-raising, Thus the names of some of the same activist participants—for example, Al Sharpton in New York City cases or Danny Blakewell in Los Angeles—often resurfaced in one crime case after another, from "Howard Beach" to "Bensonhurst" in New York or from "Rodney King" to "Reginald Denny" in Los Angeles.[18] Then, too, it is not uncommon for editors to reassign some of the same reporters from later to more recent instances. For instance, Los Angeles Times editor Leo Wilensky selected reporter Jim Newton to be the lead reporter on "Rodney King," and then again as a principal reporter on "Reginald Denny" and "O.J. Simpson."[19] Editors at the New York Times assigned reporter William Glaberson to cover both the "Central Park" and "Bensonhurst" cases, and David Margolick to cover the trial of William Kennedy Smith and then O.J. Simpson. Reporters who wrote about one high-profile crime case are assumed to have gained expertise later applicable to covering other cases as well. These reporters may have already established connections with social movement activists and community figures to whom they can again turn as a source of information. In this way, too, "intertextual" connections were forged.

Last but not least, legal participants in one case may also resurface in subsequent provoking assaults. The same lawyers may be hired or appointed, their names appearing and then reappearing in print and on television. For instance, in New York City, district attorney Charles Hynes reassigned prosecutor Ed Boyar to the 1989–90 "Bensonhurst" case after his successful prosecution of the 1985–86 "Howard Beach" case; Boyar already knew Al Sharpton among the "cast of characters" who had been involved with the earlier homicide case. Defense lawyer Roy Black became known for his expertise in handling highly profiled crime cases in both the "Lozano" police brutality case and the subsequent "William Kennedy Smith" rape case, both tried (and, in "Lozano," appealed) in Florida. Attorney Johnnie Cochran was involved with the "Reginald Denny" case and then, much more visibly, was a part of the so-called dream team of defense lawyers hired by O.J. Simpson. Later, moving from Los Angeles back to the East Coast, Cochran's name and that of Simpson-team lawyer Barry Scheck reemerged in the suit filed against New York City for the assault of a black man by white police officers in the

"Abner Louima" case. In some instances a lawyer no longer associated with a given case or perhaps retired from practice will reappear in the public sphere, creating another kind of continuity between cases as paid "legal commentator" on recent high-profiled crimes; in this capacity, their roles are evocative of a similar part played by commentators in the world of sports.

But intertextual linkages are not the only long-term consequences of provoking assaults. In the aftermath of verdicts, cultural and policy changes that are socially beneficial may be brought about. For instance, in communities affected by high-profile crimes like "Bensonhurst" or "Glen Ridge," sensitivity awareness programs (about racial and gender biases, respectively) owe some if not their entire genesis to debates that grew out of such cases and their aftermath. The passage of rape shield laws was certainly spurred by activism surrounding high-profile crimes in which women suffered victim-blaming of the sort feminists have termed "second assaults."

On the other hand, these advantages of provoking assaults seem inseparably related to disadvantages that involve locality and temporality. An individual case may have positive effects in Bensonhurst or Glen Ridge, but not necessarily across the country. Then, too, a given crime that grows to be symbolic may exercise strong effects but only for a relatively short period of time. Thus, for example, concerns about racial urban violence that followed the "Rodney King" verdict in Simi Valley led to the formation of the Christopher Commission. Yet, policy changes resulting from this commission's no doubt well-intended work seem to have had minimal long-term impact on the structural problems of racial and class discrimination that were ignited by the case. Similarly, in California, additional shelters for battered women were proposed in the immediate wake of the double homicides at issue in the "O.J. Simpson" case. But as more time elapsed, and racial discrimination surfaced symbolically on the case's other side, attention shifted away from concerns about the issue of domestic violence that the case had earlier mobilized.

FROM DEFINITION TO CASE STUDIES

I initially became interested in high-profile crimes after analyzing and writing about the "New Bedford" rape case in Massachusetts, on which the widely known commercial film *The Accused* was based.[20] In March 1983, a young woman was raped on a pool table in a bar full of men who shouted "Do it! Do it!" while the assault occurred. No one called the police. The incident soon became nationally publicized and, after extensive news coverage, became the first criminal trial to be broadcast on cable television.

In addition to attracting broad media attention, the "New Bedford" case also generated public reactions to two symbolic issues, gender and ethnic biases, that emerged and were thereafter pitted against each other before, during, and after a 1984 trial. Between the time the incident occurred and verdicts were announced, both issues inspired public protests. In the days immediately after the incident, feminists demonstrated in the city, denouncing gender biases and holding up placards that read "Rape Is Not a Spectator Sport." But by the time of the jury's verdict that convicted four men and acquitted two others, other protesters were taking to the streets to denounce what they perceived as ethnic biases. For example, some reporters covering the case referred to the defendants as "the Portuguese rapists." Indeed, many of New Bedford's large Portuguese community petitioned against long sentences for the convicted rapists, and hailed those found innocent as "heroes."

But rather than protesting anti-Portuguese discrimination or indicting the media for forging a competitive "gender versus ethnicity" framework of debate, the young woman herself was blamed by some in the community for having patronized Big Dan's Bar in the first place and then later for bringing charges. Such victim-blaming continued even after it was made public that the victim of the attack was of Portuguese descent. "Why, then, wasn't she home with her kids?" a number of women and men asked in different ways. Following the 1984 decisions in the case, ominous threats forced the woman to leave the area. She died in a Florida car accident two years later.[21]

Had the New Bedford incident struck me as a poignant but isolated case, hardly resembling other contemporary highly profiled crimes, this book would likely not have been written. However, the factors present in "New Bedford"—extraordinary media interest, incensed public reactions, and national publicity—resurfaced in later crime cases that became notorious both in New York City and nationally. For instance, like the "New Bedford" case, the highly profiled 1989 "Central Park jogger" rape case counterposed two societal discriminations: instead of gender and ethnicity, however, the later case involved antagonisms of "gender versus race." Again, controversy swelled through a combination of intensive media interest, public protest (including against media coverage itself), and consequent publicity of a 1990 New York City trial. The "Central Park jogger" case was marked by another striking feature as well: its publicity occurred close in time and place to other high-profile crimes—the "Howard Beach," "Tawana Brawley," and "Bensonhurst" cases—with which it became connected through media references.

Thus I became interested in why and how certain violent crimes emerged not only in a small city like New Bedford but in large urban settings. But rather than proceeding from only a sociological intuition, I wanted to obtain an overall gauge of which U.S. crime cases had attracted sufficient journalistic attention to become vehicles of public debate, and to ascertain whether such crime cases as the "Central Park jogger" in New York City or "Rodney King" in Los Angeles were indeed among the most well-known incidents of their time and place. To obtain this data concerning the "most publicized" cases, I conducted a newspaper study using indexes of the New York Times and the Los Angeles Times. Analyzing television news transcripts was not possible because of cost and the prolonged stretches of time required to be surveyed. The New York and Los Angeles newspapers are, however, the most well-regarded papers in their respective regions, the two media capitals in the United States.[22] Since they provide both local and national coverage, and are known to strongly influence television coverage in turn, the crimes they feature in their coverage is likely to exert an influence on other media and so become known by varied media consumers. The time period I chose to research spanned 1985–96, from a year following the "New Bedford" case's conclusion through the verdict in the trial of O.J. Simpson.

Resulting from this research, and listed in appendix B, are the top twenty cases in terms of publicity in New York, Los Angeles, and nationally. Not surprisingly, the "O.J. Simpson" case stood out as by far the most publicized case of the decade; predictably, too, the "Rodney King" case appeared among the top three cases by all three gauges.[23] I used a second criterion to decide which cases to study in detail: since I wished to investigate how and why connections emerged between high-profile crime cases, I sought out paired crime cases that had been committed and/or tried in close chronological proximity with one another.

From these dual criteria emerged seven cases on which I focused my attention. For New York City, I selected the "Bensonhurst" and "Central Park jogger" cases to study in depth: these highly profiled crimes were among the top ten most publicized cases in New York City between 1985 and 1996. Both cases attracted national attention, though stronger interest was clearly evinced by papers in New York City. Moreover, these New York City crimes were committed and tried within six months of one another in 1989 and 1990, respectively.[24] For Los Angeles, I selected the "Rodney King" and "Reginald Denny" cases. Although the "King" case was as widely publicized nationally as it was well known locally, the "Denny" case with which it became associated attracted more specifically local coverage in Los Angeles than in New York City. Moreover, while these crimes were separated by approximately a year, the 1992 assault on Denny coincided with the 1992 delivery of the Simi Valley "Rodney King" verdict; in 1993, the federal "King" trial and the "Denny" trial took place within six months of one another.

In choosing to research other cases, I wished to see whether observations about high-profile crimes culled from the study of the New York and Los Angeles incidents could also be found in cases that could not have become interconnected on the basis of geographic proximity alone. Thus I also decided to examine two crimes that garnered relatively more highly profiled mention on a national basis than specifically on a local basis in either New York or Los Angeles (see appendix B): the "William Kennedy Smith" and "Mike Tyson" rape cases. Again, these cases surfaced close together in time (both rapes were alleged in 1991, and tried in late 1991 and early 1992). However, they occurred in different cities: Tyson was accused and tried in Indianapolis, Indiana; Kennedy Smith was accused and tried in West Palm Beach, Florida. Preliminary readings of newspaper coverage in local as well as national papers indicated that the two cases were quickly interconnected, spurring my interest in tracing how and why this had occurred.

Finally, it seemed impossible not to include the case that obviously attracted more attention from the mid-1980s through the mid-1990s than any other: the "O.J. Simpson" case. Again, the "Central Park jogger"/"Bensonhurst" and "King"/"Denny" pairs received both national coverage and became particularly familiar in their respective local contexts. The "Simpson" case surpassed all other cases in local as well as national publicity, dominating crime news coverage for much of 1995 and 1996.[25] Thus the cases I chose to study in greater depth—"Central Park," "Bensonhurst," "Rodney King," "Reginald Denny," "William Kennedy Smith," "Mike Tyson," and "O.J. Simpson"—included both locally and nationally well-known violent crimes (the "Simpson," "King," and "Tyson" cases) publicized in American newspapers between 1985 and 1996.[26] In case readers may not know the circumstances of these cases, since they occurred a decade or more ago, table 1 of appendix B provides a brief overview of what happened in the cases, and when they took place and were tried.

Once having selected these cases, I relied on media texts and extensive interviews for my analysis of them. For media sources, I used national and local newspapers as my primary media sources. For each case, I read through all the coverage by the *New York Times* of original incidents and later trials, as well as reportage in at least one widely circulated local paper. For example, in addition to the *New York Times* coverage, I read all local *Daily News* coverage for New York City cases,[27] for the "Tyson" case, I read all local *Indianapolis Star* coverage, and for the "William Kennedy Smith" case, all *Palm Beach Post* coverage. To avoid relying exclusively on coverage by mainstream newspapers, I included media accounts of the seven cases in well-known local papers serving predominantly minority communities. For example, for New York City cases I drew on the *Amsterdam News*'s coverage of relevant cases; for Los Angeles cases, articles written in the *Los Angeles Sentinel.* These are the most widely read newspapers owned and operated by African Americans in these two cities.

My primary source of information, however, was interviews conducted with people engaged in some capacity with the seven selected cases. I interviewed many of the major reporters for the *New York Times* and for local papers I was perusing; some editors were included as well. Likewise, for each case I interviewed as many as time allowed of those who had become involved with the case through the criminal justice system, including many of the lawyers and, in some instances, judges and jurors. Last, I interviewed persons who were part of the public's reaction to the various cases through such activities as protesting, writing editorials, monitoring trials, or attending community meetings. I also included interviews with people who had strong opinions about cases though these viewpoints were not quoted in journalistic accounts. For instance, I taped several wide-ranging discussions of the cases in high school and college classes and, for the "Kennedy Smith" and "Tyson" cases, conducted interviews with people who worked in or near the courthouses in which the trials took place. In many of the interviews I excerpt in chapters that follow, I use respondents' names; however, in cases where people were or preferred to remain anonymous, I have either omitted or changed their names.

In sum, more than two hundred interviews were conducted over approximately seven years in four U.S. locales. In order to do research on the "William Kennedy Smith" case, I made three separate trips to West Palm Beach, Florida in 1992 and 1993; to conduct research on the "Mike Tyson" case, I twice visited Indianapolis, Indiana in 1993 and 1994. Since I live in New York City, research on New York City cases was relatively easy to undertake. To research Los Angeles cases, I visited the West Coast for close to four months in 1994 and 1995, and commuted back and forth for research purposes over the course of the next year. During this time period, the "Simpson" case was unfolding; I was thus able to conduct research on that case as it progressed, capturing people's impressions while fresh in their minds.[28]

Emerging from this research were the four traits of provoking assaults summarized above. To bring to life the genre of crime cases that I have thus far described only abstractly, this book proceeds as follows. I begin with narrative case studies. Chapter 2 chronicles the April 1989 "Central Park jogger" case and chapter 3 the August 1989 "Bensonhurst" case involving the murder of Yusef Hawkins. These case studies concentrate on events immediately following the two crimes, and show how media coverage and public reactions developed by way of a point/counterpoint interaction between the two. My intention in this part of the book is to offer a framework potentially useful when analyzing other crime cases that occur in other locales.

I then shift focus from illustrating provoking assaults to examining the nature of different parties' participation. I also introduce interviews with those related to the other five cases I researched intensively—"Kennedy Smith," "Tyson," "King," "Denny," and "Simpson"—to determine if patterns emerging from "Central Park" and "Bensonhurst" reappeared in later cases as well. Thus chapter 4 returns to "Central Park" and "Bensonhurst" to analyze the role of legal participants in provoking assaults, concentrating especially on the views of judges, lawyers, and jurors. That chapter also uses interview material from the later cases, and explores the cases' repercussions for the legal system's day-to-day operations. Chapter 5 returns to a consideration of the role of the press and, like chapter 4, expands the focus beyond the "Central Park jogger" and "Bensonhurst" cases to include the "Kennedy Smith," "Tyson," "King," "Denny," and "Simpson" instances. Chapter 6 draws on interviews with a range of public participants in the later cases to explore diverse public reactions and, in conclusion, chapter 7 assesses this book's implications for future reactions to high-profile crimes of this genre.

One more word about chapter 6: there I discuss four "social-psychic" dynamics, defensive in character, that are sometimes engendered by two-sided frameworks of debate. As explained above, substituting (or "blaming the victim") and reversing (or "defending the defendant(s)") may invert the tacit phenomenology of a crime. I also noticed a third dynamic that was sometimes common to otherwise diverse reactions—namely, exceptionalizing ("yes but" reactions). By this, I mean that parties might sometimes admit that the arguments by those on the other side of a case made valid points, but that these points were not relevant to the case at hand. Fourth, partializing (or "taking a side") takes place when people conform their considerations of a case so as to fit within the parameters of the dominant two-sided framework, even if their responses in reality do not "fit." While a detailed analysis of this topic lies well beyond this volume, I suggest in chapter 6 that the Freudian notion of "defense mechanisms" might have more application sociologically than it is often thought to have. An ongoing problem sociologists cite with the psychoanalytic tradition is the latter's analysis of defenses in terms of unconscious conflicts that hark back to an individual's childhood. In chapter 6 I consider another possibility: defense mechanisms may also stem from unconscious conflicts that have distinctly social sources.[29]

Taken as a whole, this book also pursues a pair of subsidiary themes. First, especially for those who work in the media or the legal system, engagement with provoking assaults may have furthered already existing debates over traditionally held notions of "objectivity." For provoking assaults' dual statuses as legal cases and social causes sometimes created special difficulties and dilemmas for parties striving to uphold these "norms" of traditional value neutrality. Indeed, chapters 4 and 5 reveal that journalists and those working in various areas of the law do not always agree about whether objectivity and value neutrality are even possible; divergences of opinion, too, were fascinatingly apparent.

A related subsidiary theme is that parties caught up with provoking assaults very often enlist the aid of other participants. The subjects of my research frequently relied on one or more people to carry out their work; their interdependence, not independence, was most noticeable. For example, while some parties involved with the criminal justice system think of the law as operating independently of outside influences, many lawyers I interviewed found it necessary to use media coverage to best defend their clients by altering public opinion. As some of these lawyers explained, they suspected perspectives disseminated by the media could filter into the consciousness of nonsequestered jurors despite a judge's instructions to ignore the news.

Likewise, for the "public," media coverage is a necessary (if not sufficient) condition not only of provoking assaults' very existence, but of people's ability to engage in ongoing debates during trials, at verdicts, and beyond. Interestingly in this regard, though, I often heard disgruntlement expressed both by members of that public and by journalists, each blaming the other for why a case like "O.J. Simpson" stayed in the news long after many people's tolerance levels seemed to expire. Finally, as Todd Gitlin noted in *The Whole World is Watching* about the 1960s group Students for a Democratic Society (SDS), social movement groups were even more reliant on the press by the 1980s and 1990s to make their protests over provoking assaults well known. This dependence was clear even as the media sometimes evoked activists' criticisms.

Finally, it should be noted that in the pages that follow, I focus on the cultural forms and contents of provoking assaults rather than on questions of guilt or innocence. Evaluating matters of guilt or innocence is of immense legal and moral significance, but this book is intended first and foremost as a work of social and cultural critique. Thus rather than investigating what actually occurred in a given crime, I concentrate on the workings and repercussions of crime cases from "Central Park" through "O.J. Simpson" as they developed into passionately debated social causes.

EXEMPLIFYING A GENRE
A Tale of Two Crimes

CHAPTER 2

The Rape of the Central Park Jogger

On the evening of Wednesday April 19, 1989, a young woman in New York City returned from work to her Upper East Side residence, then went for a run in Central Park. She was known to be a regular jogger, going out four or five times weekly. According to newspaper accounts, later called into question by the confession of Mathias Reyes in 2002,[1] this woman would be the first female victim of a group of over thirty youths who had roamed through Manhattan's Central Park that night. Allegedly, the youths had committed several crimes before they encountered her. Seven other crimes had already taken place, according to reports filed with the district attorney's (DA's) office: the robbing and beating of a homeless man, an attempted attack on a couple riding a tandem bicycle, and an assault on two male joggers. But, despite controversies that eventually emerged over whether the assaulted was committed by a gang or by a single attacker, no one denied then or later that the attack on the young woman was the most violent of the reported crimes on April 19. Journalism professor Helen Benedict, assuming a gang was involved, described the attack as follows:

> The gang jumped her, grabbed at her, tore at her clothes, and sexually molested her as she fought back. Using a lead pipe and nearby rocks, they beat her to unconsciousness, crushing the bones around her face, and raped her. Some of them cut her with a knife, others grabbed at her body. They left her for dead. Hours later she was found in a puddle at the bottom of a ravine.[2]

The time of the attack was between 10:00 and 10:55 P.M.[3] After being found several hours later, the victim was rushed to intensive care at Metropolitan Hospital and was listed in critical condition, facing possible death from loss of blood and skull fractures.[4]

By 9:00 A.M. on April 20, the district attorney's office and detectives from the elite Manhattan North Homicide Squad had been summoned, and were aware that an unidentified white[5] rape victim had been found. By then, the well-known attorney Linda Fairstein had appeared in her capacity as chief of the Sex Crimes Prosecution Unit with the Manhattan DA's office; she soon assigned the case to experienced prosecutor Elizabeth Lederer. Print and broadcast reporters, too, had learned about the case and had arrived at the Central Park Precinct around the same time.[6]

SYMBOLIC ENGAGEMENT: A CASE BECOMES A CAUSE

As an indication of how quickly the case had been picked up by the press, Lederer recalled hearing about the crime over the radio as she was getting dressed for work, even before she was contacted by Fairstein:

> [T]here was nothing about this case that made me think it was more than a case that fades in the first 24 to 48 hours. I don't think any of us knew, in those first days that this would turn into this. I think we all thought "It's just the initial crush of reporters, it'll die down," and it didn't. . . . I had never seen anything like it. . . . It somehow (pause) symbolized something to everybody.[7]

Note, then, that three groups were quickly affected by the event. One set of individuals was involved at the level of the crime itself, with its clear-cut violence and uncertain cause: the victim and the young men. All of the latter were African American or Latino, and Lederer began to obtain videotaped confessions on the night of April 20. Then, too, the power of the criminal justice system had been activated. Third, though hardly least in the genesis of high-profile crime cases, the press was on hand. An almost instantaneous back-and-forth communication was by now taking place between the latter two institutional actors—the representatives of the criminal justice system and the various media that had picked up the story. Journalists, for example, knew from police reports that a crime had been committed by minority males against a white female victim in Central Park, a case already considered sufficiently important that a high-level criminal justice official like Fairstein had intervened. They knew Fairstein had personally appeared at the precinct even before Lederer arrived, and that the case was being given priority treatment by the Central Park Sex Crimes and North Homicide squads of the New York Police Department (NYPD).

Clearly, such journalistic attention was necessary for the case to become a provoking assault. But this does not explain why editors and reporters were willing to accord extraordinary coverage to this particular incident. Why and how did it become the "Central Park jogger" case?

THE ROLE OF THE MEDIA IN GENERATING WIDESPREAD REACTIONS

According to a story written by reporter Don Terry for the *New York Times*, twenty-eight other reports of first-degree rapes or attempted rapes were received by the police during the week of April 16–22, 1989.[8] The victims included sixteen black, seven Hispanic, two Asian, and three white women. Yet it was only the assault on the young woman jogger in Central Park that generated high-profile media attention. When interviewed, Elizabeth Lederer suggested a possible reason why this was so: the crime took place in Central Park, which "symbolized something to everybody." Linda Fairstein suggested much the same, adding that images of "wilding" had piqued journalists' interest:

LF: Murray Kempton, the great columnist, was the first to say, never attack anybody in a landmark location. That's one element of it. The fact that it occurred in Central Park, like the Chambers case before it, is one feature that attracted attention. . . . There had been many gang attacks and pack attacks, but it was the first time that the phenomenon of wilding was reported in a criminal case, that a group of young men, in this case thirty-nine by their own count banded together and considered it sport to go into the park to assault people.

LC: Do you think that's unusual?

LF: I know it's unusual. . . . I don't know of another case like it. I think that's quite phenomenal.[9]

Indeed, in newspaper accounts soon after the rape, "wilding" was dubbed a self-conscious social practice. The term came to denote the callous use of crime sprees as entertainment by inner-city youths: "Park Marauders Call it Wilding" read one *Daily News* headline on April 22, 1989.[10] Yet other reports later claimed that the word was a misnomer, and that it had originated in misheard references by the youths to the Ton Loc song "Wild Thing."[11] Therefore "wilding" may have been a media-generated rationale for coverage, one that later shaped the perspective of other parties.

Thus, one explanation for the heightened interest in the case is that the intense media coverage resulted from the special traits of this particular case and this case alone: from its extreme brutality; the sympathy it aroused in other joggers; its occurrence in a landmark location; and its association with anomic youth violence, whether or not "wilding" actually existed. Did journalists involved at the time also perceive the case as unusual? In the words of Emily Sachar, a reporter assigned to the case for *Newsday*, "I think we in the media were stunned by the violence of the case. For most of us . . . it was just so incredible, it so offended the human sensibility. It was a horrendous visual image of thirty to forty kids. I'm a jogger myself, and the crime was horrendous."[12] Lizette Alvarez, who covered the case for the *Daily News*, observed in another interview: "[P]art of it was that we saw pictures of her body. . . . She had been beaten so horribly that we felt anger, so we almost justified it [the coverage] that way."[13]

As involved journalists, then, Sachar and Alvarez thought that the extraordinary coverage of the "Central Park jogger" case resulted from the nature and outcome of the crime itself. Indeed, one might categorize their views under what I have elsewhere referred to as "journalistic individualism."[14] By this I mean that reporters and editors often justify high-profile news coverage on the basis of the unusual traits reflected in a certain case. Such explanations emphasize what is particular and unique, rather than that which fits a general pattern, about a given story. Yet not all reporters I interviewed were persuaded that the "Central Park jogger" case was so exceedingly anomalous. Alternative explanations, at once more cynical and less oriented toward this case's special characteristics, were also forthcoming.

According to Don Terry, who wrote the story about the twenty-eight other rapes that occurred the same week as the jogger's attack, journalists seized upon "Central Park" precisely because the victim was a white, upper-middle-class woman and her attackers were minority males; the story evoked familiar social stereotypes. Another reporter who covered the "Central Park jogger" case for a national paper put it even more bluntly:

REPORTER: It's obvious. She was a white, upper-middle-class young woman, almost beaten to death by a group of young blacks and Hispanics. Everybody's worst nightmare in New York. It's not complicated. . . . It wouldn't get coverage if she was black or Hispanic. Not much. In fact, right about the same time a young black woman was thrown from a roof of a (nearby) apartment building after she was raped. And she was raped and murdered by a group of young black and I think Hispanic men. That got three stories and it disappeared. And her death was as brutal, and it had many of the same elements as the jogger case. . . .

LC: But what makes, who makes the decisions. Is it more the editors, or the reporters?

REPORTER: It's collegial. I determine, hey, this is a big story. But if my editors don't share that opinion it's not going to go anywhere. Because newspaper reporting isn't a very complicated enterprise. It's really very simple. . . . You try to be objective, you try to jump right to the main issue. And so there's not a lot of nuances. . . . If you read about a young black woman who was raped by a bunch of blacks and Hispanics in Central Park, I doubt very much whether you would be as interested in that story . . . as you would be if it was your college roommate.

LC: So you're saying the news is oriented toward a white audience?

REPORTER: Well of course! Most newspapers are. Hey, the black population of this country is only 13 percent. So who's reading newspapers in this country? Eighty-seven percent white. Sure! Again, that's a no-brainer.[15]

This reporter seems to have been expressing something other than journalistic individualism; in alluding to the assault of a raped and murdered minority woman,[16] he clearly did not view the jogger's attack as an anomalous crime of its kind. But notice that this journalist could not fully eschew journalistic beliefs in "objectivity" either. In *Deciding What's News*, sociologist Herbert Gans observed that journalists define this notion of objectivity in terms of "personal detachment" and "exclusion of values" from such matters as how and why they cover the news. "Journalistic values are seen as reactions to the news," wrote Gans, "rather than *a priori* judgments which determine what becomes newsworthy."[17] Exemplifying this observation, the national news reporter just quoted referenced the traditional journalistic credo as a practical ideal ("You try to be objective.") On the other hand, this is contradicted by the statement that the "Central Park jogger" case was not selected because editors and reporters perceived it to be an "objectively" newsworthy event, one that could be detached from its surrounding social context. Rather, the case came closer than other rapes committed between April 16 and April 22, 1989 to fulfilling a decidedly social criterion. Only "Central Park" resonated with the interests of mostly white editors and reporters in selling papers to largely Caucasian audiences, audiences whom the reporter presumed were less "interested" in hearing about crimes committed against minority women.

But another implication, too, emerged from the preceding interview. Even if partly accurate, the relatively less individualistic explanation offered by Terry and the other reporter just quoted—namely, that economically and racially oriented factors dictated journalists' interest in "Central Park"—seems too simple. If three white women were raped during the week of April 16 through April 22, why did only one of these incidents become the most highly covered violent crime case of 1989? The answer to this question requires another interpretation, one able to provide a more multifaceted alternative to the explanations proffered by journalists themselves. Turning to conclusions reached by other sociologists who have studied journalists and their practices, it has been suggested that journalists have a propensity to favor stories that provide novelty within formulaic routines; it has also been suggested that the media tends to construct oppositional categories.

In a well-known article, Gaye Tuchman surmised from ethnographic observation that journalists are often attracted to stories that are variations on standard news formulas. They seek novelty—stories unexpected in their content, proffering "sexy" pegs and angles—but only so long as such variations takes place within formats already structurally familiar and "routine."[18] Writing from more politically radical positions, other students of news have observed that the media often constructs stories in terms of an "either/or" framework, resulting in oppositions between issues and their spokespersons. As both Stuart Hall and Todd Gitlin have argued, this can have the effect of neutralizing serious social challenges, while legitimizing ideological claims about capitalistic democracy and consent. For example, in their landmark study of social reactions to a media-generated "moral panic" over mugging in 1970s Britain, Stuart Hall and his collaborators described how the press characteristically counterposes parties in situations where both sides share an interest in challenging society. Once contrary pairs are constructed, their opposition works to neutralize the significance of each; Hall contends this is a "central element in the repertoire of modern liberalism." [19] Likewise, in his study of how the U.S. media covered the rise and fall of Students for a Democratic Society (SDS) in the 1960s, Todd Gitlin stressed the use of what he called "polarization"; stories included accounts of counterdemonstrations and presented supposedly balanced pictures of "extremists" on the other side including ultra-Right and neo-Nazi groups. [20] But how do these analyses of contemporary media point toward a fuller explanation of "why 'Central Park'"?

Applying the logic of Tuchman's argument, "Central Park" ought not be conceived as an isolated incident but placed in the larger context of surrounding events. Other cases covered with equal intensity in prior years may have established "routine" themes that the "Central Park jogger" case both reiterated and varied. Looking back on highly profiled crime cases since the early 1980s, it becomes apparent that two thematic trends were well represented long before 1989. The first involved a series of race-related crime cases that provoked discussions about racial tensions in New York City, and were among the most highly covered crimes prior to "Central Park." The second involved several gender-related crime cases that had begun to symbolize women's vulnerability to male violence.

Well before "Central Park," a series of high-profile "race" cases surfaced. In 1983, there was the case of Michael Stewart, a black photographer and graffiti artist who died of multiple trauma wounds before being detained and apparently beaten to death by New York City transit police officers. That same year Eleanor Bumpurs, also black, was killed when shotguns were fired through her door in the Bronx by Emergency Service police. In 1984, the focus of media attention shifted away from murders of blacks by whites onto the highly profiled Bernhard Goetz case. Goetz was a white man who fired an unregistered pistol at four black youths he assumed were about to rob him on a New York City subway, seriously injuring two of the young men. In 1985, the racial factors highlighted by a highly profiled crime case changed again: on his way to Stanford University after graduating from a prestigious boarding school, a young African American, Edmund Perry, was killed by a white police officer who claimed to be defending himself. [21]

And, in 1986, the crime took place that would garner more publicity than all of the other cases just mentioned combined: "Howard Beach," as it was referred to in the media, was the most widely covered violent crime case of 1986 and 1987.[22] In a Queens neighborhood, a group of white youths carrying baseball bats chased four young black men out of a pizza parlor; the latter had walked into Howard Beach to use the phone when their car broke down. Michael Griffith fled in panic from the pursuers, hoping to escape; he was killed by a car after he ran onto the Belt Parkway. The case was immediately given front-page coverage in all four New York City daily newspapers. Soon thereafter, organized protests were held on the streets of Howard Beach with as many as ten thousand people attending a series of well-publicized marches that were compared to civil rights marches of the 1960s. Al Sharpton, C. Vernon Mason, and Alton Maddox garnered extensive media attention for their roles in leading these protests and for their insistent calls for redress from the criminal justice system.[23]

In 1986 and 1987, several cases concerning gendered violence also received high-profile coverage in and around New York City. In 1986, the "Robert Chambers" case dominated front-page news. Chambers, who frequented predominantly white, Upper East Side well-to-do bars and restaurants, had allegedly strangled sixteen-year-old Jennifer Levin to death in Central Park. He claimed the death to have been accidental following "rough" but consensual sadomasochistic sex with the young woman; both the victim and the defendant were white.[24] Relatively recently, then, Central Park had been the site of another well-known crime case involving a violent act committed against a white woman; in fact, attorney Linda Fairstein was already a familiar media figure herself, having prosecuted Chambers in his highly profiled trial.[25] Then, just after the first "Howard Beach" trial produced three convictions in late 1987, the "Tawana Brawley" case rose to become the most highly publicized local crime of 1988. Tawana Brawley was a young African American woman who charged that a group of white police officers had raped and sodomized her for days in upstate New York, leaving the words "nigger" and "KKK" inscribed on her body. The "Brawley" case, which merged themes of gender and racial discrimination, was the most publicized crime case in New York City immediately before "Central Park" exploded onto public awareness.

This brief history suggests that a journalistic "routine" may indeed have been established: over the course of the 1980s, the most highly publicized crime cases in New York City involved violent assaults through which problems of racial and gendered discrimination were broached and debated. Consequently, when the "Central Park jogger" rape occurred, it contained thematic elements already familiar to both the media and the public. Clearly, "Central Park" continued the theme of gendered violence raised by the "Chambers" and "Tawana Brawley" cases; it even recalled the landmark location where the Chambers crime took place. Just as evidently, since editors and reporters immediately knew that minority youths were accused of raping a young white woman, the "Central Park" case revisited the theme of interracial violence.

Yet this sequence of highly profiled 1980s cases evidence more than mere repetitiveness. Observe, too, that the identities of victims and alleged perpetrators alternated through different combinations of race and gender. These went from crimes said to have been committed by white men against a black man, to one by white men against a black woman (Stewart, Bumpurs, 1983-84), to a crime committed by a white male in alleged self-defense against a group of black males supposed to be attacking him (Goetz, 1985), to a crime said to have been committed by a white male against a white woman (Chambers, 1986), on through a crime alleged to have been committed by white males against a black man and then allegedly by white males against a black woman (Howard Beach and Tawana Brawley, 1986–88). When "Central Park" hit the news, it sustained what was simultaneously a pattern of continuity and difference by reversing the racial sociology once more: from a group of whites who allegedly attacked a young black woman (Brawley, 1988) to a group of minority males who allegedly attacked a young white woman ("Central Park jogger," 1989).[26] Tuchman's point therefore seems borne out insofar as the "Central Park" case was appealing to journalists both because of its familiar theme and because of its provision of variation on that theme.[27]

That the historical timing of the "Central Park jogger" case seems hard to explain only by coincidence suggests that editors and reporters do not select cases solely on the basis of journalistic individualism. Instead, they may engage in a more complex decisionmaking process that I call "journalistic relativism."[28] For, rather than selecting a case for its uniqueness, journalists often make cultural associations between past and present events, assessing new developments against the backdrop of cases already established. They make these relative associations out of a professional motivation to find the unexpected within the routine. Yet journalistic relativism is not a practice that is often acknowledged;[29] journalism generally has long held objectivity to be a primary value of the endeavor. Nevertheless, precisely because this customary practice requires relative assessments, editors and reporters necessarily play a role in historical events through the ramifications of their decisions regarding coverage; like all social actors, they are immersed in dynamic cultural processes that have shaped them, and that they in turn help sustain.

Relativism offers a fuller explanation than those of the participants themselves when deciding "why Central Park," because it encompasses both the individual and sociological interpretations lawyers and journalists explicitly cited. Concerning individualism: if Tuchman is right about the appeals of the unexpected, journalistic relativism allows for uniqueness to figure into case selection. In "Central Park," under the category of the "unexpected," fit case-specific traits like those cited by Lederer, Fairstein, Alvarez, and Sachar—for example, that seven other crimes were involved that night, that people empathized with the jogger's vulnerability—that may indeed have endowed this story with special "pegs." At the same time, relativism incorporates the realization that social and historical context also influence journalists' situated assessments of competing news stories; these assessments cannot help but be affected by the racialized, gendered, and class-oriented backgrounds of participants in the "Central Park" case.

Yet more than Tuchman's notion about journalists' interest in novelty within a given context is needed to understand the selection of the "Central Park jogger" case. The writings of Stuart Hall et al. and that of Todd Gitlin also call useful attention to another journalistic tendency: the appeal of stories that involve seemingly stark antagonisms between issues and spokespersons. This tendency was clearly reflected in the highly profiled race and gender crime cases of the 1980s—including "Central Park"—that readily lent themselves to building stories around the oppositional frameworks of blacks versus whites and men versus women. Then, too, the most intensively covered cases of the decade entailed thematic reversals. Recall that the crime cases to which journalists accorded extraordinary attention during the 1980s often reversed the racial identities of victims and perpetrators from one case to a next. Contrasts emerge, for example, in the movement from the "Goetz" case (1986) to "Howard Beach" (1987), and again from "Tawana Brawley" (1988) to "Central Park" (1989). Four months after "Central Park," this pattern of reversal continued into "Bensonhurst" (August 1989), where, instead of an assault alleged to have been committed by minority men against a young white woman ("Central Park"), at issue was an assault alleged to have been committed by white men against a black man.

Logically, a journalistic fondness for framing stories in terms of oppositional categories would likely affect not only why "Central Park" became such a high-profile case, but also how the case was covered. Did the character of early coverage illustrate the proclivity diagnosed by Gitlin to depict an event in terms of stark contrasts—here in terms of blacks versus whites? Let us return to April 21, 1989, when the "Central Park jogger" case was accorded top coverage in each of the city's four daily newspapers: the *New York Times*, the *Daily News*, the *New York Post*, and *Newsday*. The *Times* first reported that a young woman, a "30 year old investment banker," had been raped and severely beaten during a "spontaneous rampage" of youths.[30] However, readers were more likely to remember *News*, *Post*, and *Newsday* coverage precisely because these papers used polarizing language.[31] Not only was the term "wilding" quickly circulated by the *News* and the *Post*, as Fairstein recalled, but some editors and reporters immediately employed analogies between the young minority male defendants and "wolf packs."[32] In the *News*, for example, the April 21 headline—"Wolf Pack's Prey: Female Jogger Near Death after Savage Attack by Roving Gang"—was set in bold block letters. On April 22, the *News*'s editorial declared:

> There was a full moon Wednesday night. A suitable backdrop for the howling of wolves. A vicious pack ran rampant through Central Park. They attacked at least five people. One is now fighting for her life. Perhaps, by the time you read this, she will have lost that fight. She was gang raped. Sadistically beaten. . . . The first four arrested yesterday were juveniles, but they were charged as adults, which is right and proper. This was not shoplifting licorice sticks and bubble gum from a candy counter. This was bestial brutality. This was attempted murder. Or actual murder, if the woman they savaged does die. . . .
>
> The only way to deter these marauding bands is to use the full force of the law against them. The kid gloves have to come off. . . .Wolf packs have been roaming the subway in increasing numbers. Assaulting and robbing passengers. They've declared the subway their turf. Wednesday's wolves declared Central Park their turf. Should they be free to pick and choose their domains this way? Should the entire city be turned over to

them? That will be the message if such delinquents are treated as delinquents. They are not delinquents. They are criminals of the ugliest conceivable kind.[33]

Not only news and editorial writers but columnists, too, wrote in language that was negatively loaded and coded. Note the liberties Mike McAlary took with interpretive projection:

The cops looked hard at them and the kids laughed, one not daring to show weakness in front of another. This is why they wound up in such trouble. Each suspected rapist posed for a color Polaroid snapshot. The poses are unrepentant, the stares hard and unrelenting.

Eventually, between the jokes and singing, a demand was made. "Yo," McCray had announced, "I'm hungry." This, at least showed some need. . . .

A cop looked in and was surprised to see the kids sleeping. A few of them jerked fitfully in sleep, guilt working hard on the body. The copy was glad to see this. "Look," he recalled saying to a detective. "Humans."[34]

While terms of opprobrium were used to describe the defendants, words of praise characterized descriptions of the victim; her life was presented as a gendered embodiment of the "American dream." In the same April 21 issue of the *News* just excerpted, a feature article subtitled "Lived a Dream Life" also described how

[s]he lay unconscious, her body viciously broken, under intensive care. And all anyone could remember about her was grace, cheer and success.

The young woman whose life was jeopardized by marauding teenagers lived the way most of us dream.

She grew up in Upper St. Clair, Pennsylvania, an affluent suburb of doctors, lawyers and professionals, 10 miles south of Pittsburgh, far from the steel mills.

Her mother is a member of the school board and former Republic committeewoman. One brother was said to be a lawyer in Hartford, another an assistant district attorney in Dallas.

After graduating from high school in 1978, she headed east for Wellesley College, an exclusive women's college near Boston. She majored in economics and graduated Phi Beta Kappa. She was much more than a

Fig. 1. Headlines like this one, appearing immediately after "Central Park," set concerns about racism into motion as the media started to use "wolf pack" imagery.

brain. In her yearbook photo she appears as a pretty blond in a turtleneck sweater with an engaging smile and eyes gleaming with promise.[35]

On the one hand, then, the jogger exemplified a "pretty," young, upper-middle-class career woman; she was a "brilliant financier," a "Phi Beta Kappa graduate, employed in the corporate finance department of Salomon Brothers investment banking firm." On the other, her attackers were depicted as something almost subhuman—a remorseless "wolf pack." Hardly could the opposition between victim and defendant, good and evil, be more stark and less subtle. Looking back, some journalists expressed misgivings about the racial stereotypes they employed. According to one reporter, who preferred to remain anonymous, "perhaps we should have played our feelings more to the vest."[36] Another writer at the News thought that "wolf pack language shouldn't be used because it's become a hot button. Then I wouldn't have been sensitive to it because I thought it would be used for white kids as well." [37] (See fig. 1.) Yet a third reporter then also at the *News*, Lizette Alvarez, recalled in an interview:

LA: I thought the coverage did get out of hand, and I was part of it. . . . Now that I'm older and more experienced, I wouldn't have used the same words. . . . We were using words like "wolf pack," derogatory language. . . . People were already using the terms and you found yourself caught up. . . . It was kind of the status quo, it's sensationalistic at the *News*. . . . Now, I would try not to be so inflammatory with my writing. The media coverage of TV was also having an effect, and the jogger was characterized as basically a saint because she was very pretty, she jogged, she went to Wellesley. . . . She was the stereotype of the good girl and she took on almost mythic proportions.

LC: Could you have been more analytic?

LA: No, it's not their style. . . . I would have tried not to use those words, because it became quite an easy way to try these kids. . . . The tough thing about New York was the competition, too, from other newspapers because you knew other papers beat you to a story. [38]

Why were some journalists regretful? One cause for concern that arises in retrospect is that, as Alvarez notes, the effect of "sensationalistic" coverage may have been to "try these kids" in the press. Think of the *News*'s editorial declamation: "They've declared the subway their turf. Should they be free to pick and choose their domains this way?" By implication, the defendants who had been arrested already were portrayed as having committed the crime; yet on April 22, as these words were written and stereotypes were circulating, plans for a trial had not even begun. Although the press was well aware that Lederer had rapidly obtained videotaped confessions on the night of April 20, the accused in principle were innocent until proven guilty in a court of law.

But perhaps even more germane to reporters' assessments of their part in the case is that they could have hardly known at the time that the racial stereotypes used in their coverage would soon provoke anger and controversy from parties outside the media. Nor did they know that these reactions would swell the case into an even "bigger" story than predictable in advance. Yet without an outburst of public reactions, which journalists set into motion but did not have the power to control, it is unlikely that the "Central Park jogger" case would have grown into the most intensively covered crime story of 1989.[39] I turn now to explore some of these public reactions: Why did various publics feels compelled to respond?

AN EXPLOSION OF PUBLIC REACTIONS: CONCERNS OVER RACISM

German social theorist Jurgen Habermas argued that contemporary media have contributed to a transformation of the "public sphere."[40] Whereas large outdoor plazas or town hall meetings were the site of discussions affecting large numbers of people in the nineteenth century, collective debates in the early twenty-first century often take place through vehicles of mass communication: in the pages of competing newspapers; on television talk shows; or, most recently, on the Internet. But this does not mean that public reactions are limited to their expression in mass-mediated contexts. Rather, as suggested by interviews in which people recalled their impressions of the 1989 "Central Park jogger" case, a back-and-forth process unfolds as responses internal and external to the media interact; each is influenced by, yet relatively independent of, the other. As this dynamic played out in "Central Park," one of the strongest public reactions first expressed—outside as well as in print—was resentment about the racial stereotypes that marked early newspaper coverage.

According to William Perkins, then president of the tenants' association at Schomburg Plaza in East Harlem where many of the arrested young men lived:

WP: People felt children were being accused of something that didn't fit their understanding of those children and immediately the media began to treat them as wild animals and to dehumanize them. It became a black/white thing in as many metaphorical ways as one can imagine in this society: black boys/white woman, rape, Scottsboro, evil, good. They were effectively tried, convicted, and sentenced in the press before they even got a lawyer when you think about it. . . . People were put in a very defensive situation. I think it was the Sunday *New York Post* delivered that edition free to us at the complex with the headline "Wolf Pack." They called her the Central Park jogger, and they called them the wolf pack. There's no question that they were treating her differently. She was the victim of a very horrible experience and she was not to blame for the way the media portrayed the case. But I think there was a commercial interest involved in what sells papers. She was a symbol of white female purity, used at times justifiably and other times unjustifiably to assault the community. I don't think the preoccupation of most people was venting anger against her, just providing the boys with a proper defense given the media onslaught. This also traumatized the community, giving the impression of this as a community of wild animals. Young people going down to get a job that summer might hesitate to say where they were from.

LC: How would you characterize people's reactions?

WP: Some people thought it was embarrassing, and didn't want to deal with it at their jobs and with white co-workers. Some people were angry because there was a trial in the press, and the community was being attacked. Some people felt sympathy for the victim; others thought, what was she doing there? There were several vigils for the victim, and some for the families, recognizing they were in need of support. . . . But the media was clearly on a mission to destroy these kids and sell those papers.[41]

Evidently Perkins felt both sympathy for the jogger and dismay at the oppositional framework used in media coverage. In the words of Nomsa Brath, who also lived at Schomburg Plaza and was known by residents as a local activist, "People were very upset about the use of wolf pack language. There's a long history of these kinds of attacks on our community." Brath, too, emphasized that cynicism toward the media had not negated concerns about the young woman. She remembered several candlelight vigils sponsored "by one of the churches to show that the community did not support any criminal activity, and felt sorry for the plight of the young lady. It was a way of the community bouncing back from negative media hype about the community at large."[42] A young Latina woman who had been living in the neighborhood and attending Columbia University at the time of the rape, recalled her resentment at the newspapers for calling the suspects names "that would never be used to describe kids in Westchester":

And I don't believe that anything close to similar attention would have been given to someone who looked like me. . . . The media coverage was definitely biased. . . . However I noticed that in discussing it in my classes and even outside the classroom, among a mixed group of people, with white people in particular, the issue of race was not being confronted. . . .

I think sometimes it's just so deeply embedded in people's ideologies that it's hard for them to distinguish what is and what isn't racist.[43]

Similar reactions to these were recorded in the public sphere of news coverage. For example, the New York Times reported several vigils and flowers sent to the young woman in the hospital by six hundred families representing the Residents Council of Schomburg Plaza. But the paper also noted community dismay at racial stereotypes; William Perkins was quoted as saying he hoped for the healing of "both the wounds on her body and the racial wounds this has caused to society."[44] Another story mentioned six or seven ministers singing "We Shall Overcome" at one of the vigils, and alluding to the 1960s civil rights movement after they were surrounded by a group of reporters.[45]

Comparisons were also made between the treatment of the suspects in the "Central Park" case and racial discrimination manifested in earlier high-profile crimes that were notorious in New York City. For instance, some people mentioned the case's potential to feed the same sort of misconceptions about young black males that had led to Michael Griffith's death in the "Howard Beach" case. At the offices of the NAACP, the phones were said to have "lit up" with calls from Harlem residents outraged that the eight suspects in "Central Park" were being held in the city's jails, whereas the "Howard Beach" suspects had been released on bail in 1987.[46] Evidently, then, it was not only reporters and editors who made relative assessments of past high-profile crime cases involving accusations of racism. Members of the public, too, drew on cultural associations that had become well known from prior media usage. But if journalists were implicitly inclined by professional habit to make connections between cases, what motivated parties angered at racial stereotypes to connect "Howard Beach" and "Central Park" explicitly?

For many who participated in protests about the earlier case, Michael Griffith's death represented both a specific incident and a wider problem: "Howard Beach" became a powerful symbol of ongoing racial violence in northern cities.[47] Likewise, in the wake of its provocative publicity, "Central Park" came to be perceived as potentially damaging to more than only individual black and Latino defendants. Once teenage defendants had been subjected to stereotypical coverage, doubts were expressed about whether minority youths in general could obtain a fair trial if faced with similar charges. Consequently, the association in public discourse of "Howard Beach" and

"Central Park" tied one symbolic crime case to another; for various parties concerned about racism, the connection bolstered claims about troubling social patterns that extended beyond individual instances alone. According to Al Sharpton, one of the ministers who attended the vigil where references to the 1960s were made, protesting these and other 1980s crime cases was connected with a larger movement against racism:

> AS: No no no. It's not people who don't see it. The media doesn't see it. People—now that's my argument. The reason when people can't see it is because no one writes it that way. Let me tell you why I say this. Howard Beach happens (clap of hands).
> LC: Right.
> AS: Mrs. Griffith calls me. We start the march and we do what we have to do. Brawley happens. Same thing. Central Park. Bensonhurst happens. Same thing. Now, every case I was involved with, I was called. . . .
> LC: Everybody calls you?
> AS: All right, now, but that's my point. Now the media operates as though these are isolated incidents, but the people in the community understand it's a movement, otherwise they wouldn't have called me. It isn't like they call different people for every case. . . . So the people in the community understand it's a movement, they're relating it not just to this isolated incident, but that this has to do with racism in American society. But the media won't write it that way.[48]

Thus Sharpton made comparisons between cases for reasons, and in ways, that were virtually opposite to how journalists typically understand themselves to operate. Whereas many journalists see themselves as scrupulously apolitical,[49] Sharpton sought to expose racial patterns for expressly political purposes. As an engaged social movement participant, Sharpton emphasized his interest in making conscious case-after-case connections, and in using the media to this end.

"Central Park" symbolized other social problems, too, for parties resentful about racially stereotypical coverage; it was not only Sharpton who feared the incident's repercussions. Related discussions ensued about whether youth violence stemmed from social or individual causes. On April 24, 1989, immediately following the crime, one *Times* story described how "blacks debated what they said were the larger issues that the incident brings to light—needs for better housing, education and job opportunities." [50] Earl Caldwell, making comparisons with Claude Brown's *Manchild in the Promised Land*, opined that an African American summit taking place in New Orleans to set a black agenda for the 1990s should have been held in New York City. That agenda, he declared, had already begun to be set "after dark on Wednesday on the north side of Central Park." [51] Caldwell went on to bemoan how, with the young suspects branded as animals, little attention was paid to the "fear and racism" permeating their lives. "It will all get worse, and race will only become a greater part of the story," Caldwell declared. "The larger America does not care. . . . America has already chosen blindness, refusing to see what is happening to kids. Who then would expect America to worry, to be concerned at all, to reach out to kids from the world of dismal projects and welfare hotels and crack-infested streets?" [52]

ANOTHER SYMBOLIZED PROBLEM: INNER CITY VIOLENCE, AND THEN VIOLENCE AGAINST WOMEN

The concerns about racism were only one set of reactions to the "Central Park jogger" case. Other responses, equally impassioned, were spurred by entirely different concerns: many people, for example, were enraged not by the controversial character of media coverage so much as the violent brutality of the reported crime. Whereas for some people, "Central Park" symbolized problems of racial and class discrimination, for others, it represented the problem of inner city violence having careened out of control. A typical representative of those who felt this concern was then-Mayor Koch, whose acerbic tongue was one of his trademarks. When asked by a reporter at a City Hall conference whether there were underlying social causes of the Central Park crime such as poverty or discrimination, the Mayor retorted not to put the "blame on society." "You name me one social reason that would cause thirty-six people to engage in a wolf pack operation looking for victims," Koch asserted, "and eight or nine of them to engage in a gang bang. That's what it is, a gang-bang rape. You name me one social reason you can give to explain it." [53] And while some people angered about racism had called the NAACP to register their reactions to the media coverage, others contacted WMCA radio talk show host Barry Gray. Gray recalled he received numerous calls from listeners "inflamed about the black youth," describing their reactions to the case as "*Mississippi Burning* comes to 'Times Square.' I've heard more yells of 'nigger,' 'they should be castrated,' 'string them up' than belong in any civilized community."[54]

Some people interpreted "Central Park" to mean that greater attention should be paid to the social causes and consequences of racism. For others, the incident crystallized a need for harsher social policies aimed at tightening the individual culpability of criminals. An op-ed piece written by Bill Reel mocked the criminal justice system's ineffective liberalism; incarceration, he claimed, was not sufficiently frightening teenagers like those accused of raping the Central Park jogger. By way of remedy, Reel suggested building Quonset huts to house prisoners in low-cost jails.[55] John H. Gutfreund, chairman and chief executive officer of Salomon Brothers, Inc., the prestigious investment house that employed the young woman, wrote in a letter to the Times: "In the name of this young woman, all her friends and colleagues at Salomon Brothers, and the many other victims of equally ugly assaults, we ask: How long will the growing reign of terror in public places be tolerated?" He went on to "implore the political leaders of this city, state and nation to see and understand what is happening on the streets of our cities. . . . Only a national campaign, which mobilized all our best resources to support anticrime programs and tough measures, will save our cities for us today and for our children tomorrow."[56]

On May 1, 1989, perhaps the most dramatic example of "get tough" policies demanded in the wake of the "Central Park jogger" case appeared. The well-known real estate developer Donald Trump ran $85,000 worth of newspaper advertisements in the *New York Times*, the *Daily News*, the *New York Post*, and *New York Newsday*; he called for the reinstatement of capital punishment in a full page *Times* advertisement. Note the impact this ad was likely to have, given its size, strong wording, and emotion-laden references to the horrors of urban violence (see fig. 2):

> What has happened to our City over the past ten years? . . . What has happened to the respect for authority, the fear of retribution by the courts, society and the police for those who break the law, who wantonly trespass on the rights of others? What has happened is the complete breakdown of life as we knew it. . . . [R]oving bands of wild criminals roam our neighborhoods, dispensing their own vicious brand of twisted hatred on whomever they encounter. . . . Mayor Koch has stated that hate and rancor should be

Fig. 2. Reacting to "Central Park" as a symbol of urban violence less than one month after the crime occurred, Donald Trump took out a full-page ad in the *New York Times* urging capital punishment for the young men arrested. The size and strongly worded contents of this ad further inflamed concerns about racism, as figure 3 also indicates.

Trump's 'Kill them' ad condemned

COLIN MOORE   DONALD TRUMP

By J. ZAMGBA BROWNE
Amsterdam News Staff

A full-page newspaper ad by developer Donald Trump, calling for the death penalty in the wake of an alleged rape and assault two weeks ago in Central Park of a Wall Street executive by a gang of teens is being widely condemned.

Even Mayor Koch seemed outraged Monday by the ad Trump carried in the New York Times and three other publications, criticizing the city's justice system for allowing criminals to prey on innocent victims.

"Nobody I know of in Western society," the mayor was quoted as saying, "believes that under any circumstances would you ever impose the death penalty on juveniles."

Attorney Colin Moore who represents one of the teens accused in the Central Park attack, said he had always suspected that intelligence had nothing to do with wealth and Trump through his ad, has proved this to be a fact.

"What Trump's hysterical outburst proves," Moore declared, "is that in America, anything is possible. Even a fool can become a multi-millionaire."

The Brooklyn attorney said he did not hear Trump advocating the death penalty when Michael Stewart, Michael Griffin, Eleanor Bumpurs and Derick Antonio Tyrus were all murdered by whites.

"All of a sudden, when a white individual is attacked," *(Continued on Page 33)*

Fig. 3. On May 6, 1989, New York City's *Amsterdam News* reported that Donald Trump's full-page ad in the *New York Times,* as well as similar advertisements that appeared in other papers, was being "widely condemned." According to Colin Moore, an attorney for one of the "Central Park" defendants, this ad was reminiscent of racist attitudes prematurely expressed in the 1930s during the "Scottsboro Boys" case.

removed from our hearts. I do not think so. I want to hate these muggers and murderers. They should be forced to suffer and, when the kill, they should be executed for their crimes. . . . Yes, Mayor Koch, I want to hate these murderers and I always will. I am not looking to psychoanalyze or understand them. I am looking to punish them. . . . Let our politicians give back our police departments power to keep us safe. Unshackle them from the constant chant of "police brutality" which every petty criminal hurls immediately at an officer who has just risked his or her life to save another's. Send a message loud and clear to those who would murder our citizens and terrorize New York: BRING BACK THE DEATH PENALTY AND BRING BACK OUR POLICE!"[57]

Following the appearance of Trump's statement, Al Sharpton organized a protest outside Trump Tower. People held signs condemning Trump and demanding, with purposeful irony, "the execution of the white teenagers involved in the 1986 death of a black man in Howard Beach, Queens."[58] Thus a point/counterpoint dynamic started to operate between the respondents just described. Intensely emotional and politicized reactions sparked other reactions, outside and inside the mediated public sphere; these then occasioned ongoing coverage in turn. In this vein, *The Times* noted that efforts had been initiated by a number of the city's black clergy to raise funds for another full *Times* ad to counter the political influence of Trump's.[59]

In the May 6, 1989 issue of the *Amsterdam News*—the city's largest African American newspaper, boasting a circulation of over two hundred thousand—Colin Moore also responded to Trump, making another case comparison that reached beyond New York City (see figure 3). "Evidently," said Moore, a lawyer long associated with civil rights activism who had agreed to represent one of the "Central Park" defendants, "Trump wants to return to the Alabama of the 1940s and the Mississippi of the 1950s. If this is Trump's vision of capitalist America in the 21st century, I want no part of it." Moore compared the "railroading" of the teenagers in the 1989 "Central Park jogger" case to one of the most famous high-profile crime cases involving race and gender in twentieth-century American history: the case of the "Scottsboro Boys," which resulted in nine black youths sentenced to execution after being accused of raping two white women in Alabama in 1931.[60]

This analogy was only partially valid. Given a long history of biases in the South, it made sense regarding racism. But it was not accurate regarding sexism. Unlike in "Scottsboro," in which it was eventually revealed that two young white women had falsely accused the nine black youths,[61] the jogger in Central Park had clearly been raped. That Moore nevertheless made the comparison suggests that some "victim blaming" of the jogger had developed, though this never became the dominant reaction on the part of the East Harlem community; recall, for example, that many East Harlem residents had organized vigils to pray for the young woman's recovery soon after her assault. While therefore not necessarily representative of many community residents' opinions, a May 6, 1989 *Amsterdam News* lead news story also cast doubt on the verity of the jogger's attack. This article concerned a black woman who had been raped and killed in Fort Tryon Park around the same time; its first sentence read in part, "after the Wall Street banker, allegedly raped and beaten in Central Park by a group of teens . . . ."[62] Even earlier, the *Amsterdam News* was the only newspaper in the city to "break" the jogger's name, doing so in its April 29th lead news story on "Central Park." Yet in the May 6 story, the name of the young woman raped and killed in Tryon Park was omitted.

Thus the reality of the violence against the Central Park jogger came to be presented by some inconsistently and with a dash of cynicism, as though it was more dubious than the reality of crimes committed against women of color that had been ignored by the New York press. Shades of the "Scottsboro" comparison, imprecise in this respect, were thereby reiterated. In response to criticisms of the decision to reveal only the jogger's identity, a May 13 editorial explained that the decision

> came about as a consequence of terminal racism on the part of some few writers in the white media who have for years tried to convince us of their liberalism as well as devotion to civil liberties and civil rights. These liberals, in all things except race and sex, saw no problem at all with naming Black children who got themselves caught up in the form of terrorizing for which the Black community has apologized on bended knee, and for which those guilty will be prosecuted. . . . This is hypocritical, clap-trap bull—and this newspaper mightily resents racist white newspapers for making an effort to impose their phony morality on us, while they continue to do anything they please.[63]

Thus, once early media coverage had constructed stark oppositions between the "evil" of the accused and the "goodness" of the victim, responses to "Central Park" unfolded analogously along highly polarized lines. On the one hand were those who placed relatively greater emphasis on defending the defendants' rights to a fair trial; on the other were those whose primary aim was to protest violence suffered by the victim. This suggests that the media's fondness for oppositional frameworks also influenced ensuing public debates. As this happened, a wide range of actors outside the media—from active community figures and social movement activists to politicians, businessmen, and audiences attuned to the news—began to make the "Central Park" case into a potent symbol of several contemporary social problems. For some, the crime represented ongoing racial and class discrimination in New York; for others, it signified growing worries about urban violence. But common to both positions was that "Central Park" started to crystallize both a specific incident and general problems. Indeed, one might hypothesize that unless a particular high-profile crime rapidly provokes cultural, social, and political debate about that case's larger significance, its newsworthiness will soon wane. Conversely, if a given case becomes powerfully evocative for two sets of parties, each with their own social and political agendas—exactly as was happening in the "Central Park" case—media coverage is likely to grow through, and perhaps even beyond, forthcoming trials.

But one further point about reactions on the part of the public is equally important. While journalistic propensities certainly influence the shape and contents of debates surrounding an event, by no means are the media by themselves capable of determining audience responses. The "Central Park jogger" case reflects a more complicated story unraveling, one in which the power of mass media was at once present but also limited. The journalists covering the case could no more definitely predict the character of reactions to their coverage than they could know with certainty that "Central Park" would resound as widely as it did.

WERE OTHER REACTIONS ALSO PRESENT?

Related to matters concerning both the power and the limitations of mass media is the following query: Were the public reactions recorded in the press even representative of a possibly more diverse range of responses which may have been occurring? Research based on interviews and the use of media texts indicates that there were alternative responses—many of which did not conform to the evolving two-sided framework—that did ensue soon after the crime. Some of these responses to the "Central Park jogger" case were verbalized in relatively private conversations between friends, family, and associates. Others entailed strongly expressed political beliefs and actions that never attracted journalistic attention. In still other instances, parties frustrated by the dominant parameters of debate aired their feelings in public, though in "alternative" rather than "mainstream" media venues. Finally, situations arose in which divergent perspectives did find mainstream expression. But once the dominant framework of debate surrounding the case solidified, these perspectives did not challenge but tended to be subsumed within the highly visible structure of one "side" versus the other.

Let us look more closely at this group of not easily classifiable reactions to "Central Park." For one thing, recall that William Perkins and Nomsa Brath stressed that while they were concerned about racism, they also were very troubled by the violence the victim had endured. For Emma Jones, who worked at the Schomburg Library around the time of the Central Park jogger's rape, another problem yet was raised by the case: neither dominant side of public debate adequately captured the complexity of her reactions as an African American woman. Her reaction was to consider the symbolic meaning of several social problems simultaneously:

> Yes, there's the issue of race that played so much into it getting as much attention as it did. But also I'm a woman, and it was a rape case. So I had a lot of conflicting feelings. . . . You know, I wasn't supposed to identify with the woman who was raped, because she was white, supposedly, and I wouldn't, you know; and I was supposed to identify with the black kids because they were being persecuted because of their race. . . . So it was very difficult just dealing with the reactions of everyone, and how they were looking at the rape . . . it got to the point where it wasn't even a factor if they did it or not. It just got to the point where it kept continuing. They wanted it to continue. I mean black and white, black and white.[64]

While this young woman's words were not reported by the media, Lisa Kennedy's thoughts did appear in print but in an alternative news venue. In a May 9, 1989 special section of the *Village Voice* entitled "The Voices Not Heard: Black and Women Writers on the Central Park Rape," Kennedy portrayed a dilemma not unlike the one described by Jones:

> As a black woman, I find myself in a schizo state of mind, my body fragmented beyond thought: woman or black? Is it possible to resist the to-

and-fro of that identity, and try to speak from my body? These are the times that try my black woman's mind, when every word is measured for what it will cost my body. If I accept the premise of the coverage, that this rape is more heartbreaking than all the rapes that happen to women of color, then what happens to the value of my body? What happens to the quality of my blackness? . . . For me, the flux is always there. You live with the contradiction, I do, 24 hours a day. To bad-mouth the youths means taking a chance that my language might be used against me, against blacks. If I remain silent, or hem and haw about the outrage against women, then again I am in danger.[65]

In the same issue, Greg Tate expressed his dismay about dominant narratives in public debate that were presenting overly facile views of African American women's and men's opinions. Tate challenged as simplistic the two-sided nature of debate in which one "either" sympathized with the jogger "or" spoke out against racist media coverage; like Kennedy, he wished to carve alternative positions from within the realm of "in but not of" mainstream journalism.[66]

Notice that, whether said privately or written publicly in an alternative weekly like the *Voice*, implicit in the perspectives of Jones, Kennedy, and Tate was a shared sense of dissatisfaction. Though stressing different points, each reaction drew from only part of the mainstream media's construction of counterposed "sides." Whereas each reaction included strong sympathy for the jogger, Jones, Kennedy, and Tate also each expressed concerns about ongoing racial biases in the media and the criminal justice system. Thus, their reactions were more nuanced than the simple "pro-victim" perspective of Donald Trump—precisely because Trump's position smacked of sensationalism and racial bias itself.

But Jones's and Tate's reactions diverged, too, from many of the "prodefendant" positions that were part of the public debate. Each feared that overly simplistic positions were being portrayed as though "the" dominant opinions on race in the "Central Park jogger" case. For Jones, it did not necessarily follow from her concerns about racism, both in the media and the public at large, that one should be barred from asking whether the defendants were guilty. And Tate, angered at an April 29 lead story in the *Amsterdam News*, which made it the only newspaper in the city to disclose the jogger's identity, saw signs of victim-blaming gradually ensuing through racialized reactions to the case—simply because the young woman was white. Indeed, a May 13 editorial in the *Amsterdam News* sought to justify that paper's decision to disclose the young woman's identity on the grounds that the names of the defendants had already appeared in the mainstream press; according to that editorial, using the victim's name afterward was "a consequence of terminal racism on the part of some few writers in the white media."[67] For Tate, though, this was "knee-jerk nationalism at its most atrocious."[68]

Common to these "voices not heard," then, was that they comprised opinions only partially represented by the two highly publicized "sides" as expressed in and outside the mainstream press. Each of these reactions protested the emerging "either/or" structure of debate that seemed to demand affiliations be declared in favor of one side (relatively more sympathetic to the defendants) or another (relatively more sympathetic to the victim). Yet while these positions aimed to combine aspects of both dominant frameworks—to recognize racial and class biases, as well as the seriousness of gendered violence symbolized by the "Central Park" case—not much room for synthetic alternatives noticeably existed in the public sphere. As Tate recognized, to be published in the *Village Voice* was not the same as to be heard in the mainstream press. Far more people were likely to read and to be influenced by public reactions reported in the *New York Times*, the *Daily News*, the *New York Post*, and *New York Newsday*. But in these mainstream venues, too, were reactions being aired that fell outside the dominant two-sided framework?

In her study, journalist Helen Benedict found that one set of public reactions conspicuously omitted from public debate about "Central Park" in April and May 1989 involved gender. Benedict argued that mainstream journalists had elicited public commentary about the jogger case from just about every social problem "angle"—poverty, race, class, crime, education—except violence against women. For the most part, this account confirmed Benedict's conclusion that, compared with expressions of concern about race and class discrimination, gender bias was not an initially highlighted topic of discussion.[69] On the other hand, reactions focusing on gendered violence did surface in the form of opinion pieces in the *New York Times* and the *Daily News*.[70] Obviously, then, these perspectives on gender bias had not been omitted entirely from public debate.[71]

On May 6, two op-ed pieces by well-known women appeared in the *Times*: one by Ronnie Eldridge, then a Democratic candidate for city council and head of the Battered Women's Defense Committee, the other by then-

Brooklyn district attorney Elizabeth Holtzman. In addition, on May 7 Susan Brownmiller, author of the influential 1975 book *Against Our Will: Men, Women and Rape*, took to the floor of public debate in the *Daily News* as a feminist intellectual. All three articles stressed a similar point: the "Central Park jogger" case was not simply an act by "blacks" against "whites" (or, more accurately, in this case, by African American and Latino male youths against a Caucasian young woman). Rather, a violent crime by men against women had been committed. As Holtzman put it: "Explanations that rely on race or class alone miss the key role that gender played. The jogger was victimized because she was a woman, and the boys apparently acted out of a misguided notion of how to prove their manhood." [72] Through this set of public reactions, then, another symbolic dimension of the case was brought to public notice with political implications of its own: safer conditions were needed to protect women from violence.

Although these articles aptly called attention to the omission of gendered violence from public debate, neither Eldridge nor Holtzman criticized the problems of racial and class stereotyping that also marked early media coverage and many ensuing public reactions. These writers' focus was gender, and the sole solution they recommended entailed making society safer for women through more stringent criminal justice measures and "sex offender" programs. But by omitting mention of racial and class biases—rather than analyzing the several social problems raised by "Central Park" for diverse groups of women as well as diverse groups of men—one overly simplistic framework of debate ("black" versus "white") [73] stood to be replaced by another ("men" versus "women"). A subtle ramification of this omission was that rather than challenging the previously two-sided parameters of discussion, their apparently new perspective could be subsumed under one of the two "sides" already dominating the debate. That is, since one side already placed relatively greater emphasis on problems facing defendants, and the other stressed violence suffered by a victim, the op-eds written by Eldridge and Holtzman about gendered victimization were easy to classify as a subset of the second position.

But Brownmiller's May 7 piece in the *Daily News* risked an even more serious potential pitfall, one of commission rather than omission: subtly, her language seemed to recycle the tenor of earlier racial biases themselves. Brownmiller started by citing criminologist Marvin Wolfgang's "subculture of violence" thesis. Unlike Eldridge and Holtzman, she explicitly referred to problems of class (if not race) to

> define the phenomenon of poorly socialized, or countersocialized, young men who develop a value system of prideful physical aggression based on distorted perceptions of masculinity. Not surprisingly, the subculture of violence is located largely in the lower and lower-middle classes, where the limitations on socially approved economic opportunities—a sanctioned form of aggression—are most severe, and where blind, angry frustration is likely to collect.[74]

However, the same criticism of Wolfgang's work could be applied to Brownmiller's later adaptation of it. As with "culture of poverty" and "underclass" theories, "subculture of violence" arguments target individual characteristics as causes of behavior, but tend to overlook structural conditions that place "limitations on socially approved economic opportunities." Perhaps not surprisingly, then, Brownmiller's piece in the *Daily News* edged toward a sociobiological focus on the young men's "raging hormonal tides" and a discussion of "packs" and their characteristics.[75] It was this part of her piece that seems, in retrospect, quite provocative in the context of the "Central Park jogger" case:

> They "act out," they fight, they hit, they aggress, they bond into roaming packs with a certain predictability and frequent recurrence. Unless these biological aggressive impulses are mediated by a strong, moral value system ascribed to by their peers, the youths can find themselves in Central Park one night engaged in a brutal rampage that neither they, their parents, nor their lawyers, can explain. . . . By sheer virtue of unequal numbers, gang rape is the ultimate act of cowards. Yet ironically, the act is perceived by the sweating, jostling pack as a ritualistic expression of manhood.[76]

But was it likely in New York City at that time that references to the "pack" would not be read racially? After all, Brownmiller was writing in the *Daily News*, in which reporters' sensationalistic references to "pack" behavior had been loudly protested only ten days beforehand. No doubt, Brownmiller meant the word to signify boys' hormones out of control; she sought to emphasize problems of all "masculinities," across race and class, insofar as men may learn to treat women as objects.[77] Still, the careless use of language risked reinforcing the oppositional "blacks versus whites," and tapping earlier polarizations that existed "between women." [78] Indeed, divisiveness within the women's movement predated "Central Park." These involved schisms between what some perceived as a unidimensional "white feminism" that focused on gender biases, on the one hand, and more recent feminist perspectives that emphasized women's and men's race- and class-based differences as well. [79] In regard to "Central Park," many women of color who were not economically well-to-do feared that should they become victims of gendered violence, their race and class would result in "invisibility" rather than any attention being paid to assaults against them. [80] For this reason a racially insensitive comment about male defendants could also be perceived as problematic by, and for, women of color.

Even if Brownmiller sought to introduce a different interpretation into the mainstream of public debate, then, her *Daily News* piece fell short of this goal. By overlooking the recent use of racially charged language, Brownmiller's gender-centered perspective came even closer than Eldridge's or Holtzman's to illustrating divisions that writers in the May 9 *Village Voice* had criticized. Consequently, even in these instances, where "alternative" opinions about gender did surface in mainstream newspapers, the dominant terms of two-sided debate were not significantly challenged. Rather, social reactions concerning gender bias were counterposed against reactions concerning racial and class biases.

Thus, both media coverage and a range of public reactions contributed to the visible dominance of a largely two-sided framework by late April and early May 1989. For many reporters and editors, the 1989 "Central Park jogger" case appealed to journalists by varying "routine" themes about discrimination raised by previous New York City high-profile crimes, including the 1987 "Howard Beach" and 1988 "Tawana Brawley" cases. Befitting typical journalistic practices, oppositions were constructed in several mainstream newspapers' accounts of "Central Park": minority defendants were likened to "wolf packs" threatening the safety of city residents; on the other side, the jogger was portrayed as a gendered representative of the urban middle class, whose life was nearly destroyed by the horrifying violence committed against her. The broader public beyond the media, too, contributed to the unfolding of seemingly opposed sides. Once the "Central Park" case was endowed with symbolic significance, different parties looked to the mass media to publicize their larger concerns and to express passionate feelings—from resentment to rage—evoked by the crime and its representation. Some of these reactions targeted social problems of racial and class bias, including the stereotypical character of newspaper coverage. Other reactions centered on the need for "get tough" policies toward individuals responsible for violence, and on the specifically gendered problem of violence against women. The notoriety of the case grew, then, both through coverage of the crime and coverage of reactions to the crime. At the same time, not all reactions were given equal consideration in the mainstream media; responses that reinforced a two-sided framework enjoyed an advantage.

Here, Todd Gitlin's observations seem germane not only to the polarization of "sides" but to the emergence of clearly antagonized—and well-known—spokespersons on behalf of these sides. As in the 1960s New Left described by Gitlin, in "Central Park" too the polarized parties were clear: on one side of public debate, social movement advocates Al Sharpton, C. Vernon Mason, and Alton Maddox were each concerned about race and class discrimination the case symbolized. Indeed, their names were already well known from the recent high-profile "Howard Beach" and "Tawana Brawley" incidents. That they once again were given a voice in the media coverage of "Central Park" reflects a journalistic predisposition to turn to familiar figures even when varying the "routine" cases with which these figures were identified. Again, as sociologists of the media have observed, such "informants" are relied on by reporters working under tight deadlines.[81]

On the other side of public debate were businessmen and politicians, including Donald Trump and Ed Koch, who took up the symbolic implications of "Central Park" about rising inner city crime. Of course, Koch had also commented on cases like "Howard Beach" and "Tawana Brawley." Thus the forms of debate indulged in by journalists and outside reacting publics came to coincide; this coincidence occurred even though journalists' motives were often expressly apolitical and individualizing, and public actors' motives often unabashedly partisan and generalizing.

Media perspectives and consequent public reactions also varied among themselves. Clearly, interpretations of "Central Park" aired in the *Daily News* differed from the accounts published in the African-American-owned *Amsterdam News*, which in turn diverged from perspectives on the case published in the *Village Voice*. Moreover, while the *Amsterdam News* tended to blame the victim, important to underscore is that community residents and activists like William Perkins and Nomsa Brath took pains to stress their sympathy for the jogger; again community vigils in East Harlem were held to pray for her. Not only were the reactions of businessmen like Trump and Gutfreund opposite those of social movement activists like Sharpton and Moore, but degrees of separation existed between their reactions too, as they did among the relatively unheard responses of the public at large. But even given these variations, one wonders whether diverse journalistic practices and diverse public reactions were propelled by common motivations. Did both find something about this framework compelling?

Despite evidence of efforts to unseat it, the stubborn persistence of a predominantly two-sided framework of interpretation suggests cultural and institutional propensities that may be widespread indeed. In 1989, the story of the Central Park jogger—a young, successful white woman brutally raped and attacked by a group of minority male teens—provided a narrative framework for debating a wide range of social problems from inner-city crime to racial discrimination, violence against women, and the role of the media itself. As the controversy surrounding the case unfolded, "sides" may have been appealing because they offered relatively identifiable objects of blame through which anger at individuals, or resentments at institutions, could be expressed. For some people, the defendants were clearly the culprits; to others, media biases were greatly at fault. And this ability to offer concreteness, this crystallization of responsibility in the form of antagonized sides, facilitated a mode of debate that was at once serious and visceral, rationally argued and emotionally intense.

Chapter 3 explores whether these same observations apply to the next highly publicized crime case, which took place four months after the rape of the Central Park jogger; the murder of Yusef Hawkins in Bensonhurst, Brooklyn in August 1989.

The Murder of Yusef Hawkins

On the evening of Wednesday, August 23, 1989, four young men went to see a 1982 Pontiac for sale in Bensonhurst, Brooklyn. After taking the subway from their East New York, Brooklyn homes, sixteen-year-old Yusef Hawkins and three friends walked along Bensonhurst's Twentieth Avenue past an elementary school where a large group of white young men, and one black youth, were gathered with baseball bats.[1] According to John DeSantis, author of an account of the case, "the four black youths heard footsteps approaching. Luther [Sylvester] turned and saw a group of white men—he would later figure twenty or thirty—coming toward them further down the street."[2] Surrounding them, the larger group told the four to get out of their neighborhood. One of Yusef Hawkins's friends protested that they must be after the wrong people, but to no avail. Someone produced a gun and shot Hawkins in the chest. The shooter was later identified as a local Bensonhurst resident named Joseph Fama.

Yusef Hawkins was rushed to Maimonedes Hospital, where he was pronounced dead on arrival. DeSantis implies that the police alerted the medical examiner's office that a potentially controversial crime had been committed; contrary to usual procedures, a van arrived from the New York City Medical Examiner's office to take the body from Brooklyn to Manhattan.[3]

GENERATING DIVERSE PARTICIPATION AGAIN: ANOTHER CASE BECOMES A CAUSE

By the morning of Friday, August 25, major media as well as the city's top criminal justice officials and politicians clearly knew about the case and were paying it extraordinary attention. On that day, each of New York City's four major newspapers—the *New York Times*, the *Daily News*, the *Post*, and *Newsday*—ran the murder among their top news stories. In the *Times*, Brooklyn district attorney Elizabeth Holtzman stated that her office, with its "proven track record," had been working on the case since late Wednesday night; the police had already taken four teenagers into custody for questioning.[4] Police Commissioner Benjamin Ward angrily decried the crime, as did Mayor Koch.[5] Not only was Koch quick to comment on the case, but the other candidates running against him in his third mayoralty reelection bid—notably, Democratic hopeful David Dinkins and Republican contender Rudolph Giuliani— also issued statements about the homicide.

Like the "Central Park jogger" case, then, the murder of Yusef Hawkins immediately became a high-profile crime. Likewise, from the outset, it embroiled three sets of participants: those directly affected by the crime, as victims or perpetrators; the criminal justice system, through the rapid involvement of police and prosecutors; and the press. But even more than "Central Park," the incident that came to be called the "Bensonhurst" case immediately stimulated reactions from well-known politicians and community figures. Why? According to James Kohler, a Brooklyn deputy district attorney who prosecuted the first "Bensonhurst" trial in early 1990, the reason in retrospect was clear. The "Bensonhurst" case was unusual, he stated, because Yusef Hawkins had been killed "for the color of his skin": "There may have been racial attacks in Brooklyn but not homicides that someone could say were racial. We have two thousand murders every year in New York City. If there had been any other case like this, it would have been picked up by the media."[6] But was the uniqueness of this apparently racially motivated homicide the primary reason for media interest, as Kohler suggests? Or did a complex of other factors also influence why and how the killing was accorded more attention than any other New York City crime in the months after the highly publicized "Central Park jogger" rape?

THE ROLE OF THE MEDIA IN LINKING CASES: WHY "BENSONHURST" WAS COVERED, AND HOW

In a front-page account on August 25, *New York Times* reporter Ralph Blumenthal characterized Yusef Hawkins's killing as possibly "the gravest racial incident in New York City since the Howard Beach attack in Queens in 1986."[7]

But neither Blumenthal nor another *Times* reporter covering a related story, Clifford May, needed to have made this comparison explicit. In the context of the upcoming fall mayoral election, political candidates were tying high-profile crime cases together as a sign of worsening "racial tensions" in New York City.[8] As May reported:

All the candidates, their spokesmen said, are sensitive to the potential for incidents like the slaying to become symbols of the city's problems and to set off heated debates and even clashes. The Howard Beach incident, the accusations of rape by Tawana Brawley and the rape and beating of a jogger in Central Park are among the episodes that have taken on a larger significance and become a source of conflict among groups of New Yorkers. In a statement, Mr. Dinkins said "some already are pointing out the similarities" between the Brooklyn slaying and the Howard Beach incident. "Both incidents are shameful reminders of how serious the state of race relations is in this city," Mr. Dinkins said. "This case has the potential to further divide the city."[9]

One explanation for the media's rapid reaction to the "Bensonhurst" case, then, is that the crime reinforced an increasingly noticeable pattern of events. Whereas coverage of the "Central Park" case initially emphasized the earlier assault's uniqueness, a growing list of race-related, high-profile crimes made it unlikely that the "Bensonhurst" case would be seen as an isolated incident. Rather, and particularly in the context of an upcoming election, Hawkins's murder was quickly linked to other cases. Thus, Gaye Tuchman's point (in chapter 2) about the journalistic appeals of patterns already familiar and "routine" apply at least as much to the "Bensonhurst" crime as they did to "Central Park." The Brooklyn killing fit a preexisting theme by now explicitly recognized: editors and reporters knew that race-related, high-profile crimes had become ready topics for public debate about social problems, including racial biases and violent crime itself, that concerned New Yorkers. Less clear was the extent to which journalists admitted their own part in facilitating, and sustaining, this pattern.

Not only did the "Bensonhurst" case continue earlier trends; like "Central Park," the Brooklyn incident also confirmed Tuchman's observations by varying now-familiar themes. In contrast to the "Howard Beach" (1986) and "Tawana Brawley" (1988) cases, the "Central Park jogger" rape had involved working-class minority youths accused of raping an upper-middle-class white woman. Now, in contrast to "Central Park," the "Bensonhurst" case reversed these circumstances again: as in "Howard Beach," a group of white youths were accused of assaulting minorities; in both instances, the death of an innocent black youth resulted. But this was not the only respect in which "Bensonhurst" differed from the most highly profiled case—"Central Park"—that took place before it. For Pat Hurtado, who covered the Brooklyn crime for Newsday, the "Bensonhurst" case stimulated journalistic interest both because of its wider context and its unique characteristics:

> First, the incident happened shortly after the Howard Beach attack and shared similar elements of a black youth being attacked when he dared enter white neighborhoods. Second, there was the element of the tension between the white youths defending their turf against who they perceived were black "intruders" in some sort of West Side Story-like rumble. There was also the tragic factor that the victim, Yusef Hawkins, was a hard-working black teen from one of the worst neighborhoods in Brooklyn. . . . It was a story that ignited the imagination of editors and reporters; they like stories where you can easily see the victim, the tragedy, the villains. . . . And then I think you have an element in New York City where you have four tabloids competing to get the most out of a story.[10]

Obviously, Hurtado did not believe the "Bensonhurst" case received attention simply because, as an individual instance, it was rare. More than journalistic individualism,[11] journalistic relativism better characterizes her assessment of the case. Hurtado saw media interest as inseparable from relativistic assessments of social context: the upcoming election and similarities with the "Howard Beach" case. She also emphasized that competition among news outlets propelled coverage that became patterned; once one paper treated the story as "big," others felt compelled to follow suit. But, in addition, Hurtado deemed "Bensonhurst" interesting in its own right; it "ignited the imagination" of editors and reporters, she thought, eager to find stories in which "the victim, the tragedy" were sharply visible. Extrapolating from her assessment, we can say that the "victim" and "tragedy" involved in "Bensonhurst" varied narrative themes bequeathed from previous cases. Whereas the "Central Park rape" case provoked controversial speculation about why poor and working-class minority youths committed brutal violence—were the young men "wilding?" were they part of "wolf packs?"— "Bensonhurst" generated concerns about why white, working-class teenagers had murderously interfered with the freedom of a minority youth. With "Bensonhurst," white Brooklyn teenagers presented a social problem too: editors wanted to know why these teenagers became involved in violent crime, this time enacting racial violence and hatred.

For William Glaberson, a lead reporter covering "Bensonhurst" for the *New York Times*, another aspect to the case made for an even more compelling variation on prior cases: gender and, in particular, the role played by Gina Feliciano in the story. In Glaberson's opinion, "the media reacted because the case was inflammatory; *Newsday* did a cover story about New York in flames over racial tensions." But Glaberson was also intrigued by a unique facet of the case, namely, the

> romantic connection between her and Mondello [one of the arrested defendants believed to have been an organizer of the assault]. . . . [Gina Feliciano] was having a birthday party, and there was a sexual element insofar as it was suggested that Mondello had this relationship with her, and that therefore he was defending his virility (not just the territory).[12]

To gauge the role of Gina Feliciano in the media attention given to the crime, we must return to initial reports of the case. Blumenthal's *Times* account began by noting that white youth had been lying in wait "for black or Hispanic youths who they thought were dating a white neighborhood girl" named Gina Feliciano. On August 25, the *Daily News* headlined its front-page coverage "JEALOUSY, HATE AND DEATH." Written by Stuart Marques, who had covered the "Central Park" case for the *News*, the article began as follows:

> Fueled by jealousy and hate, a gang of up to 30 white teens—armed with a gun and baseball bats—shot and killed a black youth they mistakenly thought was dating a young white woman in their Brooklyn neighborhood, police charged yesterday. In an incident with haunting similarities to the 1986 Howard Beach racial attack, the white teens chased a small group of blacks through Bensonhurst and chanted, "Let's club the niggers," before one whipped out a gun and shot the helpless youth in the chest late Wednesday, police said. . . .
>
> Police said several white youths had a confrontation with a different group of blacks Tuesday involving the woman. They said there also was a confrontation Saturday night, in which the woman was warned to stop bringing blacks to the predominantly white neighborhood.[13]

Thus, though the "Bensonhurst" case recalled "Howard Beach" more than "Central Park" in one respect (white perpetrators had attacked a group of blacks), it was more reminiscent of "Central Park" in another. Nothing about the "Howard Beach" case entailed gender bias; Gina Feliciano, however, exemplified the issue of women's freedom to date whomever (or, as in "Central Park," to go wherever) they chose. In this respect, too, the Bensonhurst crime reiterated aspects of prior cases at the same time it was a unique instance. Not only had a black been killed in a case of racial violence by a group of whites allegedly resentful that a young woman was engaged in interracial dating, but what Glaberson called a "defense of virility" had resulted in impugning a young woman's sexual freedom.

Moreover, further analysis of Feliciano's role reveals a second reason "why Bensonhurst?" became a highly profiled crime. In addition to its obvious relationship of continuity-and-variation with the city's most well-publicized prior crimes, "Howard Beach" and "Central Park," the Brooklyn murder presented sharply opposing issues and spokespersons. Here as well, two "sides" of the story were juxtaposed against each other from the moment reporters started to write about the crime and why it occurred; as in the "Central Park" case, for journalists, this probably heightened the story's "legs."

THE EMERGENCE OF SIDES

In "Bensonhurst," the two-sided interpretations that unfolded through media coverage were as follows. One side, obviously, emphasized racism. Initial accounts of the crime stressed that some witnesses overheard shouts of "Let's club the nigger" before the fatal shooting. An article by Don Terry—the same *New York Times* reporter who had probed "why Central Park?"—focused on the "sorrow and rage" over the crime in East New York, Brooklyn, where Hawkins had lived. In Bensonhurst, Terry wrote, people felt sorrow too, but also "hate and defiance." "The black people don't belong here," he reported one white teenager stating as she stood on the corner of Bensonhurst's Twentieth Avenue and Sixty-eighth Street. "This is our neighborhood."[14] According to another resident, the twenty-six-year-old local resident Joanne Carretta, "The neighborhood is definitely prejudiced. They don't like blacks. They don't like Puerto Ricans."[15]

In the *Daily News* on April 25, beneath a headline asking "Another Howard Beach?" Jared McCallister and Geoffrey Tomb quoted Fred Hawkins, Yusef's father, angrily commenting on his son's death: "This is America. He's supposed to be able to go to all 50 states with no problem. It's 1989. This isn't Alabama, 1956. This is New York, 1989." The story proceeded to record visits paid the Hawkins family later that afternoon by Reverends Herbert Daughtry and Al Sharpton, the latter already "serving as the family adviser."[16] Indeed, Sharpton's appearance among the cast of characters immediately involved with the "Bensonhurst" case is significant. Recall that he had first become known through his role in the "Howard Beach" and "Tawana Brawley" cases; and later, of course, his criticisms of racial stereotyping in the "Central Park jogger" case were likewise well publicized. Now his reappearance in the public eye in the "Bensonhurst" case both demonstrated continuity with previous cases and signaled expectations on the parts of the press and the public that one "side" of this latest case would protest racism associated with the crime. This connection between cases was solidified even further by circumstantial coincidence. As both the *Times* and *Daily News* reported immediately, one of the three black youths attacked with Yusef Hawkins in Bensonhurst, Luther Sylvester, came from the same Trinidadian family as Curtis Sylvester, who had accompanied Michael Griffith on the night he was killed in Howard Beach. As it happened, Luther Sylvester was Curtis Sylvester's uncle.[17]

A second interpretation of the crime emerged just as rapidly as the first; here, Gina Feliciano figured prominently. The same *New York Times* front-page story that broke that paper's account of the crime also reported Keith Mondello's family hiring an attorney as their spokesperson. This was Stephen Murphy, well-known to New York City political and legal aficionados for winning the only acquittal of four defendants in the highly publicized first "Howard Beach" trial of 1987. Thus, Murphy was yet another character appearing in "Bensonhurst" after playing a visible role in an earlier race-related case. Connections between cases were therefore further reinforced by Murphy's involvement, signaling at the same time another "side" to the story—exactly opposite the one represented by Sharpton.

Murphy stated at the outset that Yusef Hawkin's murder was not at all racially motivated; nor was there any "romance" going on since Gina, spurned by Mondello, was no longer his girlfriend. Rather, Murphy contended, Gina Feliciano had "caused the confrontation by telling Mr. Mondello that she was going to bring as many as 30 youths to beat him and his friends."[18] Because of this young woman, as Murphy also asserted in an interview, young men in the community felt they needed to defend themselves and their neighborhood. The problem was "turf," he said, "territory"; by implication, violence would have erupted even if Irish or German teenagers had entered the neighborhood for the purposes of challenging local Bensonhurst youths.

Thus, two opposing interpretations of the causes of the crime were quickly constructed and bolstered by the media's propensity to see events in two-sided terms.[19] Against the side asserting the cause of racism, for example, Murphy's ready response was that the crime was caused by a battle over turf triggered by a "jealous girl." But this does not mean both sides were equally well represented in the media. Also needing to be explored is how the two viewpoints were framed. Did the opposing interpretations each work to neutralize the other's contents, as Stuart Hall and Todd Gitlin argue, thus exercising a depoliticizing effect they assert to be a common by-product of this media practice?[20] An alternative possibility, though, emerges from closer analysis of early coverage in both the "Central Park" and "Bensonhurst" cases. Rather than leading to perceptions of their equal legitimacy, media presentations of "two sides of a story"—at least in highly profiled violent crime cases—often result in one side occupying a more advantageous offensive position. The other side, by contrast, faces a disadvantage by having been placed on the defensive.

This asymmetry stems initially from violent crime cases, by their very character, differentiating offenses suffered by innocent victim(s) from the wrongs allegedly committed by perpetrator(s); this is an inherently imbalanced and value-laden distinction. But then, once particular incidents like "Central Park" and "Bensonhurst" have been selected and magnified into high profile notoriety, collective dynamics come into play *en masse*: newly cognizant publics are often outraged by news of the crime and by evidently awful victimization that has resulted. Many parties sympathetic to the "side" of victims thereafter react from a stronger offensively oriented position, reasonably as well as emotionally: charges from this vantage point seem powerfully persuasive; righteous indignation is heart-felt and understandable. Sensing this, editors and reporters are likely to believe it justified that they scrutinize the social problems which have led to such blatantly offensive crimes; around the same time, public demands for retributive redress may begin. Yet this media coverage has commenced well before a case has been tried.

By the media so reacting, a premature asymmetry arises from the offensively situated side tending to be accorded a 'public relations' advantage in the news. Sometimes, this advantage can be unfair and prejudicial because of the tenor of coverage, or due to a case's specific characteristics; on other occasions, such as when social biases are exposed, media attention may strike many members of the public as desirable and justified. In both eventualities, though, journalistic investigations in the wake of highly profiled violent cases are apt to reinforce—and, often, to aggravate—the defensive situation in which individuals accused of an agreed-to-be-shameful crime already find themselves. Moreover, at a collective level, other parties also start to react defensively as the media spotlights the background of arrested defendants, sometimes voyeuristically. In the aftermath of coverage, these parties often see themselves as having been placed, likewise, in a defensive position. It may be that some people share the same racial, ethnic, class and/or gender backgrounds as the defendants, or simply that they live in the same neighborhood. For any or all these reasons, those identifying with the defendants come to feel that like it or not, "the media" has begun treating them as though in the same category as the accused. From this comes embarrassment, outrage, or both, about the justice or injustice of journalists staring, as though a proxy for the larger society, at those affected by indirect associations with the crime.

Indeed, this analysis conforms precisely to what emerged from "Central Park." Features about the April case quickly probed the character of the neighborhood, and of the Schomburg housing project where the defendants lived. One such story by *Times* reporter Michael Kaufman, for example, stereotypically started: "The eight adolescents being held in the rape and beating of a jogger in Central Park were bound to each other by ties of neighborhood rituals of the playground and common ties of passage that began long before the rampage last Wednesday night. Some were the children of broken homes, and certainly all bear daily witness to the abounding pathology of drugs, drink and poverty." [21] Again, other stories referred provocatively to "wolf packs" and to an alleged practice of "wilding." Consequently, the youths arrested for the rape of the jogger found themselves defensively situated through a combination of three factors: the brutal character of the crime itself; outraged public sentiment (recall from chapter 2 Donald Trump's advertising campaign); and the contribution of the media as catalysts of the public response. These produced negative stereotypes long before a trial date had been set. Not surprisingly, these accounts spurred angry community reactions in those who, also vulnerable to the effects of racism, felt correspondingly affected by such generalizations. Others felt justified in their concerns about whether early media coverage made it impossible for the defendants to receive a fair trial.[22]

Four months later, did equal-but-unequal presentations of the story's two sides also characterize media coverage of the "Bensonhurst" case? Again, certainly, two polarized sides were apparent. And, again, journalistic coverage accorded an analogous advantage to parties in the "offensive" position—that is, to those sympathetic to the "victim" of the crime. But in the "Bensonhurst" case, it was those on the 'side' protesting racism who were structurally advantaged by their placement relative to the crime and its media portrayal. As Al Sharpton, soon to play an even more visible role in "Bensonhurst" than he did in "Central Park," remarked:

> [I]t was clear to us what to do in Bensonhurst, and the media had to deal with it. We were never able to grab a handle of where we could force the media to have to deal with the contradictions of the "Central Park" case. Because the problem was you were not the victim outright: a kid was being falsely accused of being the perpetrator, but how did you deal with the victimization of the young lady that was raped without looking like you condoned that?[23]

Circumstances had changed. Whereas in the "Central Park jogger" case young minority males were accused of victimizing, here an innocent young black man—Yusef Hawkins—had clearly been victimized. On the other hand, now it was defendants from Bensonhurst whose relationship to the crime put them on the defensive. Since high-profile coverage usually tends to reinforce this structurally bequeathed defensiveness, now the Brooklyn neighborhood itself would be placed under a magnifying glass of journalistic inspection; soon to be investigated was how this community, too, had nurtured young criminals in its midst.

INDIVIDUAL OR SOCIAL DISPLACEMENT? REVERSING VICTIMS AND VICTIMIZERS

"It happened in blue-collar Bensonhurst," began one *Daily News* feature about class stratification. According to reporter Don Singleton, Bensonhurst was a largely Italian American neighborhood that hadn't changed much since World War II. It was a place "where men play cards on folding tables under sidewalk trees on summer afternoons, where women chat in Italian outside the bakery in the morning, where young guys talk tough when they meet on the street." Further into his coverage, and apparently in the interests of fairness, he included both "sides of the story." Approximating Murphy's argument, one resident is quoted stating, "It ain't race. I'll tell you that. . . . I don't care if they were black, white, green or blue—it's just a bunch of punks making trouble. It ain't race, it's jerks."[24] Nevertheless, the overall thrust of the article favored those who believed racism to be, at least in part, responsible for the crime. It illustrated precisely the kinds of biased sentiments that many of the local residents seemed anxious to deny. For the most part, the neighborhood came across as prejudiced.

Said one local teenager, "Why do you go looking for a car in the neighborhood at 9:30 at night if you're black? If we walked through Coney Island at the same time of night we'd get jumped too." He pointed to the television cameras and said, "They're making too big a deal of this."[25] Similar victim-blaming on the part of Bensonhurst residents also appeared in an August 26 *New York Times* account by Michael Kaufman, the same reporter who wrote the April 25 "Central Park" story investigating East Harlem's Schomburg Plaza. This time, though, the angle of Kaufman's *Times* feature was a contrast in neighborhoods. Comparing Hawkins's predominantly black East New York neighborhood with Bensonhurst, it was the latter of these two Brooklyn neighborhoods, the mostly white Bensonhurst, that appeared in the more negative light, and that found itself in a defensive position:

In East New York, there was sorrow and fear and predictions that racist violence was turning more and more black people to the teaching of Malcolm X. . . .

On the tidy streets of two-story brick dwellings . . . where the shooting took place, the most evident responses were first of all, sympathy for the crime, and then hostility toward the media, and the 18-year-old woman whose dating of dark-skinned men reportedly aroused the anger, and perhaps jealousy of neighborhood youths like a violation of a tribal taboo. Michael Campanelli, 18 years old, questioned police explanations that the Hawkins youth and three of his friends ran into their attackers as they were responding to an ad for a car. "Why was he buying a car at 16? What does he know about cars?" asked Mr. Campanelli in an aggressive tone.[26]

Nor was it only news features that portrayed the neighborhood unflatteringly. Whereas in late April *Daily News* columnist Mike McAlary bitingly mocked the youth arrested in "Central Park,"[27] now he ridiculed quoted residents' undoubtedly gender-biased interpretations. But in McAlary's sarcastic recounting of how Gina Feliciano's role was used to rationalize the Bensonhurst murder, a note of neighborhood stereotyping is also discernible:

> She is skinny with medium-length hair, and Italian. She didn't like books and dropped out of New Utrecht High School in her freshman year. She attended secretarial school for a while, but got bored and dropped out. This happens at 18. The girl has these new friends. Some are Hispanic, a couple are black. Gina Feliciano likes them very much, her old friends say. Sometimes she invites them to her home. She has dated a black guy a couple of times. In another neighborhood, you might consider Gina Feliciano normal. But at this moment, in this city, along a stretch of 20th Avenue in Bensonhurst, Gina Feliciano is the girl that ruined the neighborhood.[28]

Still, it should be pointed out that even if stereotypes were emerging through such characterizations, alarmingly apparent was that some people in the neighborhood seemed to hold Yusef Hawkins responsible for his own victimization. Also troubling was that others were blaming Gina Feliciano for having caused the crime. But a third object of neighborhood resentment was also readily identifiable by the end of Kaufman's feature: for many residents the media, too, had become an object of hatred and blame. This becomes clear after Kaufman, seemingly concerned about balanced coverage (as had been Singleton), quoted someone who disagreed with the racially biased sentiments being expressed. "A 16-year-old boy should be allowed to go where he wants to go," this party declared. "There's no such thing as off limits, this is not Russia." But the man went on to agree with other members of the community about one source of resentment—the media. A crowd gathered around, reported Kaufman, as the man began to "become more emotional" and to demand "why has there been all this publicity?" Then "one voice cried out that the media was making this incident 'into another Howard Beach.' Another could be heard saying that the case of the Central Park jogger . . . 'was now completely forgotten' because 'she didn't die and she was a white girl.'"[29]

It seems clear, then, that not only journalists and politicians were connecting "Bensonhurst" with other recently publicized violent crime cases.

Local residents also seized on such comparisons for their own purposes: they served as a symbolic aid in expressing anger and a sense of community vulnerability once Hawkins's murder was accorded high-profile treatment. And one target of the community's anger was the media, indicted by some Bensonhurst residents for creating comparisons with other high-profile cases, and for doing so by biased selection of only certain previous crimes. But was this blame angrily directed toward the media, like the attribution of responsibility to Yusef Hawkins and Gina Feliciano, also unfair?

In one respect, blaming the media was simplistic and unjustified. A circumstantial disparity between community reactions to the "Central Park" case and reactions to the "Bensonhurst" case was that, initially, none of the quoted residents around Schomburg Plaza had openly blamed the jogger for her own victimization. While reports of the earlier crime case noted anger at the media's portrayal of the community, it was also made clear that community residents had expressed sympathy and held vigils to pray for the victim's recovery.[30] Given that media coverage of the "Central Park jogger" case was roundly criticized for its racial bias, why would mainstream editors and reporters fail to report victim-blaming in one case ("Central Park") while underscoring it in another ("Bensonhurst")? The difference may be simply that victim-blaming sentiments were aired more vehemently, and openly, in the Brooklyn neighborhood than in the one in Manhattan. If so, then this disparity may call for sensitive exploration; hardly, though, should journalists be faulted for reporting what they found.

In other ways, though, anger at the press was at once understandable and justifiable. Just as East Harlem residents were repelled by media coverage that based collective stereotypes on the acts of a few, so Bensonhurst residents sensed that journalists painted a picture of their community in brushstrokes too broad and undifferentiated. Yes, media coverage presented two sides of the story—citing both racial and territorial interpretations of the crime, and then associating most Bensonhurst residents with the latter explanation—but perhaps there were other, alternative interpretations of the crime that went unreported in the mainstream media. Moreover, while many reporters and editors believed that presenting what they determined to be both "sides" of the story constituted good journalistic practice, this practice ignored the structural disadvantages reproduced when violent crimes are highly profiled. As in "Central Park," putting both the case and the community of Bensonhurst squarely in the spotlight—and, again, long before a trial date was even set—reinforced the defensive disadvantage already facing young men thought to have committed a heinous violent crime. This media magnification also generated a sense of collective victimization among community members who, having been put on the defensive already, felt that in the eyes of the outside world they were regarded similarly as the accused.

Yet whether or not blaming the media was warranted, from the standpoint of the press, matters had come full circle: after the outcry of criticism that met early coverage of the "Central Park jogger" case, journalists reporting on "Bensonhurst" faced loudly voiced resentment again. How had this happened—that between the "Central Park" case in April and the "Bensonhurst" case in August, not only residents of two city communities but journalists themselves were placed on the defensive? Certainly it cannot be said that editors and reporters did not know they were under attack, or were unaware that they had become objects of resentment. Think back to the interviews cited in chapter 2 with several reporters who provided coverage of "Central Park." [31] They seemed to realize that media usage of "wolf pack" and "wilding" language had been strongly criticized. In the "Bensonhurst" case, interview data is not required to show that Kaufman and his editors knew that resentment, even hatred, was being directed at the media; after all, the blaming of the media was included as part of Kaufman's coverage. And reporter Pat Hurtado gave an indication of the degree of the antimedia sentiment that had been aroused:

> [T]he amount of hatred I encountered covering the trial was just amazing, because there is so much desire to blame the media. I once I found a message on my office answering machine where someone cursed me for about eight minutes. I covered every day of the case for over a year and experienced nearly nonstop hostility from the defendants' supporters. It seemed to me that in the eyes of those supporters, my colleagues and I symbolized all the frustrations and anger they felt about the case. [32]

Again, how did journalists end up in this predicament?

One answer is implicit in the above analysis: journalists did not detect that the presentation of a supposedly objective and balanced "two sides of the story" tends to produce unequal effects in crime cases. Not surprisingly, the side that finds itself defensively situated by a crime is apt to hate the "messenger." In "Central Park," then, it was people living in East Harlem who became resentful about overtly racist coverage; in "Bensonhurst," it was local Brooklyn residents who became enraged at being treated as though a monolithic community entity. Thus, one could say that the presence of media blaming in these cases was a patterned by-product of what many reporters and editors consider to be good professional practice. In the interests of fairness and "objectivity," this practice involved offering predominantly "two sides" to each (crime) story for the public's emotional and intellectual consumption. Yet this routine habit now seemed capable of producing consecutive backlashes against "the media" even though, paradoxically enough, the case's easily discernible sides were precisely one reason "why Bensonhurst" attracted journalistic interest to begin with.

RECREATING CRIME CASE POLITICS: CONNECTIONS FROM CASE TO CASE

But another answer also clarifies how the press came to be blamed for practices many journalists regarded as fair. This point leads to a fourth and final reason 'why Bensonhurst' became the City's next most highly profiled crime case after "Central Park." Perhaps members of the press found themselves on the defensive not only as a by-product of their supposedly 'objective' routine practices, but also due to a 'subjective' response they enacted on finding themselves the object of community criticisms. Hardly were journalists likely to enjoy being hated: for one thing, in terms of both their professional and economic survival, the press depended on credibility and interest to sell newspapers and maintain viewer ratings. But, just as people in the communities they covered felt, disdain and negative stereotyping of "the media" seemed to touch sensitivities in journalists too. We saw in chapter 2 how several reporters covering the "Central Park" case came to express some degree of self-criticisms. For example, according to Lizette Alvarez, "coverage did get out of hand"; other reporters, some "off the record," expressed similar retrospective misgivings.[33] The media as an institution may not be likely to apologize for their coverage of a news event, but one way in which liberally oriented journalists[34] put on the defensive by accusations of bias might respond is through a symbolic mode of redress. Subtly, reporters and editors may have reacted to community criticisms of them in "Central Park" by shifting the sociological contents, if not the forms, of the stories they next reported.

To investigate this possibility, let us retrace the development of media coverage after the breaking of the "Central Park" story. In fact, reconfigured shifts in the contents of covered stories evolved in such a way that, four months later, the appeals of selecting "Bensonhurst" for high-profile treatment may indeed have related to this analysis. But what about the other cases that occurred within the four-month period between "Central Park" and "Bensonhurst"? Do they provide insight into how journalists may have responded to criticisms directed against them?

In fact, several less-high-profile cases in the weeks after "Central Park" reflected the influence of the jogger's rape case, as explicit references were made to "Central Park" in the sparse coverage given these lesser-known, later cases. But they also may have reflected the effects of at least two of the main criticisms voiced against the media. The first criticism concerned preferential treatment supposedly accorded the "Central Park jogger" case because the victim was a white, upper-class woman; as Don Terry had already pointed out, violent assaults committed that same week against poor minority women were ignored. The second criticism was related: mainstream journalists also received complaints that they were more likely to highlight crimes alleged to have been committed by poor, minority male youths than to publicize crimes in which white, middle- or upper-class male youths stood accused.

Regarding the first criticism, then, the *New York Times* subsequently covered two sexual assaults of minority women that had also been committed in late April 1989. However, as noted in the previous chapter, whereas intensive coverage of "Central Park" initially surfaced on April 21, it took until May 7 for even brief mention that a young African American woman had been raped and murdered in Fort Tryon Park to appear in the news. Sam Roberts, in a piece of media self-criticism, commented on this discrepancy:

> [A] world of difference distinguished the two grisly crimes. The 28-year-old victim was a white investment banker, attacked while jogging in Central Park. The 19-year-old was black, identified by the police as a prostitute, and was found in Fort Tryon Park in Upper Manhattan. Which are some of the reasons why the first crime stunned New Yorkers and a nation generally numb to violence, and the second was barely mentioned by most of the media. The *Amsterdam News*, though, which caters to a predominantly black leadership, led its current issue with the headline "Another Woman Raped and Strangled to Death."[35]

Also in early May, a small story about another woman raped and thrown off a Brooklyn rooftop was reported immediately below an article about the "Central Park" case. Again, the victim was African American; and in this instance, too, the crime had not initially been reported. Pat Hurtado noted that, indeed, this story garnered much more attention after some members of the black community charged that the media had ignored the Brooklyn case. According to Hurtado,

> some legitimate news stories just die out. What has frustrated me as a reporter is how and why some people's lives become more important than others. . . . Maybe it's because American tabloid journalism in the 1990s was pretty simplistic. There was a push at the time to paint stories in terms like "hero," "victim," tragedy," "saintly." But after the "Central Park jogger" case started to get attention, there was a backlash against it seeming that newspapers only cared about the jogger because she was white and upper class. After that some stories were reevaluated such as the story about the woman who was raped and tossed from the roof. Suddenly reporters were dispatched to write about those cases that had been forgotten.[36]

Thus brief coverage of these smaller crimes appeared to result from reactions to reactions: journalists seemed to be responding to public debates over the "Central Park" case, which included, and quite prominently, critiques of the media.

Regarding the second criticism, that the media primarily focused attention on crimes committed by poor, minority male youth, consider a story that appeared in late May and was given more attention than the two tardily reported rape cases combined. Garnering more publicity than any other crime covered between "Central Park" and "Bensonhurst,"[37] this incident became known in the media accounts as the "Glen Ridge" case. In a rich New Jersey suburb, approximately thirteen white and relatively well-to-do teenagers, including the two co-captains of the high school's football team, were arrested for sexually assaulting a seventeen-year-old, mentally handicapped girl with a broomstick and a baseball bat. Although the assault took place in Glen Ridge on March 12, 1989, it was not until six weeks after the April 19 Central Park rape that the *New York Times* referred to the incident. And once again, references to the highly publicized "Central Park" case were conspicuous in this front-page May 25 *Times* story:

> Coming weeks after another sexual attack—the gang rape and beating of a jogger in Central Park—the Glen Ridge arrests seem likely to intensify public rage and anger over teenage crime and its causes. The Central Park

victim is white and the suspects are black; despite official denials of a racial motive, the park attack fueled speculation—from talk-show debaters, politicians and scholars alike about the pathology of poverty and racial resentment. . . . The Glen Ridge case contrasts with the assault in Central Park in several ways. Here, those arrested are white and are said to have known the victim, who is also white. The incident happened out of sight in the basement of a home, and it was talked about for weeks before arrests were made. Because the case involves teenage group behavior, it may send the speculation in new directions.[38]

Even though the two stories were substantively unrelated, associations between them were forged by media-generated comparisons. Evidently, connections were being made in the minds of journalists themselves. A few days later, reporters for other media outlets highlighted both class-based and race-related differences between the two cases. In a *Newsweek* story titled "Gang Rape in the Suburbs," "Central Park" and "Glen Ridge" were contrasted in a manner critical of the former case's media coverage. "Six weeks after the brutal rape and beating of a Central Park jogger," this article began,

> tabloid papers and newscasts once again confronted New York area residents with images of young faces accused of depraved crimes. The details of the attack were different but no less chilling than those of the Central Park assault. This time the setting was a small cushy suburb of well-weeded gardens and driveways studded with Mercedes and Saabs. . . . The attack drew big play in the New York papers, including front-page treatment from the *New York Times*. But the heavy attention is as much a sign of the city's fractious climate, with editors intent on demonstrating that they will train the same harsh glare of coverage on white suburban defendants that they did on the black East Harlem teens arrested in the Central Park attack.[39]

Consequently, in the four month interval between "Central Park" and "Bensonhurst," subtle alterations were discernible in the contents of which crime stories were noted by mainstream reporters and editors. Each of the two major criticisms aimed at the media appear to have generated journalistic responses. Prior to "Bensonhurst" in August 1989, several crimes against minority women had been mentioned, though cursorily and only in the shadow of the "Central Park jogger" case. And, as seen in the even more visible media attention shown "Glen Ridge," publicity had now been accorded a sexual assault allegedly committed by white and well-to-do youthful male defendants. But where did the murder of Yusef Hawkins on August 23 fit in? Clearly, the high-profile coverage given "Bensonhurst" conformed with the direction in which journalist attentions were already shifting, apparently influenced by criticisms of "Central Park." Like the coverage given the "Glen Ridge" case, then, the reporting of "Bensonhurst" provided further and even more dramatic evidence that journalists did not only highlight crimes committed by youths who were minority and poor.[40] Perhaps "the media" was not so bad, as reputed, after all.

Thus there is something ironic indeed that the initial coverage of "Bensonhurst" would again generate irate community reactions toward "the media": the reporting of the case took place in the context of journalists aiming to redress, not necessarily wittingly, prior community charges of bias and insensitivity. But now the puzzle of how, nevertheless, journalists found themselves again in a defensive predicament can be better unraveled. In and of itself, shifting which cases receive high-profile coverage cannot mitigate structural problems created by the media's purporting to cover two unequal sides as though equivalent; shifting the contents of publicized cases was not the same thing as altering their form. Still, for the most part, reporters and editors did not seem terribly cognizant or worried about the consequences of failing to change not only which stories they covered, but how.

That this omission created difficulties is illustrated by a reporter who, following the emergence of the "Bensonhurst" case, ostensibly sought to alter the way in which coverage was carried out. Stuart Marques began "an August 26, 1989 story on "Bensonhurst" with the following sentence: "Teams of detectives from all over the city searched Brooklyn last night for an 18-year-old white man suspected of killing a black teenager in the Bensonhurst *wolf-pack* attack (emphasis added)."[41] "Wolf pack" language had not been used in *Daily News* coverage of the last extremely well-known, race-related case in New York City—the late 1986 "Howard Beach" case, which, like "Bensonhurst," had also involved a violent crime alleged against white, working-class youth. Why was the term used now? In retrospect, one can speculate that Marques may have sought to make a corrective gesture in the wake of "Central Park" criticisms of the media, one which demonstrated that at least by August 1989, the *News* could no longer be accused of racially biased coverage. Yet this formal alteration did nothing to resolve the structurally analogous effects that using "wolf pack" language in any community context was likely to produce. A backlash against the media was a predictable result, and repetitively from case to case, from any such usage that reinforced the defensive situation in which both defendants—and community members perceiving themselves aligned with the accused—already found themselves.

Before investigating public reactions to the "Bensonhurst" case in greater detail, though, it is now possible to summarize the four interrelated explanations of 'why Bensonhurst?' attracted more media attention than any other case following "Central Park." The first explanation reverts to then–District Attorney Kohler's observation: statistically speaking, homicides[42] suspected of being racially motivated were not weekly or even monthly occurrences in the borough of Brooklyn. As with the "Central Park jogger" case, then, "individualistic" interpretations that focus on unusual circumstances should not be ruled out as one factor motivating media interest. But this alone could not ensure the enormity of coverage eventually accorded "Bensonhurst." A second explanation, powerful when combined with the first, incorporates the contextually oriented workings of American journalistic relativism: the "Bensonhurst" case was appealing because it continued and varied themes of earlier "race-related," high-profile crime cases. Not only did the Brooklyn case reiterate racial differences between victims and defendants from the late 1986 "Howard Beach" case; through the experience of Gina Feliciano, threads of the role of gender bias, which had surfaced to some extent in "Central Park," were apparent as well in "Bensonhurst."

Moreover, a familiar "cast of characters" in present and past crime cases solidified perceptions of both continuity and variation. Social movement activist Al Sharpton's role on the side protesting racism was long familiar from "Howard Beach" to "Tawana Brawley," and now from "Central Park" to "Bensonhurst." Exemplifying the simultaneous appeals of variety, the side with which Sharpton was aligned in this latest case shifted from the defendants' back to the victim's. Representing the legal profession, Stephen Murphy would repeat the part he played in "Howard Beach" in "Bensonhurst" by defending one of the accused white youth. That the media perceived these connections among cases is perhaps best demonstrated by the reappearance of journalists themselves. Some of the same reporters who had covered "Central Park" for the city's four mainstream newspapers were now assigned to report on "Bensonhurst"; apparently, journalistic experience covering one extraordinarily publicized case was thought to provide expertise in reporting or commenting on others. Among the journalistic cast of characters quoted here who continued to play a role from "Central Park" to "Bensonhurst" were Don Terry, Michael Kaufman, Pat Hurtado, Stuart Marques, and columnist Mike McAlary.

Then, as in "Central Park," the existence of two "sides" in "Bensonhurst" aligned as polar opposites reinforced the sense of continuity with previous cases. Thus another related factor is the clash between parties over whether racism or territoriality was at fault for Yusef Hawkins's murder. In the context of an upcoming mayoral election, in which issues of race were beginning to figure prominently, this dispute was likely to register as newsworthy. But in contrast to Gitlin and Hall's classic studies, both of which argued that media portrayals of a story's two opposing sides effectively neutralizes dissent, this analysis suggests that high-profile coverage of the kind accorded "Central Park" and "Bensonhurst" can ignite public reactions further—albeit as its unintended consequence. Soon to be seen is that protest reactions occurred not only after "Central Park," but also following the high-profile treatment of Yusef Hawkins's murder in Bensonhurst.

Media criticism, as we have seen, can also help explain why "Bensonhurst" achieved such intense publicity. The Brooklyn case surfaced in the context of a back-and-forth interaction between media coverage and public reactions to it. Even more significantly, though, tracing this dialectical interplay—between media actions and public reactions, media responses to that reaction and new public responses in turn—points up the crucial role the media plays in the multifaceted unfolding of high-profile crime cases. Although journalists still often cling to beliefs in the detached and apolitical character of their professional practice, stories are not selected solely on "objective" grounds. Journalists also choose to focus on new cases insofar as they manifest continuities and variations among cases. Further, reporters and editors are apt to evince a reaction as to how debates in the public sphere "subjectively" affects them; as engaged actors, journalists sometimes wish to alter how they are seen and assessed. Yet precisely because of ongoing adherence to norms of objectivity and political neutrality[43]—and notwithstanding that the press can also be relatively powerless, sometimes unjustly accused through courses of events—journalists are not likely to "officially" admit this aspect of their own participation.[44]

Given that more media coverage was accorded "Bensonhurst" than any other violent crime case after "Central Park," what happened next? Chapter 2 moved from analyzing media participation to investigating why and how public reactions developed after the jogger case's initial publicity. Here, I proceed analogously to explore public reactions to "Bensonhurst." Did reactions tend to be framed around the now-familiar "either/or" dualism, strongly influenced by media constructions but not merely echoing them? And, as has become an increasingly germane question, how did public reactions to "Bensonhurst" compare with those registered in the wake of the "Central Park" jogger rape case?

THE PUBLIC CONNECTS CASES: WHY AND HOW?

Whereas an extraordinary volume of media coverage of the "Bensonhurst" case surfaced at least as quickly as did attention given to the "Central Park jogger" case, so Yusef Hawkins's murder provoked public reactions even more rapidly than had the earlier crime. Hawkins was shot to death on Wednesday night, August 23; by Saturday afternoon, August 26, the first of twenty-six weekly demonstrations on the streets of Bensonhurst was held. Right away, then, public reactions erupted both outside and inside the public sphere of ongoing journalistic coverage; in contrast to "Central Park," though, angry sentiments immediately took the form of highly profiled protests. In "Bensonhurst," the City's televisions news stations and four daily papers noted that both demonstrations and counterdemonstrations were mounted by two incensed groups of participants on the first Saturday following the crime. According to Nick Ravo, reporting for the New York Times:

> The marchers, shouting, "Whose streets, Our streets," started at about 3:30 P.M. They were led by the Rev. Al Sharpton and Alton Maddox, a civil rights lawyer. . . . As angry white youths and some older local residents filled the sidewalks, a bitter racial hatred permeated the atmosphere.
>
> The whites chanted, "Central Park, Central Park," referring to the rape and beating of a white investment banker in April. Six black and Hispanic youths have been charged in that attack. The black demonstrators in Bensonhurst chanted back, "Howard Beach, Howard Beach."
>
> Later the blacks' chants changed to "Yusef, Yusef." Yusef Hawkins is the 16-year-old black youth whose death sparked the protest. The whites yelled back, "We want Tawana, we want Tawana." . . . "You couldn't get any uglier scene than this in Mississippi," Mr. Sharpton said of the march.[45]

That there were from the beginning two opposing sides in the "Benson-hurst" case expressing markedly different sentiments was not a figment of editors' and reporters' imaginations. Rather, demonstrators and counter-demonstrators personified this antagonism with a photogenic clarity even more apparent than the two sides that formed around "Central Park." But whereas journalists obviously had their own reasons for responding to the Brooklyn incident, what motivated two opposing groups of public partici-pants—their actions influenced, but not created, by the press—to quickly take to the streets?

To begin with, we should note how one reason for the public's reaction ac-cords with what happened in the wake of the "Central Park" case. As in that earlier case, "Bensonhurst" came to represent social problems far broader in scope than the killing of Yusef Hawkins alone; it, too, moved from the realm of the particular to the general. That both cases resonated symbolically in this way reinforces one of this book's previous observations: high-profile crimes that mushroom into vehicles for intense public debate are usually perceived to affect many more people than those directly involved in a given case. More-over, "Bensonhurst" echoed the "Central Park" case by coming to signify not one set of social problems but two.

To demonstrators participating in protests on the streets of Bensonhurst, the case symbolized racism. For hundreds of people who marched on Au-gust 28, most black, it was unacceptable that a young man could not walk into any New York City neighborhood without fear of deadly reprisal. If Yusef Hawkins did not possess this basic freedom, why should any person of color feel safe from racial violence? This protest differed from that in "Central Park" in a crucial way. In the earlier case, parties who "sided" with the young woman jogger expressed their indignation in assorted ways: Donald Trump purchased newspaper advertisements; Koch spoke to reporters; Elizabeth Holtzman and Susan Brownmiller wrote op-ed pieces. But there were no marches organized through the streets of Harlem to demand harsher sen-tences for those found guilty of the crime; feminists did not walk through Central Park to protest violence against a young woman who had been exer-cising her own freedom of movement. Why the contrast?

For Mary Wright, a college administrator who had attended several of the Bensonhurst demonstrations, the answer was that Yusef Hawkins's murder represented more than racism. In addition, demonstrating symbolized the need for ongoing activism in the historic spirit of the 1960s American civil rights movement. Thus "Bensonhurst" did not only signify a problem but pointed up the importance of a time-honored social movement tradition—marching—as a means of protesting that which blacks in the South had experienced for decades: discrimination through actual or feared violence. Yet, as the following excerpt from an interview with Wright indicates, there were also differences between past and present protests:

MW: I would listen to talk radio, and if there was a protest, I would go. You listen to WLIB, BAI, and you'd hear these black shows and people would call in and voice their opinions. You didn't have to go to meetings; you'd just go to the demonstrations.

LC: So you recall first going to one in Bensonhurst?

MW: No I got involved after Tawana Brawley. I remember saying "Here it goes again." Like in Howard Beach. That started and then the Tawana thing and then Yusef, and it was just like a chain reaction. . . . It's similar to what Marcus Garvey said, "When all else failed to unite us as a people, conditions will bring us together." That's what the feeling was at that time. People started to come together.

LC: Did it seem like a similar group of people?

MW: It was basically the same people. People who were coming into their consciousness about race and politics, and older people, especially who had been in movements before and things had died down. . . .

LC: It didn't feel like it was just about that one case?

MW: No, we knew that it wasn't an isolated case, because we knew family members who had been in situations of police brutality, for instance. It didn't start then. It had always been happening before Rodney King, way before then. . . . Whenever [ministers such as Al Sharpton and the Reverend Herbert Daughtry] spoke, they talked about the Tawana Brawley and the Michael Griffith situations. Everyone involved in the first two incidents were at these rallies. More people were getting involved. . . . That gave me the sense of its being a movement.[46]

Similarly, in Al Sharpton's view, demonstrations against 1980s high-profile crime cases were interconnected as part of a "movement." But, even more strongly than Wright, Sharpton understood demonstrating against "Bensonhurst" and other cases of the day to be a continuation of 1960s civil rights activism. In the 1980s, the problem of crime nationwide had come to be conceived primarily as affecting individuals; by harking back to the 1960s, Sharpton realigned the problem of crime to associate it once again with violence aimed at groups. As he put it in an interview, elaborating on why he called for weekly demonstrations as part of the public reaction to "Bensonhurst":

AS: [W]hen I was called by the family, the day after Yusef was killed, I got out to the house. . . . [T]he media was trying to say that Bensonhurst was about a love triangle and that Yusef Hawkins was dating a girl out in the area: that was the first spin on this. And that her jealous boyfriend killed him. I said, sitting in the Hawkins's house watching the news, that if we were going to get any kind of justice here, we have to make it clear about the racism in Bensonhurst. . . . [T]he only way we can do this is to march hundreds of blacks [there]: I know that area because they beat up two guys there the Christmas before we marched out there. They will come out and act ugly, and then the whole world will understand the problem there is racism, and the media will have to cover it. So I deliberately marched in Bensonhurst. And we did twenty-nine marches.

LC: Is it true, twenty-nine marches?

AS: Every Saturday, twenty-nine weeks. . . . Even with that they never called these guys "wolf packs," they never called them "animals."

LC: You knew when you marched in Bensonhurst that you would get some media coverage.

AS: Oh absolutely. After everybody saw the 6 o'clock news two or three weekends, people coming out with watermelons, calling people racial names, it would be hard to act like this was an isolated romance case. . . . [T]hat's why Martin Luther King wrote in his books that they way you fight racism is first expose it. That's why he marched in Cicero, that's why he marched in Birmingham. . . . [V]ery few of your daily reporters have a historic knowledge of the civil rights movement, so they cover civil rights activity in a vacuum rather than in a context. . . . In the sixties and seventies, we marched in white neighborhoods in the South. But if you have no knowledge of that, and arrive at the *Daily News* and the *New York Post* as a graduate of some journalism school, you'd think the most radical person in the world is Reverend Al. Which is really nonsense. So I not only have to put a family's problem on the front burner, I've got to deal with the ignorance of media people who are looking at me totally out of context. . . .

LC: But many things were different in the sixties, don't you think?

AS: The difference was that Dr. King and others were fighting in the South. The media was controlled in the Northeast. Since we are fighting in the Northeast, it's much more difficult for people to look at their own racism than if they were marching five hundred miles down the road in Alabama. You have to remember I'm marching on these publishers' houses. When I go to Bensonhurst, it's not like I'm down in Mississippi. I'm marching past a guy's house that might write for the *Daily News*. Or I'm marching past a guy's house that may advertise in the *Daily News*. So they take it much more personally and subjectively than if I were in South Africa or in the South. Because now northern racism has come to its door. And the media does not want to admit that in their own backyard they have the same problem that they [criticized] in the sixties. . . . When King came to Chicago against Daly, the same *Chicago Tribune* and others that were raising all kinds of praises when he won the Nobel prize started calling him a demagogue, saying he should get out of town. Because it's a big difference if I'm saying, "help me fight something cruel a thousand miles from here," and saying, "help me fight something around the corner." . . . Absolutely. For instance, nobody heard of Michael Griffith. That would have been a one-day story had we not marched in Howard Beach. So it's not like we run into take advantage of the media. We run in to hold the media there, and to keep it focused. . . . Like Dr. King used specific cases to dramatize what he had to do. . . . Rosa Parks was the case they used to cripple Montgomery. You need something people can look at and touch. You have to come up with some point of drama that the media will buy into. . . . And I don't think the "Left," for want of a better term, has realized that there is a problem. Maybe media activists like me did what we had to do in the times that we live in. To me, to get media attention on an issue means that I'm a competent activist. Because I'm in a media age.

LC: Because if you hadn't gotten media attention nobody would have ever heard of you?

AS: That's right. Not only me, they never would have heard of the cases. . . . But there is the tension there. The tension becomes—and you just totally crystallized the tightrope a guy like me has to walk on—if you don't get media attention, forget it, you don't exist. Your clients, your people you're fighting for, they're totally wiped out. If you do get it, as I have done in many cases, then the media says, "Sharpton is a media manipulator." So you're damned if you do, and you're out of business if you don't.[47]

Sharpton's perspective was different from those who aligned themselves on the "side" of the victim in the "Central Park" case; the latter had no history of protesting group discrimination. Clearly businessmen like Trump already possessed entrenched social and political power. On the other hand, Sharpton envisioned 1990s demonstrations to be an extension of 1960s civil rights protests that took place in Birmingham and Montgomery; but in the immediate context of 1980s high-profile crime cases, he also connected protesting on the streets of Bensonhurst in 1989 with protesting on the streets of Howard Beach in 1986. Thus, like journalists for whom continuity had its own appeals, Sharpton's reaction to "Bensonhurst" was steeped in perceptions of case-to-case connections. Unlike the press, though, he openly aimed to use these linkages for politicizing purposes. Also note the attempted link that can be traced back from Brooklyn to "Central Park." Somewhat incorrectly, Sharpton criticized journalists' wholesale omission of "wolf pack" language from their coverage of the "Bensonhurst" case, even though the press had frequently used the term in reporting the rape of the jogger.

Other relevant points, too, emerge from Sharpton's reflections. Apparently, journalists were not the only participants in the dynamics of this burgeoning high-profile crime case to treat "Bensonhurst" as a mostly two-pronged dispute. Sharpton also acted within a two-sided framework of predicted, and predictable, antagonisms. Yet while his perspective was certainly influenced by the media's take on the case, it was by no means identical with it. As a political activist, Sharpton strategized that marching in Bensonhurst against racism would bring out and expose the other "side"—namely, racists. This strategic expectation was inseparable from his understanding that the media could be counted on to record any ensuing confrontation. Here, then, was one way in which social movement organizing of the kind in which Sharpton was engaged was not simply a continuous outgrowth of, but also differed from, 1960s social movement organizing in the civil rights tradition.

For, as Sharpton's comments suggest, two motivations—wishing to demonstrate out of moral indignation, and hoping thereby to attract the attention of the media—had become so enmeshed as to be virtually indistinguishable by the late 1980s. To some social movement activists like Sharpton, this development evinced its own distinctive form of variation-as well-as-continuity relative to prior demonstrations. But before turning to what "Bensonhurst" symbolized in the perspective of the other "side"—those who counter-demonstrated—one wonders whether Sharpton's strategic expectations were borne out. Did marching on this Brooklyn neighborhood's streets expose racial reactions that the media was quick to cover?

"Tensions Up as Marchers, Residents Trade Taunts" read the August 28 headline in the Daily News.[48] "250 Whites Jeer Marchers" announced the New York Times that same day.[49] This time covering the public's reactions to the crime, Don Singleton described a "clash" between more than three hundred "angry black protesters" and "scores of jeering whites." On one side of this confrontation were demonstrators "led by the Reverend Al Sharpton, Hawkins' parents—Moses Stewart and Diane Hawkins—and Yusef's two younger brothers, who chanted 'murderers' and 'no justice, no peace.'" On the other side were the counterdemonstrators: "Many whites—some of them holding watermelons in the air yelled, 'Go home, niggers go home,' and other racial slurs." In a New York Times story, Nick Ravo described African American protesters singing gospel hymns and conducting a twenty minute rally on the steps of St. Dominic's Church, a church active in local affairs in Bensonhurst. Meanwhile, several hundred white counterdemonstrators on the street waved Italian flags and chanted taunting remarks: " 'Let the boys from Bensonhurst go,' they shouted. 'Central Park, Central Park,' they shouted, referring to the beating and rape of a white jogger there by a group of black youths in April."[50]

Thus, in several ways, Sharpton's expectations were borne out. Marches through Bensonhurst did attract media attention. This is not surprising since the media's partiality for two-sided antagonisms neatly fit with Sharpton's similar, though activist-motivated, presumption of "sides." The reports of local community residents holding up watermelons and yelling "Niggers go home" at black marchers succeeded in exposing racism. Last, following these first late August marches, other events triggered connections that no longer needed to be pointed out by Sharpton alone; other reacting parties in the mass-mediated public sphere now pointed out relationships with the 1960s civil rights movement for him.

Fueling these linkages to the 1960s, if unintentionally, was then-mayor Ed Koch. For just as Koch had spoken up to align himself with one "side" of the "Central Park" case, denouncing the crime as a "wolf pack operation,"[51] he again took a stance against Sharpton's on "Bensonhurst." Reported in an August 29 Times story headlined "Racial Link in Brooklyn Killing Divides the

Mayoral Candidates" was Koch's opinion that "black politicians and ministers were wrong to hold demonstrations in Bensonhurst"; this had only increased racial tensions, he said, stereotyping an entire neighborhood. Moreover, referring to "charges against six black youths from East Harlem in the beating and rape of an investment banker in Central Park in April," the mayor went on to remark, "It's just as wrong to march into Bensonhurst as it would be to march into Harlem after that young woman in the jogging case. The Harlem community was not involved in that."[52]

Other candidates in the upcoming mayoral election saw matters differently. David Dinkins, who would become New York City's first African American mayor if he defeated Koch in the looming September Democratic primary, claimed he would not have criticized ministers holding peaceful demonstrations in Brooklyn "in the finest tradition in our country." Dinkins, too, referenced "Central Park" in proposing a state law that would toughen penalties for crimes committed by groups: his proposal, Dinkins asserted, was aimed not only at crimes committed by "racially-motivated gangs" but at acts of "urban terrorism" like the rape of the Central Park jogger the previous spring.[53] But it was Harrison Goldin, another Democratic mayoral candidate that year, who denounced Koch even more vociferously on the front page of the *New York Times*: "New Yorkers deserve better than a yahoo mayor," declared Goldin, comparing Koch to "Southern leaders who had opposed civil rights marches."[54]

In the realm of public reaction *qua* media commentary, with no pretense to "objective" reporting, *Daily News* columnist Bob Herbert likewise decried Koch's statement. Herbert, who had immediately compared the killing of Yusef Hawkins to the Mississippi lynching of young Emmett Till in 1955 for whistling at a white woman,[55] now unfavorably contrasted Ed Koch of the 1960s with Ed Koch in 1989:

Once a long time ago, when Ed Koch was young, he went down South to fight bigotry. . . . It was, perhaps, Ed Koch at his finest. . . . At a press conference in the Blue Room at City Hall, Koch criticized the marchers who went to Bensonhurst to protest the murder of a black teenager. Thus Koch, who once marched proudly and courageously into Mississippi and Alabama, was now singing the sorrowful refrain of Deep South officials who denounced civil rights marchers as outside agitators who were unfairly tarnishing the reputation of an entire region.

We are hurrying back toward tragedies that should never happen again. The faces of the people who taunted the marchers in Bensonhurst were xeroxes of the faces that tormented the freedom riders two decades ago. The epithets and the insults were exactly the same. "Niggers go home" they shouted. They spit on the marchers and laughed and jeered. They held up watermelons. . . . Koch criticized the taunters as well, but no more strongly than the marchers. Bensonhurst will be solid Ed Koch turf come the Democratic primary, and he wasn't about to antagonize any of those voters, racist or otherwise. Leadership will have to wait.[56]

But if Sharpton thereby managed to crystallize what "Bensonhurst" signified to some parties—namely, the need to protest ongoing prejudice—what did the incident represent to those on the other "side"? One could argue that, at least for some counterdemonstrators, "Bensonhurst" was associated with an opposite perceived problem: rather than racism against blacks, the case symbolized reverse racism against whites. This point is made by sociologist Howard Pinderhughes in *Race in the Hood: Conflict and Violence among Urban Youth*. In the course of conducting interviews in 1990 and 1991 with multiracial, working-class youths in three New York City neighborhoods—Harlem, Southern Brooklyn, and the Bronx—Pinderhughes found a number of these young men expressing the same attitudes reportedly held by counterdemonstrators in August 1989. Indeed, a number of youths from Bensonhurst, whom Pinderhughes called the "Avenue T Boys," focused on what the highly profiled murder of Yusef Hawkins represented to them. The local youth asserted that their neighborhood had been "crucified" and labeled "racist" by marchers; each singled out Sharpton, a figure they especially endowed with symbolic significance as a "troublemaker." Among the youths' other comments were the following: "The problem in Bensonhurst is the blacks marching down 20th Avenue"; "Sharpton is the problem. If he'd tell his people to forget about it, everything would be okay"; "He's an instigator, he should be shot"; "I can't wait 'til watermelon season starts."[57] Even comparisons with "Central Park" came up: one youth remarked that when something bad happens to a "black guy, it's like wham—everything's all hyped up. . . . But in Central Park, if that was a black girl who got raped" by whites, "forget it, they would have castrated those kids."[58]

Delving deeper, Pinderhughes also found that coupled with such overtly racist attitudes were anxieties these young people felt about their economic future and class positions. Bensonhurst had long been a largely working-class community; it was the neighborhood in which *The Honeymooners*'s classic blue-collar protagonists, Ralph Kramden and Ed Norton, were imagined to live. But between 1959 and 1981, New York City lost 650,000 manufacturing jobs as the local economy shifted to become service-based.[59] By 1989, many working-class youths could no longer obtain the jobs they had expected.[60] In 1990, the median Bensonhurst household income was $27,125 and some families lived below the poverty line. At the same time the public school system failed to provide assistance. New York City school dropout rates rose from 13.5 percent in 1983 to 25 percent in 1987; after African American and Puerto Rican youth, Italian-Americans in New York City were the third most likely group to leave high school.[61]

Pinderhughes contends that racial tensions grew in tandem with the scarcity of jobs and greater competition for them; any preexisting biases held by these white working-class youth from Bensonhurst were now exacerbated. Thus one young man stated, "You know I been lookin' for work for a while, but I can't get a job 'cause they're giving them all to the black people." Said others: "The situation is more racial because the economy has changed. Some people are out of work and they don't like it." "Everybody is leaning over backwards to give the blacks everything. They get all the jobs."[62] Just as Sharpton saw demonstrations as continuing the 1960s tradition of civil rights activism, then, Pinderhughes's analysis illustrates how some young people on the other "side" of the "Bensonhurst" case reacted against that very tradition—by counterdemonstrating.

The attitude of the counterdemonstrators can be understood as locally incarnating a broader neoconservative agenda that by the late 1980s, writes Pinderhughes, "had achieved national prominence in current debates over civil rights, affirmative action, and racial inequality. While these teens were not well informed about a larger neoconservative political analysis, they related to its images and symbols: a black person getting a job that a white person is more qualified for, blacks getting preferential treatment, young black males as criminals."[63] And clearly one emotionally powerful symbol for contesting these heatedly discussed issues had become high-profile crime cases themselves. Thus, by the time demonstrators in 1989 Bensonhurst chanted "Howard Beach, Howard Beach" and counterdemonstrators shouted back "Central Park, Central Park" and "Tawana Brawley, Tawana Brawley," such provoking assaults had already become symbolic vehicles used to convey a much more general and ongoing range of associations than the mere "facts" of these cases. Moreover, the press was imprinting these signifiers into the larger public's cultural vocabulary through mass-mediated reiteration. All told, then, the appearance of intercase references in the public reactions of social movement activists, in the words of counterdemonstrating community residents, and in the statements of competing mayoral candidates indicated that debates about New York City high-profile crime cases had become their own form of politicized expression—indeed, politicized participation—by the end of the decade.

On the other hand, it is too simple to conclude that the prejudiced statements aired by counterdemonstrators and by Pinderhughes's "Avenue T" boys represented the feelings of all Bensonhurst residents. Other interviews reveal that for many community members, counterdemonstrators themselves were seen as an extremist minority — indeed, as racist youth. For these residents, offended by "bad elements" in the community and yet opposed to Sharpton's and other protesters' belief that racism alone was the reason for Yusef Hawkins's killing, the case's symbolic significance was at once different and related.[64] Many people in Bensonhurst explicitly criticized racism, even as they reacted defensively against the same wholesale stereotyping of their neighborhood. This frequently expressed counterinterpretation also included the following beliefs. Not willing to accept that most people in Bensonhurst were racists, many of its residents asserted that Gina Feliciano had started the whole incident by telling neighborhood youths they would be attacked by her friends. Defense attorney Stephen Murphy had already made this case to the press. Residents thus insisted that local youth had not gone out to murder an innocent young black man on the night of August 23, but rather had gathered to defend their "turf." Last but not least, many local residents agreed that "the media" itself had become a major instigator of racial tensions, stoking flames of divisiveness by portraying all of Bensonhurst— and not just an especially troubled subset of young people living within it— as at fault.

Note that this alternate interpretation had already been mentioned, and shaped, in previous media accounts. Again, the press could not reasonably be accused of plucking viewpoints from thin air: these opinions were being expressed both outside, and inside, the mass-mediated public sphere. In the words of Donna Marconi, a long-time neighborhood resident, Yusef Hawkins had been killed by "some monster." However, she also recounted being extremely upset for other reasons as well:

> **DM:** Every Saturday, the demonstrations started to happen beginning in late August, and they wouldn't stop. . . . I don't like railroading. A terrible tragedy had occurred and it should have been a time that we all came together. But it became a media circus: they loved every minute of it. . . . I'm not saying there's not racism in my neighborhood, but have you looked around? Not everyone in the neighborhood is the same.
>
> **LC:** Why do you think . . .
>
> **DM:** I don't believe he was killed because of his race. . . . The media did that. . . . I know kids around here act tough, like they're big macho men, but they're not killers.
>
> **LC:** Why do you think it did happen?
>
> **DM:** The media had a lot to do with it, and the young woman; she was a troublemaker. She was like Helen of Troy, bringing down the soldiers.[65]

Notice that even as she channeled blame toward both the media and the young woman, Marconi did not completely deny the presence of racism in Bensonhurst. Similar acknowledgments regarding racism, at the same time that Gina Feliciano and the press continued to be blamed, also characterized the remarks made by well-known community figures. According to Father Arthur Minichello of St. Dominic's Rectory:

> First of all, this was a racial incident, just like the Howard Beach case. You have a city divided over racial lines for years, you had Dinkins running for mayor. Yusef Hawkins was just a nice kid, completely innocent. I'm not sure what really happened. . . . Racism is racism, and it's not exempt from other areas, but why single out a single community? Bensonhurst and more of Bensonhurst, Howard Beach and more of Howard Beach . . . every story capitalized on "the Bensonhurst" trial, or "the Crown Heights" case, why didn't the media just call it the "Yusef Hawkins case"?[66]

John Carmine, a local businessman, stated:

> **JC:** It was a terrible thing that happened, white, black or whatever. A big part of the problem was the young lady involved. . . . She antagonized

people. . . . Then there were reporters who would only publicize what an ignorant sixteen or seventeen year old would say, not what the adults had to say.

LC: Why do you think reporters wrote about the case?

JC: It sells newspapers and gets viewers. People were upset, No. 1, that Mr. Hawkins was killed, and then the bad name they were getting, that we were all in Bensonhurst killers. When the media came down, the marchers came down also. Every Saturday, like clockwork, busloads would arrive, police officers would arrive on horses and motorcycles. . . . People were just mad at the whole situation. If the media hadn't been here, Mr. Sharpton wouldn't be here. This was also during Central Park when black kids had raped the white girl, the Central Park jogger. White people didn't go to march in Bed-Stuy. . . . It was a form of harassment to the whole community.[67]

James DiPietro, too, sought to distance himself from the racist views of counterdemonstrators. At the same time, talking with him evidenced "Bensonhurst" taking on another dimension of symbolic meaning: identification. As a lawyer engaged with the case after he agreed to represent defendant Joseph Serrano, DiPietro sympathized with the accused; his remarks could be taken to stand for the experience of Bensonhurst residents as a whole, as feelings of sympathetic alignment began to develop between community members and defendants. DiPietro himself grew up in Bensonhurst. "It could have been me," he reflected:

JDIP.: Listen, there's a lot of good hard-working people in that community that had no part in this and all of a sudden . . . they're being portrayed in the papers as a racist community, next thing you know there's marches in their community, police presence, everything else, it's just not a pleasant environment. And then you get to see some of the bad elements in your community itself . . . showing their racism . . . .

LC: So you're saying the case meant a lot to you because you're from Bensonhurst also?

JDIP.: The case meant a lot to me because there but for the grace of God could have been James DiPietro. Absolutely. It could have been me. When I was a teenager and all my friends . . . would have said, there's a big fight tonight going on round the corner, even though I was not a tough guy, I was an academic kid, I would have probably been on the corner with my friends. . . . Cause when you're a young kid in your teens, that's big-time important. . . . Now if I would have heard guns, don't get me wrong, then I'm home in my basement. But if it was a fight, guys were coming to fight my friends, I could have been on that corner. And if one of my friends, unbeknownst to me, would have pulled out a gun and killed someone, I could have been charged for the same murder. So you know, I just know what that community's all about. And I felt in my heart, you know as you get into a case and you don't feel it with every case, that some of these kids were being railroaded. And, you know, once you get that in your heart, then it becomes a cause, you know what I mean?[68]

Peppering DiPietro's comments about the community were not only references to racist "bad elements" but allusions to stratification by class—to "good hard-working people," and to "academic kids" versus "tough guys." Despite differences between DiPietro's typical counterinterpretation and the views of numerous counterdemonstrators, then, an important affinity allied them: widespread in the community was the feeling that high-profile coverage of the "Bensonhurst" case had demeaned people in the neighborhood, and made them feel "put down." Highlighting "Bensonhurst" exposed sensitivities that predated the incident; it tapped the defensiveness on the parts of many residents about their lack of socioeconomic status and their Italian American ethnicity.

This same sensitivity was still present in the community when, years later, one local resident related how she had called a *Newsday* editor to protest a reference to "Bensonhurst" in a completely unrelated story. "What in God's name did that story have to do with Yusef Hawkins?" she recalled asking the editor. "If you want to see kids going to college from Bensonhurst, I'll bring you 100. It's time to stop the bullshit. Will you stop putting us down—why can't you just let us live?" She went on to observe that "the kids here were stereotyped as 'Guidos,' in other words, as Mafioso, people who were uneducated and dropouts. They're stereotyped as kids who hang out on corners and don't work."[69] Similar defensiveness and embarrassment at how the community was being portrayed, in both class and ethnic terms, were also apparent in the recollections of a young man who had gone to school with a number of the accused youths:

I was resentful of the fact that they didn't interview me or my friends. They looked for the greatest lowlifes. . . . If you said anything good about the neighborhood, or bad about the media, you didn't get on TV or into the paper. I told that to one guy from the media: you're the ones who are lighting the fuse and if riots break out, it will be your fault. Everyone knew I was sympathetic to the fact that a young boy was dead for no reason. But the neighborhood didn't do it. One person pulled the trigger, not the whole neighborhood. . . . . I don't like to read a newspaper. Just look at Howard Beach: when Howard Beach happened, I thought what a bunch of jerks live out there. Then when it happened to us, and I saw how many lies the media told . . . now when I read in the papers Crown Heights this, Crown Heights that, I don't believe it. If the media doesn't have a crime story every day, they don't have anything to sell. . . . You know I go to school on Long Island. I live out there and when people ask me where I'm from, I'm ashamed to say I'm from Bensonhurst. The first time I say Bensonhurst, people will say, are you a racist? So I say I'm from Bay Ridge.[70]

Experiences of social vulnerability characterized both counterdemonstrators' and counter-interpreters' reactions in "Bensonhurst." We can go on to ask, however, whether parties on the case's polar-opposite "sides" were linked by shared experiences? It seemed that nothing but mutual incomprehension marked relations between those chanting "Howard Beach, Howard Beach" and those retorting "Central Park, Central Park" as they debated symbolic meanings—racism on the one side, reverse racism on the other—that were accumulating from one high-profile case to another. Under other circumstances, though, people confronting each other might have noticed something other than just their polarization into "sides." This is because two sources of potential commonality did exist—if only putatively, and though hard to glean amid equally significant differences.

First, parties on both sides felt anger and resentment at the media and its stereotyping of entire groups and neighborhoods. Donna Marconi and James DiPietro mentioned defendants being unjustly "railroaded"; by this they meant that the spotlight of media coverage encouraged the public to presume that the arrested youths were guilty, even before they were tried. Protesting the case from the other side, Sharpton believed that the "Central Park" and "Bensonhurst" cases were interconnected insofar as both manifested racism, albeit in different forms. In the earlier case, those concerned about racism also thought the youths arrested in the case were being "railroaded"—language about "wolf pack" behavior and "wilding" being used to describe their actions even before guilt had been established.[71] Yet Marconi seemed to see the dangers that those accused were being "railroaded" only in one case, not in the other. Similarly, Sharpton only noted the problems posed by negative media coverage of defendants in the "Central Park" case; he did not comment on the degree to which an analogous predicament faced arrested youth from Bensonhurst.

Both sides were also angered by other damaging effects of stereotyping. Marconi objected to ethnic and character prejudice reflected in the description of members of the Brooklyn community as "Guidos" and "racists"; "not everyone in the neighborhood is the same," she said. But treating "everyone the same" in a prejudicial manner was precisely what had upset numerous parties, including Sharpton, about journalistic accounts of "Central Park." In that case, many believed, stories about East Harlem had been steeped in ideological presumptions and had often used race-skewed terminology. Moreover, stereotyping figured in Yusef Hawkins's murder itself. It is hard to believe that, had he been Caucasian, Hawkins would have been assaulted when innocently walking down Twentieth Avenue. Even if he had arranged to meet Gina Feliciano, instead of visiting the neighborhood to see a used car, why would this be provocative but for racial stereotyping? Hawkins and his friends had not bothered anyone prior to being attacked. Yet again, though, Marconi seemed to see the problem of stereotyping much more clearly as it applied to her "side" of the case than to racial prejudice asserted by protesters. Similarly, Sharpton was not willing to acknowledge that many people living in the Bensonhurst community felt defensive in the face of collective stereotyping, as had many Schomburg Plaza residents unfairly subjected to scrutiny of the East Harlem community in toto.

Thus these opposed parties made connections, and interconnections, which were partial to their "side." In the process, they overlooked those damaging aspects of stereotyping that created shared vulnerabilities—humanly—across apparently unbridgeable racial and ethnic divides. But in theory a second commonality, too, reached across the "sides." This one had to do with class. It was not only youth in Bensonhurst who were working-class and poor, and who suffered from recently aggravated socioeconomic insecurities. As the aforementioned Times features by Michael Kaufman and Don Terry had pointed out, the economic profiles of the two Brooklyn neighborhoods—East New York (where Yusef Hawkins had lived) and Bensonhurst (where the defendants resided)—were not dissimilar. Both neighborhoods included large numbers of working-class families; again, school dropout rates in New York City were highest in African American, Latino, and then Italian American neighborhoods.

Moreover, social scientists have shown that all three groups—certainly not only Italian Americans—experienced the effects of shrinking labor market opportunities. As anthropologist Philippe Bourgois detailed in a well-known ethnographic study of Puerto Rican and African American drug dealers in East Harlem, these young men at one time had also expected to find manufacturing jobs—jobs that no longer existed. A devastating combination of racism, changes in the economy, and lack of cultural capital had coalesced to make it seem all but impossible to survive with "respect" by legal means.[72] Yet Howard Pinderhughes's interviews with African American youth around Schomburg Plaza, and with Italian American youth around Bensonhurst, found another interesting concurrence. Both groups blamed their economic misfortunes on racial and ethnic divisions far more than they faulted class-related social processes that shrank the overall "pie" of full-time, well-paying jobs available through most of the 1980s and 1990s. As Pinderhughes described, many Italian American youth in Bensonhurst were convinced that at the source of their difficulties was reverse racism: allegedly, blacks were gaining social and economic power at their expense.[73] Analogously, Pinderhughes's data on young African Americans in East Harlem revealed equally strong convictions about how racism made it impossible for them to get ahead; "whites" were seen as invested in maintaining the marginalization of African Americans.[74] Ironically, then, young people taking opposite positions—some upset about reverse racism, others protesting racism—shared a greater likelihood to act on the basis of separate racial and ethnic identifications than to criticize class-stratified inequities that disadvantaged them both.

At the same time, however, the presence and power of racism should not be overlooked as though merely a reflection of class. The situations of the two groups studied by Pinderhughes were certainly not, simplistically, entirely the same. White ethnic working-class youth do benefit from privileges related to skin color; the virulence of racial bias in U.S. history has bequeathed extraordinary difficulties for minority youth until, and including, the present.[75] And yet it is striking to note the curious disparity between racial and ethnic discriminations protested passionately through high-profile crime cases, and common class-based problems that go relatively unnoticed. Why the difference? Since the dynamics of high-profile crime cases provide one approach to answering this question, let us return to the question why "Bensonhurst" initially attracted media attention.

It has already been noticed as a recurring theme that it is a common journalistic tendency to favor stories featuring clear-cut oppositions between spokespersons and issues. Of course, this tendency is only reinforced by the legal process of adjudication, which is called upon to decide between competing accounts of what actually took place. Also examined earlier is the propensity for high-profile coverage to bequeath advantages to the side favoring the "victim." However, not yet specified are the effects this formulaic media practice, and its further reinforcement by the courts, have on defensive public reactions.

Take the "Glen Ridge" case again. Press attention to that case was noted earlier, but not the public reactions registered in the New Jersey town soon afterward. Some residents of this wealthy suburb responded strongly—and defensively—to what they perceived to be unfair representations of their community by the media. They complained that the press used its depiction of the town as a way to try and demonstrate its "fairness" in coverage. At a May 1989 Memorial Day speech attended by fifteen thousand community residents, Glen Ridge mayor Edward Callahan declared angrily that the town had experienced a "literal invasion by the national news media." He objected to the sense of "guilt and somehow embarrassment over how we are now perceived by the outside world . . . when we have also seen the name of our town unfairly treated as being part of this horrendous alleged act." [76] Even more revealing, though, was the resemblance that emerged during an interview between Callahan's reactions to journalists' focus on the New Jersey assault, on the one hand, and, on the other, defensive community reactions to media coverage of "Central Park" and "Bensonhurst." The words of East Harlem residents criticizing media coverage of the "Central Park" case and those of Brooklyn residents angered at media coverage of the "Bensonhurst" case echo in the form—however different the contents—of Callahan's response to media interest in "Glen Ridge":

EC: I believe that it followed very quickly the coverage of the Central Park rape. And there was, in my opinion, a parallel being made, you know, this can happen in Central Park, in a big city like New York, and here is . . . this big town with all these wealthy people. . . .

LC: Tell me about your impressions of the media coverage once it occurred, and people's reactions to it.

EC: In this rich town, the street, trees, the gaslights, this horrible thing occurred. . . . That was the kind of coverage. And then the *New York Post* topped it off with the famous, or infamous, front page: "Town of Shame," they called it. . . . No one ever tried to take a look at the positive side of Glen Ridge. . . . I didn't see one positive story about Glen Ridge in all that coverage.

LC: So people were . . .

EC: As angry as I am. I don't think anyone ever condoned what happened. But I think there was a general feeling of outrage that these accused kids, and they were kids at the time it occurred, had been tried, executed and hung in the press before they even got a chance to go to trial. . . . But the other interesting thing, I thought, was that this was called throughout the press coverage "the Glen Ridge" case, which always drove me crazy about the Central Park comparison. That wasn't the "New York City" case but this was the "Glen Ridge" case.[77]

Thus, Callahan thought the young male defendants in the "Glen Ridge" case were victimized by the press because they lived in a wealthy, white community; they had been "executed and hung in the press before they even got a chance to go to trial." But some people who lived in East Harlem also felt young men from their neighborhood were victimized, "railroaded," though because they were poor and of color; others didn't believe that youth from Schomburg Plaza could receive fair treatment in court, either. Brooklyn residents, too, were convinced that young male defendants in Bensonhurst were victimized, again indeed "railroaded," because they were white, working-class Italian Americans; here as well, a number of community members thought the youths' chance for a fair trial was slim.

In one respect, that similar media approaches would produce similar reactions across divergent communities was not surprising. Formally, the defendants and the town of "Glen Ridge" were both being scrutinized by the press in a way that was analogous to the treatment given the defendants and neighborhoods of East Harlem and Bensonhurst. On the other hand, Callahan's description of the New Jersey defendants' situation in unqualified terms of victimization obscured precise sociological distinctions, like ones based on class. Listening, one might gather that each set of youth interacted with the media and criminal justice system on a level playing field of social relations. But "equal" media treatment of unequal entities allowed virtually anyone who felt put upon to criticize the media and criminal justice system on the surface, as though separable from surrounding social processes by which these institutions are affected. For defendants do not engage with the media, or with the law, from equivalent positions; inequality characterizes various groups' relationships with the workings of these institutions, as well as their relations with each other.

Thus, for example, in a book about the "Glen Ridge" case wryly titled *Our Guys*, Columbia University journalism professor Bernard Lefkowitz illustrated the well-to-do community's indulgent treatment of its high school footballs stars. "Our guys" benefited from combined class-, race-, and gender-related advantages prior to their arrest for sexually assaulting one of their neighbors, a mentally retarded girl. Lefkowitz chronicles these advantages accompanying the young men to trial, and subtly influencing an unusually lenient outcome after their convictions. Although Judge Benjamin Cohen sentenced three convicted youth to seven and fifteen year terms, the young men were able to avoid serving any prison time at all until years later, when they were well into their twenties.

Clear, too, from examining then-Mayor Callahan's reactions is that he focused on certain social conflicts to the exclusion of others. Overlooked were the class-differentiated advantages just mentioned, advantages that Glen Ridge defendants possessed in the wider society long before stepping in front of a news camera or into a courtroom. On the other hand, as we saw earlier, disdain for the media was explicit. Callahan seemed to be saying that none of the defendants' problems, and by extension the town's, would have arisen were it not for journalists' nosy intervention. Note, too, that Callahan brought up interconnections between "Central Park" and "Glen Ridge." Debates over racism ignited by the prior case were blamed for causing the victimization of "Glen Ridge" by the press. Consequently, Callahan included parties concerned with racial discrimination among those whose actions and positions he resented.

It was not only parties protesting racism on the analogously defensive "side" of prior cases who evoked blame: the victim on the offensively situated other "side" of "Glen Ridge" was also incriminated. Indeed, as Lefkowitz stressed in *Our Guys* and as interview data separately confirms, some local residents suggested that the young woman who had been sexually assaulted was responsible for the crime. As has often occurred in rape cases, some people raised questions about whether her past sexual behavior had been "promis-cuous"; even though mentally retarded, some alleged she had been capable of consenting to the insertion of a baseball bat and broomstick into her vagina.[78] Gender bias is a form of ideological currency often used in sexual assault cases to attribute and reverse blame across diverse class, racial, and ethnic groups. Here, when such traditionally sex-skewed aspersions carried over from community reactions into trial transcripts, prosecutors sarcasti-cally dubbed the strategy of the young men's lawyers a "Lolita defense."[79] Thus the actions of the young woman were not overlooked but inspected as some members of the Glen Ridge community defensively blamed her as well as "the media" and activists concerned about racism in the "Central Park jog-ger" case.

But now needing to be assessed is whether these observations apply across high-profile crime cases, helping also to explain where community reactions were directed in the "Bensonhurst" case. Generally, parties in Ben-sonhurst who reacted defensively did not note disparities of class either— even though, in contrast to the young men in Glen Ridge who possessed clear advantages, class distinctions negatively affected the lives of local Benson-hurst youth. Yet counterprotests were not directed at class-based differences between this working-class community and enclaves of wealth. Counter-demonstrators did not reportedly shout "Glen Ridge, Glen Ridge!" Nor did class-based similarities mollify racial resentments by pointing out analogous community defensiveness that might have linked Bensonhurst with East Harlem through the prior "Central Park" case. Instead, intensely felt criti-cisms were directed again at forces and parties much closer to home, namely, at those seen as potentially responsible for affecting defendants' fates in courtroom battles to come. Therefore, a strong predictor of which entities will become objects of blame in high-profile cases like "Bensonhurst" seems to be what, or whom, is believed most responsible for affecting criminal jus-tice outcomes at trial.

Thus, in the "Bensonhurst" case as well, the media were immediately in-dicted. Indeed, problems with the press account for another form of blame that disparate communities seem willing to identify. Media critiques surfaced in defensive reactions to all three of these violent group-based crime cases. But it was not just the press that was criticized; parties within the dominant two-sided framework that oppose "victims" and "victimizers" were also identified by some reacting defensively to the Brooklyn case. Once more, not class disparities but racial divisions were openly resented for supposedly fomenting that "Bensonhurst" emerged at all; to some people, protesters representing race-related social movements were believed to be just as blameworthy as journalists. Both were seen as having placed working-class white defendants at a disadvantage not only in the present, but vis-á-vis symbolic interconnections that steered reporters from past high profile crimes involving perceived reverse racism to this one. Community members bitterly focused on race-based differences between the two sides, but, again, class-based differences or affinities were hardly noticed. Moreover, this particular channeling of anger was reinforced by the expectation on the parts of those responding defensively that racially divided antagonists would soon confront each other again—not on the streets, but across symbolically opposed "sides" of inner city courtrooms.

Finally, but not least in importance, there was in "Bensonhurst" the matter of gender. The pivotal role attributed to Gina Feliciano was not only one of allegedly instigating the crime; in addition, the mounting of a counterinterpretive defense depended on beliefs about her culpability. Even though this was not an instance of rape, gender-based resentments combined with race-based ones to effect a reversal of the apparent identity of victims and victimizers. What might have been seen as a nonviolent yet gender-biased incursion on Feliciano's sexual freedom became another opportunity for impassioned attributions of blame.

Thus, in sum, for those aligned on the side of defendants, social conflicts perceived as visible and immediate—directing angers provoked by high-profile crime cases toward specific criminal justice system goals—were more readily focused on than relatively remote social problems like class inequities. Such inequities did not offer easily identifiable outlets for expressing community angers and resentments; by contrast, the two-sided framework of crime cases fulfilled this function admirably. Few options besides the dominant "either/or" dualism seemed available anyway, even if they were being sought. Remember that for at least some social movement activists on the offensive "side" of the "Bensonhurst" case, two-sided confrontations had begun to figure into political strategies and expectations. These seemed to ensure predictable media coverage, enabling activists to raise symbolic points that signaled social injustices. For many people reacting defensively to the case, blaming the "other side" comported with journalistic preferences for oppositional, two-sided frameworks. Thus public reactions and media practices mutually reinforced each other: media practices fueled two-sided public reactions; public reactions on each side provided journalists with new two-sided antagonisms to cover; new media reportage of two-sided stories influenced new two-sided public reactions in turn.

This interplay between public reactions and media coverage continued through late August into early September of 1989. Confrontations between demonstrators and counterdemonstrators were repeated each Saturday. On September 3, the *New York Times* reported that five hundred protesters had returned to the streets of Bensonhurst. Again chants by demonstrators proclaiming "What we do want? Justice! When do we want it? Now!" were met by obscenities and racial epithets like "Niggers go home," "You savages," and "Long Live Africa." These confrontations made front page-news and television newscasts, impressing on demonstrators a political need to return. But as happened in "Central Park," and whether or not covered in mainstream news, did any public reactions seek to disrupt this cyclical repetition of two-sided antagonisms?

Jack Spatola, a well-respected local figure who chaired the board of Brooklyn's Federation of Italian-American Organizations, recalled that he and other community leaders organized a march in early September to emphasize that many Bensonhurst residents were themselves angered and saddened by Yusef Hawkins's murder. The purpose of this event was comparable to that of the vigil by Schomburg Plaza residents to pray for the recovery of the young woman brutally raped in "Central Park." The march aimed to provide an alternative perspective on the crime that transcended the simplicity of the "either/or" dualism. These organizers sought to distance themselves from the racism expressed by counterdemonstrators; at the same time, they also wished to counteract stereotypes implying that everyone who lived in Bensonhurst was racist and uneducated. But Spatola recalled his frustration when television and newspaper reporters ignored this event, continuing to frame the crime in terms of the dualism between protesters concerned about racism and counterdemonstrators venting racist beliefs. As Spatola recounted in an interview:

> So we came together, [State Assemblyman] Frank Barbero and the Federation, to have a prayer service the following Monday at 6 P.M. Approximately 300 families marched to the corner of 69th Street to conduct a prayer service for Yusef Hawkins, and we sent telegrams of condolences.

At the same time, Mort Downey was in Bensonhurst with Roy Innes for the other demonstration which was taking place; there were reporters around from all the major television stations and newspapers. We were coming from 75th Street and 20th Avenue where we stopped to pray: they went past us to do a TV interview. This other demonstration was playing to the cameras. . . . .So on one corner, you had 300 families with clergymen who were praying; on another you had Roy Innes and Mort Downey. And it's like a study in media: they didn't record anything. Barbero and I were amazed. We decided it was impossible to get a fair depiction of what the community really felt: it was like we couldn't have any remorse and sadness, but had to be depicted like we were all the same, like we were in some High Noon movie.[80]

Spatola's negative expectations that the march he helped arrange would be ignored by the press were borne out; no mention of this event can be found in the Times or the News at the beginning of September. But this omission had consequences: it left the dominant framework of opposing sides, reinforced by the dialectic of back-and-forth interactions between media and publics, intact. Thereafter, it was extremely unlikely that either side would discern anything other than what it expected on the part of its antagonists; each side remained trapped in its own partisan perspective, disabled by the structural dualism to even perceive feelings of those on the other side it might possibly share. Thus the hurt Bensonhurst residents felt in response to community stereotyping did not evoke much sympathy in demonstrators; all they could see was that racism was again rearing its ugly head. On the other hand, many residents of Bensonhurst could not see past all the publicity accorded marchers; they were unable to appreciate the well-founded anger marchers felt over deep-seated realities of racism. Yet the persistence of prejudice was a social problem with which, at least in terms of ethnicity, many local residents had long been familiar. Indeed, Sharpton's response to the concerns of Bensonhurst residents was to inquire why, rather than becoming defensive, the mostly white members of the Brooklyn community did not join the mostly black marchers to show their concerns about prejudice.

Without much opportunity for establishing common ground of marchers and counterdemonstrators alike, developments in late August and early September proceeded much the same as before. By the end of the month, Sharpton was again comparing the "Bensonhurst" case with previous highly pro-

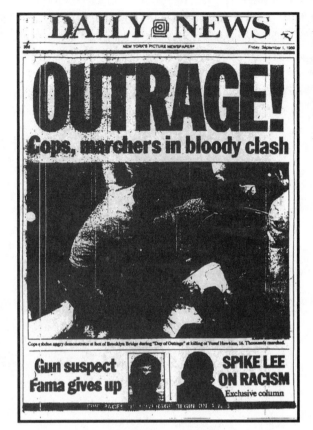

Fig. 4. About ten days prior to the September 12, 1989, primary that resulted in David Dinkins becoming the Democratic Party's candidate for mayor, protestors outraged about Yusef Hawkins's murder in August marched across the Brooklyn Bridge and clashed with police.

filed racial incidents. But now he drew media and public attention to discrepancies between the treatment by the criminal justice system of defendants in "Central Park" and the treatment of youth in "Bensonhurst." Whereas in the former case, minority youths were taken into custody without the possibility of bail, Sharpton objected, white defendants in the "Bensonhurst" case were "sent home to enjoy the Labor Day weekend."

Clearly for Sharpton and many others on the side protesting racism, demonstrating in Bensonhurst was not an isolated action but an effort to reinvigorate a civil rights movement aimed at overcoming economic, political, and cultural discrimination in the United States. However, protests in late August came to target relatively more specific criminal justice goals. Reflecting a similar linking of the general to the specific, activists expressed hope at Yusef Hawkins's August 31 funeral that the case would unite the black community to fight racism and injustice. More than a thousand people—including political leaders, religious figures, and leading artists such as Spike Lee—crowded into Grover Memorial Baptist Church to hear Reverend Curtis Wells begin his address by intoning: "Mr. Mayor, Mr. Governor, let freedom ring in Howard Beach! Let freedom ring in Wappingers Falls. Let freedom ring, yes, from Bensonhurst."[81]

That same day, a Day of Outrage march had been organized by the December 12 Movement, formed in 1987 in reaction to racism manifested by Michael Griffith's death in "Howard Beach."[82] Two years later, this march not only commemorated Hawkins's death but the then-recent killing of Huey Newton, the founder of the Black Panther Party, who had been shot to death by a drug dealer in Oakland California on August 22. Although eight thousand people walked peacefully from Grand Army Plaza to the Brooklyn Bridge, a clash between police and several demonstrators at the end of the day resulted in several injuries (see figure 4). In its coverage of this incident, a September 2 *New York Times* editorial concluded: "The temperature of the city is already overheated. Bensonhurst, the death of Kevin Thorpe, the Central Park 'wilding' case and a dozen other random incidents have made race 3 tender, exposed nerve in the city's life."[83] In this climate of spiraling concerns about unrelieved racial tensions, the Democratic primary for the upcoming New York City mayoral election was held on September 12. Though a close contest between Ed Koch and David Dinkins had been expected, Dinkins won the primary—assisted both by a large black turnout of voters and by a sufficient number of whites for whom his campaign theme of racial harmony proved persuasive.

Was there a direct relationship between the now-ensured election of Dinkins as mayor in November, the first African American to hold that office in the history of New York City, and the ongoing "Bensonhurst" case that symbolized public divides over racism and crime? Following the election, the views of some black voters who had been longtime supporters of Koch were quoted in the news: " 'To me, Koch has changed,' said one woman from Prospects Heights. 'One reason I liked him was he used to be a fighter for civil rights.' " " 'Especially because of Bensonhurst,' said another woman, '[W]e need a leader who's going to take care of the racial problems in New York City. David Dinkins is reaching out to everybody.' "[84] In addition, for some liberal white voters, Dinkins may have seemed best able to lower the "overheated" temperature of race relations about which the *Times* editorial opined. Indeed, fears of racial tensions were being discussed, in and out of news culture *per se*; for instance, Spike Lee's film *Do The Right Thing* had been released at the beginning of the summer the same year. In the film, the character Pino remarks to his father Sal, a pizzeria owner, "We should stay in Bensonhurst and the niggers should stay in their neighborhood"; after a young black male character named Radio Raheem is killed, riots against police brutality erupt in New York City. Assuming such fears were in the air, the media may have ignored local community efforts like Spatola's to point beyond "either/or" positions. But the voting public itself may have reacted by electing a mayor who promised to be a link between the two sides.

During his campaign, Dinkins had proposed a state law to combat "urban terrorism," a category within which he took pains to include both the "Central Park" rape and the "gang motivated" racial killing of Yusef Hawkins in Bensonhurst. Thus, Dinkins sought to bring together two concerns that the events of 1989 crystallized. One concern was the issue of violence in the city, as symbolized in "Central Park." The other was racial discrimination and the persistence of racial tensions as manifested in Yusef Hawkins's death. At least for the moment, Dinkins's election signaled a coalescing of these issues.

IN SUMMARY

Before shifting to an analysis of legal, media, and social movement participation in these and other cases, I would like to summarize how "Central Park" and "Bensonhurst" exemplified provoking assaults as defined in chapter 1. First, "Central Park" and "Bensonhurst" generated diverse participation almost immediately after their initial coverage. High-profile treatment by the media transformed these violent crimes into seemingly larger-than-life political symbols. But without the added ingredient of incensed public reactions—those of political leaders, social movement activists, and ordinary people living in the communities affected by these cases—"Central Park" and "Bensonhurst" would not have become "provoking assaults." Journalists were well-aware of public reactions, including criticisms of media coverage itself; these reactions endowed the cases with even greater importance and justified continued media coverage in turn. The involvement of the legal system only reinforced entrenched feelings about the cases, bringing with it another group of participants: judges, lawyers, and members of the public in the role of jurors.

Second, legal cases and symbolic causes overlapped in both instances. Reflecting the media's predilections and the dualism inherent in the legal system's framework of "prosecution" versus "defense," debates over the "Central Park" and "Bensonhurst" cases were predominantly two-sided. Partialization occurred as antagonized positions made it difficult to recognize possibly valid points made by the other side. In "Central Park," one side symbolized violence against women and fear of crime felt by urban residents; the other side symbolized biases on the parts of the media and the criminal justice system that impeded minority defendants' ability to obtain fair trials.

Partialization also occurred in the "Bensonhurst" case. This time one side symbolized the racism manifested by hate crimes directed at innocent individuals; the other side symbolized resentment over ethnic stereotyping of whole communities in response to the criminal acts of a few. Again no alternative perspective seemed possible, as arguments made on one side were roundly divorced from arguments made on the other. For purposes of the legal system, this partialized structure may have been unavoidable as trial dates approached; matters of guilt or innocence had to be determined. But given the complex sociological issues raised by both "Central Park" and "Bensonhurst," the two-sided framework of debate created as many problems as it solved. Little or no room existed for opposed sides to glean commonalities they shared. Then, too, within a legal structure supposed to produce win/lose outcomes in the form of "either/or" verdicts, one symbolic side or the other was bound to feel demeaned following trials.

Third, the "Central Park" and "Bensonhurst" cases illustrate how once legal cases and social causes become conflated and only two sides dominate discussion, reversals in the identity of apparent victims and victimizers also tend to take place. Within the confines of a restricted and partialized framework, victims are indeed sometimes blamed for their own victimization; simultaneously other sources of power in American society tend to be "let off the hook." In the "Central Park" case, the culpability of the young woman who had been attacked was not initially an issue. However, as the case wore on, lawyer Robert Burns wondered out loud whether "her boyfriend" might have been involved. In the "Bensonhurst" case, lawyer Stephen Murphy argued even before the case was tried that "Gina Feliciano" was to blame, echoing the sentiments of some Bensonhurst residents. Also clear from these case studies is that, in both "Central Park" and "Bensonhurst," "the media "was an object of enmity. To some extent, journalists did bear responsibility for publicizing the cases in ways that many parties aligned with defendants resented. Nevertheless, the sheer enormity of hostility expressed toward journalists and reporters—around Schomburg Plaza after the "Central Park" case, in Brooklyn after "Bensonhurst," and in New Jersey following "Glen Ridge"—suggested that angry feelings of nonspecific social origins may have been displaced onto comparatively more visible institutional objects like the media and its representatives.

Fourth, and finally, "Central Park" and "Bensonhurst" reveal connections drawn both in the press and within communities between one high-profile crime and another. Recall, for example, references made in the *New York Times* right after Yusef Hawkins's death to the "Howard Beach," "Central Park," and "Bensonhurst" cases as evidence of a tense racial climate in New York City. Just as evident is that the "Glen Ridge" case was perceived in relation to the crime that had received most prior publicity in New York City—namely, "Central Park." Public participants on both sides of "Bensonhurst" also linked cases together. When protesters took to the streets of that community, local residents shouted "Central Park! Central Park!" to those concerned about racism who shouted back "Bensonhurst! Bensonhurst!" At Yusef Hawkins's funeral, allusions were made to "Howard Beach" and "Tawana Brawley." Moreover, the appearance of the same public figures in different cases was striking. Al Sharpton, for example, linked the various cases in which he played a role self-consciously, seeking through those connections to forge political protest. Among journalists, some reporters—at the *New York Times*, for example, Michael Kaufman, William Glaberson and Don Terry—reported on both cases.

If "Central Park" and "Bensonhurst" thus may be considered to be provoking assaults as I earlier characterized them, how did they compare with crimes even more publicized, nationally and locally, over the next decade? In the next part of this book, I analyze interview material culled not only from "Central Park" and "Bensonhurst," but also from the highly profiled "William Kennedy Smith" and "Mike Tyson" rape cases of 1991–92; the assaults of Rodney King and Reginald Denny, highly publicized between 1991 and 1993; and the "O.J. Simpson" murder case that dominated crime news coverage from 1994 to 1996. These cases further contribute to developing chapter 1's criteria of provoking assaults. "William Kennedy Smith," "Mike Tyson," "Rodney King," "Reginald Denny," and "O.J. Simpson" also became symbolic of controversial social problems; as before, each of these later cases were framed as antagonistic and unfolded through mostly two-sided debates. In each case controversy again emerged over whether victims were as innocent as they appeared (and apparent victimizers as culpable). Last but not least, vestiges of partialized dissatisfaction remained following courtroom verdicts; and reminiscent of "Central Park" and "Bensonhurst," these later cases sometimes featured parties familiar from earlier cases.

On the other hand, though, the following three chapters focus on the vantage point of differing participants in provoking assaults. Chapter 4 explores legal actors' strategies and perceptions from earlier cases through later ones; this chapter concentrates on the consequences of legal cases becoming conflated with social causes in provoking assaults. Chapter 5 returns to a consideration of the role of the media. Chapter 6 assesses the views and behaviors of community participants, social movement activists, and other members of the public at large.

FROM DIFFERING VANTAGE POINTS
"Smith," "Tyson," "King," "Denny," and "Simpson"

CHAPTER 4

In *re* the Legal System

The previous chapters traced the interaction of media and community participation in the burgeoning of the "Central Park" and "Bensonhurst" cases as
"provoking assaults." Now I turn to the legal system's distinctive contribution to the dominance of a preset, dualistic framework of sides. In assessing
the trials of the two 1989 New York City cases and other well-known trials
through the mid-1990s, this chapter centers on the participation of legal actors—in particular judges, lawyers, and jurors. I draw from the views expressed by parties to "Central Park" and "Bensonhurst," as well as those involved with the 1991–92 trials of William Kennedy Smith and Mike Tyson,
the 1992–93 trials of Rodney King and Reginald Denny, and the 1994–95
criminal trial of O.J. Simpson, in order to investigate two central themes.

First, to what extent is the legal system at the root of the two-sided framework typical of provoking assaults? For more than only an influence that
manifests itself at trials, the spirit of the law accompanies cases like "Central
Park" and "Bensonhurst" all along—from the time the crime is committed,
through the subsequent explosions of media coverage and public reactions,
to when the case finally is tried in the courtroom. Second, how does the law
react once high-profile crime cases have mushroomed into provoking assaults? Here I highlight the problem of "enmeshment," which is a distinct
trait of provoking assaults. By this, I mean difficulties that ensue once a legal
system based on ideals of objectivity and impartiality must process individual
cases no longer easily distinguishable from social causes.

Enmeshment, as just explained, appeared in this book's "Central Park"
and "Bensonhurst" examples, as well as in the later "William Kennedy

Smith," "Mike Tyson," "Rodney King," "Reginald Denny," and "O.J. Simpson" cases of the 1990s. While responses to it varied, this chapter posits that provoking assaults of the 1980s and 1990s challenged the presumption of "objectivity" that underlies the legal system's credibility. As legal scholar Paul Gewirtz has written, "Maintaining the boundary between the courtroom and ordinary life is a central part of what legal process is all about. Distinctive legal rules of procedure, jurisprudence, jurisdiction, and evidence insist upon and define law's autonomous character—indeed constitute the very basis of a court's authority." [1] Yet it is precisely the "boundary between the courtroom and ordinary life" that provoking assaults tend to blur, and the possibility of legal autonomy they call into question.

EVIDENT *A PRIORI:* THE INFLUENCE OF THE LAW

Before addressing the specific dilemmas faced by lawyers, judges, and jurors in trying the provoking assaults that are the subject of this chapter, evident *a priori* is that the law exercises a structural influence on all crimes brought before it. In the interests of discovery, legal cases routinely develop in the institutionally mandated form of sides; to resolve questions of guilt, the side of the defense is divided from that of the prosecution. Thereafter all courtroom events are judged through two-sided parameters; evidence starts to be amassed, and merits/demerits to accrue, to the side of the prosecution or the defense. Moreover, since someone has either committed an illegal act or they have not in criminal as well as civil cases, the veracity of one side's or the other's arguments must be decided by the close of trial. Hoped, and expected, is that jurors' assessments will be concretized in a verdict delivered back to the court in guilty or not guilty, "either/or" form.

What this means for provoking assaults particularly is that, long before trials occur, the public and press know that highly publicized violent incidents—of murder, assault, rape—will eventually be processed through the legal system. Soon after the commission of such high-profile crimes, members of the public are likely to take sides in the widening court of public opinion. In "Central Park," for instance, Donald Trump, sympathetic to the prosecution's side, took out full-page ads in the *New York Times* to express his anger about inner-city youth violence. On the other hand, those aligned on the defendants' side emphasized what seemed to them to be racialized presumptions of guilt. In "Bensonhurst," now on the prosecution's side, activist Al Sharpton and others strongly protested racial prejudices implicit in Yusef Hawkins's murder. And on the defendants' side, now it was local Brooklyn residents who worried whether accused young men could receive fair trials, regardless of race or ethnicity, given the extraordinary publicity accorded the case.

Thus the sides in specific criminal cases evoked concerns about broader, more general causes. For example, in "Smith" and "Tyson," on the prosecution's side, feminists voiced pretrial concerns about victim-blaming sentiments expressed against the women who had brought charges in those rape cases. In "Tyson," on the side of the defense, local groups mounted protests against what they perceived to be racist media coverage. In "Rodney King," on the prosecution's side, many people expressed anger about racist police brutality the case seemed clearly to symbolize. In "Reginald Denny," concerns about racism were evoked by the side of the defense, since the assault of the white truck driver occurred hours after a Simi Valley 1992 verdict acquitting police officers of brutality sparked outrage.

Perhaps most famously, two symbolic sides had formed even before the first trial of O.J. Simpson for murder opened in 1995. On the prosecution's side, many parties felt Nicole Brown Simpson's murder symbolized society's failure to assist victims of domestic violence. And even before detective Mark Fuhrman's obvious racial prejudices surfaced, others on the defense side thought it was Simpson himself who needed assisting, insofar as he was yet another African American man facing potential mistreatment by a biased criminal justice system.

Moreover, the legal system influences not only the two-sided form but the two-sided contents of provoking assaults. Previously I discussed the cultural effects of the media in producing "partialization"; here, the idea is salient as a particular by-product of the legal system. To help jurors decide between divergent interpretations of events, lawyers invariably build arguments "partial" to the side they represent. Dominant narratives are mounted: these are interpretive strategies tailor-made to emphasize points beneficial to a lawyer(s)' own side, either the prosecution or the defense. At the same time, they background other points perceived as detrimental to one or the other side's interests. Even if these "other" points contain important kernels of validity, they are treated for legal purposes as though irrelevant.

While this structured divide serves a defensible legal function, it introduces complications in high-profile cases like provoking assaults. Now both a legal case and a social/political cause, or causes, are at stake. As legal cases, concrete issues must be decided: in the first "Central Park" trial, did these three young male defendants actually rape the jogger? In the "Tyson" case, did the famous defendant in fact rape a young woman named Desiree Washington in the Canterbury Hotel? Did, or did not, O.J. Simpson actually murder his wife Nicole Brown Simpson and her friend Ronald Goldman in Brentwood, California? However as social/political causes, not only the particular but the general must be adjudicated; society's faults, too, are by extension indicted in such cases. Yet crimes like "Central Park," "Tyson," and "Simpson" manifest social problems—women's vulnerability to violence, racial stereotyping in the media, biases toward wealth or poverty—too complicated to neatly fit the two-sided framework into which they are forced.

In retrospect the dominant narratives that attorneys employed in these cases often translated pretrial debates into legal arguments. From early on, assorted individuals and groups not part of the legal system might as well have been working as public counsel *pro se*. For soon after the commission of these crimes, parties upset by the events or by media coverage of them— community leaders, social movement activists, politicians, religious leaders—began to build, and to repeat, points (again, a dominant narrative) of points partial to the side they favored. (See the discussion in chapter 6 of the formation of dominant narratives through public reactions to the "Tyson" and "Simpson" cases.) Thus, just as the legal system exerts a structural influence in shaping the two-sided formal structure out of which public debates emerge, so public debates influence the arguments—that is, the dominant narratives—that lawyers eventually present in court. For example, in "Central Park," a protest first made by public advocates on the defendants' side— that the defendants were "railroaded"—later became a point of contention about how well particular lawyers had, or had not, used this argument to defend their clients. In the "Reginald Denny" case, some parties' anger at the apparently political prosecution of defendants later resounded in the defense side's approach.

Structural traits of the law thereby bring one result into being: through provoking assaults, social problems are framed and debated legalistically. This was earlier illustrated by how media and public reactions to "Central Park" and "Bensonhurst" became aligned with one or the other side in each case. But what are the ramifications for the legal system of its becoming the focus of symbolic attentions and collective hopes?

My research underscored distinctive issues that lawyers, judges, and jurors face when involved with provoking assaults. Common to all three groups were dilemmas generated by the overlapping of legal cases and social causes, that is to say, by the enmeshment that is typical of provoking assaults. But the experience of members within each group also differed insofar as some of them expressed more traditional understandings of the law and legal system than did others, who opted for a more modern understanding. Some members of the groups expressed aspects of both traditional and modern positions, leading me to surmise that these parties' impressions are best arrayed along a continuum connecting traditional and modern outlooks rather than as themselves neatly describable in "either/or" terms. It should also be noted that my usage of "traditionalist" and "modernist" in this chapter to describe such disagreements diverges from that suggested by Gary Minda in his book *Postmodern Legal Movements: Law and Jurisprudence at Century's End*. What Minda refers to as modernist I allude to as traditionalist—namely, the tendency to envision law as a realm "objectively" separable from its social context. What he refers to as postmodernist I allude to as modernist—namely, the conviction that law is better envisioned as part of the social fabric, both influenced by and influencing culture.[2] I chose to use "modernist" rather than "postmodernist" for the simple reason that legal parties I interviewed might not explicitly associate themselves with the latter term and debates that have developed about its meaning. But while our terminology differs, common to both Minda's and the ensuing account are depictions of internal disagreements that evolved from the 1960s through the 1980s. As Minda recounts:

> The autonomy of legal thought was relatively secure as the 1970s began but then events, both internal and external to law, caused legal thinkers to question their faith in law's autonomy. The Age of Faith had passed; the Age of Anxiety had finally arrived. . . . Doctrinal legal scholars correctly saw these new "law and" movements as challenging the central core of beliefs of autonomous, objective law. . . . It is only now becoming clear that the new legal discourses of the "law and" movements of the late 1970s and 1980s have themselves become transformed by a general disenchanted condition that has affected contemporary legal scholarship—*postmodernism*. By the mid-1980s, new scholarly trends in the legal academy consumed and modified the structuralist and determinist modes of the early 1970s and 1980s. Early "law and" scholarship, wedded to a foundational

and structural explanation of law, adopted an antifoundational and more skeptical explanation of law.[3]

ON THE PART OF JUDGES

The cases I studied posed at least three problems specifically relevant for judges: (1) controversies surrounding their selection to hear the case; (2) handling extraordinary media coverage, particularly television coverage; and (3) the challenge of keeping jurors "impartial" in the face of intense media coverage at each trial stage.

Exemplifying the first issue, contention over which judge would oversee the "Central Park" and "Bensonhurst" trials soon suggested that these cases' symbolic and legal dimensions had indeed begun to overlap. Whereas judges who were assigned to hear cases under the jurisdiction of New York City usually had their names selected arbitrarily from a rotating wheel, court administrators bypassed this custom to make special appointments in both instances. In the "Central Park" case, administrative judge Milton Williams chose Thomas Galligan to hear the case, stating that an especially "qualified" party was needed for such a high-profile trial.[4] Similarly in the "Bensonhurst" case, as indictments were handed down and demonstrators and counterdemonstrators garnered increasing media coverage, state court justice Thaddeus Owens was picked outside the wheel to preside over the trials.[5]

Objections greeted both selections, especially from lawyers who worried the appointments would be detrimental to their sides. In "Bensonhurst," several defense attorneys speculated off the record that Owens's appointment was symbolic in a case laden with charges of racial bias: Owens was African American. In "Central Park," defense lawyer Jesse Berman characterized Galligan's selection as extraordinarily pro-prosecution, implying it reflected the Manhattan district attorney's determination to win a conviction in the notorious "Central Park jogger" rape case, at a time when fears about violent crime had escalated in New York City. As Berman, the lawyer for defendant Steve Lopez, described his impressions of Galligan:

JB: Procedurely and substantively everywhere along the line the judge did whatever the DA wanted. He wanted to make sure there were convictions in the case. And nobody got a fair shake in my opinion.

LC: Why would the judge want a conviction?

JB: Well, it was his nature

LC: From what you knew of him previously?

JB: Well, Judge Galligan has a reputation as a very pro-prosecution , very hard anti-defendant judge. Defendants refer to Riker's as "Galligan's Island," and he visibly detested all the defendants from day one.

LC: Why did you feel that?

JB: [H]e . . . routinely denied any application for anything, routinely granted everything the prosecutor wanted. Now it may well be that the prosecution was correct in some of the people they got convicted. . . . I mean, it was a terrible crime. . . . It's just that I don't know to this day which kids were guilty.[6]

But it was not only in the "Central Park" and "Bensonhurst" cases that the selection of judges raised questions about an instance's relationship to politics. In the "Mike Tyson" case, too, some parties sympathetic to the defense felt Indianapolis judge Patricia Gifford's selection was motivated by the determination to obtain a "prize" conviction. Gifford was known locally as a "pro-prosecution" judge, especially experienced and tough in dealing with rape cases. The district attorney at the time, Jeffrey Modisett, remembered questions being raised along those lines by well-known lawyer Alan Dershowitz, but strongly denied that any improprieties in the selection of Gifford as judge had taken place.[7]

Once judges were selected, the second problem mentioned above had to be dealt with: given the extraordinary publicity surrounding provoking assaults, to what extent would judges allow the press, particularly television cameras, into their courtrooms? In the "Central Park" case, Thomas Galligan held out adamantly against Court TV:

TG: You're aware of the attention a case is getting. I wrote a decision about why I wouldn't allow TV: Tim Sullivan's boss, Steve Brill, was just starting Court TV at the time so he was very interested in having the Central Park jogger case as the lead case, and he also felt substantively it was a case of such interest.

LC: Do you think it's inappropriate in general?

TG: No, not in general. But there were very specific factors in this case because of the type of crime and the testimony of the victim and the age of the defendants (who were juveniles). Let's assume they were given juvenile offender status, the record is sealed. Then suddenly their faces are all over the media. This was my principal reason. And also concern for the victim, absolutely. I allowed the victim to be in court but would not allow them to sketch her.[8]

In addition, Galligan was concerned about whether lawyers would "play" to the [television] cameras.[9] In the "Tyson" case, this problem of double visibility—being watched by people in and outside the courtroom, by those immediately and not-so-immediately involved—was also cited by Judge Gifford as the primary reason for her opposition to the presence of television cameras. Although the court "ended up with closed circuit television" anyway, she explained her lingering doubts:

PG: I guess, generally speaking, that my first opposition to cameras in the courtroom is that I think it makes witnesses and attorneys act differently than if they weren't there.

LC: How about judges?

PG: Well, I thought about that, too, because we did end up with closed circuit television and at the beginning I was aware that the camera was there, but I was not after a while. I was aware that people could hear what I was saying, more than in the courtroom. Yes I think it probably affects judges too.[10]

But whereas Galligan weighed this problem in 1989 when *Court TV* was just beginning to televise trials like "Central Park," the "Tyson" case was tried in Indianapolis in 1992, just months after millions of people had watched the television broadcast of the William Kennedy Smith trial in 1991. During that interval, a gradual shift seemed to have occurred: judges found themselves increasingly pressured to open their courtrooms to mass-mediated scrutiny by the public at large. By 1991, Gifford stated that television coverage of "William Kennedy Smith" had influenced her thinking about allowing cameras in the courtroom:

PG: I think there is always a problem as long as we try to maintain the secrecy of a victim. She can be photographed outside or in the courtroom, either way. Obviously from having watched what I did of William Kennedy Smith, it didn't work too well half the time. So I think that it is a problem.

LC: What did you think when you watched the coverage of Kennedy Smith?

PG: I didn't really watch that much. . . . I saw the victim on 20/20 or something later. My general conception was that it was a media circus as opposed to a trial. . . . I don't think that's good in any situation.[11]

Despite these reservations, Gifford agreed to closed circuit television coverage once intense media coverage appeared inevitable. Though only fifty seats were available (including lawyers on both sides, and the families of victims and defendants), over 150 news organizations applied for admission to her courtroom. She took care to put in place special measures. For instance, concerned that the reporters would not get the story "right," Gifford agreed to daily answer legal questions submitted by the media. The judge came to this decision after investigating how judges had handled high-profile cases in the past:

> The Center for State Court Administration was in the process of writing a book. They spent a good deal of time going and talking to judges who had handled trials. . . . Some of the suggestions indicated that how you decided to deal with the media depended on the judge's personality. Some people were not comfortable talking with the media and they obviously shouldn't. Some people felt they shouldn't talk to them at all. But if people wanted to, one judge recommended that he thought it would really help and I thought I would rather have them report accurately. They felt like I was really trying to help them with their job.[12]

Gifford also mentioned that to further prepare for the trial, she had considered calling the judge in the "William Kennedy Smith" case to discuss matters that might apply to the "Tyson" case. The striking aspect to Gifford's preparation for trial was not only that she felt compelled to react thoughtfully to the crush of media coverage, but that her responses were arrived at by making comparisons between high-profile cases. Evidently some legal actors were also perceiving the emergence of a case-after-case phenomenon that created patterned practices in high-profile trials.

In an interview conducted after the public interest surrounding the "Glen Ridge" case, tried in 1993, had died down, Judge Benjamin Cohen mentioned that he had developed his own "theory" of high-profile crime cases over the course of his experiences. In his view "Glen Ridge"—which concerned a group of star New Jersey high school athletes who had assaulted a young, mentally retarded girl—attracted media coverage for several reasons, one of which involved "Central Park":

> I think there are a couple of factors that, in my opinion, probably gave rise to the case receiving so much attention from the press. First of all, I have a theory that whether it's a legal case in court or any other story, once a story achieves a critical mass in the press, it then takes off. If you see something on *NBC News*, then *CBS News* and *ABC News* are going to follow that story. . . . Another factor is that the Glen Ridge incident, as you may recall, occurred quite close in time to the "Central Park jogger" case in New York City. There were of course many differences, but the juxtaposition, that this can happen among white kids in the suburbs, may have also contributed to the focus in the press.[13]

Indeed, before the trial of the "Glen Ridge" case in 1993, Cohen also received requests that cameras be placed in the courtroom. Like Gifford, he felt they "distort the process. I think lawyers, even judges, and others who are involved in the case, witnesses for example, can't help but be affected when they see a TV camera rolling." But Cohen could not just ignore media-related problems:

> There were requests , and thankfully for me, before the case was assigned to me, the assignment judge of the county had dealt with all the pretrial matters. The ground rules he established were, number one, there were no cameras or tape recorders of any kind allowed in the courtroom.[14]

This problem of media influence on jurors—before, during, and after trials—posed a third special issue for judges trying provoking assaults. Given that the media would be present, with or without television cameras, how can jurors be protected from resulting coverage so that the judicial process remained "impartial"? In each of the cases I studied, judges prepared to face this dilemma early on—as early as jury selection—by overseeing lengthy *voir dire* processes that went well beyond measures taken in ordinary cases. In "Central Park," approximately 350 prospective jurors were questioned. In "Bensonhurst," over three hundred persons were queried early on about whether they could stay impartial given stories about Yusef Hawkins's 1989 killing, an incident about which most New Yorkers had at least some knowledge. In the "Central Park" case, more than fifty questions were posed to potential jurors aimed at determining whether press and television coverage had "unduly" affected them. Galligan also told jurors in no uncertain terms that "race was not involved" in the "Central Park jogger" case.[15]

Yet Ronald Sullivan, covering the jury selection process for the *New York Times*, was not convinced that Galligan really believed race to be an irrelevant subject. According to Sullivan's account, six of Judge Galligan's questions probed potential jurors' attitudes about race: for instance, jurors were asked whether they or their families had ever attended a racially segregated school, and whether they believed people are "racially discriminated against in this county."[16] As these questions suggest, Galligan may in fact have been quite concerned about whether debates over racism aired in the media prior to trial—for example, were racial stereotypes used? could young men of color get a fair trial in New York City?—had tainted the judgment of potential jurors.

In the "Bensonhurst" case, too, concerns about racism emerged with jury selection. The reporter covering courtroom proceedings for the *New York Times*, William Glaberson, intimated that many prospective jurors would be familiar with previous controversies surrounding "Bensonhurst," whether or not a judge declared them irrelevant. Glaberson wrote that "the bitterness that emerged after Mr. Hawkins's death would haunt the trial" as potential jurors saw "white supporters of the defendants on the right side of the room behind the tables where the defendants were sitting. Far across the broad aisles reserved for the jurors, a group of black people sat behind the prosecution table."[17] By this account, the polarized division between sides that had been so visible on the streets and in media accounts was reflected in the courtroom.

After jurors were selected, judges again took special precautions to protect them from media or other outside influences. For instance, in "Central Park," the jury was instructed daily to ignore the media. As Galligan described:

TG: [T]hey were told not to pay attention to any media accounts, and I think by and large they did this.

LC: Wouldn't sequestering the jury have been necessary to ensure it?

TG: There are practical problems with sequestering. I think it might create more psychological problems. I really do think that fundamentally jurors do act conscientiously. . . . I tried to impress upon them that what the media says is not what the case is about. It's what *they* say: they're the jury. It's not what the press thinks: it has to be decided *solely* on the basis of what you hear in the courtroom. When people have this responsibility, they take this seriously.[18]

The judge also put the jurors and the public at large on notice: "This case will not be decided on the street, or radio, or TV, or the paper. It will be decided on the evidence in this courtroom." [19]

On the other hand, judges had varying perspectives on the issue. Judge Gifford, who heard the "Tyson" case, believed that jurors could not be protected from media influences unless sequestered:

> PG: [I]f if they were not sequestered it would be a definite influence on them. It's very difficult to tell people to go home and not listen to the radio and watch the television when that's all that is on.
>
> LC: This was a sequestered jury, right?
>
> PG: Yes that's why I chose to sequester them. . . .
>
> LC: How about before they were sequestered?
>
> PG: They all knew. In questioning they were asked if they had read or knew anything about this case, and they all admitted that they had. Those who indicated that they had already formed an opinion were excused. Most of them did not have any opinion one way or another. Or at least they said they didn't. [20]

Judge Cohen expressed yet a third approach to this problem. Although not sequestering the "Glen Ridge" jury in 1993, he was closer to Gifford than Galligan in worrying about jurors' ability to withstand outside influences:

> Repeatedly, I said, "look, I don't want you to read the accounts of this case in the newspapers. Have your family members if you want cut out the clippings, and after the trial is over you can look at them. Don't watch TV accounts. But if you should be exposed to these, accidentally or otherwise, I want to know about it." So virtually every day, I and the attorneys monitored the press collectively, and my staff did also. If there was anything reported by the local papers that were covering the case or the TV stations that people watched that was likely to run a risk if the jurors saw it, we were especially careful the next morning to ask, "Did any of you see, watch or listen to any of these accounts?" I said, "I'm not going to yell at you if you tell me you did." Whenever any juror did, we brought him up alone to sidebar and asked him, "What did you see? Did it affect you? Is it going to be a problem for you to continue to remain fair and impartial?" [21]

Cohen summarized his experience with jurors by saying, "[I]n my opinion, for the most part, jurors really rise to the occasion. I mean, you have to understand the process they go through. They're told before they even come into the courtroom that this is important business, particularly when they get on a case like this." Nonetheless, alluding to the dilemmas of enmeshment, Cohen also stated that jurors "knew they are a little part of history in the making and that everyone is watching." [22]

IN RE LAWYERS

Lawyers in high-profile crime cases also confront special issues, only some of which are similar to those faced by judges. The overriding concern of the judges is to preserve the legal system's aura of impartiality, perhaps especially in high-profile cases like provoking assaults. On the other hand, the role of lawyers in the courtroom demands partiality; theirs is an adversarial function.

Below I target four issues germane to the role of lawyers in provoking assaults: (1) their appointment or hiring (by clients); (2) jury selection; (3) media relations; and (4) legal strategy. As already discussed, the first three of these issues also apply to judges but the fourth does not. The creation of legal strategies to be used in a case is strictly a matter for the opposing attorneys, and reflects their respective partiality. Interestingly, in the context of high-profile cases, lawyers' attitudes toward jury selection, media relations, and legal strategy often comprised an interrelated worldview about how to best defend or prosecute high-profile crimes. However, these views can differ markedly among lawyers whose approaches can be deemed relatively more "traditional" or "modern." For a traditionalist, legal autonomy is a goal to be achieved even if external influences interfered in the process. Striving to maintain a boundary between the courtroom and the world without, traditionalists are likely to avoid media contacts wherever possible. On the contrary, believing media influence to be unavoidable, a modernist attorney hopes to use such coverage in a client's interests. Differentiating their views, too, traditionalist lawyers seek to defend or prosecute a case on its own terms despite surrounding social controversies. On the other hand, modernists tend to incorporate symbolic controversies into "partialized" strategies aimed at advancing their clients' interests.

To some extent, this distinction between lawyers also applies to judges. For example, Judge Galligan emerged as more of a traditionalist, asserting that the legal system can remain "objective" even amidst a barrage of media coverage; on the other hand, Judge Gifford seemed to be more of a modernist. Further, the more traditionalist judges (such as Galligan) were confident that jurors could distinguish outside media influences from the evidence they evaluated inside the courtroom. Other judges (Gifford and Cohen) believed that sequestering jurors helped to protect them from media influences.

Let us begin, then, with the appointment or hiring of attorneys. While the process of assigning a judge to hear a high-profile case often resulted in controversies, choosing lawyers often evinced continuities. Yet the process of choosing both judges and lawyers seemed greatly affected by past cases that had likewise garnered symbolic notoriety. For example, in the 1989 "Bensonhurst" case, Charles Hynes, the district attorney for Brooklyn at the time, assigned Ed Boyar to prosecute the racially charged incident; like Hynes, Boyar had already gained some experience with high-profile cases when prosecuting "Howard Beach." On the other side of "Bensonhurst," Stephen Murphy was engaged to defend Keith Mondello. Murphy, too, was well known from "Howard Beach," having procured the only acquittal of a defendant in that 1985 crime case.

Prior to the "Central Park" case, Linda Fairstein was known for her involvement with sexual assault cases; she had prosecuted the highly profiled murder trial of Robert Chambers, the Upper East Side "preppy" teen accused of killing Jennifer Levin in 1986. While Fairstein herself did not prosecute "Central Park," she selected Elizabeth Lederer to be the state's lead prosecutor. Although such continuities were not initially present on the defense's side of "Central Park," a connection with past high-profile cases was later established. Feeling her son was not well represented at his 1991 trial, Sharonne Salaam engaged a lawyer extraordinarily well known for his work as a defense attorney during the 1960s—William Kunstler—to take the convicted youth's case on appeal.[23]

Nor were continuities in attorney selection limited to these instances taking place in 1989. Attorneys from well-known 1990s cases often were rehired as their name recognition grew with media coverage that forged, in this way and others, connections between crimes. For instance, after appearing frequently in the news when he successfully defended William Kennedy Smith, Miami defense attorney Roy Black was a more recognizable figure when his name reappeared in the context of appealing the also highly profiled "William Lozano" case. That case involved a Cuban police officer who shot two African Americans on a motorcycle in Miami in January 1989; after Lozano was initially convicted, Black won the case insofar as Lozano's conviction was overturned on appeal.

Similarly, in the "Tyson" case, Alan Dershowitz joined the side of the defense's case on appeal. Like Kunstler, Dershowitz was already known for expertise in appealing high-profile crimes; indeed, after "Tyson," Dershowitz reappeared as part of the so-called Dream Team representing O.J. Simpson in 1995–96. Another example of continuities between lawyers in these cases is exemplified by Johnnie Cochran, who was already established as a defense lawyer in Los Angeles before he came to be one of the leading courtroom figures defending Simpson. Prior to that case, Cochran was hired by Reginald Denny in the "Reginald Denny" case that grew out of the "Rodney King" verdicts acquitting police officers in Simi Valley. Then, following his success in the "Simpson" case, Cochran resurfaced in several notorious New York City cases, in particular the one in which Abner Louima brought charges of police brutality against Justin Volpe. Cochran thus moved from a high-profile crime case career targeting potential racist abuses of the Los Angeles Police Department (LAPD) to one involving potential abuses within the New York City Police Department (NYPD).

Certain lawyers, then, accumulated special expertise in prosecuting or defending symbolic high-profile crimes from the 1980s through the 1990s. Once hired or appointed, though, the lawyers confronted one of the same issues that judges faced: jury selection. Now viewed from a lawyer's standpoint, a core issue again was whether potential jurors had been exposed to pretrial coverage, and if so, whether they could remain impartial when asked to assess evidence at trial. Several lawyers therefore treated jury selection as having the utmost significance. This was true for Roy Black. Jury selection was "key to winning the Smith case," he asserted, and therefore the stage in a trial most likely to affect its ultimate outcome. One is reminded as much of a sociologist as a lawyer by Black's description of how he researched the "Kennedy Smith" and "Lozano" cases to uncover which potential jurors were most likely to believe, or doubt, his clients:

RB: One thing that lawyers have learned in the last twenty years is that up until the 1960s, there was a hundred years of social science research that we had left untapped. And what was most of this research about? The interaction of small groups of people and decisionmaking, which is exactly what a jury trial is. . . . [T]here's a tremendous amount of information, both in the literature and with experts, academics, that could easily be adapted for use in trials. . . . Today we have trial consultants that do far more than just jury selection, you know, working in demonstrative exhibits, preparing witnesses to testify, working out issues in cases. In big cases I do focus groups, mock trials.

LC: What else do you do?

RB: We do polling, there's different types of polling. In Lozano's case, we did real scientific polling for the jury with telephone interviews, three or four hundred people in each location, in which the survey instrument was designed by social scientists. Then we had people going to interview people in shopping malls, just to get ideas. . . . I had students go out and just stop people to ask them about the case. . . . Then we would do the focus groups, where we would do a very short presentation of each case, then ask questions and we would show them our demonstration exhibits and ask them what they thought of it, how this would affect them, which things they liked and what they didn't. We didn't do any real mock trials; we didn't have the time to do that.[24]

Not all attorneys agree with Black that outside social science research to help with jury selection is required to maximize a client's chances for a positive outcome at trial. Black himself described contact with a defense attorney on the "Tyson" case prior to Dershowitz's entering the case on appeal. According to Black, the lawyers defending Tyson subscribed to a philosophy quite different from his own:

RB: I had a lot of communication with his [Tyson's] lawyers on the first trial, prior to his trial. Since our cases ["Smith" and "Tyson"] were so close . . . I made a number of recommendations of things that they ought to do in Tyson's case.

LC: Did they do them?

RB: I don't think they did. No, I really emphasized the part that they really had to work on was the jury selection and doing polling, jury questionnaires, getting expanded questions to jurors. I told them that was the key to winning the Smith case, and in fact I recommended using the same [jury consultants] that I did because they not only got through a month of jury selection, but they stayed there for the whole trial. What better preparation could there be than that? But the lawyers [in the "Tyson" case] didn't seem to want to use jury consultants.[25]

This difference between lawyers defending Kennedy Smith and the original defense team in the "Tyson" case about outside advice from jury consultants also extends to a third issue that lawyers, like judges, encountered. For some, not only were juries understood to be potentially affected by pretrial coverage, but attorneys realized as well that the extraordinary attention shown cases by the press would continue throughout trials, even as they disagreed about how best to react. On the other hand, some lawyers were not interested in communicating with parties who regularly mediate between the worlds inside and out of the courtroom—namely, print and television reporters. Indeed, two Washington, D.C. lawyers initially involved with Tyson's defense, Vincent Fuller and Kathleen Beggs, expressed this view. According to Fuller, he was too busy during the trial to watch or read what was being reported. And, as Beggs described the position they shared,

> Vince never talks to the press. Nor do I. You run the danger of saying something in the early stages of a case that might come back to hurt your client once the facts are better known. In most states, you also run the risk of breaking the rules of ethics.[26]

James Voyles, a local lawyer handling Tyson's defense, expressed a similar attitude:

> I have a general view about most cases. Media does play a part in analyzing people's thought processes, not just in "Tyson" but in any case: you never know about the effect. We sought and received a gag order to prevent anyone—attorneys, police officers, agents of both sides—from talking. We never met with the media at all. The other side has a spokesman with the press but no one on our side. In all criminal cases, there's a predisposition against the defendant. This is not special about this case: the media is permitted to go into an individual's background before the case even though whatever happened between Tyson and [Robin] Givens may have no bearing on this particular case. Yet there were negative implications about his past conduct that you can't prevent from getting in the media.
> These presumptions do get into the media, and then into jurors' minds. You'd be surprised if people may not have seen some information.

But you just have to rely on the jury. . . . I'm against television coverage. I have had no reason to doubt that it has some effect on participants.[27]

Note that neither Fuller, Beggs, nor Voyles denied media influence on jurors; they simply felt that talking to the press would only exacerbate their client's already precarious situation. Fuller and Beggs thought the media had already prejudiced jurors in the "Tyson" case, commenting about Indianapolis prior to their arrival to defend Tyson:

KB: Indianapolis is worse than other midwestern cities. People didn't like Tyson or us because we were out-of-towners.

VF: From the day it broke, the press was against us. . . . [T]hey convicted him before we got there.

KB: The whole pretrial press coverage about the case was that it was a continuation. They dredged up stuff about him as a street thug.

VF: Absolutely. The local sentiment was already pretrial against Tyson: presumptions of guilt at its worst.

KB: And it was extraordinarily racist. We knew it was the home of the KKK; if David Duke had run for governor of Indiana, he would have won.[28]

Moreover, Fuller and Beggs felt the timing of the case—tried several months after William Kennedy Smith was acquitted for rape, and after Supreme Court nominee Clarence Thomas was accused of sexual harassment—had lessened Tyson's chances of acquittal. In Fuller's words, "The Kennedy case hurt us." Said Beggs, "It was hard to have two things happening prior. Popular sentiment in Indiana was that Kennedy Smith was guilty; he was a rich kid who bought his way out, and they weren't going to let Tyson do it."[29]

Contrast these attitudes with the relatively more modernistic ones expressed by Alan Dershowitz when, following Tyson's conviction, he agreed to argue the case on appeal. For Dershowitz, to ignore the media was to deny its influence on a case's final outcome—whether one approved of this influence or not. Whereas Roy Black accorded jury selection priority, Dershowitz emphasized the importance of using the media as a legal tool:

LC: At what stages does the media affect this process? Does it affect jury selection?

AD: It affects everything. There is nothing it doesn't affect. We live in a world where everybody watches television; everybody has a point of view about these cases. No matter how hard you try not to let it affect your judgment, it always affects your judgment. Helping the media shape the perception of a case is the single most important thing a lawyer can do.

LC: Was that true twenty years ago?

AD: You go back and read what is called "legal realism," a development that started in the 1930s. It's very close to . . . but of course, in those days, we didn't have mass culture. It's not so much that postmodernist theory explains so much, it's that we have a change in the mechanisms for transmitting public culture. Let's say an event occurs: for example, Michael Milken is let out of jail. It will be covered on CNN, which means it's covered all over the world. How the spin is put on will affect how millions of people think about Michael Milken. . . . These public perceptions affect everyone. . . . They affect judges, they affect Supreme Court justices. Feminist theory had an enormous impact on getting the Supreme Court to decide *Roe v. Wade.* But *Roe v. Wade* isn't decided by the Constitution, it's decided by the fact that Justice Blackmun told me that his daughters influenced him on that decision. When I argued the von Bulow case, I argued it on television. The appeal was on television. Everyone in New England saw the argument that day. I said to myself, I'm not arguing to those guys: I'm arguing to their wives, their spouses, their peer groups. I want to make it thinkable. . . . I would have said the same thing twenty-five years ago, that the judiciary is influenced by the public. But I would have said that the influence is less pervasive. There is a real qualitative difference because there are only four new outlets in the world that matter. That is the four television networks and CNN, and the newspapers don't really matter anymore. . . . Let me tell you what I tell my law students when I have a jury case. If you have a jury case on Monday, do not spend the weekend in the library, spend the weekend on the train, in the subway, flip the television stations, find what everybody is watching, go to see the most popular movies. I want you to be involved in popular culture on Monday. I want you to the use the language of *LA Law.*

LC: You're a sociologically oriented law professor.

AD: Oh absolutely. . . . I want you to know what the jurors are thinking. You can't know everything. You can't know who had a fight with their spouse that night; I wish you could. It would be great to be able to make analogies from that point of personal life. I say on Monday, in your opening argument, mention the Bible. Sixty percent of your jurors will have read the Bible just twenty-four hours ago. Find out what the preacher spoke about. If you're in a city like New York, don't read Brandeis and Cardozo: the jurors never heard of them. Speak their language. Know what people are talking about.[30]

This worldview distinguished Dershowitz's defense from the one proffered by Tyson's more traditionalist lawyers during his Indianapolis trial. For, according to Dershowitz,

had I been his trial lawyer, I would have tried his case in the press. . . . Whenever I come into a case my client has already been tried and convicted in the press. . . . Mike Tyson's lawyer never spoke to the press and he [Tyson] was already an animal. I would have tried very hard to change public opinion the day I got into the case. I would have Mike speak. I would have spoken. . . .

LC: So you would have gone to the press much earlier?

AD: Absolutely. . . .

LC: Would TV coverage have helped?

AD: Absolutely. I'd have loved to see Tyson's appeal on television. Had it been on television the strategy would have to be different. Because when the goal is going to have a trickle down impact, you have to argue it somewhat differently. Remember you're arguing to an audience that knows more facts. The jury knows only a few facts, because the jury has these airtight compartments, whereas the public knows much more. So they see it through a different filter and so you have to be very careful how you argue to the public and the jury.[31]

Indeed, during the time he was working on Tyson's appeal, Dershowitz strategically used popular cultural venues. For instance, following our interview in early 1993, Dershowitz invited me to accompany him to the *Maury Povich* show where he appeared along with several jurors flown in from Indianapolis for a discussion of whether Tyson's conviction should be reversed. My notes of that occasion read:

Fascinating to watch Dershowitz acting on the *Maury Povich* show as though he were in a courtroom—he went out of his way to assure a heavyset woman that she didn't make a mistake the first time around but that she didn't have enough evidence. . . . [A]pplause seemed to shift from initial opposition to Tyson to more support for him as the show continued.

[Dershowitz] was trying to establish that there should have been reasonable doubt, that there wasn't enough evidence to convict Tyson. He must have been satisfied because, at one point, he managed to get the two jurors on the show who said they wouldn't change their mind to admit that new evidence would have made it harder for them to have convicted Tyson.[32]

Like Dershowitz in this regard, Roy Black also evinced a modernistic approach insofar as he recognized that the influence of the media, because unavoidable, had to be "worked with":

LC: You were saying you can't get away from cases like this being publicized?

RB: Yes, it's inevitable that this is going to happen, and there's nothing you can do to stop it. You have to try to remedy the situation, not even remedy it—you have to recognize that it's there, and you have to sort of work with it, some way. Because there's simply no way you're going to be able to stop it from occurring. In this day and age, once the case captures the public fancy, it's going to have a life of its own, and all you can do is react to that in some way.[33]

Black, like Dershowitz, speculated he would have devoted more attention in the "Tyson" case to "humanizing" the defendant, since the press "always made the young woman look virginal, and he looked like a brute: all that publicity has to have some effect on potential jurors." And indeed, when defending William Kennedy Smith, Black did "work with" publicity in two ways: first, by fostering good relations with the media; and, second, by striving to portray Kennedy Smith positively. Although Black himself did not discuss his doing this, several reporters who covered "William Kennedy Smith" in 1991, like Dershowitz when interviewed, used a term usually associated with two-sided political campaigns—"spin"—to describe defense efforts to foster public and media impressions of "Willie" as a "nice guy." Despite this spin, or possibly because of it, these reporters were more favorably impressed by Black's work than they were with the more remote-seeming approach of Moira Lasch on the prosecution's side. As Christine Stapleton, the lead reporter for the *Palm Beach Post*, recalled:

CS: Oh, but you know spin control was just ridiculous.

LC: What do you mean by spin control?

CS: The way they manipulated the Kennedy name. It was just brilliant, you know, the PR. Well, the whole thing was very carefully orchestrated. Right down to what Willie was wearing, that all of a sudden he comes up with this little puppy McShane.

LC: He didn't have the puppy before?

CS: No. Yeah, they came down, and he'd just gotten a puppy. Sunday morning, just out of the blue they called up certain media and said come on down to the compound, we're going to do a photo shoot of Willie and McShane. . . . They called the writers, they called the [Palm Beach] *Post*. . . . There was another person going around saying, "I'm handling all the media requests for Willie" that had gotten be to too much, and she gave out a phone number that she had—she was staying at the [Kennedy] compound. . . . His mom was always there too. You know that's important, when you have your mom every single day walk in and walk out with you and sit behind you, then all your favorite cousins come in.[34]

Stapleton recounted how Roy Black talked with the media each day at a prearranged spot, a practice that contrasted sharply with prosecutor Moira Lasch's avoidance of the press:

CS: Moira did not deal with the media at all, and that was a big mistake she made.

LC: Why was it a mistake?

CS: Because, you know, I talked to groups of lawyers about this. When a reporter comes up to you, you don't have a choice: we're going to write this story whether you like it or not, so you can either be cooperative or uncooperative. When a reporter comes up to you, even if you can't say anything to them, be polite, be nice. Maura was as nasty as she could be. . . . She's an excellent lawyer. She has a brilliant legal mind, and she's very organized and she can prepare a case, and she's the most thorough person I've known, but she's not good in front of a jury. She has one of the flattest affects. People want to see *LA Law*, and she doesn't look like or act like Susan Dey; it's not even close.[35]

Perhaps decisions by lawyers to use or ignore the press reflect regional differences in attorneys' mindsets. For example, some of those I interviewed thought Dershowitz's media-friendly approach had an "eastern" tinge to it, something that worked against him among lawyers and judges in Indianapolis. By local cultural standards, his style was considered pushy and obnoxious. But the adoption by lawyers of traditionalist or modernist approaches must be more complicated in these cases since some local Indianapolis lawyers developed good relations with the press, while eastern lawyers (for example, the Washington, D.C.–based Fuller) chose not to deal with the press at all. On the other side of the "Tyson" case, for instance, Indianapolis lawyer Greg Garrison remembered having good relations with reporters at the same time he was suspicious of the media's effects on the criminal justice system:

> The media can get in the way. They were nice to me and I was nice to them; we never refused to talk to them. We wouldn't give them any inside scoops during the trial though they treated me like I was some intergalactic star.[36]

Just as differences among lawyers were not explicable solely by regional factors, they were not simply a function of class: both Tyson and Kennedy Smith could afford to hire expensive attorneys to defend them, yet the former initially received a more traditional defense than the latter. On the other hand, class was not entirely irrelevant to these cases either. In the 1989 "Central Park jogger" case, the fact that the accused youths were not well-to-do meant they could not afford a high-priced defense of any kind. In the end, what matters most may not be class *per se* but the possession of "cultural capital" as understood by sociologist Pierre Bourdieu: there may be a sophistication, a kind of legal "know-how," that some lawyers more than others bring to high-profile crime cases. In this light, looking back on how he handled Yusef Salaam's defense in "Central Park," lawyer Robert Burns wondered:

> [I]s there anything that I would have done differently in the course of defending the case? . . . . I think I would have been much more sensitive to the power of the press. . . . I was naïve as far as the press was concerned. I did not realize the degree to which they would take sides. In a subtle manner, taking sides.[37]

As it happened, Burns himself was the object of intense scrutiny from the media, and eventually from parties sympathetic to the defense, because of other serious legal problems reported during the 1990 trial. For instance, his calling Yusef Salaam to the stand was widely thought to be a blunder not only for his client's case, but because it was potentially incriminating for the other defendants as well. It was also a matter of some controversy in the "Central Park jogger" case that four New York City newspapers had portrayed the defendants in racialized terms presumptive of guilt. Therefore, looking back on the case after taking Salaam's appeal, William Kunstler agreed with Burns that sensational media attention to "Central Park" had rendered the defense's position tenuous. Once the case and the cause of (gendered) violence had melded on the prosecution's side, attorneys had a "hard row to hoe." Nonetheless, Kunstler criticized the performance of earlier attorneys, intimating that they had failed to exhibit legal savvy by not "humanizing" the defendants in "Central Park":

WK: When you're dealing with a high-profile case, it's sort of a feeding frenzy.

LC: How?

WK: Oh, it erupts in the media. Then it becomes a two-edged sword for the defense because the higher the profile, the more access defendants and their counsel have to the media. On the other hand, of course, the prosecutor gets a lot of detrimental material. In the jogger case, you had the age-old syndrome of white woman, black man, sexual crime, and so on. Because no matter how you slice it in America, sexual relations or assaults between black men and white women occupy a different status than any other, virtually, any other type of crime. And so in the jogger case when you had all of that, and then make it a middle-class white woman, a woman who worked for a stockbroker's firm, you have an even worse situation. If she had been of a poor socioeconomic class background, there would been even less stir. This has been true of American life since the slave ships arrived. And then, I think, Donald Trump had taken an ad. . . . [T]he youth were portrayed as wilding, beasts and so on, and so you have an instantaneous public reaction against the defendants. Engendered by the media, by the prosecutor, . . . by everybody that had an axe to grind. At any rate not that the jogger wasn't terribly, terribly abused, okay? Nothing like that. . . . It's just that the identity of the victim and the identity of the attackers racially, and even her economic identity, played against the defendants from start to finish. It permeated the judge, the jury, the press, people on the street. . . . I don't think they ever really had a chance. Unfortunately, the lawyers were not what I call political lawyers, they were not very good lawyers to start with. And secondly they didn't know how to respond, say, by having a press conference with the families. They needed some way to humanize . . . .

LC: To humanize the defendants?

WK: Yes, that was not done in this case at all. And so the defendants went into this trial with a hard row to hoe, believe me. The fact that the jury was out so long, I mean eight or nine days, suggests that maybe this jury—under different circumstances, maybe the defendants would have had a shot. But that did not occur.[38]

What can be concluded is that, for lawyers like Dershowitz, Black, and Kunstler, media relations themselves are a key component of legal strategy. But key to legal strategy is also how one plans to argue the case substantively, a decision that also may be affected by the case–cause enmeshment distinctive to these instances. In provoking assaults, both the prosecution and the defense are engaged with crimes well known to the media and public alike. How, then, should lawyers handle symbolic controversies these cases quickly evoke? One option is to simply ignore how cases and causes have become enmeshed. A lawyer choosing to proceed this way would concentrate primarily on the merits of his or her case to the exclusion of debates about larger social problems that case evokes. Such an approach would therefore reflect a traditionalist orientation, one that presumes the courtroom proceedings can (and should) take place without "external" influence from the media or society intervening.

A second option is the reverse of the first: a prosecutor or defense attorney explicitly or implicitly brings political and social events into the courtroom, incorporating pretrial debates into arguments on behalf of one's client. (See, for example, figure 5.) This obviously equates with what I earlier described as the modernistic approach, accepting and attempting to use blurred legal/ social lines. Finally, and possibly in conjunction with this second approach, a third strategy can be employed by lawyers seeking to reverse the identity of victims and victimizers within the two-sided framework of the legal system, arguing that accusing parties in some way contributed to, or "provoked," their own victimization. This tack is obviously more likely to be taken by attorneys for the defense.

In the cases I studied, lawyers used the second and/or third approaches more often than the first. Since most people, from reporters to jurors, were

SIMPSON: Cochran Urges Jury to Send a Message With Verdict

Defense attorney Johnnie L. Cochran Jr. shows jury the door to freedom for O.J. Simpson if he is acquitted on double-murder charges.

Garvey, Jenner
in Audience

Fig. 5. A *Los Angeles Times* headline suggests that defense attorney Johnnie Cochran was purposely using case/cause enmeshment as part of his legal strategy by urging the "Simpson" jury to "send a message" with their verdict.

aware of impassioned debates preceding these cases, lawyers often referenced—whether in opening statements, over the course of a trial, or at summation—symbolic controversies. By way of illustration, I describe four instances in which attorneys strategically used case–cause enmeshments and attempted to reverse the identity of victims and victimizers, or both. These lawyers' approaches also exemplify how dominant narratives may be used to transform pretrial debates into a substantive part of trial strategy. Further, the ensuing sections analyze why modernistic strategies may have succeeded with jurors in some cases but not others.

THE FIRST "CENTRAL PARK" TRIAL

On the defense side of this case, first tried in 1990, lawyers attempted to incorporate pretrial debates regarding race and class discrimination into their legal strategies. Since forensic evidence against the accused had not been found, the prosecution in "Central Park" came to rest its case overwhelmingly on confessions obtained in an Upper Manhattan police precinct the night of the crime. These confessions were obtained without the presence of lawyers and, in at least one case, by a defendant who communicated soley through family members, who were themselves not fluent in English. The confessions, then, were arguably "coerced" from young people who hardly possessed cultural capital of the kind that, for middle- or upper-class youths, would likely have resulted in the immediate appearance and participation of well-paid lawyers.

In fact, several lawyers for the accused attempted to make precisely this argument. For instance, when interviewed, Michael Joseph described his efforts on behalf of Antron McCray, the defendant he represented in the "Central Park" case, to introduce evidence about how

> [t]his client, this young man, was coerced into making a statement. One of the things I argued to the judge is that the jury should be able to understand—"Who is Antron McCray—Alan Dershowitz?" You know, somebody who is fully aware of what his rights are, fully able to deal with the police as an equal? . . . Yet the judge ruled that this evidence would not be permissible.[39]

Similarly, Peter Rivera, the lawyer for defendant Raymond Santana, characterized his client's confession as unfairly obtained. According to Rivera, coercive police methods had aimed at making Santana say exactly what prosecutors wanted to hear.

Nonetheless, these lawyers had not developed a "coordinated" strategy, something also noticed by *New York Times* reporter William Glaberson:

> [D]efense lawyers have been notable mostly for what they have not done. After three weeks of testimony and fifteen months of news reports detailing the prosecution's version of events on that Wednesday night in Central Park in April 1989, the defense has yet to present a comprehensive alternative theory of the case. . . . Instead, the scattershot cross-examination by the lawyers, who were appointed by the court because the defendants could not afford private counsel, appears aimed at raising doubts among the jurors rather than providing them with a single perspective on the evidence.[40]

While race and class discrimination seemed the dominant narrative on the defense side, gender discrimination was a pretrial issue potentially germane for the state: the jogger's assault evoked collective anger at violence against women, especially among affluent urban dwellers increasingly fearful about inner-city crime. And, on this side of the case, prosecutor Elizabeth Lederer did seem to effectively bring feminist issues into the courtroom by highlighting, simply but vividly, the rape's brutal character. This was the dominant narrative, the cause counter to racism, on the part of the prosecution. As Ronald Sullivan wrote, again in the *New York Times*:

> A Manhattan prosecutor described in graphic detail yesterday how a group of youths attacked a woman jogging last year in Central Park. . . . Ms. Lederer said the youths so viciously beat the woman, an investment banker at Salomon Brothers, that she has no memory of the attack. . . . Reading from a transcript of Mr. McCray's videotaped statement, Ms. Lederer described how the youths charged the woman, knocking her down. "Everybody was just hitting her. We all took turns getting on top of her. I kicked her. I just kicked her," she quoted Mr. McCray as saying. She then quoted Mr. Santana as saying: "She was screaming for help. She kept screaming, and then someone hit her with a brick and she became quiet." Ms. Lederer read from Mr. Salaam's statement to detectives in which he said the attack "was fun" and admitted striking the jogger with a pipe.[41]

Several jurors from the first "Central Park" trial confirmed this approach's impact. According to one of these jurors, "Yes the case was very complicated . . . lots of evidence. There was also an emotional side to it. I had to try to keep a clear head, to keep my anger level because of the pictures we saw and what they did to her. It's one thing to hear about it, another to see pictures. You have to put everything together. It's emotional when you look at the faces of defendants, which showed indifference, no compassion, total recklessness."[42] Another juror recalled:

> [A]fter the pictures presented in the court about the condition that this woman was in, I think we were all horrified. It was terrible.
>
> **LC:** So it had a large impact?
>
> **REPLY:** Yes it did. And then when she finally came to testify, we got a chance to see her. . . . I think it was important for us as a jury to see the woman who was the subject of the attack.[43]

Lederer herself described the connection she perceived between pretrial concerns about gender discrimination and the prosecution. She was sensitive to the issue of violence against women, and felt that feminist concerns had heightened people's interest and concerns about "Central Park":

I think that it was a case that people could identify with, it was a gender case, it was a male/female thing because it was a sexual assault. It was a class case for many people because it represented a very affluent victim, and in fact the people in Central Park that night were largely people who work out and go running or biking at 8:00 or 9:00 P.M. at night and people who were working in high-pressure investment banking types of jobs. . . . It became a focus for many people who could identify with just the fear that random violence provokes . . . everybody identified with her.[44]

Although Lederer believed gender issues were relevant to the prosecution's side, she went on to deny that racial biases also pertained to the case:

EL: Many women would come up to me and say, "It could have been me." But, despite all those things, it also became a racial issue.
LC: Was that your feeling, that it became a case that was seen in terms of race . . . ?
EL: It seemed as if the attorneys for the accused were playing with that issue. I was very aware of that in the openings, and in the summations. You know, it wasn't about that. . . . And I knew that there were all these voices that were trying to look at it in terms of race, but I really felt it was about gender. But it was such a weird time. I remember looking out the window one day and seeing a big circle of Guardian Angels, and saying, "Oh god, what side are they here on? What side are they here for?" It ended up they were on the prosecution's side but initially I couldn't tell.[45]

Lederer's assistant in the case, Timothy Clements, likewise stated that, in his view, the case had to do with violence against women rather than racism. There was no factual basis to think there was a racial component to the case, based on anything that was said."[46]

Analyzed from afar, then, the prosecution did incorporate a pretrial issue (violence against women) into the courtroom while also engaging in "partialization." By this I mean that attorneys who make strategic use of symbolic pretrial debates broach only those aspects of provoking assault debates relevant to their side. Indeed why would they raise points apparently detrimental to their client(s)' interests? Still, in the intricate social world that precedes and in which crime cases like "Central Park" take place, a number of points can be valid at once. In this case, the crime committed against the jogger did come to symbolize a larger problem of violence against women; at the same time, race and class biases may have affected whether and how accused parties confessed. Partialization therefore has the effect of simplifying, if not oversimplifying, how we think about social issues that form the backdrop of these crimes.

The defense in "Central Park" also sought to introduce symbolic issues in a partialized manner, this time emphasizing race and class biases rather than gendered ones. Why, then, did its efforts seem less fruitful than the prosecution's, with the eventual result that all three defendants were convicted? One explanation, already noted in considering various strategies for handling the media, is simply that the defense did not argue its symbolic side of the case powerfully. It was not only Glaberson writing in the *Times* and a high-profile defense attorney like Kunstler who questioned the defense's efficacy. Jurors, too, suggested that had a stronger case been presented, they might have found arguments about race and class prejudice more compelling. One juror, for instance, recollected being torn between gender-oriented sympathies that inclined toward the prosecution and ethnic sympathies that inclined toward the defense:

> The foreman made it very clear from the beginning that race shouldn't be a factor, but nonetheless we're all human beings. It's hard not to be empathetic toward someone whose situation you understand; at the same time, you're trying not to be biased in your thinking.[47]

According to another juror:

> Well of course, the prosecutors, I think, really were prepared. . . .
> **LC:** And you didn't have as good a recollection of the defendants' lawyers?
> **REPLY:** No I did not. . . . I think they could have been better prepared. I really do. I don't know whether they were court-appointed attorneys or what. But they could have done a better job up there. They did not seem to have the kind of skill that Lederer had in getting to the real heart of the case. And also, getting across to the jury the things that would be defending their client. Too many things were left floating, so to speak. And that's why we felt that they were letting things slide under the gate. Not pinning everything down.
> **LC:** Do you think they could have made a stronger case?
> **REPLY:** I think they could have.

LC: What could they have done to sway you more?

REPLY: Well, be better prepared. You know, when you get up to question a witness, particularly when they were cross-examining the policemen who were involved. And particularly the detectives who were, I think, the ones who got the confessions and taped them. They might have done a better job in trying to dispel their testimony. Or find flaws in their testimony. Just like they're doing with O.J.: his lawyers are now saying everything in the world possible to defend him. . . . And these attorneys didn't do that.[48]

This juror's comment about O.J. Simpson's lawyers "saying everything in the world possible" intimates that racial biases were not perceived as relevant to, even if they were being used in, the so-called trial of the century. Still the juror thought "better prepared" lawyers might have stirred doubts in jurors' minds, as happened in the "Simpson" case, about whether evidence in the earlier "Central Park" case had been fairly obtained.

A second reason for the prosecution's success was that its symbolic issue, violence against women, emanated from the victim's side, a person whose attack evoked immense public sympathy. Not only had she suffered obviously horrific injuries, but pretrial publicity consistently portrayed the young woman's life—a portrait that Lederer reiterated in the courtroom—in approving terms. Thus the state had an advantage from the start: the prosecution represented the party against whom an awful wrong had been committed. This meant the defense could employ the third strategy sketched above—reversing the identities of victims and victimizers—only at risk to itself. Nevertheless, late in the trial, defense lawyer Robert Burns did engage in victim-blaming by implying that the jogger had not *really* been raped; only her boyfriend's semen, he told the jury, was definitely identified on the young woman's body. This tack apparently backfired for several jurors; one later angrily characterized this late change in strategy as yet another indication that the defense had poorly represented the accused.

Thus the first "Central Park" trial exemplifies lawyers making use of symbolic controversies to strategic advantage. In so doing, the prosecution was favored from the outset. Representing parties with whom the public sympathized or identified after media saturation of the crime, prosecutors benefited from strong emotions—desires for justice, anger at evident injury—that accrued to this side. On the other side, though, defense attorneys could have adopted several strategies in response. As "Central Park" also illustrated, one option was to argue a symbolic countercause; partialization facilitates this possibility since it ensures that two opposed arguments remain clearly separable throughout the trial. While this strategy did not work in "Central Park," underscoring race and class biases more effectively might have facilitated the defense's goal of raising doubts in jurors' minds. Such doubts may have been further fueled, especially given the extreme physical violence of the crime, by the lack of forensic confirmation that firmly linked these defendants to the crime. Another option for the defense—victim-blaming—was clearly inappropriate and almost sure to backfire in this case, given the degree of sympathy accorded the victim.

THE FIRST "BENSONHURST" TRIAL

Looking back from a prosecutor's vantage point, the "Central Park" and the "Bensonhurst" cases had certain similarities at the same time that each was obviously different. For one thing, in the later case, the state again stood to benefit from deep public sympathy a horrific crime had aroused. Yusef Hawkins was killed when he and three friends on their way to look at a used car were assaulted by between thirty and forty youths in this Brooklyn neighborhood; once more, an evidently innocent person had been victimized. Second, as in "Central Park," it was clear that a symbolic issue, a well-known cause, was closely associated with the prosecution's side. Because the victim and his friends were black, and his attackers overwhelmingly white, a dominant narrative during the pretrial stage was that Yusef Hawkins's murder was a hate crime, which could be tied to civil rights violations of the 1960s. Last but not least, prosecutors in both cases confronted limited evidence. In "Central Park" confessions existed but not forensic confirmation. In "Bensonhurst," virtually no one was willing to come forward to testify that they saw a particular youth attack—or, key for the prosecution, that they saw defendant Joseph Fama shoot—Yusef Hawkins. Several witnesses eventually testified for the state, though their credibility was questionable.

It is not surprising that, like Elizabeth Lederer in "Central Park," prosecutors in "Bensonhurst" also tapped public indignation about the crime and its symbolism in presenting their case. Consider, for example, Spike Lee's assertion in a Daily News guest column on August 31, 1989, the day of Hawkins's funeral, that "Bensonhurst was the modern-day urban equivalent of the lynch mob." These sentiments were echoed by prosecutor James Kohler's assertion in his opening statement in a Brooklyn courtroom on April 17, 1990: "Keith Mondello was going to murder a black man; it didn't matter which black man. Yusef Hawkins innocently appeared on the scene, and his fate was sealed. . . . To call it anything else but a race riot would demean and trivialize the death of Yusef Hawkins."[49]

Moreover, according to Ed Boyar, already experienced in prosecuting bias crimes from his previous successful prosecution of "Howard Beach," the lack of evidence available to the state stemmed from a "wall of silence" regarding racial attitudes. Many people suffered from "Bensonhurst amnesia," Boyar declared solemnly to the jury during the 1990 trial of the first two major defendants, Joey Fama and Keith Mondello. "They hear nothing: the silence of Bensonhurst," he stated. "They see nothing: the blindness of Bensonhurst." And, as Lederer attributed interest in the "Central Park" case to larger public concerns about gender, so Boyar believed this "amnesia" related to deeply engrained prejudices that made the "Bensonhurst" case so socially and symbolically significant:

> If you don't think Bensonhurst and Howard Beach are neighborhoods where many people hold racist attitudes, think again. You walk three guys down a street and the same thing is going to happen. It's not like this was an isolated incident. . . . It's like all blacks need to be out by sundown. They can cut your lawn, but when the sun goes down, you've got to be out. It's like the song, "you've got to be carefully taught."[50]

Thus Kohler and Boyler reiterated impassioned public protests about racism in their prosecutorial arguments; this was the dominant narrative, the "cause" now argued, on their side. But the "other side," as represented by defense attorney Stephen Murphy, also used sentiments expressed pretrial to develop a dominant narrative on the defense side. Recall from chapter 3, chronicling initial media coverage and public reactions to the "Bensonhurst" case, that many local residents felt the defendants had been "railroaded." Rather than seeing the accused youths as racist, people in the neighborhood said they believed the case to be one of mistaken identity and fighting over "turf" set off by a young woman's threats. As this side saw it, Gina Feliciano had let it be known that minority friends with whom she had been spending time planned to "beat up" local youths on the night Hawkins and his companions happened into Bensonhurst. She was therefore seen to be at least partly guilty for the killing. As one reporter at the time recounted: "The fault, in the eyes of much of the neighborhood, lies with Gina Feliciano, who lives in an apartment over the candy store and who, among other things, violated the mores of the Italian-American community by dating black and dark-skinned Hispanic men. . . . 'She provoked everybody,' said Carmen Mercado. 'It's a sin.' " [51]

Now in his opening statements at the "Bensonhurst" trial on April 17, Stephen Murphy, likewise seasoned by his past experience with "Howard Beach," transmuted this community interpretation into a legal strategy that sought to focus blame on the "victim's side" of things. When Murphy rose for his opening statement, he "pounded the lectern and began a blistering attack. . . . She's a contemptible liar and her mother is a contemptible liar. . . . She's responsible for this whole thing." This evoked a warning from Judge Thaddeus Owens that "Miss Feliciano is not on trial here." William Glaberson, who had also covered the "Central Park" case for the *New York Times*, described the later confrontation between Murphy and Feliciano in virtually literary detail:

> Ms. Feliciano, in black culottes, a starched white shirt and black and white vest, rarely backed down in the face of shouts, accusations and sarcasm from the lawyer. . . . "You mean to say," Mr. Murphy asked, his voice climbing toward a shout, "you saw all these people with all these guns and everything and you didn't say anything?" Even before he finished with the question, Ms. Feliciano was gesturing and yelling back at the lawyer. "That's right," she shouted. "I seen what I seen." . . . For a minute, Mr. Murphy seemed to have her confused about what room she was in her mother's second-floor apartment when she saw something on the street below. Then, she said she knew what room it was. "Are you sure of that?" Mr. Murphy asked. "No," she said with dripping sarcasm, "I'm making it up." "It wouldn't be the first time," the lawyer shouted at the teenager. [52]

Whether or not purposefully, Murphy's strategy thereafter restated the countercause on behalf of many in the Bensonhurst community. This amounted to the same dominant narrative heard before—that local residents had been unfairly labeled as racists and had consequently been "victimized" by the media; simultaneously, Murphy's argument reiterated many residents' sentiment that Feliciano, too, was at fault. This approach in effect reversed the identities of victim and victimizer insofar as, obviously, Feliciano had not committed any crime. Paradoxically, it was her right to date whomever she pleased—a feminist issue in itself—that arguably was impeded by local youths' and some residents' reactions to the coming of "minorities" into the neighborhood.

In view of the potential pitfalls that accompany a strategy of "victim blaming," why did Murphy—a well-known and respected defense attorney who had won an acquittal for one of the "Howard Beach" defendants—engage in it anyway? One answer is that, as a matter of strategy, it was crucial to call into question Feliciano's credibility: she was the only person who had come forward to testify that she saw Joey Fama shoot Yusef Hawkins. A second answer is that class and status differences between the victim in the "Central Park jogger" case and Feliciano may have suggested to Murphy that he could sway, not just offend, jurors by aggressively questioning Feliciano. Then, too, Feliciano herself had not been physically, brutally assaulted; the gender-based victimization she experienced was much more difficult to discern. Finally, it was telling that while Feliciano was blamed for the crime by many community residents, and now was also blamed by a defense attorney in the courtroom, her case had not attracted visible feminist support. Although several representatives of the National Organization of Women monitored this first "Bensonhurst" trial, as they had the "Central Park" case, public protests about racism and ethnic discrimination were far more noticeable in "Bensonhurst" than objections regarding victim blaming raised on feminist grounds.

For any of these reasons, or for all of them, Murphy may have believed his best strategy was to question Feliciano's credibility, while arguing the countercause that the attack on Hawkins and his companions was a matter of protecting the community's "turf." Simultaneously, it seemed that Murphy was also personally persuaded by the argument that Feliciano had provoked the situation:

SM: The "Bensonhurst" case was a horror show. The kid [Hawkins] wasn't doing anything wrong. . . . I mean everyone's not a good guy or a bad guy. In "Bensonhurst" the black kids involved were very nice kids. None of the complaining witnesses were bad guys . . . except for Gina Feliciano. . . . [I]n truth she provoked the situation . . . and she didn't come off that nice. When she came up with an attitude, I didn't think I'd have much trouble. She was going to fight me back, and that's a big mistake with me. If you're going to come at me head on, then you're going to have to answer the questions as fast as I can fire them at you.

LC: Did you feel badly about tearing her apart?

SM: Well, there's one way to sell your client out: not to be willing to be the bad guy.

LC: What's the media's part?

SM: To make it a headline case, you need a great white shark eating a half-clad woman, and racial overtones. You need basic ingredients to feed the media. The media seems to thrive on these things. If the cases hadn't become racial, would "Howard Beach" or "Bensonhurst" have been anything exceptional without that racial element they wanted?[53]

In sum, attorneys on both sides of "Bensonhurst," as on both sides of "Central Park," used legal strategies that intimately linked the cases with—and were traceable back to—the symbolic issues responsible for these crimes mushrooming into provoking assaults in the first place. Moreover, in both cases, the prosecution won. In the first "Central Park" trial, all three defendants were convicted and, in the first "Bensonhurst" trial, accused shooter Joey Fama was found guilty. Stephen Murphy's client in the case, Keith Mondello, was acquitted of manslaughter charges; this controversial verdict displeased protesters sympathetic to the prosecution's side, and may have stemmed in part from Murphy's relatively greater experience defending such high-profile cases. On the other hand, even though Mondello was acquitted of manslaughter, he was convicted and sentenced to ten-to-fifteen years in prison on a series of lesser charges. Thus Murphy's strategy of arguing the community's "cause," while using Gina Feliciano to reverse the identities of victim and victimizer, did not manage to offset the prosecution's overall case.

However, in the "Rodney King" and "Reginald Denny" cases—the former first tried in Simi Valley in 1992, the latter in Los Angeles in 1993—defense attorneys succeeded in neutralizing advantages initially favoring the state. In both instances, the defense prevailed. At the Simi Valley trial of "Rodney King," lawyers argued a countercause and reversed the identities of apparent victims and victimizers in a characteristically partialized argument. In "Reginald Denny," a symbolic countercause was presented without resorting to blaming the victim. I turn now to elaborating on the legal strategies adopted in these cases.

Starting once more on the state's side, "Rodney King" ought to have been far easier to prosecute in 1992 than "Central Park" and "Bensonhurst" in 1990. The state possessed a videotape made by a local bystander, George Halliday, showing white officers from the Los Angeles Police Department in the act of beating Rodney King, a black man, on the ground with batons. Through the videotape, the case seemed to speak for itself more than any other police brutality case in U.S. history. As in "Bensonhurst," the dominant narrative of the prosecution—the cause—was that a clear-cut and unmistakable manifestation of racism had occurred. Yet all four accused LAPD officers were acquitted in a trial that took place in Simi Valley, California. The startling verdict set off the now-historic "Los Angeles riots," sometimes also referred to as "the Los Angeles uprising," during April 1992.

When interviewed, Terry White, the lead prosecutor for Los Angeles County at the Simi Valley trial, characterized the venue change that an appellate court had granted the defense as one—if not the—key factor in the defense's winning the acquittals. He also expressed the view common to trial lawyers that jury selection is the most important part of a trial. By extension, where a case is tried, its venue, is also crucial since it determines the pool from which jurors are selected. Thus, when the first trial of the "Rodney King" case was moved from urban Los Angeles County to the mostly white and politically conservative Ventura County, White knew the case would not be an easy one to prosecute:

> Out of five hundred jurors brought in for jury selection, there were only eight blacks in that whole group. If you only have eight people to start with, the chances of any black person getting on was slim. . . . We had a discussion about how preposterous it was to have an all-white jury. And I can tell you that the day we went back into court to do jury selection, I thought we were going to lose the trial because the jury was so defense-oriented. Initially, just looking at the jury pool, I thought we were going to lose. Once the evidence was presented, though, we thought the case was going well. . . . For once in my life, I thought the media were being accurate; all the media seemed pro-prosecution. Then, on the day it was over, we thought we had convicted at least Powell and Koon [two of the accused officers]. I started to get worried when days went by [without a decision].

But still no one expected what happened. . . . Yet I never felt the case was a slam dunk as the media said—and no one in our office did.[54]

White never "felt the case was a slam dunk" both because it was tried in Simi Valley and because he thought police officers were difficult to prosecute in general:

I felt strongly that there should be convictions, but I knew right from the beginning that it would be difficult. . . . Many people respect police offi- cers, and are willing to give police officers a good deal of leeway. I'm not talking about police officers who rape or rob, I'm talking about officers who commit a crime while in the middle of their duties. In my mind, all of them were guilty. You can talk to community activists who think about po- lice brutality but, for the average run of the mill guy, many people out there like cops. So I thought this was going to be a difficult case even before Ven- tura County.[55]

Several conclusions can be drawn from White's remarks. First, at least in theory, the prosecution in the first "Rodney King" trial ought to have had a greater advantage than prosecutors in either "Central Park" or "Benson- hurst." Whereas the state in the previous cases confronted serious eviden- tiary limitations, in "Rodney King," the prosecution possessed a seemingly unimpeachable recording of the assault. But, second, precisely because the state possessed this videotaped evidence—which had been played and re- played on local and national television—the defense was able to mount a compelling argument for a change of venue. As the appellate judge ruled when granting the change, urban residents were so saturated by the tape's televising that 85 percent of Angelinos were already convinced the defen- dants were guilty even before a trial; finding "impartial" jurors seemed im- possible. Thus, paradoxically, the very piece of evidence that should have made the case "open and shut" for the prosecution ended up being used to the defense's advantage. Still, this does not explain why one particular county over another was selected. Why move "Rodney King" to conservative and rel- atively homogeneous Ventura County rather than to a diverse metropolitan region comparable to Los Angeles, like San Francisco's Alameda County?

Former Los Angeles County district attorney Ira Reiner responded cyni- cally to this question, mocking the notion that concerns about impartiality were all-important. Reiner, whose tenure in office was clouded by both the

Simi Valley acquittal and the Los Angeles riot, was likely echoing the prosecution's side of things when he stated:

IR: As you look about at the various places where the judge could have sent the case, you cannot make a rational argument why the case should go to Ventura County. . . . If there is a need to change the venue because of media saturation, moving the case to a contiguous county that is mainly dependent on Los Angeles County for virtually all of its major news media obviously doesn't address the problem. There really is no doubt for anyone involved in this case what the judge's motives were: it was a matter of personal convenience. If he sent it to Ventura County, he would be able to commute by car and would not have to be away from home five nights a week. I expect also, in all fairness to him, I'm sure he felt that it did not matter where this case was sent, that the verdict was preordained. He'd seen the videotape several thousand times like everyone else had.

LC: Were you surprised by the verdict yourself?

IR: Oh yes! Utterly surprised, we all were.[56]

A more charitable, yet not altogether different, reading of the judge's action came from Michael Stone, himself a veteran police defense attorney who became engaged with "Rodney King" after agreeing to represent accused police officer Larry Powell:

MS: The reason the Court of Appeals granted the change of venue, while it would not in other cases, was that Los Angeles had "publicity plus." Not only had there been pervasive, adverse publicity about these officers, but there was a political firestorm in Los Angeles involving Chief Darryl Gates, Mayor Tom Bradley, and the Police Commission, and police use of force policy. It was "publicity plus politics" that tipped the scale, the court said.

LC: But why Simi Valley in Ventura County?

MS: What happens in a change of venue grant is that the Judicial Council surveys counties in California to find one that can accept the trial. They usually give three counties to the trial judge who then makes the selection after hearing the opinions of the parties. In our case Alameda, Riverside, and Ventura Counties were given to us. In terms of demographics Alameda County is racially mixed, and approximates the same demographics as Los Angeles County. There's no question that if we went to Alameda County there would be at least 50 percent minorities in the jury pool. I was raised up there, so I know the area. This was not where I wanted to try the King case, not given the prejudgment, and the prevailing opinion that this was a racially motivated beating of a black motorist by white cops. I wanted a jury that would at least listen to our case, if not presume innocence until guilt was proven. The prosecutors wanted Alameda County because they realized that they would have a much better chance with a racially mixed jury. Ventura County is conservative and the black population is only about 2.5 to 3 percent. It's generally very conservative, but it's also very close. . . . In terms of proximity to where the crime happened, the Ventura County courthouse in Simi Valley is much closer to the scene of King's arrest than the Criminal Courts building in downtown Los Angeles, which is where the trial was located before the venue change. Judge Weisberg selected Ventura County because you've got witnesses to think about, the needs of the defense and the prosecution to think about, and the costs to the taxpayers. If he moved to Alameda County, everyone would have to move up there, three hundred miles to the north. All the witnesses would have to be transported up there at taxpayers' expense. It would have made no sense.[57]

Note that while White and Reiner spoke from the side of the prosecution and Stone from that of the defense, all three agreed that the question and determination of venue had a powerful influence on the case. While the state would have been more likely to prevail had "Rodney King" been tried in an urban center like Los Angeles or San Francisco, the social and cultural composition of jurors drawn from Simi Valley amounted to a gift bestowed on the defense. Legal strategy and the sociological profile of place reflected modernistic outlooks on the parts of these attorneys. Rather than thinking of the "Rodney King" trial as a laboratory of impartial considerations, they pragmatically evaluated factors in and outside courtroom walls.

This point about the entanglement of the legal system with social context may seem obvious now, but in "Rodney King" it was not apparent to everyone. According to Michael Stone, reporters covering the Simi Valley trial failed to perceive that Halliday's videotape was likely to be "read" differently in Ventura County than in diverse urban areas. In this respect, then, the tape may not have been so "objectively" indisputable after all. Stone's strategy was therefore to encourage jurors in Simi Valley, already sympathetic to police perspectives, to "re-view" the evidence in light of the case urged by the defense:

MS: This was a use-of-force case. It's a question of whether they used justified or improper use of force. . . . The one thing that made it different was the media. Other than that, there was nothing unusual about it. This was not a particularly extravagant or noteworthy use of force. It was captured on video and watched by people. . . . That's why it became a symbol of the oppression of the African American male by majority white police departments, even though it was not a symbol of that at all.

LC: Can you tell me more about the defense that you used?

MS: . . . They showed this one snippet over and over, which is the worst looking, because King is apparently doing nothing but trying to defend blows. That was the impression I had going in, but I suspected that there had to be more to this. And of course, when I met Larry and I understood the facts, I understood that it was not the beginning of the scene but really the very end of it. It had been precipitated by a 100-mile-an-hour chase on the freeway and an 80-mile-an-hour chase on the circuit streets, the appearance of PCP ingestion, with a very large African American male, 6'4" 250 lbs., with extremely buff upper body development . . . who continually refused demands to . . . be taken into custody after his two comrades had followed every order. . . . Cops are taught that you don't ever try anything with a duster; they'll rip your throat out. So King started to fight and wrestle and they couldn't get his arms behind him. He started to rise and they zapped him with the first of his set. . . . And down he went. And all the cops must have thought, "Phew, I'm glad this is over." But within seconds he started to fight it off. He stood up, can you imagine the sight of this large man, getting up with his body convulsing. So Koon hits him with a second blast and down he goes again. That's when the video begins. But you never saw that part of the video because the media didn't show it. They had it but they didn't show it because it was inconsistent with what they were trying to suggest this was about. Nobody was interested in seeing something where it looked like the cops might be doing the right thing. When the video begins, you see Powell standing behind King with his baton out. . . .

LC: So you felt like there were media distortions?

MS: Oh absolutely. . . .[58]

Clearly, Stone's way of reacting to the prosecution's initial advantage in "Rodney King" was, like Stephen Murphy's in "Bensonhurst," to construct a countercause: it was the police, not King, who were experiencing unfair treatment. This interpretation was an attempt, also evident in "Bensonhurst," to reverse the identities of apparent victims and victimizers. It became the dominant narrative on the defense's side of the case. In Stone's "re-reading," the full videotape did not depict a fearful King being brutalized by police officers. Rather, the police officers had reason to fear a physically intimidating person who might be under the influence of drugs. In effect, Stone argued that King had "provoked" his own victimization. Simultaneously, he constructed a partialized legal argument from which considerations that might overlap with the other side's point of view were obviously excluded. Stone did not place the impressions he recounted of officers' reactions to a "very large African American male" in the wider context of white-dominated police forces having historically intimidated, and indeed in many instances brutalized, black men. Instead, he felt that "symbolic" concerns about the "oppression of the African American male" were relevant only to the state and to a pro-prosecution media invested in distorting what had occurred.

Indeed Stone was quite critical of the media's role in the riots that took place in the wake of "Rodney King," even while emphasizing the strategic importance of a defense lawyer's being "media savvy":

MS: I was in favor of cameras in the courtroom in this case because I thought the public has to understand this case, or else history will write it as being a racist, brutal police abuse case. . . . I don't think [the media] reported our case accurately . . . [T]hey all thought we were going down.

LC: So you think there was enormous surprise . . . . .

MS: Precisely, which is why there were riots. That's what kicked it off, because people were unprepared. . . . I blame the 1992 riots in Los Angeles, in terms of the spark, the catastrophic sparking of the thing, on the media and secondly on the politicians.

LC: You blame it on the media for the reasons you've just been outlining?

MS: Right. Here we are after ten weeks of trial with the general public who are familiar with the case through media coverage believing that there is no defense. . . .

LC: So you felt that the media made an error of omission that put people in a position to be surprised. Were you surprised by the riots?

MS: Yes, I was blown away by it. . . . I don't think that a lawyer should try his case in the media. But in a case like this where the media is already involved up to its eyebrows, you have to combat this. You've got to be media savvy.[59]

Thus Stone was modernistic not only in his attitudes about the media but in seeing the worlds inside and outside the courtroom as inextricably linked. In retrospect, Stone knew that even though he won in Simi Valley, the defense eventually "lost the war" in 1993 when the "Rodney King" case was retried in a California federal court; even though Stone mounted a defense similar to the one before, the officers were convicted. One of the reasons Stone lost the second time around was that the context changed again: the federal trial took place in downtown Los Angeles. But the defense attorney also felt he lost because:

MS: In high-profile cases like "O.J. Simpson," like "King," the "Kennedy" rape case, all our notions of jurisprudence and how the system works go right out the window. That's what sets these cases apart. It's a phenomenon. Does that mean we throw out the system? No. It's such a small percentage of the cases that go to trial, yet it's a significant one because of the effect these cases have. . . . I was disgusted with the results [in the "Reginald Denny" case], and again I think this has to do with politics in South Central Los Angeles. . . . There was always this linkage in the media in people's statements, "Well if the officers in the "Rodney King" case were acquitted, then these guys [in the "Reginald Denny" case] shouldn't be convicted." There's no linkage there. That was an out and out, unprovoked attempted murder. And every one of them should have been convicted.

LC: Why do you think they weren't?

MS: Because it was politics and fear of a riot, just like our guys were convicted. Because it was assumed, maybe accurately, that if they were convicted again, that we would go up in smoke.

LC: Do you think LA has the potential to go up in smoke again?

MS: You bet . . . because little has changed. There has been little improvement in the quest of the African American community for equality, justice and integration into the system. . . . [In "Rodney King,"] I may have won a battle, but I lost the war in terms of changing public opinion about the real facts of this case.[60]

In the immediate aftermath of the first "Rodney King" case, another high-profile incident took place in the Los Angeles area when four young men were accused of pulling Reginald Denny from his truck and assaulting him. Attorney Edi Faal was hired to defend Demian Williams, one of the accused. Like Michael Stone, Faal was sensitive to issues of context; he, too, understood that enmeshment had affected the "Denny" case by the time he took on Demian Williams's defense. However, as opposed to Stone, Faal did not doubt that racism in the LAPD posed ongoing problems for African Americans and other minorities. Whereas Stone was known to excel at police defense work, Faal discussed openly his view that police brutality in Los Angeles County was routinely ignored. Given these different outlooks, it is worth asking how their strategies compared.

As in the "King" case, Reginald Denny's assault was captured on videotape by a camera crew that hovered above in a helicopter; from an evidentiary standpoint, then, the defense found itself disadvantaged again. The tape showed Denny, a white man, being pulled from his truck and beaten by four black youths on the same April 1992 afternoon the acquittals of the police officers in "Rodney King" were announced. Thus the assault occurred in direct response to the "Rodney King" verdicts; the two cases had a cause-and-effect relationship with one another. Yet, despite recordings that captured both incidents on tape, Faal's defense diverged from Stone's in two striking respects.

The first is that Faal did not seek to reverse the identities of victims and victimizers. Even if Faal had been willing to employ a victim blaming strategy, however dubious it might be from an ethical point of view, he knew it would likely backfire. Like the Central Park jogger in New York City four years earlier, Denny was widely perceived locally and nationally as an innocent victim. Faal reasoned that "anyone who had seen the video of Reginald Denny would invariably condemn the attackers. Denny was an innocent man who did not do anything to his attackers, so the media sympathy for him was understandable. This was not a case like Rodney King where I could attack on the other side, because I cannot attack Reginald Denny. It became very difficult."[61]

A second difference is that Faal sought to clearly connect previous high-profile crimes to the present one. Faal realized, just as this book seeks to make clear, that provoking assaults of the 1980s and 1990s were interrelated. For in the "Denny" case, not only media accounts and public reactions but the very crime itself in question was an outgrowth of the "Rodney King" incident.

But Faal encountered difficulties in making this argument, as sociological as it was legalistic, in the courtroom. Initially, the defense attorney tried to contrast the relatively more serious charges brought against the so-called LA Four in "Reginald Denny" with the relatively lighter charges brought against police officers in the "Rodney King" case. In "Reginald Denny," the four defendants faced accusations of torture, aggravated mayhem, and attempted murder. After going through thousands of pages of material on police brutality cases in Los Angeles Country from 1984 onward, Faal and his legal associates were unable to find one case where the same charges had been filed against a Los Angeles police officer. From this Faal concluded that prosecutors were using the "Reginald Denny" case, in effect symbolically themselves, as a way of responding to the LA riots that followed the announcement of the Simi Valley verdicts in the "Rodney King" case:

> In "Rodney King" the police officers were accused of assaulting Rodney King. Assault is a much lesser crime than attempted murder. . . . In "Reginald Denny," the torture charge carries a mandatory sentence of life imprisonment.... So that was discrimination, it was symbolic. We cannot lose sight of the fact that the Los Angeles riots of 1992 were probably the worst riots in the United States in modern times. Something of significance was that the police fled, abandoned the streets, and the streets were taken over by lawless gangs and hooligans. That is very significant because I think this was a large part of what motivated the politicians, district attorney, and the chief of police to come up with the serious charges against these defendants. And also the city had to send a message that this type of conduct is so threatening to the community at large that it will not be tolerated. But these are political considerations and I reject that political factors ought to be considerations in the filing of criminal charges.[62]

But Faal's attempt to explicitly compare the two cases in court was disallowed; to argue that the state's reaction was politically symbolic appeared to be literally and figuratively inadmissible:

> To allow cases to be compared would expose the unfairness and the disparity in the way that minorities are treated in the criminal justice system. . . . I wanted to show discriminatory prosecution in this case which,

under California law, would have meant the case would be dismissed. But you have to establish the evidence, and the judge wouldn't allow me to bring the evidence.[63]

On the other hand, Faal did succeed in indirectly linking the "Reginald Denny" and "Rodney King" cases by calling academic experts to testify about collective behavior following the Simi Valley verdicts; sociology thus made its way into the courtroom through the back door. Faal's aim was to show that the defendants, at the time of the incident, did not have the "refined state of mind" necessary to be found guilty of attempted murder; rather they had been part of a "senseless mob." This argument became the dominant narrative of his defense:

> **LC:** Did you make any reference to the "Rodney King" case?
>
> **EF:** Yes we did in relation to the mob argument. Milling is a sociological action; it is a response. In this case, there was an announcement in Simi Valley that the police officers in the "Rodney King" case had been found not guilty. Much emotion was afoot, and people ran outside and were expressing their anger, which created a milling effect. Other people started running to the intersection. All of a sudden you had an angry crowd. . . . What we explained to the jurors is that crowd behavior is a very complex sociological phenomenon, and that there are different forms of crowds and types of crowds. We were able to show that the conventional crowd, such as a rally or people going to a movie, has a clear objective and location. Before you get to the location you know what you're going there for and what is expected of you. Those crowds are acting in a civil manner. This though was a dysfunctional crowd, a leaderless crowd, a crowd without objective. . . . What happened is that you had a congregation of people who were angry and engaged in thoughtless acts of violence. . . . Apparently the jurors agreed. We believe they accepted that theory.[64]

Faal's strategy may have indeed persuaded jurors that these two high-profile crimes were interrelated: his client, Damian Williams, was found not guilty of aggravated mayhem (which carried a sentence of life in prison), though Williams was convicted of the lesser charge of simple mayhem. The lawyer's approach also suggests an analogy between trends in journalism, as previously discussed, and the law. Chapter 2 distinguished an American journalistic individualism (which treats stories as though discrete from one another) from an American journalistic relativism (which treats stories in relationship to one another, thereby depicting more precisely what reporters and editors actually seem to do). Now Faal's strategy suggested that individualism can also characterize legal strategies and philosophies; parties in the law may also treat cases of the provoking assault variety as though unconnected and separable from one another. Presumably, the judge in "Reginald Denny" felt this way in disallowing Faal's efforts to explicitly mention the "Rodney King" case. The judge must have thought the earlier case was irrelevant to the present one being tried. However, here again, relativism may more accurately than individualism describe how media and legal decisions are actually made. Like editorial decisions, legal ones are often affected by consideration of events both inside and outside the courtroom. Yet such subtle political concerns may go unacknowledged, institutionally taboo given the "objective" practices conventionally still alleged in the mainstream of both the media and the law.

Faal's strategy may have reflected this sort of legal relativism, but it was also pragmatic. As a defense attorney, he sensed, much more simply, that he could not represent his client effectively unless he connected "King" and "Denny." Not much later, defense attorney Johnnie Cochran evinced a similarly relativistic awareness—and an analogously pragmatic interest in bringing external political events into the courtroom, again, indirectly—when, in 1995, he represented O.J. Simpson at his trial for murder. Cochran's allusions to racism in the "O.J. Simpson" case would have had far less impact were it not for the "Rodney King" and "Reginald Denny" cases, which had left in their wake concerns about racially discriminatory police brutality.

THROUGH JURORS' EYES

Provoking assaults affected the jurors I interviewed in a number of different ways. Most had heard about the highly profiled case they were to be a part of before being selected as jurors. At the jury selection stage, lengthy questionnaires and the careful questioning by the judge and lawyers made it plain that the case bore special status; potential jurors were asked pointedly if they felt they could remain objective in the glare of media exposure. During trials, as William Glaberson reported about "Bensonhurst," jurors could tell a case was unusual simply by looking out into the courtroom. The press was notably in attendance, and the presence of a well-known figure like Al Sharpton reminded jurors that racial tensions existed both at and outside the trial.

But it seemed to be at the deliberation stage, when they could finally share their impressions openly, that jurors first encountered difficulties. At this point, according to several jurors who served on the first "Central Park" and "Bensonhurst" cases, two dilemmas became manifest: first, the challenge of separating the evidence about the case from political pressures surrounding it (most jurors believed they could make this separation, though their remarks hint at contradictory tensions not so easily resolved); and, second, heightened pressures compared with those in ordinary cases to reach an "either/or," guilty or not-guilty verdict. In this section, I elaborate on each of these problems, and relate how they came to be interwoven.

Jurors who sat on the first "Central Park" and "Bensonhurst" trials recalled feeling outside pressures before and after deliberations. One juror on the trial exclaimed:

> [JUROR]: No, I certainly wasn't happy that I was on that case!
> LC: No?
> REPLY: Well, for one thing, it was going to be controversial. And being on a jury with such a controversy, I said, well I could be someplace else.
> LC: When you say controversial, what comes to mind? What was your sense of how it might be controversial?
> REPLY: Well, you know, one of the things is that people, the general public really looked at each individual juror and said, "You're responsible for this." . . . It got very personal. To me, they even called up and said, "We're going to get you" and "You'll pay for this."[65]

Another juror, who served on the first "Bensonhurst" trial of alleged shooter Joseph Fama, described measures taken to shield jurors from the swirl of activity surrounding the case that only had the opposite effect of increasing their awareness of external controversy:

> [W]e would come down to the courtroom to hear testimony back, ask questions of the judge, so everyone would be there. That's when I knew, saw the people camped out and the news vans. Then on the fourth night, there were five times more news vans at ten o'clock. On the sixth or seventh day, we got off the elevators and they had blanked out all the win-

dows. They didn't want us looking out. Prior to that we'd come and gone out of the elevator, they had screens like you'd put around a desk area, sound-proof screens. Now anywhere by the elevator bank, jury room or courtroom, all the windows were covered. Then you really knew something was up. But we didn't know exactly what, which was good. The only thing I can remember was being in the jury room, a small eighth-floor room on the corner in the back by Adams Street, and we could hear this chanting. We all went to the window and we could just see the beginning of this big group of people coming down Tillory Street. They were still kind of far away, but we could hear them. Instantly the court officer said, "Ok, we're all getting out of the room." He walked us down to the middle of the hallway and into the stairwell, made us sit on the floor. Like an air raid drill, so that we couldn't see or hear anything, which was smart. That was very stressful. In fact, one person started crying right then and there. We tried to tell jokes and calm her down and relax about it. But that was a clue of how intense it was.[66]

Arguably, then, jurors in such high-profile cases faced a difficult and contradictory dilemma. On the one hand, as Judge Cohen observed, jurors "knew they were a little part of history in a case like this. That everyone's watching." Under the glare of media and public attention, they clearly understood that once a crime grew to have symbolic significance, verdicts were likely to be read as political statements—whether as a vindication of one side's arguments or a rejection of the other's. But jurors were at the same time expected to uphold the justice system's impartiality by bracketing out surrounding social pressures that might otherwise taint their consideration of the case. How else could defendants receive a "fair trial"? With this aim in mind, they were firmly instructed not to talk about the case with anyone, not even fellow jurors, during the trial, and to avoid media coverage of the case.

Thus jurors in provoking assaults were asked to operate, in effect, with a dual and divided consciousness: at once aware that cases/causes had become enmeshed, and exhorted to ignore outside influences so as to remain "objective." Thereafter, like judges and lawyers who also experienced by-products of enmeshment, jurors had little choice but to react; like judges and lawyers, too, not all jurors reacted similarly. For instance, external pressures to think of the first "Central Park" trial in terms of racial discrimination seemed to produce a backlash in the minds of the seated jurors. As a "Central Park" juror recollected:

Al Sharpton performed every day in the court, down in front of the court . . . made it more of a story for the people who were interested in that kind of racial overtone . . . .

LC: What was he doing?

REPLY: He was rabble rousing as far as I'm concerned. But we didn't stop, the jury just went in and out, we knew he was there, but we never stopped to see what was going on. Yeah, we knew that he was down there, you could hear him making statements.

LC: Why did he get so involved in the case?

REPLY: He gets involved in everything like this where he thinks he might be able to get a little publicity for Al Sharpton. He tried to . . . I think he tried to make it into a racial thing. I think that's probably one of the things he's very great in doing. Puffing things up.[67]

Another juror confirmed both that attempts were made to bring race-based debates into the courtroom and that the jurors had been instructed to ignore these efforts. According to this juror, the case had had little to do with gender or race: "Well, I mean, we were told right at the outset, this is not about racism, that isn't what it's about, and we all agreed, and that was the last time that the whole subject was ever discussed." Moreover, according to the same juror, the racial backgrounds of the jurors overall had had little or no effect on their deliberations:

[JUROR]: So you know all of the shenanigans that went on in the court-room, when you saw Tawana Brawley show up (laugh) and all that, it was, uh—I kept thinking, if they knew what is actually going on—cause this isn't about race at all. It was about trying to weigh the evidence. Of course, there wasn't any evidence except for the confessions.

LC: So you think that it was a misperception on the part of outsiders to think that it had anything to do with . . . .

REPLY: Yes, of course. I mean, that it got a lot of attention in the press may have had something to do with the fact that these were black kids and the woman was white. But that was the press, not the judicial system, or the jury, or anything that had anything to do with what went on in the jury room.[68]

One can interpret these comments as reflecting a traditionalist orientation. The "Central Park" jurors were convinced that, even in the face of outside pressures, the legal system inside the courtroom and the external social/political world outside it had been kept separate; they felt they had preserved the criminal justice system's commitment to impartiality, even knowing that the case had become racialized.

Some jurors in other provoking assaults, however, were more modernistic in accepting a case's broader symbolism; such jurors recognized how case and cause become, in these instances, enmeshed. Consider the views expressed by Tonya Bailey, who served as foreperson of the jury in the first "Bensonhurst" trial of Joseph Fama. Even prior to being selected, Bailey said she thought cases like "Bensonhurst" were symbolic of larger issues like racism. She was familiar with high-profile crime precedents to the "Bensonhurst" case such as "Howard Beach"; having grown up in the South, she had observed the realities of racism first-hand. In addition, Bailey believed that by the time the "Bensonhurst" case was tried in 1990, race relations in New York had reached a "crisis point." Thus serving on the "Bensonhurst" jury offered an "historical opportunity"; it far transcended ordinary jury duty to become one of the most "important events of her life." But note from her comments that, like all the jurors I interviewed, Bailey also carefully followed the judge's instructions to avoid news coverage of the case; like the "Central Park" jurors, she was committed to upholding the principle that the accused be given a "fair trial." Mostly, then, the modernistic influence Bailey evinced was her belief that, as part of the jury, she would be contributing to social change through the symbolic statement a verdict in such highly profiled cases can make. For Bailey suspected that a great deal was at stake in the "Bensonhurst" case:

TB: I am quick to speak up and I did say that we want to be careful about this, because it is so high profile and there could be repercussions. Well, I mean, you don't want to say something that comes out the wrong way and then you're lambasted in the press for it. . . . Well, even when I was home, I didn't read [the newspapers] during the trial. I had people saving everything for me so that when I got out I could review it all and see what was going on. . . . I read headlines later that Al Sharpton said, "We'll burn the town down . . . ." I do believe at this time that had a not-guilty verdict come back, what happened in Los Angeles would have happened in New York. . . . The

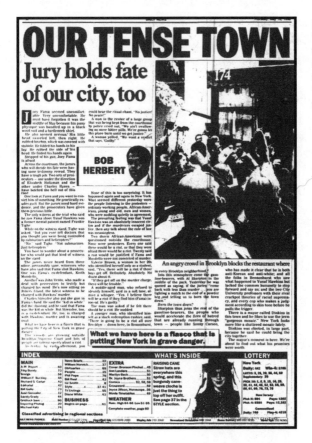

Fig. 6. Media coverage of the "Bensonhurst" trial confirmed that a legal case and social cause had become enmeshed for New York City jurors in the "tense town" awaiting their verdict.

first person I saw after coming out, other than my husband, was a woman who lives on my floor. . . . [S]he said to me as we got out of the elevator, "Good job, you saved the City's ass!" That shows how much tension there was. The sense was a lot could happen depending on how this verdict goes.

LC: So even if you couldn't read the papers, if you were sitting there, you had that sense?

TB: Yeah I had that sense.[69]

In referring to "what happened in Los Angeles," Bailey made retrospective allusion to the Rodney King case and the Los Angeles rioting that erupted following the acquittal of police officers in Simi Valley.

Bailey did not describe herself as alone in perceiving the case's symbolic significance. Other jurors, she recollected, likewise realized that their deliberations were taking place in a racially charged environment and were concerned about how their verdict might affect that climate. (See figure 6.) The experience of another juror illustrates the second difficulty mentioned above—namely, reaching a clear-cut "either/or" verdict under circumstances of heightened social scrutiny. Granted, this juror said, the prosecution had successfully convinced him that accused shooter, Joey Fama, had been present at the crime scene. But the juror was not initially certain that there was sufficient evidence to convict Fama of murder; however, after reviewing the evidence again, this person became satisfied as to Fama's guilt. In such situations, the difficulties of reaching a clear "guilty" or "not guilty" verdict can become entwined with the challenge of separating a high-profile crime from a social cause. Indeed, once a verdict was reached, the juror believed it was an important one because of the symbolic meaning it conveyed:

[JUROR]: By the time we did reach a unanimous verdict, I thought there's a message in this verdict so this will be what will be important.

LC: What did you feel the message was?

REPLY: Unfortunately I think the message was lost on everybody. To me, the message was that society does not tolerate mob behavior. If you think you can hold someone down while someone else rapes him or her, while someone robs them, society will not tolerate that. We were twelve people from different walks of life, who all know in their communities, in their homes and in their families what society and people expect. This is behavior that we won't accept. For me it meant for everybody: it didn't mean just black people don't have to be afraid. They had made a documentary about Yusef Hawkins, it just happened right during the Crown Heights thing. Al Sharpton wasn't there that night because he was in Crown Heights. His wife was there, Yusef's mother, father, and Lenore Fulana. She stood up and praised Al Sharpton. She said he put that boy I jail. I raised my hand and said, "Excuse me. No he didn't. I did, along with my eleven fellow jurors. We spent nine weeks of our lives, and we're the ones who made that hard decision. Al Sharpton had nothing to do with this." They were talking that day about how that day they had gone and painted a mural for Gavin Cato, the little boy who had been hit by a car in Crown Heights. I said, you should be ashamed of yourselves. You're going to put up a picture of that boy who was hit by a car next to Yusef Hawkins and you can't even mention Yankel Rosenbaum's name. That's whose face you should put, because he was killed for the exact same reason: an angry mob thinking as one, without thought, that was going to kill the first Jewish person they saw, who had nothing to do with that little boy getting hit by a car. They didn't make the connection. I went home and cried like a baby. I went through so much and obviously, no one learned anything from it. There was no message in that.

LC: Do you think many people on the jury felt that message was important to convey?

REPLY: Not in the deliberation. When we reached the verdict, though, we talked about what it would mean: it sent a message to society that everybody's life is valuable, a black life is as valuable as a white life, and we won't tolerate mob behavior of any kind.

LC: At that point did you use that kind of language?

REPLY: Yes.[70]

At least one juror in the trials of the "Central Park" defendants also experienced difficulties reaching an unambiguous "either/or" decision. This juror had not been fully convinced of one of the defendants' guilt, and worried that fellow jurors might have been swayed more by the horror of the crime than by "the facts" presented at trial:

[JUROR]: But you have to understand they were just so horrified. . . .

LC: The other jurors?

REPLY: Yes. Or at least some of them were. You know, it was an appalling recitation that they heard of the events, of what had happened. . . .

LC: But are there two separate issues there? One is that an appalling, horrendous crime occurred. And then there's a second question . . . .

REPLY: Did they do it. (Laugh) Well, of course . . . .[71]

But the juror also sensed there was little room for ambiguity: "Well, I mean, the option allowing for ambiguity, under criminal law, as I understand it, is to vote not guilty if you have doubts. Which I did in this case.[72]

While these examples reveal divergent attitudes among jurors, note that the verdicts eventually handed down by both juries favored the prosecution: all three defendants in "Central Park," as well as the accused shooter Joseph Fama in "Bensonhurst," were convicted. One reason for these outcomes has been mentioned before: in both cases, the state possessed the advantage that dreadful acts of violence had been committed against innocent parties whose gender or race had apparently affected how and why they came to be assaulted. In each case, then, public outrage over the crimes and their broader implications provided the state with ready-made dominant narratives, easily transposable from public debates into legal narratives tailored for the courtroom.

But this advantage at trial could be gained by the prosecution in each case only by competently connecting case and cause, thereby tapping collective public emotions the provoking assault had stirred. (Indeed, jurors I interviewed for the "Central Park" and "Bensonhurst" cases sounded, in general, positively disposed toward prosecutors.) Once that connection was made, the state had a good chance of winning regardless of whether jurors' attitudes reflected a traditionalist or modernist orientation. This does not mean that jurors render verdicts without in-depth consideration of evidence: on the contrary, each juror I interviewed impressed me with the degree to which his or her duties were approached with gravity and sincerity. Yet neither the evidence jurors received, nor the quality of lawyerly presentation they encountered, necessarily brought them to a clear-cut verdict. Instead, as just illustrated, gray areas emerged. Given such areas, it was easy for interpretations to continue developing in the same direction to which pre-trial influences—including, of course, the media—had already inclined them. Thus, with good prosecutorial work, the state in both "Central Park" and "Bensonhurst" were able in the end to reap pretrial advantages.

In moving toward this chapter's own summation, though, just as clear is that the defense sometimes manages to offset the state's *a priori* advantages in provoking assaults. This occurred in the "King" and "Denny" cases, despite videotaped recordings that armed the prosecution with unusually strong evidence; even in the "Bensonhurst" case, the prosecution's victory was muted when Keith Mondello, represented by Stephen Murphy, was convicted of lesser charges but acquitted of manslaughter. Of course, sometimes evidence does turn out to be definitive for the defense or the prosecution: perhaps DNA identification shows beyond doubt that an accused person is innocent (as happened many years after the first trial of the "Central Park" case defendants described earlier in this chapter), or evidence from documents and/or witnesses proves too overwhelming to refute. But as "Rodney King" indicated, and "O.J. Simpson" further confirmed (at least for those who were convinced of the credibility of the state's evidence in that case), even apparently foolproof evidence can frequently be (re)interpreted in multiple ways.

Granted that such cloudy areas exist, then, one strategy the defense often uses to offset the state's advantage entails the construction of a countercause as its own dominant narrative. This can be done in at least two ways, each requiring the convergence of other factors. First, as illustrated by attorney Michael Stone's characterization of the police and Rodney King as victim and victimizer, respectively, a defensive countercause seeks to reverse the identities of the parties. Yet this countercause was only "workable" because the first "Rodney King" trial took place in conservative Simi Valley. In Los Angeles County, or in much more progressive-leaning New York City, such a strategy would have almost surely backfired.

Second, a defensive countercause may rely on making implicit or explicit references to history and politics. In the 1990s, as I have argued, some of these cultural references were to other recent high-profile crime cases that had been tried near in time and that had become symbolic of the same social problem—for example, racism as expressed through a series of police brutality incidents. Thus Edi Faal in the "Reginald Denny" case, and Johnnie Cochran in the "O.J. Simpson" case, developed countercauses that put the state itself on the defensive. Neither lawyer's strategy centered on blaming a victim, but on the contention that counteroffenses had been committed by the "powers that be." Faal argued that without the Simi Valley acquittal of police officers in the first "Rodney King" case, which came to symbolize an ongoing history of racialized police brutality, the "Reginald Denny" assault would never have occurred. Two years later, Cochran made indirect use of these same Simi Valley verdicts in "Rodney King" to increase the plausibility of the claim that the Los Angeles Police Department planted evidence against O.J. Simpson. Again, the success of these legal strategies was context-dependent: had Faal and Cochran been forced to try their cases in Simi Valley, their arguments were far less likely to have been effective.

Another strategy is equally, if not more, potent for the defense: the possibility of altering the social context of the trial by obtaining a change of venue (and, by extension, changing the pool of potential jurors). Here, the defense argues that negative publicity is so great in the locale where a provoking assault occurred that it must be tried elsewhere for a fair trial to ensue. If a defense attorney is clever and/or fortunate, and even slightly sociologically oriented, s/he will try to locate the new trial in a county where residents are likely to be favorably disposed toward the defendant. Yet clear from the cases I studied was that judges' opinions are even more decisive in procuring venue changes. Consequently, the most germane issue may be whether a judge's views and that of the defense are in sync. Obviously the prosecution was unable to prevent "Rodney King" from being moved from Los Angeles and, far worse, to a conservative county that bestowed an *a priori* advantage upon the defense. Similarly, after the "Lozano" police brutality case was first tried in Miami, Roy Black managed to obtain a change of venue to Tallahassee, Florida, where jurors' attitudes tended to be much more sympathetic to the police: thereafter, on appeal, the defense won. In New York City years later, a change of venue was procured by the defense in the "Diallo" case, which also involved police brutality. The case was moved to Albany County where attitudes toward police were more sympathetic: again, the defense prevailed. Had "Diallo" been tried in New York City, though, this side would have had a more difficult time winning a case; without a change of venue, the prosecution might have reaped advantages tending to accrue from pretrial publicity.

According to attorney Roy Black, quoted earlier on this point, it is jury selection that is most important in determining a trial's outcome. Clearly, venue changes affect jury selection by altering the pool of potential jurors. But sometimes, as in the "William Kennedy Smith" case, it may turn out that the place where the alleged crime occurred seems best suited to the defense. When defending Kennedy Smith, Black, with the help of a leading expert on jury selection, concluded from polling research that Palm Beach was, ironically, the area in Florida most likely to contain jurors sympathetic to the defense. On that basis, he did not push for a venue change. But Black was extremely concerned about which jurors he selected. He and the jury consultant he had hired were seeking like-minded jurors sympathetic to the defense's case. Yet I was struck when interviewing jurors in the "William Kennedy Smith" case that some expressed surprise—according to one it was "coincidental"—that they got along so well. Indeed, after the trial had ended, the jurors met several times socially because, as another also put it, "we got along so well, even though we were so diverse." The process of jury selection had resulted in a group of jurors, though, who may not have been as diverse as they seemed. This helped the defense offset the prosecution's initial public relations advantage.

We have seen that judges, lawyers, and jurors experience the effects of enmeshment in different ways and with varying levels of awareness. These levels of awareness range from purposeful and explicit (e.g., lawyerly strategies like juror selection in the "William Kennedy Smith" case) to unconscious and implicit (e.g., some juror reactions to such strategies as in the "Kennedy

Smith" case just described). But regardless of the myriad repercussions for particular participants of legal cases' enmeshment with social causes, provoking assaults point to a larger and more genuinely thought-provoking challenge. Returning full circle to Paul Gewirtz's assertion, these cases suggest that indeed the "boundary between the courtroom and ordinary life" is difficult to credibly maintain once crimes have been subjected to mass-mediated magnification and subsequent public scrutiny. Put differently, provoking assaults demonstrate that the conventional notion of legal objectivity—kindred to the idea of objectivity conventionally used in the social sciences—itself deserves scrutiny in the light of mass-mediated cases that clearly reveal the interpenetration of law and society.

This chapter has explored legal dilemmas posed by provoking assault cases, while pointing beyond these dilemmas per se. For even if judges are concerned about the influence of juror exposure to media coverage in provoking assaults, still jurors obviously have preexisting conceptions of crimes (influenced no doubt again, though in other ways, by popular culture and media images) in more ordinary cases as well. Even if lawyers draw on previously developed public reactions to build strategies in provoking assaults, still they tap popular ideas when building arguments in ordinary cases too. Ambivalence about a case and the struggle to reach a clear-cut verdict also characterize jurors' decisionmaking in mundane legal cases. Thus while provoking assaults evoke special precautions, they also highlight the social character of crime cases in general.

CHAPTER 5

More on the Press: Journalistic Divides

Journalists depend on others, whether spokespersons of the criminal justice system or activists in communities, to generate news about "provoking assaults." Without the media's own participation, however, these highly profiled cases would likely not exist; reporters and editors actively deem some crimes, not others, to be worthy of special attention. I have already explored this relatively autonomous role of the media, concentrating on journalistic philosophy and stated criteria of story selection. But while chapters 2 and 3 focused on the "Central Park" and "Bensonhurst" cases, I now want to consider why journalists thought the "William Kennedy Smith," "Mike Tyson," "Rodney King," "Reginald Denny," and "O.J. Simpson" cases merited extraordinary attention.

For the most part, journalists involved with these cases expressed a worldview similar to the one aired by reporters and editors involved with "Central Park" and "Bensonhurst." Nevertheless, just as lawyers differed in their attitudes toward provoking assaults (see chapter 4), the journalists I interviewed also diverged among themselves. Not surprisingly, reporters who worked for established mainstream newspapers frequently saw their role differently than did journalists employed by alternative papers. However, even within the same mainstream venues, journalists' views were often stratified in a way reminiscent of philosophical differences among lawyers. Most reporters who covered provoking assaults described themselves in relatively "traditional" terms; some expressed a relatively more "modern" orientation; others fell somewhere in-between.

Traditionally oriented journalists tended to voice three interrelated attitudes toward their craft. First, regarding news philosophy, many journalists recalled legal traditionalists in holding that "objectivity" was both possible and desirable. They believed news stories ought to be presented "fairly" and with the utmost consideration for telling the "truth" about events. This value placed on objectivity usually coexisted with a belief in the journalist's own neutrality, thereby sidestepping complex issues about how or if "truth" even exists. If anything, many journalists seemed committed to an apolitical self-image; reporters were supposed to be observers of events, not active shapers of them.

Second, regarding news presentation, most traditionally oriented reporters tended to believe that good journalism meant airing "two sides" to every story. Insofar as journalists felt they should not express their own opinions, this practice was part-and-parcel of a wider dedication to objectivity and neutrality.

Third, regarding story selection, traditionally oriented journalists covering 1990s cases continued the pattern previously found in the 1989 "Central Park" and "Bensonhurst" cases: again, reporters felt the "Kennedy Smith," "Tyson," "King," "Denny" and "Simpson" cases had been selected for extraordinary coverage largely on the basis of their uniqueness. Stories that became highly profiled were perceived as interesting or important in themselves, rather than as interconnected with historical or sociopolitical events, including (as we shall see later in this chapter) those deemed "journalistic precedents" by the media itself. Once more, attitudes toward story selection went hand-in-hand with the ruling commitment to objectivity.

But not all journalists I interviewed subscribed to this traditional orientation. Some could best be deemed modernistic in believing it neither possible nor desirable that reporters shy away from social engagement. Frequently such dissenting reporters who covered the "Smith," "Tyson," "King," "Denny," and "Simpson" cases worked at alternative newspapers; sometimes, though, they worked for such mainstream papers as the New York Times and the Los Angeles Times, where they disagreed with colleagues about the role of the media. Exemplifying an alternative position in the broader world of American journalistic thought, disagreements in the 1980s and 1990s surfaced between traditional journalists and those who advocated a "public journalism"; the latter called for the press to play an active role in interpreting events. According to journalism professor Jay Rosen, who worked with reporters from alternative newspapers to promote public journalism, implicit in this notion was a rethinking of objectivity, this "official doctrine" dating back to the 1920s and 1930s that permitted "journalists to speak of 'informing the public' without worrying about how a public got formed in the first place."[1]

It is interesting that most critics of mainstream practices were well aware that objectivity—which aims at separating "fact" and "opinion," and presumes that reporters can and ought be politically detached—has not always characterized American journalism. Rosen and others were familiar with the work of well-known media critic Michael Schudson showing that U.S. newspapers were originally owned and operated by political organizations; only later in the twentieth century did they become concerned about attracting readers who had no partisan affiliation. Therefore the idea of journalistic objectivity developed alongside mainstream newspapers' efforts to maximize their profits by enlarging their audiences.[2]

But notwithstanding these differences, the traditional journalistic outlook predominated among those who covered both the earlier "Central Park" and "Bensonhurst" cases and the later "Smith," "Tyson," "King," "Denny," and "Simpson" cases for mainstream newspapers. Moreover, corresponding to each of the traditionalist attitudes earlier described—news philosophy, news presentation, and story selection—were noticeable discrepancies between reporters' self-assessments of their ideas and practices, and what they actually seemed to be doing. Perhaps, then, as was concluded in chapter 4 in the context of the law and the legal process, studying provoking assaults of the 1980s and 1990s reveals the limitations and contradictions in this other powerful social institution—the media.

While many journalists faithfully adhered to dominant journalistic principles, two developments between "Central Park" and "Simpson" called into question objectivity's own accuracy. First, news coverage became increasingly diversified. By the time of the "Simpson" case, there was hardly a newspaper publisher or editor who did not sense a vulnerability to larger socioeconomic and cultural trends; competition within and among variegated media had grown, and lines between "news" and "entertainment" were becoming blurred. crossing more and more spectacularly. Second, at the same time journalists' ability to believe in their own independence—and in their power to select stories on manifestly "objective" grounds—may have been shaken. Here, "Simpson," the so-called trial of the century, played a cumulative role in raising questions about how social differences among journalists, especially racialized ones, may have affected perceptions of O.J. Simpson's guilt or innocence. In sparking controversy over whether "subjective" opinions affected news coverage itself, the "Simpson" case made it difficult to ignore the kaleidoscopic character of journalists' own socially constructed interpretations.

This chapter also recounts gaps I noticed between journalists' statements about, and their actual practices of, story presentation and story selection. Allegedly, a "two sides to every story" approach was fair to all parties concerned. Yet as happened with "Central Park" and "Bensonhurst," partialization again characterized the media's coverage of a number of 1990s cases. Whether or not intended by reporters and editors, a partialized one side "versus" another framework of debate seems again to have exerted a divisive effect on how later cases were perceived. Finally, while many reporters insisted they selected these 1990s cases because of their individuality, in practice, cases selected for high-profile coverage evidenced case-after-case themes and patterns rarely discussed or discerned by journalists themselves. From this springs further evidence that journalistic relativism offers a superior description of how cases are actually selected than the currently still-dominant claims of individualism.

To document the thesis that provoking assaults of both the 1980s and 1990s revealed limitations in the dominant journalistic worldview, I next expand on the contradictions noticed in each of the three areas—news philosophy, news presentation, and story selection—but, this time, in reverse order. The status of journalistic "objectivity" underlies much of what follows, and I conclude with an assessment of its viability.

INDIVIDUALISM IN THEORY, RELATIVISM IN PRACTICE

Why did reporters accord extraordinary high-profile coverage to certain 1990s crime cases? According to Christine Stapleton, journalists labeled the "William Kennedy Smith" case a major story immediately after a woman pressed rape charges against Smith in July 1991. Stapleton, the lead reporter on the case for the *Palm Beach Post*, recalled:

cs: Well, I knew Sunday afternoon, that it would be the biggest story that we'd ever covered, probably the biggest rape case of the decade at least.

LC: Why were the media interested? What were the factors?

CS: Well, the obvious ones. I just think it was the Kennedy name and that it was in Palm Beach. I don't think if it had been a Kennedy and it had been in Gary, Indiana, it would have the same . . . .

LC: Why?

CS: Because Palm Beach has this reputation as a place of decadence, like film noir. Palm Beach is known as a very decadent place sexually, the drinking and the drugs and everything else. I think Palm Beach had a great deal to do with it.[3]

One of her colleagues at the *Palm Beach Post* agreed that the "Kennedy name was the main thing. Another acquaintance rape case was scheduled to start, but the defendant's name was not Kennedy so it got much less coverage."[4] Nor did this interpretation appear limited to print journalists. Local television reporter Robin Kish likewise commented:

There was a lot of mystique surrounding the story right away. First, in terms of interest, you have a family as akin to royalty as you can get in the United States. Second, a woman is accusing a royal and you don't know who the accuser was. Another part of the Kennedy mystique was historical charisma and their interplay with women. There were people who were always interested in the Kennedys, going back to Chappaquidick. So you have history repeating itself not verbatim, but in a way the public can relate to as a soap opera. The media ate it up and, once the lawyers got involved at least on the defense side, the story started to feed upon itself.[5]

In 1991, only months after the "Kennedy Smith" story catapulted into local and national notoriety, another highly publicized "date rape" surfaced: a young woman accused heavyweight champion Mike Tyson of raping her in a hotel room in Indianapolis, Indiana. Even though the "William Kennedy Smith" and the "Mike Tyson" stories diverged in an often-noted racial sense, reporters thought celebrity explained both crimes' appeals. But just as Stapleton cited other factors also, so Joe Gelarden, the lead reporter for the *Indianapolis Star* on the "Tyson" case, described a confluence of elements including race: "Glamor, celebrities, money, and a racial element. . . . The fact that the case is about a big black man, a black celebrity. . . . Another element here was that Desiree (Washington) is a suburban kid, not a street kid. She's a product of the middle class, she had a scholarship to college, was member of an exchange program to the Soviet Union. Some amount of class identification with her made the case interesting to people also."[6]

Another reporter who covered the case for the *Star*, Barb Berggoetz, put it only slightly differently: "[W]e couldn't be outdone by national and international coverage. This is our hometown. Also, Tyson was a big person in the black community and outside. There was sports, sex, celebrity."[7] Local television reporter Neal Moore also pointed to the role of celebrity in explaining the Tyson case's appeal. According to Moore, who covered the story for Channel 8 in Indianapolis:

> The fact that Tyson was a worldwide celebrity and brought journalists from around the world made it the biggest case Indianapolis had ever seen. Members of the general public were there throughout the trial. There was vocal support for Tyson as a fallen celebrity black hero.[8]

The Kennedy name, Tyson's renown as a boxer—these were the common reasons given for the high-profile treatment given those cases. But compare them with the statements of journalists about why they thought the "O.J. Simpson" case mushroomed to unprecedented notoriety only two years later. For Leo Wilensky, the metropolitan editor at the *Los Angeles Times*, the decision to accord the "Simpson" case extraordinary coverage in June 1994 was easy once police charged the former football star with the murders of Nicole Brown Simpson and Ronald Goldman:

> **LW:** A case like this is interesting because it's O.J. Simpson, but I have to say a couple of things from our standpoint. We viewed this case a little bit differently than some other papers do: it was a local story. It was a grisly double murder, to begin with. It involved a person who is one of the most well-known, recognizable figures in the country, if not the world. It has other aspects to it like the whole spousal abuse issue. For us, it holds the potential of being able to really use our powers to educate the public as to how the system works and how it doesn't work under pressure.
>
> **LC:** So you feel the murder . . . .
>
> **LW:** Yes, you don't find incidents of double homicide. In fact, we went back and couldn't find an instance that we know of in which a celebrity was involved in even a single homicide other than Fatty Arbuckle.[9]

Jim Newton, one of the two lead reporters Wilensky assigned to the case, had this to say:

> [T]he crime was very personal, very brutal, but the obvious reason was that he's famous, arguably the most famous person ever tried for murder. It happened in Brentwood, the fact that she was beautiful, it's a "life style" story. . . . But the most fundamental reason was that he was famous and likable. . . . It's not a story that the fate of the city turns on, but it's a hell of a read, it's a tale, a tragedy of epic proportions. . . . The "O.J. Simpson" case was not really a question. I don't think we have to apologize for writing about something if it's not boring. Our concern is wanting to be fair, sober, not to handle mistakes. . . . But there was never a moment at the paper when anyone doubted the story on the front page.[10]

To Michael Janofsky, a general assignment reporter sent to do early coverage for *New York Times*, fundamental to the story was Simpson's personality. This was the reason, Janofsky opined, interest in the case extended far beyond Los Angeles:

> O.J. Simpson is a guy who crosses lots of lines, so much so he becomes a kind of "everyman," successful in generally regarded white venues like advertising, television, acting. It's not that they're necessarily white domains but as a public person, he's so charming and comfortable to be with for many people that he has developed lots of constituencies. . . . I also think Americans are fascinated by "heroes," with rich people, with upper-class life styles and with success. And yet there's something about O.J. . . . I think because of his humble background, he also resonated with people who saw him as a good guy who succeeded. The other thing is he's so visible—first as a football player, salesman, and then star.[11]

Evidently, then, journalists covering or editing all three stories—"William Kennedy Smith," "Mike Tyson," and "O.J. Simpson"—attributed media interest largely to the status of individuals whose names the cases came to bear. Rather than reflecting on what broader symbolic social meaning the cases might have or on how they connect with an historical chain of similar stories, journalists felt the crimes received attention because they were interesting in themselves. In each case, this interest was a blend of the appeal of celebrity with circumstances unique to that particular story, such as location (Palm Beach) in the "William Kennedy Smith" case.

Thus, these views could be said to evince "American journalistic individualism," which, as we have seen, incorporates journalists' commonly held belief that cases are chosen for high-profile coverage because interesting *sui generis*. The emphasis is placed on what is unique and special, not typical and general, about particular instances. Indeed, journalists also cited unique circumstances when asked "why Central Park?" and "why Bensonhurst?" One reporter said the jogger's rape attracted unusual coverage because it was committed in a "landmark" New York City location; another cited the disreputable but "fascinating" character of Gina Feliciano as an element of the Brooklyn case's appeal. Of course, in the "Kennedy Smith," "Mike Tyson," and "O.J. Simpson" instances, the celebrity of the defendants accounted to a large extent for journalists' perceptions of their uniqueness. As sociologist Joshua Gamson has observed:

> [C]elebrity is a primary contemporary means to power, privilege and mobility. Audiences recognize this when they seek brushes with it and when they fantasize about the freedom of fame and its riches and about the distinction of popularity and attention. They recognize it when they assert their own power to tear down the star. They recognize it when they seek to watch and be a part of the media spectacle. They recognize it when they speak admiringly of the celebrity's capacity to achieve, maintain, and manage a public image: if fame is power, the capacity to achieve it is an even greater one.[12]

But since "Central Park" and "Bensonhurst" were not "celebrity cases," the American journalistic individualism reflected in those cases signal a more deeply ingrained perspective than can be explained by the powerful appeal of fame alone.

Of course, it is not unreasonable for reporters to assert that a famous name and notorious locale added interest to "Kennedy Smith" and "Central Park," nor that the varied class backgrounds of Desiree Washington and Gina Feliciano heightened interest in "Mike Tyson" and "Bensonhurst." This claim seems even more persuasive in the "Rodney King" case: how could an element of existential uniqueness not have figured in media decisions to give it intensive coverage? If George Holliday had not happened to be present with a camera to videotape King's beating by a group of Los Angeles police officers in March 1991, the "Rodney King" case would not have become a well-known cultural reference. Consequently, "why Rodney King?" struck many journalists as something of a rhetorical question.

But the problem with individualism is that it does not explain enough. Remember that the "Bensonhurst" case provoked media interest in 1989 both for case-specific reasons and due to the timing of this crime's occurrence in relation to other incidents that included "Howard Beach," "Tawana Brawley," and "Central Park" as cultural markers. Nor were these earlier cases publicized simply for their uniqueness; like "Bensonhurst," each signaled concerns about race relations in New York City that transcended the unique factors of a given case.

Analogously, editors and reporters did not appear to highlight the "Kennedy Smith," "Tyson," "King," "Denny," and "Simpson" incidents solely on the basis of uniqueness. As with "Central Park" and "Bensonhurst," the sequence of these extraordinarily publicized crimes suggests that journalists also make decisions about the coverage to be accorded a story on the basis of how it relates to earlier cases. To show this, let us look back at the "Simpson" case. Clearly editors and reporters believed this crime to have been unique; journalists were largely responsible for dubbing the case "the trial of the century." In retrospect, though, it makes little sense to say that the "Simpson" case received extraordinary publicity for case-specific reasons alone. For the coverage given to the 1994 double murder continued, as well as varied, themes that had been debated through the vehicles offered by three prior strands of provoking assaults: namely, cases relating to gender, race, and class discrimination in the United States.

Regarding the first pre-"Simpson" strand, gender-related cases, the murder of Nicole Brown Simpson continued the debate over the problem of violence against women through crimes alleged against well-known men. Simpson was arrested in 1994 and charged with having murdered his ex-wife in a fit of jealousy and rage; the issue of domestic violence was immediately emphasized as news stories recalled battering charges Nicole Brown Simpson had lodged against her husband in 1989. But "Simpson" was not the first crime case of the 1990s to ignite discussions of gendered violence. In 1991, the "William Kennedy Smith" and "Mike Tyson" cases also brought "date rape" into mass-mediated public awareness. Moreover, between the time rape charges were filed against Tyson in July 1991 and Kennedy Smith was acquitted in December that same year, another feminist issue received high-profile attention. At a televised Senate hearing held in October 1991, Anita

Hill accused Supreme Court nominee Clarence Thomas of sexual harassment. Although no trial ever took place, the event was accorded nearly as much publicity as the "Kennedy Smith" and "Tyson" cases.

Interviews produced no evidence that connections among these cases were contrived by members of the media. Instead connections seem to have resulted from ordinary, quite unconscious media practices. As noted in part 2, where I drew on the work of media scholars Herbert Gans, Mark Fishman, and Gaye Tuchman, journalists are attracted to new stories that both repeat and vary the themes of older ones. And, in fact, both continuities and variations wove their way from "Kennedy Smith" to "Tyson" to "Thomas" to "Simpson." While both "Kennedy Smith" and "Tyson" were rape cases, identities of accused and accusers varied from the first of these extraordinarily high-profile cases to the next. In March 1991, a well-known white man was charged with assaulting a white woman; in July 1991, a well-known black man was charged with assaulting a black woman. Then again, from "Tyson" to "Simpson," the accused party was a black man. But this time both the alleged crimes and the identities of victims varied: Simpson was arrested for allegedly murdering a white woman and a white man (though Ronald Goldman's murder received relatively less attention).

Clearly, then, both continuities and variations ran through these 1990s stories. Moreover, by the time the "Simpson" case broke, a pattern had formed of symbolizing feminist issues through these media-selected, high-profile crimes alleged against well-known black men. Although the U.S. Senate eventually confirmed Clarence Thomas as a Supreme Court justice in October 1991, Thomas was by then the most well-known symbol of sexual harassment in U.S. history. While William Kennedy Smith and Mike Tyson were both tried for rape, only Mike Tyson was convicted. For this reason, and because his February 1992 conviction came after Thomas's confirmation, "Tyson" followed "Thomas" to become an analogously well-known symbol of rape; each man became symbolic of crimes linked with specifically feminist concerns. One can visualize this evolving pattern simply as follows:

FEMINIST ISSUE	SYMBOLIC REPRESENTATIVE
Sexual Harassment	"Clarence Thomas"
Rape	"Mike Tyson"
Domestic Violence	"O.J. Simpson"

Note that this "Thomas–Tyson–Simpson" sequence of 1990s high-profile crime cases satisfied the media propensity for both "routine" and "novel" stories, for both continuity and variety, that Tuchman and others observed when studying the traditional practices of mainstream newspapers in the 1960s and 1970s.[13]

A second pre-"Simpson" strand involved race-related cases: here, "Simpson" also continued a pattern of debating racism, and "reverse" racism, through high-profile crime cases of the 1990s. On March 3, 1991, George Holliday videotaped Rodney King's beating and presented the tape to the media. Approximately two weeks later, on March 16, Korean grocery store owner Soon Ja Du wrongly killed an African American teenager named Latasha Harlins; after a jury conviction, a Compton judge sentenced Ja Du only to community service. According to *Los Angeles Times* reporter Andrea Ford, the "Rodney King" case was therefore perceived in relation to a longer time line of incidents involving persons of color—especially, but not exclusively, African American men—being treated unfairly by the Los Angeles criminal justice system. In Ford's opinion, a more modernistic than traditional one, anger that erupted in rioting after the April 1992 acquittal of police officers in Simi Valley expressed frustrations that had long been accumulating through prior incidents from "Latasha Harlins" to "Rodney King."[14]

Moreover, amid confrontations set off by the Simi Valley verdict, the beating of white truck driver Reginald Denny by a group of African American youths in April 1992 resulted in debates about "reverse" racism. The trial of this high-profile crime case, obviously linked to the outcome in "Rodney King" in time and substance, produced a controversial verdict in April 1993: the accused youth were acquitted by a jury willing to place their actions in the extenuating context of the Los Angeles riots. In the sensitized context of mid-1990s Los Angeles social and political unrest, Simpson's color was likely to tap journalistic associations with previous "race" cases even if these connections were not consciously made. At a minimum, journalists were alerted to whether and how race might influence events—which is precisely what happened once tapes revealing former police officer Mark Fuhrman's racial prejudice cast doubt on the behavior of the Los Angeles Police Department in the "Simpson" case also. Thus viewing "Simpson" relatively—namely, in light of other race-related cases, from "Latasha Harlins" to "Rodney King" to "Reginald Denny"—only strengthens the argument that media interest in "the trial of the century" resulted from a combination of case-specific and broad contextual factors.

Third, a strand of celebrity cases pre-dated "Simpson," which only continued the pattern of interest in crimes alleged against men who were either born wealthy and well known, or would become so. I have already mentioned the journalistic "common sense" that "Kennedy Smith," "Tyson," and "Thomas" attracted interest due to each man's fame, respectively, as a Kennedy family member, a boxer, and a Supreme Court nominee. But predating the "Simpson" case was also the trial of the Menendez brothers, intensively publicized nationwide in late 1993 and early 1994. At issue was what had motivated two brothers from Beverly Hills to shoot and kill their parents. The defense claimed the murders resulted from years of sexual abuse by their parents. However, since the brothers stood to become millionaires on their parents' death, the prosecution countered that the crime had been spurred by greed. The common thread linking the "Kennedy Smith," "Tyson," "Thomas," Menendez brothers" and "Simpson" incidents, then, was interest in why people apparently enviable on the basis of fame or wealth may nevertheless commit acts of violence or coercion.

More than merely "celebrity," then, this last strand of cases also suggests that class plays a role in cultural interest accorded these cases. For some people, the cases allowed resentment to be vented at those whose wealth seemingly coexisted with unscrupulousness, with hidden anomalies in their characters. For others the cases occasioned protests against mistreatment, including racism and child abuse, from which even wealth did not necessarily provide protection. Whichever interpretation is adopted, the cases provoked debate about whether justice could be attained more easily, or perhaps not at all, when the rich are accused of serious crimes. In sum, the preexisting strands of interest to which "Simpson" was heir permitted strong, public feeling.about distinctions of gender, race, and celebrity/class to be aired.

Stemming from this analysis is the conclusion that journalistic interest in a case's uniqueness is too superficial an explanation for why the "trial of the century" was treated as such. Could it have been merely coincidental that the "Simpson" case continued and varied the three preexisting strands of thematically interconnected highly profiled crimes? More persuasive is that unique factors combined with the case's place in relation to a line of prior incidents resulted in its being more interesting to journalists than other crime cases that might, alternatively, have been accorded extraordinary publicity. But why, then, was it unusual rather than common for editors and reporters to mention this relationship between "Simpson" and prior themes?

One possibility has already been suggested—namely, that for journalists to include prior high-profile crimes among "surrounding historical events" would highlight an unavoidably selective dimension of journalistic activity itself. Journalistic relativism provides a philosophical alternative to individualism—namely, that crime cases are accorded high-profile coverage not only for what is unique about them, but also for where and when they occur. A relativistic explanation suggests that at some points in time, a given crime case may or may not be noticed and accorded extraordinary publicity; relativism admits, rather than overlooks, journalists' semi-autonomous power to affect history through their own decisionmaking.

Indeed, high-profile crimes that become provoking assaults may place journalists in a self-contradictory position. On the one hand, conventional wisdom—and the faculty of many journalism schools—still maintain that editors and reporters should remain "objective," value neutral. On the other hand, journalistic choices in these cases seem in actuality to be made relative not only to history in general but media history in particular: "in fact" processes of selection are affected, and in no small measure, by journalistic precedents. By journalistic precedents, I mean that once prior cases have been given extraordinary media attention, they in turn influence which future stories are selected for attention. Older stories exert social pressures by their past predominance; in so doing, they take on virtually a life of their own. However, journalistic precedents most often go unacknowledged because they reveal members of the media to be active rather than detached social actors.

This is both different yet similar to attitudes toward precedents held by parties working within the legal system. Unlike journalists, many judges and lawyers do perceive their roles as active ones: they are engaged in creating an ongoing body of legal theory within which precedents greatly matter. On the other hand, like journalists, many judges and lawyers believe just as strongly in an ideal of legal "objectivity." Thus, in this context at least, distinguishing legal actors from journalists may be mainly that the former see themselves as active, not passive, pursuers of "truth." For our purposes, then, whereas lawyers and judges consciously and explicitly draw on precedents to support their arguments or decisions in the courtroom, for journalists, the influence of precedents tends to be unconscious and implicit.

Indeed, this influence is meaningful: once particular cases have been accorded high-profile coverage, a media investment has been made; and given such investments, it is not likely that future related cases, or new stages in the same case, will be ignored. For instance, once enormous attention was devoted to the state trial of the Rodney King case in Simi Valley, the 1993 federal trial of "Rodney King" in downtown Los Angeles was almost guaranteed ongoing coverage. Analogously, once journalists intensively covered the criminal trial of the Simpson case in 1995–96, the civil trial that ensued in 1997 was virtually ensured coverage as well. Journalistic precedents continued to mark crime coverage in the late 1990s, too, when, as this book's chapter 1 noted, a trio of police misconduct cases called the criminal justice policies of New York City Mayor Rudolph Giuliani into question. Once allegedly sadistic police brutality by then-officer Justin Volpe against a Haitian immigrant named "Abner Louima" received coverage beginning in August 1997, a journalistic precedent had been set. Thereafter, it was far more likely that the "Diallo" case, involving an unarmed Guinean man killed by police officers shooting forty-one bullets, would also receive high-profile coverage when the shooting occurred in February 1999. In turn, once the "Louima" and "Diallo" cases became well-known precedents, a third story about the killing of African American "Patrick Dorismond" in March 2000 was likely to attract attention too; this case involved an African American man who was shot to death, allegedly by accident, by a police officer in Manhattan's Port Authority bus terminal. Rather than eliciting coverage only because newsworthy in and of itself, as individualism would claim, the "Dorismond" case was also notable because it followed soon after journalistic precedents as real in their consequences as those found in law.

Other evidence also bolsters the case for journalistic precedents, whether or not consciously acknowledged. In researching this book, I used the "All-News" category of Nexus/Lexus not only to learn which cases during 1985–97 received most coverage, but when case references ebbed or flowed from the time of an alleged crime's occurrence through the present. For example, I checked how often key words like "Tyson" and "rape" appeared not just in 1991 and 1992, when the alleged incident and its trial occurred, but in every other year from that point onward.

In the "Tyson" case, not surprisingly, I found enormous coverage when the story first surfaced; high-profile attention continued through Tyson's conviction at the end of his February 1992 trial. Predictably, too, references to the case sharply declined afterward through 1993, but then increased in late 1994. Why the rise? When I looked at the contents of particular stories, it appeared that references to "Tyson" were sometimes recalled in the later, thematically interrelated context of "Simpson." I found similar cross-references to other instances that thereby became interrelated in other pairs of 1990s cases as well—most notably between "William Kennedy Smith" and "Tyson," "Rodney King" and "Reginald Denny," and "Diallo" and "Dorismond" (the latter involving an African American man shot to death, allegedly by accident, by a police officer in Manhattan's Port Authority bus terminal). Even if editors and reporters did not explicitly say they were linking new cases to journalistic precedents of the recent past, their practices manifested the making of cultural associations nevertheless.

In analyzing media coverage, I also noticed that cases from the late 1980s (including the "Central Park jogger" case) sometimes became entwined with early 1990s cases. For instance, references to "Central Park" reappeared amid a controversy during the "William Kennedy Smith" case over whether victims' names should be used in media coverage of rape cases. On August 18, 1991, Deirdre Carmody referred to both "Central Park" and "William Kennedy Smith" in her New York Times coverage of this issue: "When the identity of the victim or complainant is known by many people, as it has been in Palm Beach and as it was by many people in the Central Park jogger case last year, some editors argue that the name should be published." [15] And, on April 26, William Glaberson described in the same paper a "debate on journalistic values" about "Kennedy Smith" that led a Times editor to wonder "whether the broad press coverage of the Central Park jogger rape case and the use of the victim's name by some relatively small publications meant that she no longer had privacy." [16]

This "debate over journalistic values" became an issue when, although established newspapers usually omit rape victims' names, the New York Times and other papers broke with this convention after NBC News revealed the identity of Smith's accuser. In response, this time the media did turn a self-reflexive eye on journalists' own practices and effects, treating the "leak" of the alleged rape victim's name, and the intramedia debate that resulted, as a story. Yet, as noted above, reporters did not connect the question of why they became interested in the "Kennedy Smith" case with earlier precedents of covering rape cases they themselves had helped to set.

Last, that journalistic decisions about coverage of a story are made on relativistic, rather than solely individualistic grounds, is evidenced by looking at who was assigned to cover particular stories. As occurred with coverage of the "Central Park" and "Bensonhurst" cases, editors at major newspapers sometimes assigned the same reporters from one high-profile story to cover a later one. For instance, before writing about the "William Kennedy Smith" case, New York Times reporter William Glaberson had earlier reported on both "Central Park" and "Bensonhurst." In another instance, at the Los Angeles Times, editor Leo Wilensky employed Jim Newton as one of the lead reporters on the "O.J. Simpson" case; Newton had previously covered both "Rodney King" and "Reginald Denny." New York Times reporter Seth Mydans also worked to some extent on "Simpson" after he, too, wrote a large number of stories about "King" and "Denny." Prior to becoming the lead reporter covering the trial of the "Simpson" case for the Times, reporter David Margolick had done a significant amount of coverage of the "William Kennedy Smith" trial. Not only, then, did covering high-profile crimes seem to have become a media specialization, but cases like "King" and "Denny" were taken to provide reporters with useful pre-"Simpson" experience, suggesting that earlier cases were treated, even if not explicitly or consciously, as relevant precedents.

At least when surveyed from afar, the movement of crime cases from "Central Park" in the late 1980s to "Simpson" in the mid-1990s shows that the reasons given by journalists for selecting high-profile crimes, and the patterns evinced by actual selections, were not identical. Of course, this does not mean that all journalists see story selection predominantly in terms of the story's uniqueness When interviewed about the "Rodney King" case, recall that reporter Andrea Ford insisted that outrage at the 1992 Simi Valley verdict acquitting police officers in that case was inseparable from frustration over previously racialized high-profile crime cases like "Latasha Harlins." Obviously Ford did think of media-highlighted events in terms of their relations with one another rather than in solely individualistic terms; in the mainstream context of the Los Angeles Times, which had assigned Ford along with Jim Newton to cover the "Simpson" case, her understanding at the time may have been more unusual than standard. Yet Ford's position makes clear that, like lawyers, journalists disagree among themselves even in "mainstream" contexts about the validity of the traditional tenets of individualism and objectivity, even as these largely continue to be upheld.

But what about news presentation—did discrepancies between theory and practice surface here, too, particularly among journalists working in mainstream contexts? On this point, perhaps it was not a gap between journalists' theory and practice that emerged so much as one between journalists' intentions and their effects.

INTENDING TO BE FAIR; PARTIALIZING IN EFFECT

In the eyes of many reporters who worked for well-established newspapers, objectivity entailed presenting "two sides to a story." For instance, when asked if he believed in journalistic objectivity, *New York Times* reporter Michael Janofsky responded in a way that joined fairness and two-sidedness under the umbrella of good journalism:

MJ: Absolutely . . . we succeed far more than anyone else in maintaining objectivity and the highest journalistic standards. No other paper reads like ours, it's solid.

LC: What accounts for this?

MJ: It's the *New York Times*.

LC: And how would you define objectivity?

MJ: Fairness to all parties, innocent until proven guilty. . . . There's also no place for my opinion. I was told when I went there, don't worry about your style, worry about your tone. And the tone is even-handed. If there's two sides to a story, we have to try to tell the two sides.[17]

On the other hand, for a critic of traditional journalistic philosophy like Jay Rosen, two-sidedness enables reporters to depict themselves as objective parties standing on allegedly neutral ground between antagonized positions. In actuality, journalists may be seeking cover, or "refuge," for their own inadmissible engagement. As Rosen suggests:

[B]y writing their stories from the midpoint between opposing sides, [journalists] conjure up a world in which opposing sides dominate the scene. Many public controversies can be described this way; but if refuge is what the describers are seeking, as much as truth, there is more refuge available if the arena is habitually seen as a world of polar opposites, with two sides battling to win, both distorting the truth to gain advantage, while the journalist enjoys the advantage of a middle position.[18]

To some extent, as argued in chapter 4, it may be the "partialized" structure of the legal system that bequeaths to the media a two-sided framework within which to report on crime cases. But, as also contended earlier, the press has its own reasons for using this framework. According to traditional journalistic philosophy, presenting "two sides to every story" is fair. Which is it, then: does the standard practice of framing stories as conflicts between polar opposites result in fairness or unfairness?

Two ways of answering this question come to mind. One entails looking closely at a particular case to see whether two-sided framing definitely occurred and if, as in "Central Park" and "Bensonhurst," this framing was divisive in its consequences. The second involves probing whether divisive consequences ensued as an effect of one side "versus" another coverage cumulatively as high-profile crime cases moved, thematically and sequentially, from the late 1980s into the mid-1990s. I explore each of these possibilities by turning to the "Tyson" case that, along with the "Kennedy Smith" case, began the pre-Simpson strand of 1990s gender-related cases just discussed. Was the "Tyson" case covered by mainstream newspapers in a partializing manner? In other words, did news stories tend to position one party against the other in such a polarizing fashion that neither side seemed capable of acknowledging any valid points in the other side's perspective, with the result that no viable "third position" or alternate perspective seemed possible?

Several newspapers framed the "Tyson" story as an adversarial dualism by using sports analogies in their coverage. For instance, on January 28, 1992, *New York Times* reporter E. R. Shipp wrote of the forthcoming trial that "the most important fight of Tyson's life had begun"; a few days earlier, on January 22, the headline of a *Times* article by Phil Berger declared the "Tyson" trial "A Drama That Will Rival the Ring When Tyson Faces His Accuser." Included in Berger's piece were references to the lawyers on each side, Gregory Garrison for the prosecution and Vincent Fuller for the defense, in language that likewise alluded to boxing: "According to Athel Micka, a reporter for WISH-TV in Indianapolis, Garrison's is a style not unlike Tyson's in the ring"; moreover, Berger added, "While Tyson may be the most prominent fighter of his time, for Garrison, the adversary is Fuller."[19] If the elite *New York Times* was making analogies to the world of boxing that only further framed the case as a polarized dualism, other newspapers were just as—or more—likely to do so. And in fact, not surprisingly, the win/lose paradigm was even more starkly presented in the *Daily News*. In that paper, on January 26, the headline read "The Main Event: Rape Trial Tyson's Biggest Fight Yet."[20]

Moreover, within media coverage of the "Tyson" case, partialization—which, as we have seen, entails constructing two-sided frameworks that set parameters for ensuing public debate—emerged through the use of opposite characterizations of accused and accuser. Some of these contrasts were reminiscent of early coverage of the "Central Park jogger" case in that Manichean-like oppositions reappeared: before, on one side was the "goodness" of the jogger and, on the other, the "vicious" wolves that had attacked her. Notwithstanding the fact that the attack on the jogger was brutal, such reportage only tends to create prejudicial assumptions even before defendants enter the courtroom. In the "Tyson" case, Berger counterposed accused and accuser in the *New York Times* as follows:

> Against the hulking Tyson, a one-time juvenile delinquent, will come the petite plaintiff who, by all accounts, is a model teen-ager. She is a college freshman from Coventry, Rhode Island who, as one of the lawyers in the case put it, "looks like 12 years old—not like 18. She's very articulate, very small. She's nice. She's sweet. She's naïve."[21]

In the *Daily News*, near a boxed outline of "The Life and Times of Iron Mike" that included reports of Tyson's crashing a car and allegedly having battered ex-wife Robin Givens, the alleged victim was described as "diminutive and pretty, brainy and chatty, her town's true love. She was a cheerleader and class president, Sunday school teacher and Kmart cashier, outstanding high school sophomore and student representative to Moscow. She didn't have a serious boyfriend. She wanted to be President."[22]

Mainstream coverage of "Tyson" also frequently made comparisons with the "William Kennedy Smith" case. Press coverage of the two alleged crimes commenced near in time: reports of the "Kennedy Smith" case hit the news on April 3, 1991 and the "Tyson" case on July 28, 1991. The trials of the two cases were even closer together: the Kennedy Smith trial ran from Decem-

Fig. 7. Comparisons drawn between the "William Kennedy Smith" and "Mike Tyson" cases illustrate the journalistic propensity to draw stark contrasts.

ber 2 to December 11, 1991, and the Tyson trial from January 27 to February 10, 1992. Consequently it is not surprising that on September 20, 1991 the *Daily News* ran a story with the headline "Tyson and Smith: Same, Different" that included a sidebar entitled "Comparing Cases." (See figure 7.) In the course of this comparison, the young woman who accused Tyson of rape was described as an "18-year-old honor student and beauty queen from a small town in New England. She is a college freshman on a scholarship and has long been heralded as a kind of local celebrity in her town for her many outstanding achievements." In contrast, the description of the woman who accused Kennedy Smith of rape was brief and nowhere near as glowing; she was described simply as a "31-year-old single parent who lives in a posh residential neighborhood in Jupiter, Fla." Comparisons between Tyson and Kennedy likewise nourished contrasting impressions: Tyson was "[b]orn and raised in Brownsville, Brooklyn. He has been described as a 'serial but-tocks fondler' and a 'ticking time bomb' "; on the other hand, Kennedy Smith was "[b]orn into one of America's most powerful and privileged families." True to the "same but different" theme, though, is that for both men the *News* also reported that other women had come forward with accusations of past sexual assaults.[23]

As in the "Central Park jogger" case, too, each side in "Tyson" became as-sociated with a symbolic cause. On the prosecution's side, again, the cause was gender: the state in "Tyson" drew on feminist arguments about violence against women when insisting that a woman has the right to say "No" to un-wanted advances at any time. On the defense's side, again, the cause was rac-ism. Fears of discrimination were sparked both by the contrasts within media coverage just described and by rumors that the Klu Klux Klan had long main-tained its headquarters in Indiana. On January 28, the *Daily News* reported that eight black leaders had gathered in the courtroom's lobby to show support for Tyson, worried that "as things are now, an American of African-American an-cestry shall once again be Marion County's victim of injustice." Among the activists present was Al Sharpton, familiar from the "Central Park" and "Ben-sonhurst" cases, who "equated Tyson's trial to a legal lynching and said he will march tomorrow in Indianapolis in Tyson's support."[24]

Further reminiscent of the "Central Park" case was that, once these public reactions turned into organized concerns about the case's symbolic mean-ings, journalists covered this development in turn—tending to juxtapose the two symbolic sides against one another. Once more, in the "Tyson" case, gender issues were depicted as opposed to issues of race in public debates and media presentations; no allowance seems to have been made for the pos-sibility of any "third" or alternative perspective. The antagonized perspec-tives in "Tyson" were aired both in and out of the courtroom. At the trial, Berger wrote, activists on the two sides were present, one representing the symbolic cause of race and the other (in the form of the Guardian Angels) the cause of gender:

> Most of the crowd that was gathered inside the building seemed to be in Tyson's corner; as soon as he walked in, cheers went up and a few people whistled. But on Market Street outside the courthouse, a group of red-bereted Guardian Angeles marched in protest against Tyson and his pro-moter, Don King. . . . As Tyson made his way up the cordoned-off stairway

to Judge Patricia J. Gifford's second-floor courtroom, where his trial on rape charges was beginning, another woman offered her support, crying out "They got you guilty, but this ain't no Mississippi."[25]

At a greater distance, a *Daily News* story quoted young boxers in New York City who were sympathetic to the side of the defense. Declaring themselves "for" Tyson amounted to their being "against" his accuser; it seemed incumbent on people to "take a side":

> "I think that girl got over-reactive," Sanders said. . . . "We got guys feeling up girls every day," said Mauhana Ali Childers, a twenty-year-old welterweight. "But they don't say nothing. She probably turned him on, he came onto her and she probably sort of whispered, "Stop. She saw a gimmick. . . . Come on. Somebody set him up."[26]

It is noteworthy that throughout this ongoing interweaving of public reactions and media coverage,[27] a defining feature of provoking assaults manifested itself: both sides claimed victimization. In an October 21, 1991 *New York Times* article, Berger posed such characteristically somersaulting victim/victimizer claims in just-as-typically "either/or" terms: "Has he [Tyson] been a sexual aggressor with a compulsion for taking advantage of women, as some have charged? Or has Tyson been, as he and his supporters assert, a victim rather than the victimizer, a celebrity whose wealth and fame have made him a target for women seeking money, notoriety or both?"[28]

But what if, as in the "Central Park" case, aspects of both gender and racial discrimination were relevant to the "Tyson" case albeit in different ways? Clearly, "Tyson" was symbolic of gender-based discrimination; it called attention to the problem of rape and to victim blaming that still too often ensues if women assert their right to have, or not to have, sex. In addition, charges of racial bias seemed to have some legitimacy. Media coverage may have indeed put Tyson at an unfair disadvantage by creating pretrial caricatures of his "brutishness" compared to his accuser's apparent "wholesomeness." (Similarly, media coverage may have put Kennedy Smith at an unfair advantage by creating pretrial impressions of his prestigious family background.) In other words, the case may have symbolically highlighted multiple social problems requiring redress if both women and men across different races and classes are to be treated fairly by the media, by the criminal justice system, and in civil society generally. These problems persist alongside, but are not identical to, the critically important legal issue of guilt or innocence.

The major flaw of the partialized framework used by the media in its reporting is that, as a mode of public debate, it is too rigid, discouraging more sociologically complex alternative positions from flourishing. And precisely because this partialized framework places more nuanced perspectives at a disadvantage, it may in effect result in unfairness to one or both parties, which is ironic given that journalists often think they are ensuring fairness by presenting "two sides to every story." No doubt journalists may defend their approach by pointing to the two-pronged structure of the legal system, where defendants are found to be either innocent or guilty. Indeed, an "either/or" structure *is* bequeathed by crime cases such that "win/lose" cultural analogies with sports appear, in one sense, justifiable. But, at another level, the public may not be well served by a convention of traditional journalistic philosophy that limits the parameters within which issues provoked by highly profiled cases are debated. Thereafter does the world tend to be envisioned in too cardboard a fashion, making it more likely that "either/or" social antagonisms will be recycled rather than questioned as problematic formulations in and of themselves?

This case of my own—namely, that partialized media presentations are not harmless in their effects, however well intentioned—is strengthened by cultural associations with "Tyson" in later cases, after the "Tyson" case had died down. As argued above, among the most highly profiled stories in the country in the next years were other cases involving well-known black men that grew, through media coverage and public reactions, to be symbolic of "second wave" feminist issues. Again, after Kennedy Smith was acquitted in 1991, "Tyson" arguably became the most highly profiled symbol of successfully prosecuted rape until that date. In 1992, "Clarence Thomas" became what at the time was the most notoriously well-known case of sexual harassment in U.S. history. In 1994, the "O.J. Simpson" case came to symbolize— and at a seemingly unprecedented degree of highly profiled visibility— domestic violence and its insidiousness.

As already analyzed, this sequence of highly profiled, symbolic gender-related cases (re)incarnated the media's fondness for variety within continuity. At the same time, though, it silhouetted stark social antagonisms by situating social movement issues (and their iconic symbols) on opposite sides. The case-after-case progression of high-profile crimes pitted concerns about sexism historically associated with the feminist movement against concerns about racism. In so doing, tensions within the second wave feminist movement, frequently perceived by women of color as a "white movement" inadequately sensitive to the significance of racial differences, were simultaneously aggravated. This is because, as I have argued elsewhere,[29] the resulting pattern in effect played gender against race both within and between high-profile crimes of the provoking assault variety. To visualize this I return to the "Tyson–Thomas–Simpson" schema presented above, relabeled to highlight this point:

Playing Gender against Race: A Media-Assisted Pattern in Effect

FEMINIST ISSUE	SYMBOLIC REPRESENTATIVE
Sexual Harassment	"Clarence Thomas"
Rape	"Mike Tyson"
Domestic Violence	"O.J. Simpson"

As chapter 6 documents, social movement and other public reactions to "Tyson" and "Simpson" often did develop in opposition to one another. Aligned on one side of each case were many parties sympathetic to feminist concerns; on the other were groups formed by those concerned that racism would lead to differential criminal justice prosecution of successful black men. By the time of the "Simpson" case, this pattern of juxtaposing issues of gender and race had already been long in formation; in the 1980s and 1990s, it stretched, arguably, from "Central Park" through the "Tyson–Thomas–Simpson" succession of highly profiled incidents. In this respect too, then, "the trial of the century" was not unique.

Perhaps, then, intense reactions to the "Simpson" case resulted both from its unusual character as a double homicide and from its placement in relation to recent journalistic precedents. For, no doubt, reactions to "Simpson" were intense. This can be confirmed simply by asking: Do you recall where you were when the verdict in the Simpson criminal trial was announced? Rarely does anyone answer "no," and ensuing discussions reveal that many felt constrained at that moment to make a choice, to "take a side." Was one "for" Simpson's acquittal, hoping the cause of racial justice would be served by a verdict that symbolically rebuked the Los Angeles Police Department's methods and tactics? Or was one "for" Simpson's conviction, thereby hoping that the cause of gendered justice would be served by a verdict that symbolically

Fig. 8. As these images from *Newsweek* magazine suggest, media coverage of the "Simpson" verdict contrasted reactions by race among college students and used headlines that emphasized opposing interpretations of "whites versus blacks."

rebuked a known batterer and possibly a murderer as well? What did one answer, how did one feel, if the wish were that symbolic recognition be accorded the social problems of gender as well as racial biases?

I vividly recall my own whereabouts and feelings when learning of the "Simpson" verdict. It was an hour before I was scheduled to teach a course on "Gender, Race and Class" to over a hundred Barnard and Columbia students; immediately I wondered how to deal with the multifaceted issues and perspectives the jury's decision no doubt would raise. Clearest in my memory, though, is that administrators' and students' reactions were, or rapidly became, polarized. College administrators of various races who usually chatted together were suddenly talking in small white-only or minority-only groupings. Some students of color who had gathered as part of a larger crowd awaiting the verdict on television in the Student Center cheered when they heard "Not guilty." Other, mostly white, feminist students began to cry. When we discussed the verdict in class, several white feminist students walked out after several black students expressed satisfaction with the verdict; other students of color, male and female, groaned when they heard feminist students, again mostly white, airing their disgust. (See figure 8.) If other reactions than these polarized "pro" and "anti" ones were possible, they were unlikely given the partialized parameters into which the "Simpson" case—like other highly profiled crime cases before it—had been forced to fit both by the media and the conventions of the legal system.

As stated at the beginning of this chapter, not all journalists concurred in their attitudes toward story selection or news presentation. Some differences among editors and reporters corresponded to whether they worked at mainstream or alternative papers, though there was a variety of feelings on the parts of those working in these venues as well. But for journalists at both mainstream and alternative newspapers, still another result may have emerged from the cumulative progression that extended from "Central Park" and "Bensonhurst" through the three strands of pre-"Simpson" cases (gender, race, and celebrity-related high-profile crimes) explored above. By the time of the public's impassioned "either/or" responses to the "Simpson" verdict, it may have become difficult for journalists not to self-reflect, at least to some degree, on their own reactions. Cracks may have become visible in the armor of the dominant philosophy: it may have become harder than ever for journalists to take refuge in the powerful tenet of objectivity.

I hope to show this last discrepancy—between allegiance to objectivity and experiences that cast doubts on its ongoing credibility—by describing two kinds of increased self-awareness that provoking assaults spurred in journalists by the time of the "Simpson" verdict. The first development arguably produced greater difficulties in ignoring racial differences in journalists' own perceptions; the second involved growing vulnerability to socioeconomic competition, that is, how journalists' place in a global capitalistic world also made objectivity harder (if not impossible) to defend.

ALLEGING OBJECTIVITY, EXPERIENCING RACIALIZED DIFFERENCES AND ECONOMIC PRESSURES

Soon after the "Simpson" case first surfaced in mid-1994, I asked several journalists whether the case would have received as much initial coverage if Simpson had been white. According to Leo Wilensky, the metropolitan editor of the *Los Angeles Times*, the answer was "Yes":

LC: Let's just say the story had been Kevin Costner, that a white celebrity had been a suspect. Do you think it would have been as much of a story, or do you think there was additional interest because O.J. Simpson was a black man, and because interracial marriage was involved?

LW: Well instead of saying Kevin Costner, I'd say Arnold Schwarzenegger. . . . Because of the name recognition, yes, I think there would have been just as much coverage. I didn't know for a few days that Nicole was white. I really don't believe there would be [a] difference. I think that in fact O.J. Simpson, while black, is not thought of as a black superstar. I think he was a sort of cross-over hero: whites, blacks, everyone loved him.[30]

According to Dennis Schatzman, though, a reporter who provided most of the "Rodney King" and "O.J Simpson" coverage for the largest African American owned and operated paper in Los Angeles—the *Los Angeles Sentinel*—the answer to the same question was a resounding "No":

> It would have been a big case but would it have been as big without the racial factor? No. We must be honest with ourselves. Anyone who lives in Southern California would be lying if they did not think that race would not be a factor in this particular case. You have a black defendant and white victims; most importantly one of the white victims is a female. I think we all know how race with respect to black males/white females is a hot button issue within most of America, black, white and otherwise. So to say that a high-profile case such as this, involving all those elements has no racial factors involved is just wrong.[31]

Part of the difference in their perspectives can be attributed to Wilensky's being white and working for a mainstream paper, while Schatzman was a black reporter at an alternative venue specifically oriented toward emphasizing overlooked distinctions of race. But another explanation—related, but not reducible, to racial differences—is that, overall, the two journalists had divergent understandings of journalism. Remember, as we saw earlier (see text of this chapter accompanying note 9), Wilensky thought "Simpson" was selected for high-profile coverage predominantly on the basis of its uniqueness; he was less likely to see racial factors, or the series of high-profile, race-related crimes that preceded "Simpson," as relevant to initial interest in the case. On the other hand, Schatzman did not see the "Simpson" case in the context of gender- or celebrated-related cases, but rather as part of a series of other recent incidents he believed to manifest racial biases toward black men in the criminal justice system. Soon after Simpson's arrest in 1994, following the now-famous car chase down a Los Angeles freeway, Schatzman claimed to be the only reporter who objected to the use of handcuffs by the Los Angeles Police Department (LAPD). In voicing this objection, he immediately linked "Simpson" with other cases where, in his opinion, black men had also been presumed guilty prior to their trials:

> Why was he handcuffed? O.J. Simpson gave no reason to believe he would be a threat at that point. I contend that's the way they treat black men here and other people of color: if they're not handcuffed, they may be beaten or even killed. That's consistent with the way the LAPD has often treated high-profile African American men. Case 1, Joe Morgan, who played baseball for the Cincinnati Reds and the Houston Astros, was arrested and beaten at the LAX airport because officers said he "looked" like a drug dealer. Number 2, Jamal Wilkes, formerly Keith Wilkes, born and raised here, played basketball at UCLA and for the LA Lakers, was stopped in his car in South Central, dragged from his car, beaten by the police and then later released.[32]

Such philosophical differences, inflected by racial ones, also extended to views held by other journalists concerning objectivity. For instance, though Ed Boyer worked at the *Los Angeles Times*, he did not express traditionalist leanings in this respect. When asked "Do you still hold to the notion of objectivity in the media?" Boyer, who had covered the "Reginald Denny" case for the *Times*, responded:

> I never have. I mean, somebody has to make a decision about what goes in here. And what page it goes on. That's subjective. . . . You can pick up any number of journalism texts, you can talk to any number of news people, you can talk to professors, and they'll all give you a notion, you'll get all kinds of abstract notions of what news is, or what the news story is. But I think the best concept of news and a news story is that a news story is whatever an editor decides to put in his paper that day. That's pretty much what it boils down to.[33]

Another young reporter who covered the "Reginald Denny" case for a Los Angeles paper felt that the ideal of journalistic objectivity had been contaminated by cases that brought social issues of racial injustice, and parallel injustices in media coverage, to newfound awareness. Just as many reporters at mainstream papers linked individualism and objectivity, so relativism and the impossibility of objectivity became interrelated in this young reporter's experience. She recalled the process of making this connection, as well as her move from working as a stringer for the *Los Angeles Times* to reporting for the *Sentinel*:

"Rodney King" was a consciousness raising event for my generation. It was the first real example of just how intense the situation has been for African Americans, and how little ground has been covered truly. . . . The verdict was so unexpected and so blatantly unfair, at least from my perspective, that I was one step away from wanting to explode. There was no objectivity to be had. Many people felt that way, including black journalists, though I commend them for trying to cover the trials as fairly as they could nevertheless. . . .

LC: You could have stayed at the *LA Times*, but did the Rodney King case affect your going to work for an African American publication?

REPLY: It did actually. By the time of the "Reginald Denny" verdicts, people were tired. We'd had a number of trials back to back, we'd had a lot of emotions out there. There was a feeling the defendants were not going to go scot-free, that's for sure. . . . I went back and forth, being bombarded with videotape of the beating of Reginald Denny.[34]

She described two schools of thought in the "Reginald Denny" case: older NAACP members, many of whom had very little sympathy for the defendants; and members of her generation in their twenties and thirties, whose sympathy with the defendants was so strong as to possibly blind them to their culpability. Notice Brown's references to "Rodney King" as well as "Reginald Denny" as she explained the younger group's feelings in decidedly relativistic, rather than more traditionally individualistic, terms:

LC: What were the sources of the younger generation's sympathy?

REPLY: . . . It seems like they put a number of statistics together to look at the bigger picture, the racial disparities. Looks are deceiving but the way it balances out African Americans, especially males, come out at the lower end of the totem pole. The defendants in "Rodney King" and "Reginald Denny" end up representing two racial groups, obviously. It's almost impossible not to put those two cases together and come up with "here we go again," another double standard.[35]

It is important to emphasize that not all reporters of color debunked objectivity and perceived cases in relativistic terms; not all white reporters clung to the older ideal of journalistic objectivity. Although influential, racial differences were not simply determinative of journalists' diverging views. For some reporters could not readily be categorized as strictly traditionalist or modernistic in their approach. Among African American reporters, Ed Boyar viewed objectivity cynically but agreed with Leo Wilensky, more than with Dennis Schatzman (the latter also African American), that a double murder committed by a white celebrity would have been as highly publicized as the "Simpson" case. Said Boyar on this question, "Had it been a guy like Arnold Schwarzenegger, it would have been just as big, there'd be a frenzy: yes, I really believe that."[36] Nor did all white reporters at mainstream newspapers, as a group, necessarily embrace objectivity. According to one New York Times reporter, journalists were split about journalistic objectivity regardless of race; he recounted how some reporters held to a more "poetic," others to a more "scientific," view of the media's role.

But even if not determinative, different experiences in a racialized society clearly affected many journalists' attitudes toward the still powerful media credo. One reason for this stems from the fact that most reporters and an even higher percent of editors at major mainstream papers like the New York Times and the Los Angeles Times are white. As sociologist Darnell Hunt noted, the racial demographic of employees at U.S. newspapers was still dramatically discrepant in 1995 as the "Simpson" case was being covered. In that year, approximately half of American newspapers employed no journalists of color, and blacks comprised less than five percent of the press at daily newspapers.[37] Mainstream journalists' claims to being objective and sociopolitically neutral therefore tended to strike Latino and African American reporters, even more than whites, as belied by the sociology of the workplace itself: allegedly balanced and evenhanded diverse social backgrounds were not represented in newsrooms supposedly committed to norms of neutrality. This gap between the ideals and actual practices within the institution of print journalism was particularly noticeable to reporters who were themselves directly affected by racial imbalances. This point, too, was underscored by Boyar:

LC: Has the newsroom gotten more diverse at a place like the *LA Times?*

EB: At the time of the "Simpson" case, the reporting staff had changed slightly. But the editing staff on the Metro Desk included no African Americans.

LC: It hadn't changed much is what you're saying?

EB: No, I mean, the whole country's press core descended on Los Angeles for the riot. So friends of mine from all over the country were here. And they'd walk into the newsroom and say [about the lack of racial diversity], "I don't believe this." [38]call

Not only did overt racial disparities call attention to who was doing most of the reporting in cases, it also pointed up how journalists' evaluations of media coverage also tended to vary in patterned ways with differences in racialized experiences. For example, the young Los Angeles reporter quoted above thought that objectivity was "not to be had" for black reporters covering the "Reginald Denny" case. But she also implied that white reporters could not be fair unless self-critical about racial politics in and outside mainstream newsrooms.[39] Dennis Schatzman was even more vocal about race-related biases. According to Schatzman, the "white media" tended to presume guilt when it came to violent crimes committed by black men; pre-"Simpson" patterns continued to affect which evidence was highlighted, or omitted, in media accounts that eventually influenced public perceptions of guilt or innocence. When interviewed after the "Simpson" criminal trial had ended and the civil trial had begun, Schatzman contended:

DS: The civil trial is just a rehashing so there's more influencing the jury through the media. The media was and has been by and large entirely anti-O.J. Simpson. When you look at it, you see this trial signifying nothing other than retribution. For the retributive mind you have the right venue which is one not sympathetic to O.J. Simpson. . . . So what happened is that the media ignored certain evidence and wrote only about things that tended to support the guilt of O.J. Simpson. They did absolutely no objective journalism.

LC: Do you think this was a widespread feeling among young blacks?

DS: Oh absolutely. There's a whole history to this . . . we saw it going back to the riots. We've seen this acquittal in Simi Valley. . . . It goes back to the old bugaboos again. Black people are used to this; we knew the fix was in with the media and the criminal justice system right from the beginning.[40]

Implicit in both reporters' comments, then, was the view that media coverage of cases stretching from "King" and "Denny" through "Simpson" had been biased rather than objective, especially with regard to how questions of defendants' guilt or innocence were portrayed. In this respect, interest in the "Simpson" case may have manifested an accumulation of ongoing social dissatisfactions that simultaneously exposed sharp divisions among reporters that were often if not determinatively affected by race. For the kinds of racial distinctions described above were not only taking place among blacks; among white journalists who worked at established newspapers, the "Simpson" verdict prompted a degree of self-reflection. For instance, in a special section in the *Los Angeles Times* written after the "O.J. Simpson" verdict, journalist David Shaw called attention to charges that journalists of different races had covered the Simpson case differently. This suggests that a mirror had been turned inward, to some extent across race, in the aftermath of "Simpson."[41]

Not only did racial differences among journalists, as cumulatively manifested through the "Simpson" case, call implicit attention to objectivity's discrepancies. In addition, journalists were feeling increasingly uneasy about their ability to make "independent" decisions as increasing competition among news media was building. Shaw cited findings from a *Los Angeles Times* poll that more people learned about crimes from television than newspapers. When asked where they found their "best information" about the Simpson case, 45 percent of Los Angeles County residents cited national television; 38 percent responded daily newspapers; and another 35 percent specified local television. These results confirmed worrisome trends of which editors, like Leo Wilensky, were already aware:

LW: There has been an evolutionary perspective sparked by the onset of television news and aggressive television news. Television is driven by the image, but we can't make the picture move; we aren't that compelling. We have to become more enterprising, more thoughtful because newspapers have lost readers. The only things we can bring to it is more depth.

LC: Does becoming more thoughtful, does that call objectivity into question?

LW: Well, you have to be very careful with that. Every story, let's face it, has a subjective dimension but we have to maintain our standards of fairness. We also know with Los Angeles as a focus of so much tabloid journalism, and as a media center, that this story ["Simpson"] would have its tabloid features and probably be one of the biggest tabloid stories because of the people involved. So after the first day or so, we knew shows like *Current Affair, Hard Copy*, were going to go wild and the networks would probably respond.

LC: In that case, were you forced to cover the case whether you wanted to or not, since everyone else was going to cover it?

LW: Well, we thought of it as an important story to begin with. I think we'd be remiss if we didn't cover it for a whole variety of reasons I've touched on. But I think there are papers, certainly the *New York Times* . . . if you look at their coverage, they seemed to not want to deal with this, and they didn't deal with it. I'm not even sure if they had a first day story or not, they dealt with it in little tiny stories. It took them a while before they got into it at all, and they'd probably tell you that's because it's just a sensational story, not their kind of story. I'm a big fan of the *New York Times* but in stories like this, they tend to hold back. But now they're into it too. They realized the potential and the importance of the story after the chase that Friday.[42]

On the one hand, then, newspapers had an advantage over television in being able to provide more detailed and "thoughtful" coverage; only print reporters were granted the time and space to develop stories in depth. On the other hand, no longer was it obvious that media consumers preferred an in-depth orientation to viscerally immediate TV news watching. Moreover, this problem reverberated in such a way as to influence the relationships among newspapers—even between mainstream newspapers. According to Wilensky, even the most prestigious of U.S. newspapers, the *New York Times*, was no longer free to cover only the stories its editors deemed genuinely newsworthy. According to one reporter who preferred to remain anonymous, editors at the *New York Times* did not originally think the "Simpson" case significant. However, once other major papers like the *Los Angeles Times* devoted front page attention to the story, the *New York Times* was under pressure to follow suit. According to another reporter, David Margolick, assigned by the *New York Times* to cover Simpson's criminal trial:

DM: You know, the *Times* has trouble striking the right note on stories like this. We floundered some trying to devote the proper amount of space to a story like this, not to get caught in a tidal wave of publicity on the one hand, not to ignore it on the other. You know, once upon a time our inclination might have been to ignore it. But we can't anymore. . . .

LC: Why?

DM: Well, you know, because these kinds of stories are just too important. It means something that if so many people and other good papers are paying attention, by definition, it's really important. And I'm sure for commercial reasons too. I mean, this doesn't enter into my equation but I think that if the *Times* were to ignore this story, readers would complain. They want it. They want it but they want it in a certain way.[43]

Not only editors but other reporters at the *New York Times* also expressed doubts about whether the "Simpson" case was sufficiently newsworthy to merit the publicity it received. As Seth Mydans asked regarding competition between "legitimate" and "tabloid" newspapers, "Would the *Times* have covered the O.J. Simpson story ten years ago? We didn't cover Heidi Fleiss, and the Michael Jackson story was covered only grudgingly." In Mydans's view, covering "Simpson" reflected the *Times's* powerlessness to resist trends toward commercialization affecting the media as a whole. For Mydans did not see much in the way of substance to warrant the saturation by "Simpson," especially compared with the "King" and "Denny" cases:

I believe the O.J. Simpson case has very little to tell us in comparison with Rodney King. It's rather insignificant apart from its prurient interest. Yet you find commentators saying how significant it is. I object to the extent of coverage and even the panic. . . . I believe one day we'll wake up with a headache and say, what were we doing? We didn't cover the "Rodney King" case as thoroughly as we're [the media collectively] doing "O.J. Simpson." There were three times in history we sent in half a dozen outside reporters to L.A.: the L.A. riots, the L.A. earthquake, and the "O.J. Simpson" preliminary murder hearing. I may be underestimating the "Simpson" case insofar as it taps into people in really visceral ways but in comparison with "Rodney King," the latter was (a) a stunning event given the ferocity of the beating, (b) it symbolized racial injustice, an extremely important issue for the country, and (c) it became an event for Los Angeles as a city. . . . In "Rodney King," I felt I was chronicling important issues well beyond the details of the blows. . . . I don't find that symbolic significance in the "Simpson" case. I don't see how the outcome of this case will affect American history and whatever happens to anyone else.[44]

In contrast to other mainstream reporters I interviewed soon after the "Simpson" case emerged, then, Mydans was quite willing both to express his opinions and to make relative comparisons between cases and the amount of coverage they had received. Yet Mydans did not cite another possible theory—namely, that the enormity of attention eventually devoted to "Simpson" may have resulted from causes both inside and outside the media. For perhaps the "trial of the century" generated extraordinary interest due to journalistic precedents set through three strands of prior, interrelated crime cases. Rather, in this respect, he too tended to perceive "Simpson" as anomalous and unique:

> We all grouped around to justify why [we] were all spending so much time on this. We played around with spousal abuse, but it wasn't about spousal abuse anymore than Lindbergh was about kidnapping. The "Simpson" case grew up like a mushroom because we were fascinated with the "Simpson" case, not because of race or surrounding issues. . . . Now the story has died out, the press has totally lost interest. I thought that we would have weeks of coverage afterward as in "Rodney King," but it's shrinking. "Rodney King" became a symbol of something; it's the opposite of "Simpson." People were fascinated with "Simpson" *sui generis* as an individual.[45]

Mydans's remarks imply that mainstream journalists did not always feel they could afford to make decisions based on historical significance apart from commercial considerations. Rather, for Mydans, the individualistic criteria for story selection used in the celebrity-oriented "Simpson" case reflected heightened socioeconomic pressures: faced with intensifying competition within print journalism itself and among other media outlets, journalists sometimes responded by publishing material that "fascinated" and "entertained" the public, whether or not they considered stories newsworthy themselves.

Therefore, just as provoking assaults illustrate dilemmas confronting the legal system, they point as well to challenges facing the media. It should be clear that, albeit in different ways, ideals and practices were often out of sync in both the legal system and the media in the mid-1990s. Yet equally notable is that divisions existed among parties within each of these institutions. In the case of the legal system, not only judges and lawyers but even jurors' views about that system ranged from traditionalist to more modernistic. Analogously, while the attitudes of editors and reporters varied from mainstream to alternative newspapers, the fact that journalists working for the same "elite" newspaper differed in outlook evinces basic philosophic differences among them. Evidently some reporters did not think of a given high-profile crime in terms of its uniqueness (e.g., Dennis Schatzman of the *Los Angeles Sentinel*, Andrea Ford of the *Los Angeles Times*, and Seth Mydans of the *New York Times*). Others doubted that objectivity was a suitable keystone of journalistic philosophy (e.g., Boyar of the *Los Angeles Times*).

Still, on the whole, especially at mainstream papers, the journalists who covered provoking assaults from the "Central Park jogger" to the "Simpson" case were more likely to report ongoing beliefs in the interrelated ideas of individualism and objectivity. Common to these beliefs is a presumption that decisions about coverage can be made without acknowledging the media's own interaction—its power and its powerlessness—with social and historical events. Yet this chapter suggests that, in practice, journalists' actions may well have contradicted their self-perceptions: editors and reporters have made such decisions on both relativistic and individualistic grounds, even while tending to admit only the latter. For too blatant to result simply from coincidence were thematic connections that unfolded near in time between the highly profiled "Central Park" and "Bensonhurst" cases but also, as we have seen here, between "Smith" and "Tyson," "King" and "Denny," and from both sets of cases to "Simpson." More convincing is that editors and reporters made connections actively and, at least in part, on their own as they enacted habitual preferences for the novel as well as the routine, and as they reassigned staff and interrelated the high-profile crime cases that received coverage. As in the law, then, journalists drew on their own brand of precedents.

Ironic, too, is that while a sequence of interrelated high-profile crime cases involving issues of gender, race, and class came to fruition in the "Simpson" case and beyond, this last example was viewed by many journalists as the most individualistically chosen of all, that is, as "the" trial of the century. Furthermore, the very chronology of cases from "Smith" to "Tyson," and from "King," "Denny," and "Menendez" on to "Simpson," placed the status of "objectivity" under examination. One reason is that wide-ranging debates about race, class, and gender biases that wove their way to "Simpson" made it hard to ignore socially "subjective" differences in reporters' own standpoints. Moreover, by the time of the "Simpson" trial in 1994, editors and reporters were describing a world of growing inter- and intramedia competition and blurred boundaries between news and entertainment that raised doubts about whether they were free to do as they pleased. As a consequence, journalists' situation was characterized in some ways by active involvement and in others by a more passive intuition of professional vulnerability.

Perhaps, then, provoking assaults in the 1980s and 1990s illustrate a time-lag between the conventions of older journalistic ideals and the visibility of recent practices. But whether or not ideology catches up, at the time of these cases many reporters still shied away from expressing their own opinions about the stories they were covering. Not so for the next chapter's group of participants. In turning to diverse reactions of everyday newspaper readers and television watchers, as well as of several community and social movement activists, it becomes apparent that provoking assaults were used precisely as a vehicle through which ideas—and openly political ones at that—could be voiced once journalists brought particular crime cases to public notice.

CHAPTER 6

Taking Sides: *Diverse Public Reactions*

Unlike a lawyer who defends or prosecutes a case or an editor who decides to accord a crime high-profile status, most people hear about "provoking assaults" second-hand. They may learn about a particular incident by reading the newspaper, watching late-night television news, or finding it prominently featured on the Internet. But regardless of how people initially learn such high-profile crimes occurred, afterward, what are their effects? In chapter 4, I investigated problems that overlapping cases and causes create for the legal system; in chapter 5, I explored how these instances challenged, in the late 1980s and early 1990s, some of the media's traditional notions and practices. In this chapter, though, my purpose is at once different and related. Here I analyze the ramifications of provoking assaults not for the legal system or the press, but for the "public" at large—an obviously wide-ranging group whose reactions to high-profile crimes range from boredom to fascination to indignation. While the interviews I conducted show that some members of the public are apt to express dissatisfaction with the "either/or" framework within which provoking assaults are debated, it is more common, I found, for people to take this framework for granted, improvising reactions in and around it.

Let me begin by summarizing types of actions myriad audiences express; these can be deemed official, protest, and conversational. Official reactions emanate from diverse parties who feel that, as prominent community members, they ought to comment on controversial crimes. Such a reaction was exemplified in the "Central Park" and "Bensonhurst" cases by then-mayor Ed Koch's public remarks about each incident, and also by the need clearly felt by mayoral candidates David Dinkins and Rudolph Giuliani to offer their "takes" on the events. The category of official reactions includes as well the roles played by diverse local community activists and religious figures, many of whom sought to prevent ethnic and racial antagonisms from escalating.

Though they may sometimes overlap with official reactions, protest reactions are motivated explicitly by parties' advocacy for one side or the other, expressed through rallies, the formation of defense groups, or other critical actions. Even if they are not directly affected by a given incident, people may respond to its symbolic implications. Thus, a number of minority youths protested the shooting of Amadou Diallo in 1997 New York City, just as then-mayor Rudy Giuliani was up for reelection, prompted by their worries that they too could be victimized, any day, by police overreactions. Likewise in Los Angeles, when police officers were acquitted in Simi Valley of assaulting Rodney King, members of the public who themselves felt threatened by police brutality lodged protests. Protest reactions were also apparent in the "Central Park" and "Bensonhurst" cases: the National Organization of Women urged feminists to monitor the first trial in the "Central Park" case to guard against sexist arguments; and during the "Bensonhurst" case, as in previous high-profile crimes like "Howard Beach," Reverend Al Sharpton and other activists led weekly protests against manifestations of racism.

The third category of public reaction, conversational, is the broadest. Most people respond to provoking assaults not because of their official positions or because inspired to attend rallies and public protests, but simply when a given case becomes an ongoing source of discussion in their lives. If a crime has occurred near a person's home, he may feel especially connected to the case, and is likely to be affected by news accounts and to become caught up in conversations—and sometimes in arguments—about the case when talking with family and friends. In chapters 2 and 3, strains of such heated debates enlivened interviews with people who lived near Schomburg Plaza in East Harlem and near Bensonhurst, Brooklyn. Moreover, conversational reactions are subject to change, something that became especially apparent to me while conducting interviews about the later 1990s cases. For example, many initially heated responses to the "O.J. Simpson" case over time became tired and cynical ones. "I'm sick of hearing about it," several people said disgustedly, expressing an antimedia sentiment that ironically conveyed its own engaged passion.

This chapter explores these categories of public reactions to the "William

Kennedy Smith," "Mike Tyson," "Rodney King," and "O.J. Simpson" cases of the early to mid-1990s. I conducted interviews about the "Kennedy Smith" case in 1992 and 1993 in West Palm Beach, Florida, concentrating on areas where the case was likely to be discussed and seeking out community figures overtly involved. Several years later I made two trips to Indianapolis, Indiana, interviewing a range of parties in that city during the period that Mike Tyson's criminal conviction was appealed. In Indianapolis, I spoke with several community figures who held governmental positions, with people involved in protests on both sides, and with varied persons I met at the local courthouse and at bars, restaurants, and malls.

Finally, I conducted a large number of interviews in the Los Angeles area on the "Rodney King," "Reginald Denny," and "O.J. Simpson" cases, talking with a number of well-known community leaders and activists about the "King" and "Denny" cases. Interestingly, I found that some of the same individuals involved with "Rodney King" later became caught up with, and were asked by the media to comment on, "O.J. Simpson" as well. In the "Simpson" case, I conducted three sets of interviews in the Los Angeles area—one soon after the crime happened, the second several months before the criminal verdict was announced, and the third soon after the verdict—with, wherever possible, the same parties.[1] Among those interviewed were ministers, public officials, high school students, activists involved with long-standing and newly formed (because concerned about "O.J.") social movement groups, and people I met at meetings, cafes, and bars around Los Angeles. Since I could capture the immediacy of people's reactions only in the "Tyson" and "O.J. Simpson" cases (and, in the "Tyson" case, only when people were reacting to the also highly profiled appeals process), this account draws disproportionately on these examples.

What emerged from these interviews were strikingly mixed responses to the later cases. The cases both spurred charged political debate and generated apathetic cynicism (and strong antimedia sentiment) in their wake. At one and the same time, debates over these provoking assaults bespoke changes in the way people were discussing social problems and fomented divisiveness in the form of angered attitudes toward social movements and their representatives. Accordingly, this chapter shows the ambivalent effects and consequences of provoking assaults.

I commence by illustrating two ramifications of provoking assaults that seem appealing from the perspective of participating publics. First, the cases provide an everyday conversational vehicle for debating social issues in a way that marries emotion and logic in lively argumentation. Unlike fictionalized popular cultural genres that evidence widespread interest in crime in the United States, these cases actually happened,[2] invoking the "real" authority of law and attracting ongoing news attention. Thereafter, members of the public may hold forth as virtual participant-observer detectives, analysts, amateur lawyers, and news commentators. Moreover, as writers who study narratives have argued, such cases are able to combine emotion and logic because they are single incidents magnified writ large. Obviously they involve stories, and usually contested stories at that; as a result, they engage participants more avidly than would abstract discussions of crime and criminality. In this regard, as Patricia Ewick and Susan Silbey have observed, the law has a deep familiarity for many Americans in many aspects of everyday life:

> The law seems to have a prominent cultural presence as well, occupying a good part of our nation's popular media, providing grist for both news and entertainment. We watch real and fictitious trials on television, often unable to distinguish fact from fiction. We share jokes about lawyers. We hear reports of crimes and criminals on the nightly local news. And, if the success of authors like John Grisham is any indication, millions of us devote hours of our leisure time reading stories about crime, courts, lawyers, and law.
>
> Thus the law is experienced as both strange and familiar; an episodic event and a common feature of our lives; deadly serious and a source of humor and entertainment; irrelevant to our daily lives and centrally implicated in the ways these lives are organized and lived.[3]

Second, such high-profile crime incidents inspire discussions that move easily from the particular to the general, and from the legal to the political. Because provoking assaults are at once legal cases and social causes, they offer a way of "talking politics."[4] This second appeal of provoking assaults makes the cases particularly germane for at least some protest-oriented reactors. Ideas about social movement issues can interweave throughout a given incident, eventually affecting the contents of debates in future high-profile crime cases and possibly in other cultural contexts as well.

I next turn to provoking assaults' more complicated aspects from the perspective of participating publics. Arguably the advantages and disadvantages of these cases are two sides of the same coin. On the one hand, the cases offer a ready conversational vehicle for concretely discussing—and, from protest reactors' perspectives, publicizing—social problems. On the other hand, dissatisfactions generated by the two-sided legal structure and mass-mediated magnification of these cases can stir what I call "social-psychic dynamics" into being by way of reaction. These dynamics share certain features of the familiar defense mechanisms studied by Freud. However, whereas Freudian defense mechanisms arise unconsciously to cope with conflicts rooted in an individual's childhood experiences, the dynamics discussed in this chapter stem from distinctly, though still unconscious, social sources. Yet precisely because they work within individuals in ways analogous to Freudian defenses—as explained below, for example, to displacement and reaction-formation—the operation of these dynamics are best envisioned as at once "social" and "psychic."

Here the specifically "social" factor that stirs social-psychic dynamics into play is as follows. Because provoking assaults are both legal cases and social causes, they provoke discussion of but cannot fully resolve the problems they evoke; once again, a verdict can only officially address/redress the case at hand, and then only for one "side." Afterward, though, how are frustrations energized by social discriminations that also seem implicated in these crimes' broader genesis—for example, anger likely to be felt at impossibly vague entities like "society" and the "media"—to be expressed? Perhaps in defense against this amorphousness, people sometimes channel responsibility onto parties that provoking assaults provide closer to hand—for example, onto victims—inside these crime cases' two-sided, and therefore relatively concrete, structure. But this may make it easier to overlook, and eventually even to forget, such cases' general implications. Consequently, what is in one sense a culturally satisfying advantage of provoking assaults becomes, from this vantage point, dissatisfying as well. Indeed, through extended conversations, I did notice apparently social-psychic dynamics recurring in the energized reactions on the part of some the 1990s cases. These dynamics struck me as defensive in character for reasons explained later in this chapter where I define and illustrate four dynamics in greater detail: substituting, reversing, exceptionalizing and, again, partializing.

Revisiting partialization in this context—not as a structural by-product of the legal system (see chapter 4) or a journalistic convention (see chapter 5) but as a cultural "fact" that affects diverse public reactions—brings up a second disadvantage of provoking assaults. For just as these cases both provide an attractive conversational vehicle and stimulate social-psychic dynamics that can operate defensively, so they both offer a way of "talking politics" and potentially impoverish the complexity—one could say the sophistication—of resulting discourse. On the one hand, shifts in how we view social problems can and do occur through these cases. On the other, if the sources of those problems are multidimensional, the dualistic structure framing such cases diminishes the likelihood that people will able to acknowledge what is valid in each side; more likely, they will remain "partial" to the side they already favor. A specific incarnation of this disadvantage may affect social movements' efficacy insofar as people come to envision several discriminations symbolized by a given crime case in "either/or" terms (as in reactions that only saw "gender" or "race" discrimination in the wake of O.J. Simpson's acquittal at his criminal trial), triggering possible reactions of backlash against valid claims on both sides.

Let me turn, then, to explore these advantages and disadvantages in the "Tyson," "Simpson," and other cases of the provoking assault variety that surfaced in the early to mid-1990s.

PROVOKING ASSAULTS AS VEHICLES FOR POLITICIZED DEBATE

Provoking assaults serve as vehicles for "talking politics" insofar as they convey dominant narratives, by which I mean the justifying stories that begin to emerge out of a high-profile case (and the media's coverage of it) that explain why people are partial either to the prosecution's or the defense's interpretation of events. Similar themes emerge as these narratives circulate; all the while improvisations, too, occur. Such themes-and-variations evolve both within and across cases, elongating debate over time; as this happens, cases are discussed not as an individualized, but as an ongoing and interconnected network of continually evolving narratives.

Many people I interviewed in the Indianapolis and Los Angeles areas reported that "Tyson" and "Simpson" were definitely topics of daily conversation when the appeal in the former case and the trial in the latter were taking place. In Indianapolis, a number of people responded that they had grown "tired" of hearing about "Tyson"; however, once Alan Dershowitz took the case on appeal, people started to discuss the case again. In Los Angeles one young man, a white hospital worker, said very early on in the "Simpson" case,

"Yes . . . it comes up in conversation." When asked how it did so, he responded, "It depends on the context. If I'm with people I don't know, I hear jokes about it. Occasionally I meet patients on my job who, because they're stuck in bed and seeing a lot of TV, are following it. Yeah, I think in response to the press and the newspaper headlines, people are talking about it. . . . I even have relatives in another country who ask about it."[5] Another young man, an African American, explained that "it actually comes up about a few times a week . . . just the progress on what's happening in the case, what's happening lately. You know, . . . after that it always develops into the question of do you think he really did it."[6] One young woman among a diverse group of Los Angeles high school students said that her "family was really upset, going on about [the "O.J." case]. You know, my father said they kept making it seem like he was guilty before there was a trial."[7]

In Santa Monica, on the outskirts of Los Angeles, a group of retirees admitted that while "sick" of the "Simpson" case, they discussed it each morning when they met at a local café. Some in this group said they thought the case served an "entertainment purpose"; others blamed their interest on the media's having "taken ["O.J."] and run with it." According to one man:

It's the topic of conversation in Los Angeles. Absolutely. As well as around the world. Wherever you travel, if you say you're from L.A., that's the first question that's asked, is about the trial. Because the media's taken it and run with it. And we're all sort of prisoners of the media, I guess. And being in Los Angeles, that's just part of living here. . . . I think that if it wasn't on television, I think the trial would have been over by now, and I don't think people would have been that interested in it. . . .

LC: So it's the number one topic. But you said earlier you were tired of it?

REPLY: People say they're tired, but they're still drawn into it. You can't escape it. And I often kid, what will people do when it's over? I think there will be tremendous withdrawal in this city. Just, a lot of people, especially elderly people, people that are home a lot, have devoted their day to watching this trial. This has become a part of their life. And I think it will be interesting to see what will happen when it's over. . . .

LC: Can you envision another case arising that would fill that void maybe?

REPLY: You can never say never. . . . [E]very day, people think that the biggest thing that could ever happen, happened. So it would be impossible to say that there will never be another trial as big. Who the heck knows?

Evident in several group contexts was that arguments often evolved wherein different, and opposing, opinions were expressed. For instance, when talking over lunch in an Indianapolis restaurant approximately seven months after Mike Tyson was found guilty of rape, three young people—a white woman, a black woman, and a white man—disagreed in their respective takes on the case, becoming progressively more and more impassioned. The contentious issue was whether the young woman involved in "Tyson" should have acted differently on the night in question:

BEVERLY: Okay, now, let me ask you this. Why did she wait forty-eight hours to report . . . .

RICK: She was, look it, first of all, she was only eighteen years old, she was probably scared, didn't know what to do, and in shock. You know what I'm saying?

BEVERLY: But, but, if a guy called you up at 1:30 in the morning, like . . . what are you doing?

LOUISE: That's just the thing though, like my feeling is she shouldn't have done all that.

RICK: She didn't . . . .

LOUISE: I'm saying she does have a right to say no, but I'm saying as a woman you do have a responsibility to look at his background.

RICK: Look at his, yeah, look at his background. Look at his wife. Yeah, really.

LOUISE: Look at his wife. He's done patted everything on the butt. Openly, openly. Well, that's the thing where I don't think she should have went because he was so openly flirtatious.

BEVERLY: Well, why did she go? Because she was after something.

RICK: Yeah, but then, again, she was only eighteen.[8]

Six months later, when "Tyson" again became news with Dershowitz's agreement to handle the case on appeal, the theme of the young woman's victimization or culpability continued to drive conversations. In a cafeteria near the courtroom where "Tyson" was initially tried, two men became involved in a loud controversy. As my notes on this conversation read:

"She was just a golddigger," said one man obviously cynical of the young woman's motives. "Is that bad for me to say as a white male?"

"Yeah," said the other, "it doesn't matter what time or why she went up here. For him to act that way . . . ."

"Yeah but, Danny, history repeats itself," the argument continued. "You're a history major. All down through history there's been gold-diggers after men's money."

"Okay, but if she was after his money, she would have tried to sleep with him and develop a relationship . . . it took courage to go against the press . . . ."

"Look, have you read Tyson's appeal? He's trying to show there's a civil suit being filed for money—that's what Dershowitz is trying to do."

"And that means she was a golddigger and that she wasn't raped? She is not a golddigger just because she sues."

Note that dominant narratives—explanations that recur in many people's accounts of why they took one or the other side in a highly profiled crime case[9]—can be discerned through such disputes. Opinions were likely affected by the mainstream media's recounting of public reactions; in turn, media accounts and subsequent public reactions may influence strategies later used by some lawyers (see the account of this transition in chapter 4). Still, as in the "Central Park" and "Bensonhurst" cases, not everyone took a side in the "Tyson" and "Simpson" cases; as described below, some individuals were dissatisfied with the limitations they perceived in the "either/or" framework.

In the "Tyson" case, people favoring the prosecution's side reflected variations on a dominant narrative that "no means no." For those taking this position, it didn't matter why the young beauty contestant went to the boxer's room. If she never expressed or withdrew her consent to sexual relations, they felt, a rape—an act of violence—occurred. As one party exemplifying this perspective, a white policeman, declared:

I don't care if she stripped down naked in front of him, no means no. Even if there was petting involved and there's foreplay and all of a sudden she changes her mind, and didn't feel comfortable, no means no. I don't care what the circumstances are. That's my opinion. . . . I think the man's got a problem. He's been known in public to be a butt fondler, for lack of better terms . . . .

LC: Do you think when you cross that line it's rape?

REPLY: Yes, that's right.

On the other side of the case, virtually the opposite position prevailed: a "what was she doing there?" narrative dominated the remarks of numerous parties who thought Tyson was innocent or should at least be extended the benefit of the doubt. Wonderment was voiced about how any young woman going to a hotel room with Tyson would not have known that this man, a widely reputed "womanizer," wanted sex. The theme of "ulterior motives" underlay this dominant narrative: perhaps the young woman sought a relationship and/or to procure a lucrative book contract about her experiences with Tyson? As one woman put this dominant narrative partial to the defense:

> Myself being a professional lady who has also been approached in these ways, there's a way to get out of it. What was she doing there? There is no reason for me to go out at two o'clock in the morning if I don't have intentions of doing what I thought I was doing. . . . I would have had second thoughts about going anyway. I don't know if she was thinking "Well, I'll get a chance to be with Mike Tyson and I'll just go," but even in the limousine it was stated that he was fondling over her then. If he was doing that I would have had reservations of going up to the room myself. In the second place I don't know if maybe she was going to get something out of him money-wise, and it didn't turn out that way. . . . She tried to state she was a virgin, but she wasn't. It was even quoted in bits and pieces in the media that she even had a child. Now I don't know how true that is, but it's factual that she wasn't innocent. Because if she was that innocent and a virgin I just don't really think she would have ventured out at two o'clock in the morning.[10]

A young man expressed virtually the same sentiments:

> Well, now, the point is, she went there one, two o'clock in the morning to the hotel. . . . I mean, she goes there that time, you have to know what you're going there for. You're not going there to watch television. So it's basically her fault. I personally think that maybe they made the plans to get together, maybe he promised her things and didn't give them to her afterward, she's upset about it and cries. . . . So you know I think that, you know, something probably did happen but I don't think it was rape.[11]

One young woman, who worked for the Indiana Black Expo that sponsored the beauty pageant where Mike Tyson met the young woman who later accused him of rape, elaborated a kindred view:

Most African Americans here think he was innocent, and it didn't have anything to do with gender. Many people question her credibility: what the hell was she doing with him at two in the morning, a total stranger? Pageant officials said she broke their rules . . . she's clearly intelligent and couldn't be so naïve as to think Mike Tyson wouldn't make advances to her physically. . . . I think she knew exactly what she was doing . . . it seems like she almost planned it.[12]

Further probing reveals that most of those expressing one or the other dominant narrative also had strong feelings about how the "Tyson" case symbolized race and/or sexual relations more generally. In this way, discussing "Tyson" became an instance of, and an opportunity for, politicized debate; conversations were about, and not about, this case *per se*. Thus virtually everyone I interviewed who expressed the "what was she doing there?" narrative also aired concerns about racism. For instance, after stating about Tyson's accuser that "if she was that innocent and a virgin I just don't really think she would have ventured out at two o'clock in the morning," the woman who described herself as a "professional lady" added, "I think Indiana is a racist state. I do think the judge he had was racist." Others sympathetic to Tyson's side of things also discussed the young woman's "responsibility" and racial injustices in the same conversations. Consider the comments of Billie Breaux, an African American state senator interviewed after Tyson's appeal:

If you take a look at Mike Tyson's life, he is not good at how to treat people, right? He's not tactful, he's a man of the streets who became famous but no one ever stopped to teach him right or wrong. This doesn't excuse him, right? But the young lady was educated, on her way to college; certainly she should have been apprised of how females and males relate enough to know that you don't leave your room at two o'clock in the morning. . . . Because minority women have been put upon since slavery, we have a deep respect for our bodies; we abhor anyone taking advantage of our bodies; this happened to our mothers and grandmothers. At the same time, we have a responsibility to carry ourselves in such a way that we are not suspect. In other words, people do not as a rule take advantage of you if you carry yourself in a proper, upright manner. Again this isn't true in all cases, okay? Generally, though, most people would not expect a woman to leave her room at 2 A.M.. At that age, we have to take respon-

Fig. 9. Several protests were held in Indianapolis to express support for Mike Tyson and concerns about racism. Some people also aired resentment toward the young woman who had brought rape charges against the famous boxer.

sibility for the decisions we make; someone can come into my home and we have no control over that, but whether I go out with someone is in my control.

But Breaux also expressed concerned about race relations in Indiana:

[It is] hard to find a minority person in Indianapolis who feels Mike Tyson received a fair trial. . . . I think the case is important because one of the things we all know is that prison sentences are loaded for minority males. If a person like Mike Tyson who has money can get waylaid in the criminal justice system, then those without money certainly are going to have trouble. I also think the case points up how you have two justice systems: one for the rich and white, and one for the poor and minority.[13]

One local activist tied cynicism about the young woman's motivations to a similar critique of local racism. He described Tyson's accuser as a "golddig-ger" who seemed unconcerned that her accusations and testimony might have resulted in Tyson's being "railroaded," given long-standing racial prej-udices in the state:

You have to understand Indiana. Indiana is a unique creature: the old boy network is self-perpetuating. These judges will find a way to rule not on the law but on the politics of the situation. . . . A majority of African Americans—a 3 to 1 majority, I would say—took the vocal position that Mike was railroaded. . . . [T]here was a sense among working women, professional women, that Desiree was lying and Tyson was railroaded.[14]

Views such as these, voiced by people sympathetic to Tyson, engendered not only talking about politics but marching as well (see figure 9). As Reverend Stacy Shields recounted, protests were organized soon after Tyson's indictment to respond to concerns about discriminatory treatment stirred by the case:

SS: Yes we called a rally here . . . the first major rally that we had was at the Christ Missionary Baptist Church.
LC: Was that before the trial?
SS: Yes.
LC: How many people came to the rally?
SS: They said it was a couple of hundred but it was near a thousand . . . the next thing we did was we decided that officials respond to votes. So we decided, being the Baptist Ministers' Alliance, to mount a drive called "Mercy for Mike Tyson," because everything seemed against him. We set as our goal 3,000 local signatures. . . . Before the trial was over we had [them].
LC: What did it say on what you were signing?
SS: "Mercy on Mike Tyson." Because he never once said that he did not have relations with the woman, but he claimed that it was consensual. So we were saying have mercy for him.
LC: Was it calling for him to be found innocent?
SS: No, no, no. Mercy does not mean that you have to find a man guilty or innocent. Rather, if he is guilty, we would like to give him a chance.[15]

On the case's other side, the "no means no" narrative similarly provided an opportunity for politicized dialogues. People sympathetic to the prosecution stressed the case's gender-discriminatory aspects, focusing less, if at all, on racism. For instance, the police officer quoted above as saying "no means no" said he had heard about, but did not agree with, charges of racial bias in the "Tyson" case. "You know, I've heard [the charges of racism]," he said.

"But every time I hear it, it's not from the majority of the black community but from a small portion. . . . I do know that there's supposedly a strong political hold of the KKK in the Martinsville area of South Indianapolis. That's no secret." But he had not "seen any type of [racist incidents], like cross burnings or any type of serious harassment, since I've been in the department."

Likewise for Naomi Tropp, long involved as an activist with the issue of violence against women [16] and who "watched the entire trial from beginning to end," the symbolic issue needing to be stressed in the "Tyson" case was not race but problems facing women who are rape victims. Not only did the young woman involved suffer violence, Tropp felt, but she clearly endured victim-blaming from a larger community resentful at her "bringing down" a successful black man. In Tropp's opinion, Tyson's accuser was hardly a "gold-digger": if money had been this eighteen-year-old young woman's primary objective, why hadn't she accepted a lucrative offer to settle out of court? Rather, she said, the young woman went to the boxer's room because she was raised believing Tyson was admirable: "[E]very man in her family thought he was a hero. They were always talking what a great guy he was, they were always watching his boxing matches." Moreover, Tropp believed the trial resulting in Tyson's conviction had been fair; for this reason she was angered when, on appeal, Alan Dershowitz reinjected the issue of racism by suggesting Judge Patricia Gifford had been biased:

> The people that I know can't stand the way he [Dershowitz] handled it. . . . I mean, we think the way he handled this has been really sleazy. He has been trying the case using the media, and saying things like "Judge Patricia Gifford is a racist": to me that's just not excusable. I mean he's supposed to go in there and see if there were serious errors . . . during the trial, [to help determine whether] the conviction should be overturned and there should be a new trial.[17]

Tropp also thought it "oversimplistic" to portray the two sides of the case as neatly polarized—with, supposedly, all blacks in Indianapolis supporting Tyson and all whites supporting the young woman. She believed the sociology of "Tyson" more complicated. For one thing, Tropp posited that class played at least as much a role as racial background in forming people's perspectives; the more educated a person, the more likely to support the young woman who, Tropp emphasized, was also black. Then, too, while social factors influence group opinions on a broad scale, a particular political position

Iron Mike's A No-Show

By Jessie Mangaliman
and Jeremy Quittner
STAFF WRITERS

About 125 people joined a vigil in Harlem last night to protest violence against women — a vigil former heavyweight champion and convicted rapist Mike Tyson declined to attend.

Tyson went shopping on the Upper West Side and met with supporters who are planning a homecoming for the ex-champ today and called last night's protest an "Anti-Mike Tyson Vigil."

Jill Nelson, a member of African-Americans Against Violence, had invited Tyson. The group had denounced organizers of a Tyson homecoming, and planned the vigil in memory of women victims of violence.

"We believe in the power of redemption and strongly support men who want to change their violent and abusive behavior," Nelson said.

"I think it's telling that the vigil in support of victims of violence is being called an 'Anti-Mike Tyson Vigil.' That speaks volume to where [homecoming organizers] are coming from," said Donald Suggs, a member of African-Americans Against Violence.

But the Rev. Al Sharpton, chairman of the homecoming committee, said Tyson "will speak out" at a news conference today at the Apollo Theater. He will also announce a donation to a charitable organization that runs youth programs.

"It seems hypocritical for a group to say Tyson should not make any public appearances including press conferences . . . but then invite him to their public vigil," Sharpton said yesterday.

Also yesterday, the Majlis Ash Shura, of the Isla-

mic Leadership Council of Metropolitan New York, voted to participate in the welcome activities for Tyson.

"Once he [Tyson] is free and clear to the rest of society, the question we ask is what is his attitude for the rest of his life? He has done that formally by becoming a Muslim. He is saying he is going down a new road. That's what we are committed to, helping him stay on that road," said Shaykh Abd'allah Latif Ali, general secretary of the council. Tyson has adopted the Muslim name Malik Abdul Aziz.

Former heavyweight champion Floyd Patterson, who was nominated yesterday by Gov. George Pataki to lead the state Athletic Commission, said Tyson could renew the popularity of boxing, even though he has a felony conviction.

"Well, he served his time, didn't he? I think he's learned his lesson," Patterson said.

Bob Liff and The Associated Press contributed to this story.

Harlem marchers condemn violence against women.

Newsday / Daniel Sheehan

Athletic Commission Nominee Floyd Patterson in Tyson's Corner, Page A52

Fig. 10. Attempts to transcend the dominant two-sided "gender against race" framework also characterized some public reactions after Tyson's release from prison in 1995. For instance, some women objected to apparently condoning violence against women by giving Tyson an enthusiastic "homecoming." At the same time, these women were also well aware of violence and discrimination that both black men and women have historically experienced.

is certainly not confined to any one class, race, or ethnicity. For this reason, it is not surprising that among Tyson's detractors in Indianapolis were not only white feminist-oriented activists like Tropp but several African American women who had a different but also critical perspective on the well-known boxer.

For example, in the words of another woman, an active member of a Republican-leaning local group called the "Black Family Forum" that advocated "family values," Mike Tyson was a "poor role model who had a problem keeping his hands to himself. . . . That's why we addressed it as a moral issue, that this was a celebrity gone awry." While the Black Family Forum carefully avoided taking a position on Tyson's guilt or innocence, her personal opinion was a variation on the "no means no" dominant narrative:

I can give you my opinion. And this is going to be simply my opinion, not the opinion of the Black Family Forum, okay? I just want to make that perfectly clear. . . . My opinion is if a woman is laying there stark naked and if she says no, she means no. I don't care what she did to lead up to it. If she means no, she means no. That is how I feel.

LC: And if you continue it's a rape?

REPLY: It is nothing for her to be in his room at 2:00 or 3:00 in the morning. I was in the Ms. Black Expo pageant several years ago. There are parties all night long. It wasn't like it was a Sunday School convention. It is a party atmosphere. You have a bunch of young girls who are away from home. And here he is a big star. He's rich, a big star, a celebrity. There's a limousine. Taking pictures with him. . . . I can really see how, in her youth, she got pulled into this thing. Probably got in way over her head. I'm sure she did. Yes, it was bad judgment to go in his room. It really was, but I still feel I can see how it happened to her. And if she said no then he should have stopped. Simple as that.[18]

Another woman who was active in the Black Family Forum expressed resentment at depictions of Indianapolis's black community as monolithic—whether this impression was conveyed by the media or by a few often-quoted local black leaders: "You can look at us and see we have different skin complexions. She has higher education than I do. And we're both black. She's from the West, I'm from the Midwest. What person can come in here and speak for the both of us? It's not fair."[19]

For some people, then, feeling compelled to "take a side" was itself problematic. (See figure 10.) One person who worked around the Indianapolis courthouse where Tyson was tried explained her annoyance at a political framework that seemed to demand an "either/or" choice between civil rights and women's rights, and asked "Where as a black woman does my experience fit in?":

I'm angry because I want justice for everybody. I want civil rights for women and for minorities, for both. . . . And you don't persecute one person while taking away the rights of the other. . . . Indiana's very strong now about prosecuting domestic violence case(s). . . . So I think this has something to do with this trial too. That they were making a point that "we're going to protect women at all costs." But at the same time, I worry did they do that while they took away somebody else's rights? That's my only concern. On the other hand, especially within the black community, there's just been such an overkill on "free Mike Tyson," and I think everybody's missing the whole point. They're saying he didn't get a fair trial, but there are more saying that the man's really innocent. But they didn't come to her defense like that. And I mean, you're talking about a black man and a black woman [in the "Tyson" case]. Why was that?[20]

Clearly, then, public reactions to "Tyson" represented an array of responses ranging across the dominant narratives "What was she doing there?" and "no means no" to frustration with the dualistic "either/or" framework in which the case was cast. As part of this public reaction, various parties tapped into the circumstances of the "Tyson" case as a way of provoking broader discussions of gender and racial biases. This, then, illustrates a primary trait of provoking assaults: the cases and the dominant narratives they reflect provide opportunities for passionate yet reasoned politicized debate on what are often much broader societal concerns.

At the same time, from the perspective of whose response is protest-oriented, the "Tyson" case exemplifies a second, albeit more ambiguous, trait: cultural shifts occur as one side's protests influence, perhaps unwittingly and in contradictory ways, parties on the other. Thus provoking assaults are important to some social-movement advocates; the cases have the potential to alter, at least to some extent, widely held public attitudes. For example, peppered through my interviews with several parties who invoked the defense's dominant narrative "What was she doing there?" with respect to the "Tyson" case were allusions to the feminist "no means no" narrative already circulating in the wake of the recently decided "William Kennedy Smith" case. (William Kennedy Smith was acquitted in November 1991; Tyson was convicted in February 1992.) But while these parties conceded the validity of the "no means no" argument generally, they did not think it applied to "Tyson." Thus, while Billie Breaux commented, "This doesn't excuse him, right?" she went on to add that the young woman in question should have known better than to endanger herself by going to Tyson's room. Similarly, after watching a television program about "date rape," Reverend Charles Williams agreed that, "true enough, society needs to understand that no means no," but proceeded to question its relevance to "Tyson" *per se*:

I was looking at Oprah Winfrey, for example, she had on some women about "date rape." And one of the girls said that she went to this university . . . she said that she was in the room with this guy she liked. They were passionately hugging and kissing and petting. He attempted to take her clothes off. She stopped him. After about a half-hour of conversation they started up again and this time he raped her. Now, the responsibility to me at that point lies with both of them. But . . . you can't say he's all wrong or he's all right. This doesn't mean I justify what he did. . . . But then there also has to be a responsibility on the part of both people. Both people are human beings who are intelligent. In [the "Tyson" case] I sympathize with her but I just don't see how . . . . She said to me [at Indiana's Black Expo] she wanted a picture with him. You got to understand, a lot of women were asking for pictures with him. So when he was holding her his hand dropped on her rear, which he probably does all the time. That doesn't make it right, so that's not the issue. But she said to me that when she said she didn't appreciate it, he stopped. So I was just shocked about the whole thing after Black Expo was over.[21]

Several other people who expressed the "no means no" position said they were concerned about racism overall, but not in "Tyson." For instance, Naomi Tropp agreed that racism was a significant issue in Indiana, adding that she made every effort daily to recognize its insidious everyday effects; however, as quoted above, Tropp simply did not believe the "Tyson" trial had manifested racial bias. Consequently, while each side in "Tyson" ultimately committed itself to either support for Tyson or his accuser—citing and then dismissing the other side's arguments in explaining its own—these interviews nonetheless reveal an evolving American cultural terrain. By the 1990s, it could not be blithely presumed that conventionally sexist notions about women's alleged culpability in rape cases, nor racially biased media coverage and criminal justice practices, would any longer be accepted if and when brought to highly profiled public light. Rather, as the "Tyson" case exemplifies, older conventional presumptions had become matters of contention and public debate.

Provoking assaults' utility as a vehicle of politicized debate, and the possibility of thereby shifting cultural attitudes, can be seen to have grown through connections that linked a progression of highly profiled crimes. Again, positions that became dominant narratives in the 1991 "Tyson" case were publicized only months earlier in the "Willliam Kennedy Smith" case. By the time of the "Tyson" case, not only was the feminist "no means no" argument familiar, but it had also previously been counterposed against the "What was she doing there?" theme. Among those who developed the feminist-oriented argument used in "Kennedy Smith" was Denny Abbott, at the time the coordinator of the Palm Beach County Victim Services Agency. In

1991, Abbott wrote several *Palm Beach Post* articles about unfair questioning to which rape victims were still subject, arguing that women's "no" ought to provide protection from public condemnation let alone violence:

> When the word "no" from a woman carries the same weight in a bar as it does in a church . . . then perhaps it will no longer be necessary to provide anonymity. . . . I have heard dozens of comments recently suggesting that dress, location or time of day, for example, in some way makes the victim responsible for the crime. Sadly, much of this type of condemnation comes from women and demands the notion of equality and fair treatment regardless of sex. Rape victims should be treated with the same respect and compassion accorded other crime victims. They are not. They are, therefore, justifiably fearful of the public scorn and humiliation that may result from public exposure.[22]

On the other side of the case, variants on the "What was she doing there?" narrative had also been aired. As in the "Tyson" case, some women and men cynically questioned why the young woman went home with Kennedy Smith on the night the rape was alleged. Said one young woman who worked near the courthouse where the case was tried, "I think she was very wrong, going at 2 A.M. to someone's house; that suggests she's really a hussy. This is strictly my opinion, but I think she knew what she was getting into; I certainly wouldn't go back to someone's house I didn't know. It's common sense . . . and now they're offering her $1 million to tell her story.[23] A young man, approximately the same age, expressed the same take on the matter that later resurfaced in "Tyson": "I think she put herself in a very compromising situation. Anyone who goes to a bar and is out on the beach at 3 or 4 A.M. . . . she must have known what he had in mind."[24] While these interview excerpts hardly show one side influencing the other, they do confirm that contentious themes were both continuing and varying from one high-profile crime to a next.

Moreover, comparative connections between these and other cases may have created virtually a high-profile crime case "infrastructure" of debate. According to Reverend Charles Williams, not only the "Kennedy Smith" case but the "Clarence Thomas/Anita Hill" incident spurred discussion in Indianapolis during "Tyson." "Oh they were talking about them, all three of them," Williams recalled, "Everyone in the streets [were] talking, whites and blacks." Women were angry at losing "two solid victories," the first when Kennedy Smith was acquitted of rape charges and the second when Thomas's

Supreme Court nomination was confirmed despite Hill's accusations of sexual harassment. On the basis of this chronology, Williams believed that by the time of the "Tyson" case, the media and some members of the public were "on a campaign to convict this man" to symbolically compensate for prior losses.

Nor were case-after-case comparisons limited to discussions of gender from the "Kennedy Smith" and "Clarence Thomas" through the Mike Tyson cases. Interviews with various parties show that critiques of racism, too, could be tracked from case to case, as in the linkage of the "Rodney King" and "Reginald Denny" through the "O.J. Simpson" case. For instance, some people perceived the "Simpson" case as merely the latest incarnation of a long string of cases attesting to ongoing prejudices. As Cecil Murray, a well-known Los Angeles minister, observed:

> Did the "O.J. Simpson" case polarize America or has it revealed a polarization that's already there? I think the latter. It has merely revealed where we are, the revelation of an existing status quo. White America can go into denial when things are reasonably quiet, thus, after the [Los Angeles riots in April 1922,] things quieted and there was no furor. Here comes another explosive issue and whites begin to react again. But blacks just feel it, the steady day-to-day pull. To give you an instance, if we had not had a video of Rodney King, there would have been no way to convince White America this happened. If we had not had the tape of Mark Fuhrman, there would have been no way to reveal to them that this is happening. So this is a discovery for whites and it's just disdain and history for American blacks.[25]

Others reacted to perceived connections between "Rodney King" and "O.J. Simpson" by taking specific actions—perhaps joining protest groups or, as sisters Linda and Rose Johnson responded, sitting in on a series of Los Angeles trials entailing alleged racism. Remember, from this book's part 2, Al Sharpton's conviction that activism around interconnected New York City race-related high-profile cases—from "Howard Beach" through "Central Park" and "Bensonhurst"—reinvigorated civil rights activism that could be traced back to the 1960s. Similarly, now in mid-1990s Los Angeles, for the Johnson sisters, observing case-after-case trials from "Rodney King" to "Reginald Denny" to "O.J. Simpson" reinforced a commitment to racial equality their mother had nurtured. Linda Johnson stated that between 1992 and 1996, she attended the state and federal trials of the police officers accused of assaulting Rodney King; the trial related to Reginald Denny's assault in the immediate aftermath of the Los Angeles riots in April 1992; and most recently, in 1995, the criminal trial of O.J. Simpson. After recounting staying up all night to be admitted to the "Rodney King" trials, Linda said that by the time that "Simpson" was tried, she was accustomed to arriving early in the morning to ensure her admission:

LC: Are you still the first one in line?

LJ: Yeah, I was the first one this morning. . . . I get here between 5 and 6 A.M. . . . When "Rodney King" happened, the world didn't know what the LAPD was like, but we knew, black people in the community knew. . . . And poor Reginald Denny, I think he just got caught up in it. 'Cause I don't think it was a personal attack on him, I think he was in the wrong place at the wrong time, and he could have been anybody who was white that it happened to, because they were mad. . . . It's a built-up anger. They got mad at the system, and the system is just like a word, right? People have to find somebody to represent the system. And then this happened: if Simpson was convicted, it would be like just another slap in the face.[26]

For some individuals, rather than allowing continuities to be asserted, case-after-case associations facilitated the making of distinctions. For instance, in the opinion of a twenty-five-year old UCLA student who identified himself simply as "Edwin," the "Simpson" case was less meaningful than either previous celebrity cases like "Mike Tyson" or prior police brutality cases like "Rodney King." As he explained, many of his young African American friends thought Tyson was a more admirable figure than Simpson, an assessment Edwin shared:

E: Well, yeah! Mike Tyson, now Mike Tyson is one of my idols. It's not that I look up to him and want to be him, but he's like the idol of my generation. He's my age, and he achieved a whole lot real quick at a young age. And he's just an idol to me because he's a fighter, literally. And mentally. I mean, he's always out to overcome odds. Always, always, always. And he has not overcome some of his difficulties, but he's just a personification of a young black male. Just fighting, struggling, always being against something. You know. I think that's why he's more accepted [within the black community.] If you listen to rap songs or whatever, Mike Tyson is mentioned all the time.

LC: Can you say where specifically?

E: Oh gosh . . . a million people mention him. You can think up any rap record and they will refer to Mike Tyson in there somewhere. He's more of a symbol. You know. A symbol of a fighter, in all ways. And that's how black males consider themselves. . . . On the other hand, O.J. Simpson doesn't fit in that category. . . . He was always accepted, you know, as a quote-unquote handsome black man. And he never really had to struggle.

LC: So even if he's different from Tyson . . . .

E: Yeah [African Americans would get behind him.] Yeah. I think that's just stems from, I guess the term is "nationalism." You know, for your race or whatever. I mean, you don't want to believe [Simpson] did it. You don't want to. Even though he might have. You see, the thing that I've noticed about black people is that they might not like one of their celebrities, a black celebrity. But when he's in trouble or when anyone's in trouble, black people are usually behind him. . . . They would still get behind him.

Edwin also used comparisons between "King" and "Simpson" to explain why he was "kind of removed" from the "Simpson" case's outcome:

E: I'm kind of, overall, I'm kind of removed from it, because it really doesn't make any difference to me.

LC: Doesn't affect your life?

E: Exactly. Exactly. . . . I was much more emotionally involved in the "Rodney King" case. But more so even than that, "Latasha Harlins." I don't know if they made a big fuss about that in the newspapers . . . but that's what started it all.

LC: 'Cause people were so upset about it.

E: Oh my god, yes. Yes. I mean . . . Rodney King, I mean, he got to live and fight, he had to go to court. But you know [in the "Latasha Harlins" case,] this was a little girl who was killed. There's a big difference. A big difference. That right there . . . that right there will lead to rage. . . . There's no excuse for that. . . . "Simpson" had a totally different feel. I mean, I regard the "O.J. Simpson" case as one of those Beverly Hills mysteries, you know? You know, it's like a . . . to me, it's a high-class crime.[27]

This assessment of the "Rodney King" case as being more politically meaningful than "Simpson" was echoed by a group of Los Angeles high school students interviewed in a history class at Fairfax High. In the words of one Latino student, the "Rodney King" case "should have been shown [by the media]. Because, I mean, that's police brutality. That affects us all. That affects everybody." [28] On the other hand, "they just publicize the 'Simpson' case because he's O.J. I mean because he was a great football player and an actor and everything." [29]

The two advantages of tracing the connections among provoking assaults seem to converge in the experiences of those quoted above. The cases both offered vehicles for politicized conversation and debate, and aided in making social movement issues more familiar, as one highly profiled crime symbolizing discrimination(s) after a next surfaced through the early to mid-1990s. For many public participants in this process, however, the "pros" and "cons" of provoking assaults were, ironically enough, two sides of the same cultural phenomenon.

ON THE OTHER HAND: SOCIAL DEFENSE MECHANISMS AND PARTIALIZED CONVERSATIONS

The unprecedented amount of media coverage accorded the dual homicides alleged to have been committed by O.J. Simpson allowed time and opportunity for diverse public reactions to unfold. Because I interviewed a number of the same people at three different stages of the "Simpson" case,[30] I could track how dominant narratives evolved in response to newly reported developments. For example, after the defense introduced tapes revealing prejudiced statements made by police detective Mark Fuhrman, discussions of racial bias increasingly figured in people's impassioned reactions on both sides.[31] As in the "Tyson" case, then, people used variations on the themes of dominant narratives to elaborate their reactions. But what were the dominant narratives in "Simpson," and do they illustrate frustrating and/or satisfying aspects of this case, and arguably other cases as well?

Not surprisingly, dominant narratives in the "Simpson" case revolved around assessments of the defendant's guilt or innocence. Parties sympathetic to the prosecution were initially, or later became, convinced Simpson had committed dual murders: "It's the evidence," people explained in different ways. As in the "Tyson" case, parties on this side also frequently mentioned gender-related concerns. But whereas this gender issue in "Tyson" was an alleged rape, in "Simpson" it was a matter of alleged domestic violence. Among those inclined to support the defense, many believed O.J. Simpson was, or *might* be, innocent: "It's a set up." And as in the "Tyson" case, parties sympathetic to O.J.'s defense expressed general concerns about embedded racism in the media and criminal justice system. In "Tyson," a history of racial prejudice throughout the Indianapolis area was specifically cited; in "Simpson," the focus was on the Los Angeles Police Department's reputation for police brutality and misconduct.

Many of those on the side of the prosecution immediately or soon came to believe Simpson's guilt had been established. But, later, often added to this view was that racism had little or nothing to do with the case; as the verdict approached, a number of people predicted Simpson would be "let off." Those partial to the defense usually expressed reverse sentiments. Some commented that even if Simpson did beat his wife, he was not necessarily a murderer; later, after the emergence of incriminating tapes made by Fuhrman, racial bias was perceived by this side as key to the case; finally as the verdict approached, many of Simpson's supporters anticipated he would be convicted.

As in the "Tyson" case, numerous parties' reactions did not conform to a racialized white-versus-black scenario that stereotypically came to be associated with these differing prosecution "versus" defense positions. For instance, expressing prosecution-partial reactions outside the courtroom was one woman who described herself as a "Chicana woman of color" and deplored "racial oversimplifications." She recalled an older African American gentleman who during the trial had driven a Cadillac decorated with quotes from Martin Luther King to deride the crimes he believed O.J. had committed. This Latina activist, who became closely involved with the Women's Action Coalition (WAC), described her annoyance at a framework out of sync with her own more multidimensional reactions, at once passionately against racism and convinced of Simpson's guilt. In her words:

> It's just the weirdest thing to me . . . when the tapes came out against Mark Fuhrman, first it sounds like when you're saying O.J. Simpson is guilty you're against black people, or the black community, or that you're for the LAPD. And, in my case, nothing could be closer to the truth.[32]

Indeed, in contrast to one-dimensional frameworks that counterpose "gender versus race" or "white versus black," this young woman had heard reports that, in addition to Furhman's expressed racial prejudices, he was known among fellow police officers for anti-feminist sentiments and activities.[33]

Let us turn to elaborating the pro-prosecution dominant narrative that emerged as the case progressed. Take, for instance, one conversation with a husband and wife, both white, interviewed in Westwood prior to the "Simpson" verdict:

LC: What made you feel this way [about "Simpson"]?

H: It's the evidence! I mean, nobody went over there and sprinkled blood.

W: I feel that the lawyers are going to get him off (both laugh). . . . I give the credit to the lawyers because they get paid to get him off and he's gonna get off on that ground alone. . . . [A]n average person hasn't got a chance.

H: Oh, yes, and the case has nothing to do with race. Absolutely not.

W: Not in Los Angeles.

H: I think the race issue has been brought up because they're trying to prove that he was innocent. . . . I'm so disgusted with our legal system, and the law has to be changed to tighten it up a little. It's just too much leeway.

LC: Why are you disgusted with the legal system?

H: Because it allows attorneys to twist the facts and confuse everybody, and jurors are not brilliant attorneys, to understand all the statutes and all. And they're gonna be influenced by a lot of things. So I don't know whether the jury system works in these cases anymore. . . .

LC: What do you think will be the outcome of the case?

W: We all think he'll get off. . . . as long as there are blacks on the jury, he'll get off. . . . [I]t's black against white . . . a racist problem. They're afraid that there will be another riot.

H: . . . I think it's good people against bad people. You know, during the "King" trial, the jury was all white. And the policemen were let off. So the blacks can say, well, it was an all white jury, how come the police were let off? They weren't being fair, they're prejudiced, and think that all white people should get off, even if they are guilty.[34]

These opinions entailed relative assessments—that is, interconnecting case outcomes between "Rodney King" and "Simpson"—rather than evaluations of the "Simpson" case by itself. Apparently some people suspected jurors would use the "Simpson" verdict to symbolically compensate for the resented acquittal of police officers in the 1992 "Rodney King" verdict that ignited protests in Los Angeles three years earlier. Similarly another group of "young professionals," as they characterized themselves, also predicted acquittal by jurors fearful of further rioting in Los Angeles. In the words of this group, comprising two Latino men and one white woman:

M1: Yeah, people are scared of a riot.
LC: You think now, still?
M1: Yeah.
M2: Absolutely.
F1: It doesn't take much in this city.
LC: What do you mean it doesn't take much in this city?
M1: We had a gigantic riot here before. And people are scared of a riot. I think they're absolutely wrong. I don't think there'd be anything but whenever you have a person of color in a high-profile trial like this, people think it's possible.[35]

According to another young man interviewed in Santa Monica, who likewise expressed sentiments sympathetic to the prosecution, "I think the evidence that we've gotten from the media, with a certain amount of skepticism even then, points to the strong possibility or even probability that this man is a murderer. You know, you hear this and that. But that's been my opinion generally." As the conversation went on, his companion added, "I think the whole race thing, it's unfortunate. He just plain happens to be of African American descent. But I don't think that it has anything to do with it. Except for being just another way that his lawyer can try and manipulate the trial."[36] A local real estate broker aired such sentiments even more forcefully:

LC: Have you been following the "Simpson" case?
REPLY: Not particularly. I was at first, now it's disgusting.
LC: What's disgusting about it to you?
REPLY: Well, they bring all this information which I think deters from the track, and it seems like they have their minds all made up, and then they bring in this other piece of evidence that I don't think shows any bearing on the case at all. . . . I think he's guilty (pause) . . .
LC: Have you felt that from the very beginning, from early on?
REPLY: From all the information that was portrayed at the time. I still do. And they keep going over and over, over and over this piece of information. . . . And I think we're, just, we're dragging it out. It should come to a conclusion.

Note that the person just quoted also asserted that the case had nothing to do with race, even as she expressed a racially charged view:

No, I don't think there's any racial prejudice in this at all. . . . I don't think that has any bearing on it. I think it's just that he has been in the limelight for so long. And at first people wanted to believe he wasn't guilty. But the longer it drags on, the more they feel he is guilty. And the pertinent evidence of the gloves, and the shoes, and everything. And the blood in his car. That wasn't planted. But they keep belaboring the point, and bringing it in . . . so Fuhrman called the black people "niggers." Does that make O.J. any less guilty? So that's why I'm disenchanted with the whole thing. And I would rather listen to something else.[37]

On the other side of the case were, of course, contrary opinions. As one administrative assistant at a Los Angeles university described, she and her friends initially thought Simpson was guilty and would have to "pay" for killing two whites. However, once news of Fuhrman's overtly racist tapes emerged, the opinions of these same parties—many but not all of whom were, like this person, African American—changed:

Well, the day after two people were killed, this is the truth, I said he was not guilty. . . . He did not do this crime. It's one thing beating up your wife. I know this sounds horrible, but it's one thing beating up an individual and it's another matter of killing them. . . . And I want you to know I thought all of my friends were going to kill me.

LC: Is that right?

REPLY: Yes. They did not agree with me, he's guilty cut and dried. There are two white people here that have been killed and someone has got to pay and I said "why him? why him?" . . . And then all of a sudden, there were all these things that were breaking . . . the Fuhrman tapes. . . .

LC: So most of the evidence could have been, in fact, set up by the police.

REPLY: That's right, it's all circumstantial really. . . . Then [after the Fuhrman tapes surfaced,] that very evening one friend called me back, she didn't apologize, but she said to me, "you're right. I've been watching the case everyday and you are right." Well then, other phone calls later on, started coming and they were calling me and saying, "You know, you really stuck by your guns. You said he wasn't guilty, and now we feel the same." I got many phone calls. From different nationalities. I was very pleased. . . . And, oh, yes, race comes into play. And, it's a racial thing. It's a black thing, an African American thing, whatever you want to call it.

LC: What do you mean, exactly, it's an African American thing?

REPLY: Um. How should I say this? I'll just tell you how I feel about it. Blacks are abused more than any others. . . . We're not safe, you're not safe from the police either. None of us are safe. Please believe me.[38]

Like this administrative assistant, another woman discussed how some whites she knew thought O.J. was innocent, while some African Americans and Latinos thought he was guilty. This young woman also believed that, where race was concerned, reactions to the "Simpson" case were no less multifaceted than in "Tyson." Yet she, too, echoed themes about planted evidence and racism that often surfaced on the defense's side of "Simpson":

LC: The polls show that there's a big racial difference in attitudes. Does that seem true to you?

REPLY: Seventy-five to eighty percent of the white people I know say he's guilty. Of the people in the black community that I've talked to, 75–80 percent say he's not guilty. . . . But there's black people who say that O.J.'s guilty, and there's a lot of white people who say that he's not guilty. . . . I feel that [Simpson] was framed. And I don't know who framed him. I can't say for sure the LAPD framed him. But I believe the LAPD perpetuated whatever happened. They might have seen something, and they did the rest. To make it look like he did it. . . . [Regarding Furhman,] most white Americans think that there's no way that he planted that glove. They don't even wanna think it. That's what hurts me because they can think that O.J. killed these people with no doubt. But they can also think that Fuhrman did not plant the glove without any doubt in their mind, do you know? . . . No, they can't believe that Fuhrman did it. It just shocked them. But it wasn't a shock to the rest of us, because a lot of people have been in Fuhrman's custody, and they know. How many black people he's arrested. And he has probably dogged every last one of 'em. . . .

LC: And do people talk about what happened to Nicole Simpson if he didn't do it?

REPLY: They have different theories. . . . Well, some people say that he might have been at the scene but he didn't do it. Some people said that maybe it was a drug deal, and he didn't pay up. Maybe a drug deal that Faye Resnick ran a tab up on. She ran a tab up on him, Nicole knew about it, Nicole confronted her. . . .

LC: Oh. That's a new one. I hadn't heard it.

REPLY: Yeah. Well that's the one I created (laugh).[39]

At first, this young woman predicted Simpson would be found guilty. However, once lawyer Johnnie Cochran succeeded at raising what she perceived to be "reasonable doubts," she could imagine an acquittal. Thus her views did not simply accord with the dominant narrative summarized above; rather, like several people partial to the prosecution, she too expected jurors would use the "Simpson" verdict to compensate for the injustice of the first "Rodney King" verdict: "people might be pretty mad about this too [the "Rodney King" acquittal verdict] if Simpson was convicted. Just like another slap in the face."[40] More often, though, parties partial to the defense predicted Simpson would be found guilty, expecting prejudices in the criminal justice systems would link one case to the next. As one young man declared, "You know. I think he's going to jail. And I think they're gonna break him, take all his money, too. I think he'll go to jail for a long time, and he'll be broke. But, you know, I'm hoping that this isn't the case.[41]

These variations on dominant narratives in the "Simpson" case have the same benefits as in the "Tyson" case. Obviously "Simpson" also provided a conversational vehicle for discussing politics, symbolizing social movement issues previously debated in "Rodney King" and other well-known cases in Los Angeles and nationwide. But I will also use the "Simpson" case to exemplify a more complicated picture. Amidst amid the public's ongoing improvisations on dominant narrative themes, certain social-psychic dynamics— substituting, reversing, exceptionalizing, and partializing—figured in the reactions to the case on the part of some, usually those who favored the defense.

First, substituting (or "blaming the victim") is a social-psychic dynamic in which parties sympathetic to one side of a case redirect the alleged responsibility for a crime away from the accused to others, such as the victim or the media. This process clearly echoes Freud's concept of "displacement," though it broadens the concept by extending its applicability beyond the individual to a group context. For an illustration, consider the following comments about Nicole Brown Simpson made by a woman interviewed in South Central L.A.: "You know, the media painted her as a saint, and she was not, she was close to a (pause) . . . . She's dead now and no one wants to make her look awful but she wasn't a saint and she had a temper." Another young woman described hearing Nicole Simpson called "bad names" outside the courtroom during the second half of the "Simpson" trial: "They say she wasn't the angel that the Browns are making her out to be. And wasn't a proper mother that people are trying to make her to be. . . . But, yeah, they called her a lot of names. . . . I've heard [that she was promiscuous] hundreds and hundreds of times.[42]

By no means, though, was this dynamic confined to public reactions on the defense side of "Simpson." Rather, the "what was she doing there?" dominant narrative expressed by many of those who were partial to the defense in the "William Kennedy Smith" case itself implied the presence of substituting as just defined. And given how this narrative recurs in one case to the next, the dynamic similarly appeared in the reactions of some who were partial to the defense in "Tyson." Moreover, I showed in part 1 how "substituting" also occurred in "Central Park" and "Bensonhurst," when other parties (including the victim herself/himself and members of the media) were sometimes blamed for a crime's genesis. Recall too in the "Bensonhurst" case how Gina Feliciano was blamed for the "turf fight" that led to the killing of Yusef Hawkins; in one woman's opinion, "She provoked the whole thing! It's a sin." In like fashion, in the "Glen Ridge" case, several local residents referred to the retarded young woman as "promiscuous," thereby redirecting blame away from the high school football players charged in the assault.

But sometimes substituting can also occur—and again on the part of groups, not only individuals—when parties sympathetic to the prosecution in a given case are upset by the verdict handed down, that is, by defendant's being found innocent. Candice Kim, for example, an assistant to well-known progressive Asian American activist Angela Oh in Los Angeles, felt that anger expressed at Korean storekeepers in the aftermath of the 1991 acquittal of police officers in the "Rodney King" case was misplaced. The verdict was unfair, she thought, but so were some people's reactions to it:

It [the Los Angeles riots] was a wake-up call, it raised our level of consciousness. We're not taking racism for granted anymore, like it will disappear if we leave it alone. Korean Americans were blamed: many Korean Americans had businesses in predominantly Latino and African American communities where there was a lot of resentment. . . . If you look at the area where the riots occurred, there was a history of neglect, but who was to blame for it? It became Koreans and, in this sense, we were scapegoats.[43]

According to Oh herself, this redirecting was not only undeserved but ironically depoliticizing: "Many storekeepers didn't even know who Rodney King was. You always blame the weak but why wouldn't you burn down City Hall? If you make a political statement, make a political statement—don't go after poor immigrants."[44]

A second social-psychic dynamic, reversing ("defending the defendant"), was also at work in some public reactions to these high-profile cases. Like substituting, reversing was more often than not a part of the reactions of those favoring the defense. But instead of emphasizing a victim's faults or degree of alleged responsibility (as does substituting), reversing focuses on the defendant's situation in such a way that, as the case evolves, the alleged victimizer comes to be seen (to some extent) as victim. Correspondingly, people come to feel sympathy toward a defendant and his/her predicament rather than, potentially, indignation at his/her alleged crime. Because such reversals often entail asserting the opposite of what is apparently the case, this dynamic echoes the process of reaction formation, though again in a group context.

In the "Simpson" case an aphorism that summarizes the contents of dominant narratives on the defense side—"It's a set up"—itself intimates the occurrence of reversing in some people's reactions. Consider, for example, the words used by the administrative assistant quoted earlier to express her sense that Simpson, too, was wronged:

> I'm not saying that he did everything or he didn't do everything. I'm not placing the blame anywhere, except that DNA testing can be contaminated. . . . I heard something that a detective said, "O.J. was the victim." It sounded as though they had already decided he was guilty instead of innocent. . . . .You understand what I'm saying. Not the victim that died, but he was a victim. They had already made up their minds that he was guilty. . . . Let's just say that when you're a failure at something that you should've been doing, you gotta find a scapegoat. I'm not saying that the person who's name I'm not mentioning thought O.J. was going to be it, but O.J. happened to be it. . . . [O]ne of the detectives was looking for a scapegoat and O.J. happened to be it.[45]

Once again, reversing was not exclusive to the "Simpson" case. In "Rodney King," the dynamic was played out again on the defense side when someone who preferred to remain anonymous told me that King had "brought on his own beating." He believed the police officers had been defending themselves, and were now being victimized by "anti-police forces." In the "William Kennedy Smith" case, a number of those sympathetic to the defense thought Kennedy Smith was basically a "nice guy" from "a good family"; at the same time, the young woman who returned to Kennedy Smith's compound was said to bear responsibility for whatever took place. Many people thought Mike Tyson was also unfairly treated by a criminal justice system and mainstream media only too eager, in 1991, to convict him of rape. And, recalling once more the cases in part 2 of this book, several people partial to the defense in the "Bensonhurst" case believed the young men accused of Yusef Hawkins's murder were "railroaded." In the "Glen Ridge" case, several people felt prosecutors, freshly influenced by the "Central Park" case, were overly zealous in pursuing indictments of well-to-do, white football players accused of assaulting a mentally retarded young girl.[46]

Of course, rather than presume that reversing is merely defensive—a claim that risks painting such dynamics as false or illegitimate—a counterargument should also be considered. For reversing can certainly serve at least one positive purpose, voicing the legitimate possibility that a person charged with a crime is in fact innocent. In the 1989 "Central Park jogger" case, a number of community activists believed the young men arrested were not victimizers but victims, "railroaded" by negative media coverage and by prosecutors eager to procure convictions in a notorious highly profiled crime. Yet, as discussed in this book's preface and at the beginning of chapter 2, new information surfaced in 2002 that called into question the convictions of the "Central Park" defendants. A convicted felon named Mathias Reyes admitted having been the only one to brutally rape the victim in a crime that, if media accounts of the time were believed, was supposedly a "gang rape"; in addition, whereas virtually no forensic evidence linked the actually committed young men to this crime in 1989, Reyes's DNA matched that of the rapist nearly a decade and a half later. How, then, is reversing necessarily disadvantageous for defense-partial persons expressing protest reactions—or, for that matter, for wider audiences engaged with provoking assaults?

Perhaps one answer lies in the dilemma of enmeshment, which I discussed from the perspective of the legal system in chapter 4: namely, provoking assaults render legal cases and social causes inseparable. This has complicated repercussions for parties responding defensively through protest reactions and, in different ways, across broader publics as well. On the one hand, reversing may well prove valid in cases where, as in "Central Park," forensic evidence is absent or skimpy and enormous pretrial publicity seems to have branded a defendant guilty prior to trials. However, on the other hand, defensive social-psychic reactions like reversing and substituting can arise even where there is quite strong evidence that a defendant is guilty. This is because, still, some parties are likely to react defensively, rebelling from media-magnified associations between individual defendants and groups that often emerge in these cases.

Note that in each of the pre-"Simpson" examples cited above—"William Kennedy Smith," "Tyson," "Bensonhurst," and "Glen Ridge"—lessening (reversing) the defendant's perceived responsibility for a crime entailed increasing (substituting) the victim's responsibility for it. Thus reversing and substituting often—though they need not, either in "Simpson" or other cases[47]—go together in the reactions of those favoring the defense. Why? One answer is that both social-psychic dynamics cooperate defensively. This is so in a literally legal sense: shifting responsibility onto another party, and reversing apparent victimizers and victims, are time-honored strategies for defending an accused party in court. But, in high-profile crimes of the provoking assault variety, defendants have also been accused in mass-mediated courts of public opinion. Thereafter defense mechanisms may be stimulated in a figurative, though also significant, collective sense.

For some people sympathetic to the defense in these cases sense that, in highly profiled crimes, not only the defendants but a social entity with which they are associated, or with which they sympathize and/or identify—a racial and/or ethnic group, a neighborhood, even a symbolic entity traditionally endowed with authority (as a celebrity or politically renowned family like the Kennedys)—has also suffered by the media's coverage. Substituting or reversing may thereafter arise defensively indeed—whatever the circumstances and evidence in a given case—rechanneling responsibility not only away from the accused but from this unfair/unappreciated symbolic elision of defendant-and-social entity against which at least some people are sure to rebel. One of the young men previously quoted when interviewed about the "Simpson" case poignantly expressed his indignation at persistent media stereotyping of African–Americans: "Do you know what? Sometimes I think that whether or not O.J. is guilty, I can't afford for him to be guilty. Where would that leave me given everything else that's happened?" Similarly, in the "Bensonhurst" case, some working-class whites in this Brooklyn neighborhood may have felt they could not afford the defendants to be guilty because, by extension, the respect they had for themselves and their community would be tarnished. A number of people in Glen Ridge apparently felt threatened by the possible impact of such high-profile exposure on their pride and valued sense of neighborhood insulation.

But from such reactions, especially in cases where the evidence points toward at least the reasonable possibility that a defendant is guilty, two concomitant problems can also later arise. One is that the very act of rechanneling emotions away from a defendant's potential culpability may affect how much energy is available for dealing with broader issues of social responsibility. Something larger is at stake in provoking assaults: people may have reason to be angry at careless media associations drawn between accused individuals and groups with which they sympathize or identify; likewise good reason may exist for objecting to historical mistreatment of minority groups by local criminal justice systems, for example, in Los Angeles or New York City. Yet specifically social anger at institutional sources of discrimination—for example, media or criminal justice system practices—can be diluted to the extent that defensive reactions, which accord apparently specious blame to a victim and/or exoneration to an apparent victimizer, recycle people's energies only within the dualistic framework of a case. In this respect substituting and reversing (though spurred by distinctly social problems and tending to occur in commonly affected groups of people) resembles the workings of a Freudian defense mechanism like displacement, which functions on an individual level. As with an individual, redirecting group emotions can be costly insofar as the actual object of a group's past ire is spared; at the same time, some other entity that is relatively (or entirely) innocent may unfairly feel the brunt of the group's ire. And all this can happen unconsciously, consonant with and perhaps reinforcing individualistic propensities that are themselves highly characteristic of American culture.

Another problem, subtler still, is that once anger at societal entities is channeled onto victims and away from defendants, stereotypes may be reinforced rather than diminished. Once defense mechanisms like substituting and reversing emerge in situations where they appear to be unfounded, any lack of careful distinguishing between political causes and the seeming "facts" of a case at hand may render protesters' critiques less credible—even subject to caricature. Such a failure to distinguish between a "case" and "cause" can also occur where protesting parties are not responding defensively but offensively, that is, they are supporting the prosecution's side. For example, the highly publicized and eventually notorious 1988 "Tawana Brawley" incident—never tried both because evidence against white police officers who had allegedly raped the African American teenager did not surface, and because a credible counterinterpretation of events did. This certainly detracted from activist Al Sharpton's ability to credibly use symbolic incidents of this kind—that is, provoking assaults—to make larger political points. In reaction some segments of a larger public—including, perhaps, those who previously held one or another prejudice or already sympathized with the prosecution—may feel justified in expressing cynicism about these claims and associating them with the gender, ethnic, racial, or class-based group who has made them. Paradoxically enough, such specious associations may be precisely what angered some protesters in the first place. To the degree this circularity of stereotyping unfolds, then, an "excuse" may also conveniently materialize for overlooking aspects of social critique that can be valid regardless of whether a defendant committed a particular crime. Here is another side of the coin indeed: in one respect provoking assaults seem to facilitate cultural shifts while, in another collectively unconscious sense, they may help to keep older biases firmly in place.

A third socio-psychic dynamic, exceptionalizing ("yes, but" reactions), involves the admission that the social concerns of the opposing side may be valid, but that they don't figure in the case at hand. Thus, as already discussed, some parties inclined to support the prosecution in the "Tyson" case agreed that racism is a problem in Indianapolis and American society nationwide, but not in "Tyson" *per se*. And, as previously quoted, several people inclined to support the defense agreed with the feminist principle that "no means no" in general but, again, not in "Tyson" in particular. Evidently, while agreeing that racism and gender discrimination were problematic, these parties questioned their relevance to an accused group or person with whom they sympathized or identified.

Similarly, in the "Simpson" case, recall that numerous parties partial to the prosecution were convinced of the Los Angeles Police Department's reputation for brutality, as revealed through the "Rodney King" and other cases; still, as some explained, they did not believe racism was a factor in the "Simpson" case at all. Likewise, among parties favoring the defense, many people strongly condemned the dangers of domestic violence on the whole; yet as several stated, including two women who reported their own experiences of battering, the evidence of domestic violence did not necessarily mean O.J. was a murderer. Consequently this third dynamic seems to offer a social-psychic compromise: on the one hand, exceptionalizing implicitly acknowledges provoking assaults' larger context, that is, sociocultural change; on the other, by dismissing the immediate relevance of the other side's claims, these claims may undergo a kind of defensive neutralization.

But, as with reversing, might exceptionalizing not be quite legitimate, and appropriate, in certain instances? Perhaps, on the prosecution's part, the gathering of evidence did not seem to involve prejudice and its expression; imagine, on the defense's, that indeed care was taken to disentangle larger social issues from the apparent innocence or guilt of an accused. Yet, as is again the same with reversing, exceptionalizing is likely to arise even if this dynamic did not appear appropriate in specific instances. For think what it would mean not to exceptionalize, that is, to admit that points made by the other side are legitimate. From a legal standpoint, the rigidity of the line between "us" and "them" within a dualistic framework might then start to dissolve. As a result, one's ability to argue effectively on the prosecution's side (e.g., if the LAPD was admittedly guilty of past racism, might the state's case against O.J. indeed have been a compromised one?) or on the defense's (e.g., if some batterers are admitted to veer obsessively out of control, might O.J. indeed have been guilty?) would be potentially threatened; the other's arguments would become entwined with one's own, rendering it less concrete but more potentially multidimensional.

Not exceptionalizing could also provoke anxiety by interfering with a person's ability to maintain distance from problems highlighted by the other side—whether prejudices or misbehavior the prosecution's side may have exhibited or awful violence a party (or parties) on the defense side has been accused of committing. Take, for example, the 1989 "Glen Ridge" case discussed in part 2 (for exceptionalizing, too, surfaced in cases prior to "Tyson" and "Simpson"). In "Glen Ridge," some defense-partial parties expressed the view that while violence against women was certainly a valid concern in society as a whole, "our guys" did not contribute to this problem[48]; they believed a consensual act, not a crime, had occurred. But what would it have meant for such parties to allow that young star football players from their home town might have sexually assaulted a vulnerable young woman? This admission might have been difficult indeed, calling forth introspection into how, and why, such a crime could be committed by young men so highly regarded in one's own community. Perhaps then, in reaction against difficult feelings that hint at degrees of collective responsibility, exceptionalizing offers one line of defense.

The fourth, and last, social-psychic dynamic is partializing ("taking a side"). This refers to public reactions that strictly separate points made on one side of a case from arguments proffered on the other. The prosecution argues "versus," and only versus, the defense; instead of admitting a case's complexity and sometimes uncertainty, parties generally envision the other side antagonistically—in "us versus them" terms rather than shades of gray. As before, this dynamic echoes a defense mechanism on the level of the individual, which the British psychoanalyst Melanie Klein called "splitting"—a mechanism that manifests as an inability to merge "good" and "bad" aspects of a parent. Here again, though, the roots of this reaction lie in sociocultural sources, not in the childhood of an individual.

Like substituting and reversing, partializing and exceptionalizing sometimes surface in pairs; each dynamic works to maintain distance between the arguments of two sides. Of course, not all public reactions entail partializing or exceptionalizing; as already seen, some people rebel from simplistic "either/or," "good/bad" frameworks of discussion in particular cases. Still, most people's dominant narratives tend to presume one side's antagonistic relationship with the other. For instance, in the "Tyson" case, most people who felt the defendant had been harmed by racism did not see the case as equally troubling from a gender-based perspective. Rather, by impugning an alleged victim, dominant narratives in that instance offset feminist arguments about "no meaning no."

In the "Simpson" case, "either/or" perspectives also dominated in narratives that juxtaposed "it was a set up" against "it was the evidence." But I would go even further to contend that partializing marked many, if not all, public reactions—across official, protest, and conversational sorts alike—in each of the cases examined in this book. Certainly partializing was present in "Central Park" as some people focused on the racial aspects of that case, while others focused on issues of gendered violence and public safety the crime grew to symbolize. Equally striking was the presence of partializing in the "Bensonhurst" case where one side protested concerns about racism and the other side the stereotyping of a neighborhood; seldom did the same party recognize both problems simultaneously.

Of course, again, one could counterargue: partializing, evidently common in reactions to provoking assaults of the late 1980s and the early-to-mid 1990s, may well be satisfying, not dissatisfying, to many people. Might not many people derive satisfaction, and indeed pleasure, from unalloyed expressions of one-sided feelings? Here too, though, several disadvantages of this dynamic are inseparably present. For one thing, across the high-profile crimes I studied, many people expressed figurative as well as literal fears of what would happen if they failed to partialize, that is, failed to take the side they were "supposed" to. For example, in the "Simpson" case, a woman frequently involved in protest activities in favor of the defense was hesitant even to mention doubts she sometimes felt. This person was expected to be "pro-O.J." and believed friends and associates would ridicule or shun her if she switched sides or expressed frank concerns about culpability in the case. While these anxieties were anticipatory, other parties in different cases described actual threats of punitive retaliation: several jurors told me they received death threats from anonymous outside parties invested in particular verdict outcomes. Thus many people came to feel, or were blatantly told, that partializing was expected of them; taking sides was experienced as culturally normative, and opposing it was potentially dangerous.

Note, then, that partializing as a cultural dynamic is "normalized" not only by legal structures (see chapter 4) and by traditional media practices (see chapter 5), but receives even further reinforcement through public reactions to provoking assaults that pressure people to take sides. As a result, open public discourse is likely to be impoverished. For example, most of the cases analyzed in this book—from "Central Park" to "O.J."—came to symbolize more than one social problem, frequently counterposing gender and racial discriminations. But even if these discriminations are both implicated in public discussions of a particular crime, partialization makes it unlikely that multifaceted considerations can be synthesized: only one side, one "type" of discrimination, can "win." Consequently, someone or some group will be disappointed by a verdict's "win/lose" outcome; dissatisfied parties may call for a new trial, seeking to retry the case as an appeal at the federal court level or as a civil proceeding. This is precisely what happened when parties dissatisfied with O.J. Simpson's acquittal in criminal court obtained a retrial, and thereafter a different outcome, in civil court. Likewise, in the "Rodney King" case, parties frustrated by the acquittal of police officers in a California state court obtained a retrial, and a different outcome, in a downtown Los Angeles federal court.

While the partializing dynamic cannot be said to be merely or even primarily advantageous in its effects on how provoking assaults are discussed, it does make it likely that some degree of ongoing public dissatisfaction will continue from case to case: as just discussed someone, or some group, will be disappointed by particular case outcomes. Even more broadly, though, people may find themselves frustrated—whether or not the source of this frustration is consciously articulated—by the straitjacketed terms of debate itself. Indeed, many of those whom I interviewed about the "Bensonhurst" case told me that they had grown weary of hearing and talking about it. The same was true for the "Tyson" and the "Simpson" cases. Several social movement leaders, out of a sense of frustration, refused to talk to the media about particular cases lest the complexity of their views be simplified and misrepresented. For instance Joe Hicks, well known for his 1960s activist work in the Southern Christian Leadership Conference and later the director of the Los Angeles Multi-Cultural Coalition formed in the wake of the "Rodney King" case and the Los Angeles riots, was reluctant to speak with reporters when asked to comment on the "Simpson" case. "Why stay away from it?" I asked Hicks, who was concerned with both racial and gender discrimination. His answer was that the effect of the verdict was to create a "polarized" situation "in a very ugly way."

Public reactions to high-profile provoking assaults, as we have seen in this chapter, have been widely varying and ambivalent. But the question remains as to what the analysis here bodes for how we respond to future provoking assaults that are virtually bound to arise.

STEPPING BACK

CHAPTER 7

High-Profile Crimes and American Culture

A good friend and author of a number of books on gendered, racial, and class-based inequalities in the United States has joked with me over the years about the standard format she adopts in her books' conclusions. These, she wryly observes, are her "What is to be done?' chapters. I wish to end this book in a similar vein, by speculating on its repercussions for the varied parties—journalists, people involved in myriad capacities within the legal system, social movement activists, community figures, and relatively disinterested bystanders—whose standpoints vis-à-vis "provoking assaults" I have explored. For while this volume does not lend itself to making clear-cut policy recommendations, as do my friend's books, it does have implications for change.

Recall the query first raised in this book's introduction. Do high-profile crime cases of the provoking assault variety bode a new and important form of politics, a position exemplified by activist Al Sharpton? Or, as defense lawyer Roy Black argued, do these cases distract us from underlying problems in the media and the legal system that are structural in character? A third alternative is one at which I have hinted all along: by their character, provoking assaults are intrinsically ambivalent phenomena that have socially advantageous and disadvantageous aspects at the same time.

Perhaps the best way to untangle that "What is to be done?" question is to review this book's arguments overall. First and foremost, I have sought to analyze the role of high-profile crime cases in contemporary American culture. I began with the observation that violent cases involving controversial issues of gender, racial, and class-related social problems frequently received extraordinary media coverage, locally and nationally, from the mid-1980s through the mid-1990s. Chapter 1 (and, in more detail, appendix B) explain how I came to this conclusion based on a quantitative study of national and local newspaper coverage in New York, Los Angeles, and Chicago. Yet the prominence of these cases can also be explained qualitatively in a way that may be predictive of whether future crimes will, or will not, be accorded unusually intensive coverage.

The narrative studies of the 1989 "Central Park" and "Bensonhurst" cases that constitute chapters 2 and 3, and many of the public reactions reviewed in chapter 6 concerning early to mid-1990s cases, document that provoking assaults provided one—not the only, but certainly one—mode of political debate through these decades. Then, too, in each of the cases I discussed— "Central Park," "Bensonhurst," "William Kennedy Smith," "Mike Tyson," "Rodney King," "Reginald Denny," and "O.J. Simpson"—issues concerning gender and/or race discrimination were seen as particularly symbolic. From this, one conclusion (which may also be predictive) emerges. These highly profiled crime cases may have risen to prominence, receiving extraordinary coverage, precisely because they engaged passions of a distinctly political kind; the cases provided an opportunity for people more and less involved to debate controversial social issues of the day and place. Moreover, they emerged at a time when social movements of the 1960s and 1970s had both made their mark and were moving, relatively speaking, onto the defensive. At such a moment, people may have been especially interested in high-profile crime cases that provided ways of continuing to argue about the depth and breadth of gender, race, and class-related discriminations in the United States. As I argued in chapters 2–4, media proclivities of interconnecting past and future incidents facilitated the public's capacity to use this vehicle of debate in the mid-1980s through mid-1990s.

If this broad conclusion just stated is valid, two factors may be seen to increase the chances that a future case will become extraordinarily publicized news as a provoking assault. The first is whether a case taps current concerns about a particular social problem in such a way as to become symbolic; the second is whether, in addition, a case is or can be linked to recently forged journalistic themes and patterns, that is, to what in chapter 5 I called "journalistic precedents."

For example, consider the "Kobe Bryant" case that surfaced in July 2003 when this well-known basketball player was accused of rape. The criminal charges against him were eventually dismissed on September 2, 2004, but intensive pretrial publicity made me wonder whether this instance would develop into a provoking assault. Had the case gone to trial, one possibility was that rapes alleged between acquaintances (so-called date rapes) were so thoroughly discussed in the "William Kennedy Smith" and "Mike Tyson" cases of 1991–92 that the issue itself would not have been, by late 2004, sufficiently "provocative" to maintain the American public's interest in the case. On the other hand, the media quickly drew connections between "Kobe Bryant" and earlier cases, and forged the familiar dualistic framework for covering the case—a typical feature of provoking assaults—even before the trial was due to occur.

Consider, for instance, the title given by editors at ABCNews.com—"Echoes of OJ?"—to August 1, 2003 coverage of the "Bryant" case prior to its dismissal. The news story proceeded to explain: "The revelation that one of the lead investigators in the ["Bryant"] case was also a key figure in a racial profiling case could provide the defense with an argument that the investigation of Bryant, a prominent black athlete, was carried out unfairly, as the defense argued in the case of O.J. Simpson." On August 5, 2003, David Schoenfeld of ESPN.com reflected: "If the Kobe Bryant sexual assault ever gets to trial, it won't match O.J. for 'Trial of the Century' status. But it should crack the top 10 sports trials of all time." Then, on Sunday August 31, 2003, another Internet news story about the "Bryant" case commenced as follows:

> The *Associated Press* reports that race may become an issue in the Kobe Bryant case. Polls already show more blacks are sympathetic to his plight than whites. And many compare Kobe's case to O.J. Simpson's—in which the vast majority of people think O.J. got away with murder. Two CNN/USA Today/Gallup polls conducted in late July and early August found that 63% of blacks surveyed felt sympathetic to Bryant, compared to 40% of whites. . . . Both blacks and whites mentioned O.J. Simpson, whose acquittal at his criminal trial for the 1994 deaths of ex-wife Nicole Brown Simpson and her friend Ronald Goldman divided the groups.[1]

Note that two sides—the opinions of blacks and those of whites—have been juxtaposed in this excerpt through what I have called in this book a "partializing" process. Left out, though, are more nuanced considerations such as where the opinions of Latinos fit in (or, for that matter, subtler differences between groups such as, say, Jamaican Americans compared to African

Americans and Italian Americans), or the possibility that many people hold more complex views altogether. Thus if this recent incident had become another "gender versus race" case—continuing the pattern of counterposing one form of discrimination with respect to another (as in the "Central Park," "Mike Tyson," and "O.J. Simpson" cases)—"Kobe Bryant," too, might have mushroomed to the status of a provoking assault in the course of arousing, and dividing, political passions and debates.

Still, none of this explains why symbolic issues of gender and racial discrimination *per se* became the focus of so many highly profiled crimes in the 1980s and 1990s rather than other social problems—say, corporate crime or governmental corruption. It is true that among the top ten cases receiving the most news coverage between 1985 and 1996 (see appendix B), two instances—the "Michael Milken" and "Charles Keating" cases—were corporate crimes involving savings and loan bank scandals. To these may be added the later, highly publicized "Enron" case of 2002. Yet, on the whole, more national and local publicity was accorded violent crimes like the "Central Park jogger," the "Rodney King," the "Mike Tyson," the "William Kennedy Smith," and the "O.J. Simpson" cases—"Simpson" receiving by far the most coverage of all—than the corporate crime cases. Again, why?

By way of responding, I point to the argument in chapter 1, where I traced (1) rising public concerns about violent crime as a social problem, (2) controversies surrounding issues of "identity politics" concerning gender, sexuality, and race, and (3) a larger-than-ever explosion of inner- and intramedia competition. Again, without a conjuncture of these three historical factors, the series of cases discussed in this book might not have garnered quite so much media attention as they did. Certainly in 1989 editors and reporters knew, and public opinion polls confirmed, that crime—especially crimes involving interpersonal violence in urban contexts—was high on Americans' lists of social concerns. Simultaneously, by the late 1980s, substantive issues raised by the 1960s feminist and civil rights movements were being argued again in view of the backlashes that occurred in response to advances already made.

High-profile crimes provided social movement groups a way to further their cause. Through the "Central Park," "William Kennedy Smith," and "Mike Tyson" rape cases, and vis-à-vis the issue of domestic violence raised by the "Simpson" case, feminists could powerfully reiterate their claim that violence against women was unacceptable. Then on the opposite side of the

"Central Park" case, and through the "Bensonhurst," "Rodney King," and on the opposite side of the "Simpson" case as well, antiracism activists knew these cases also had the capacity to concretize prejudices like those still sometimes manifested in media practices and brutal police actions.

But, of course, not everyone agreed. Once the main framework of debate was structured dualistically, and even though some people rebelled from this framework, chapter 6 showed how in both "William Kennedy Smith" and "Tyson," many people went back and forth only within the "no means no" and "What was she doing there?" dominant narratives associated with the prosecution and defense sides of these cases, respectively. In "O.J. Simpson," many people debated the "gender versus race" problems that case came to symbolize. Those convinced of O.J.'s guilt, for whom the case starkly exemplified domestic violence and its ills, offered variations on the dominant narrative "it's the evidence" theme, while parties who favored the prosecution thought the whole thing was a "set up."

Arguably, then, provoking assaults from the mid-1980s onward married rising concerns about crime felt by larger numbers of people with profound shifts taking place in cultural consciousness about gender and racial discrimination that were the legacy of 1960s. Whatever else most Americans may disagree about, heinous acts of violence against innocent parties—murder, assault, rape, precisely the crimes alleged in these instances—remain universally condemned. Consequently social movement groups on the defensive by the 1980s may indeed have sensed that a "Bensonhurst" or "Rodney King" crystallized the ugliness of prejudice in particularly undeniable form. Or was it undeniable? For, in "Rodney King," even a seemingly transparent act of police brutality caught on tape was called into doubt by a legal interpretation— namely, Rodney King threatened the officers, not the other way around— that convinced at least one set of Simi Valley jurors in that case's first criminal trial in April 1992. Thus the two-sided, "either/or" form of these cases not only enabled arguments but counter-arguments, allowing not only movements but countermovements a mass-mediated forum for their views.

Cultural negotiations, then, took place through provoking assaults: new ideas were challenged and absorbed; changes occurred and stimulated backlashes. Moreover, when all this is combined with the third factor in the historical "conjuncture" alluded to above—that, by the 1980s, more competing mass media existed than ever before—the sources of provoking assaults as a complex linkage among cases that combine public and social movement concerns with multimedia opportunities for political debate should be clearer.

Once selected for high-profile media coverage, provoking assaults grow to encompass the participation of multiple parties. Of course, this includes journalists and editors who allow through their coverage a given crime to become and remain highly profiled, as well as actors in the legal system. But further, and just as critically, these cases soon "provoke" myriad community and social movement participation—generating wide-ranging public reactions from less directly involved persons—as they attain symbolic status. In other words, as an incident evolves to become a legal case, it develops into one or more social causes. Once this happens, the media draw connections between past and present incidents, creating a common nexus of cultural reference points that encourages comparative discussions.

Yet this book suggests not only that provoking assaults were cultural vehicles of politicized debate and of change in the 1980s and 1990s, but, just as centrally, that disadvantages as well as advantages accrue to this medium. For another trait of provoking assaults is that, when legal cases become social causes, a two-sided "prosecution versus defense" framework is created not only by traditional media habits of telling "two sides to every story" (see chapter 5) but through the structure and assumed practices of the legal system (see chapter 4). Important to note is that, by this interpretation, this "habit" is not voluntarily entered into by individuals, nor is it a reflection of a duality somehow inherent in all of us: rather, when viewed from this vantage point the "either/or" dualism appears as social constructions that became institutionalized. Thereafter members of the public, from community and social movement activists to people who discuss cases at work or among friends or family at dinner (see chapter 6), tend to reinforce this two-sided structure of debate: dominant two-sided narratives unfold even as rich improvisation occurs in and around them. This is not to overlook those occasions when people rebel against the perceived limitations of this framework of interpretation. On the whole, however, I noticed that the tendency toward "partialization" tended to be dominant.

I have defined the term "partialization" as a process through which people channel their thoughts and feelings in support of, or against, one of two sides. Once this occurs, a seemingly unbridgeable chasm separates the antagonists; valid points of partial validity that may inhere in one side are likely to be overlooked by the other. Of course in some situations—such as when adjudicating clearly "either/or" questions of guilt or innocence, or, for example, in sports—clearly separating one side from the other is appropriate. However, precisely because provoking assaults concern not only legal cases but the social problems they symbolize, debates that take place within the narrow parameters of a dualistic framework often confuse and oversimplify much more complicated matters.

Other dilemmas emerge from the two-sided character of provoking assaults. A "win" or "loss" in any legal case resolves only that particular case, leaving unresolved the general class of problems that case grew to symbolize. Moreover, if the arguments of both sides contain some degree of validity— as I have argued, both gender and racial discrimination did figure in different ways in both the "Central Park" as well as "O.J. Simpson" cases—"either/or" verdicts allow only one side to "win," thereby gaining social legitimacy. But even so, the media and some resentful members of the public at large (those who were on the side that lost) may seek to stimulate ongoing connections between cases by seeking reversals through retrials. Thus, for instance, parties outraged by O.J. Simpson's acquittal at his criminal trial were especially eager for a civil trial to produce a different outcome; similarly, parties outraged by the prosecution's loss in the first "Rodney King" trial pushed, and eventually "won," when the case's retrial in federal court reversed the outcome in the Simi Valley state courtroom.

As described in chapter 6, partialization in provoking assaults also bequeaths at least four social-psychic dynamics, defensive in character, that sometimes arise in people's reactions to these cases. In addition to partializing (or "taking a side"), I called two of these dynamics "substituting" (or "blaming the victim") and "reversing" (or "defending the defendant"). The former refers to debates that typically arise over whether an alleged victim should bear some degree of responsibility for their own victimization; the latter alludes to reinterpretations of apparent victimizers as possibly victimized themselves. Strikingly, some degree of substitutive "blaming the victim" occurred in each case this book considered. I referred to the fourth dynamic as "exceptionalizing" (or "yes but" reactions), in which people sometimes concede a general point made by the other side while denying its immediate applicability in the case at hand.

Taken together, these dynamics have the subtle collective consequence of letting social responsibility "off the hook"; ironically, the conflation of cases and causes tends to guarantee that "larger" factors figure somewhere in provoking assaults' backdrops. Yet systemic analyses do not usually result from discussion of these cases and the questions of economic, racial, and, gendered discrimination, and/or the character of the media, they raise. Instead, debates tend to volley back and forth within the structure of the two-sided framework of a given case, for example, was the (apparent) victim really victimized? Was the (apparent) victimizer in fact the victim? Perhaps, then, the four social-psychic dynamics explored in chapter 6, and reviewed here, operate unconsciously in defense against the inadmissibility of social responsibility in these cases. In this respect—that they are not necessarily consciously known or admitted—I envision the dynamics as akin to Freudian defense mechanisms. Yet they differ from these insofar as they have distinctly social sources (rather than being rooted in childhood experiences of the individual) and appear in similarly situated groups or subgroups. Further study of social defenses along the lines introduced in this book would likely be fruitful.

Overall, much seems to change and not change through provoking assaults. On the one hand, cultural shifts have certainly occurred in the wake of these high-profile crime cases. On the other hand, the partialized mode of discussion characteristic of provoking assaults recycles parties' energies from side to side, and from individual case to individual case, such that at last more is promised than delivered by way of lasting social transformation. Again, though, what do provoking assaults bode not only in general but for the specific parties engaged with them?

THE LEGAL SYSTEM

In chapter 4 I argued that, through the late 1980s and into the 1990s, these crime cases implicitly posed challenges to notions of legal "objectivity" that presume the world inside and outside the courtroom can be neatly separated. For provoking assaults make social enmeshments between law and society plainly visible. As a result, provoking assaults create special challenges, for instance, for judges who must consider whether jurors can actually be free of outside influences in cases to which they were already exposed through the media's coverage. Judges must further determine if cameras should be allowed in the courtroom or whether changes of venue requests should be granted (an issue especially thorny if highly profiled crimes receive national attention).

I suggested that, as seen in the light of provoking assaults, judges as well as lawyers differ in their approaches along a continuum that ranges from "traditionalists" to "modernists." A traditionalist judge and lawyer continue to maintain the possibility of a strict demarcation between the courtroom and the world outside. A modernist judge or lawyer, on the other hand, tends to admit that lines separating the courtroom and the outside world have become blurred, and proceeds on that basis. For instance, a modernist judge might anticipate that jurors were already affected to some degree by high-profile news coverage, and might find themselves unwittingly exposed to media accounts again as a case progressed. Rather than denying such influences, this judge might figure it into his or her decisionmaking process by, perhaps, urging jurors to speak up if particular problems related to exposure were to arise.

Lawyers' responsibilities at trial obviously differ from that of judges insofar as they are expected to be partial. But differences between traditionalism and modernism in the legal system also affects lawyerly strategies for representing a case. I was struck by the degree to which attorneys who perceived the synthesis of cases and causes that characterize provoking assaults often had an advantage in arguing their cases. For one thing, since modernist lawyers usually presume that jurors were or may become aware of media developments, they are more likely to incorporate media relations into their overall strategies. Second, modernist lawyers (whether they saw themselves as such) often recognized how the enmeshment between case and cause could become iconic. Thus, for example, the prosecution in the "Central Park" case and the prosecution in the "Bensonhurst" case made indirect or direct allusions to larger symbolic issues. These were, respectively, the problems of a city in which a young woman could not jog freely in a public park without fear of assault and rape, and wherein a young black man could not walk in any neighborhood he chose without fear of suffering a violent and racially motivated attack.

On the defense side of cases, and regardless of whether one agrees with particular strategies and the outcomes they may have produced, Johnnie Cochran's famous "playing the race card" in "O.J. Simpson" was a clear example of some of this book's arguments. Indeed, Cochran effectively alluded to the historical effects of the "Rodney King" case without overtly mentioning it; in other words, he framed the "real-world" context of "O.J. Simpson" outside the courtroom while arguing the case within. In the same way, as we saw in chapter 4, defense attorney Edi Faal in the "Reginald Denny" case tried first explicitly and then implicitly to tie that attack on a white truckdriver at the corner of Florence and Normandy in Los Angeles to the "collective psychology" already created by "Rodney King." Indeed, on the defense side of that prior case, lawyer Michael Stone also relied on "context" to make his own kind of reversal, arguing in the specific setting of Simi Valley that police officers, who face dangers on a daily basis, were threatened on the night in question by Rodney King (not vice versa).

Finally, jurors also perceive the enmeshment of cases and causes typical of provoking assaults; their attitudes, too, may range along a traditionalist-to-modernist continuum just as may the approaches of judges and lawyers. A number of jurors I interviewed in the "William Kennedy Smith" and "Central Park jogger" cases believed they had upheld the legal institution's objective status. Others, including several jurors in the "Bensonhurst" case, took relatively more modernist positions by consciously perceiving the law as a place where justice could be upheld inside and outside the courtroom simultaneously.

No doubt, to many people, these observations will not be surprising. It is hardly news that law and society are interwoven; nor is this book unique in noting philosophical debates that divided legal scholars in the 1980s and the 1990s. For instance, in concluding *Postmodern Legal Movements*, Gary Minda depicts developments in legal theory (and the forging of "critical legal studies") that have separated traditional perspectives from newer ones such as interest in poststructuralist and postmodern perspectives.[2] Again, though, provoking assaults may be distinctive in their ability to vividly illustrate legal and social/political enmeshment because of their magnification of "ordinary" legal processes that results from competitive intra- and intermedia publicity.

THE MEDIA

In chapter 5, I argued that in the 1980s and 1990s, these high-profile crime cases also called the journalistic assumption of "objectivity" into question. As with the legal system, provoking assaults sometimes challenged the ideal that conventionally presumed journalists should, and could, separate themselves—their own personal perspectives and priorities—from events they covered. Indeed, I have contended that these cases may have been one of many influences that, over time, fueled debates about precisely this issue within the media.

In chapter 4, I discussed divisions within the legal system as between traditionalists and modernists; in chapters 2 and 5, I referred to differences within the media as between individualists and relativists. Those who expressed what I called "journalistic individualism" believed cases were selected for high-profile coverage because of their inherently interesting characteristics. On the other hand, those who expressed "journalistic relativism" saw their practices more contextually. In contrast to individualists, this latter group of journalists' relationship to their subject matter, and their power to shape public perceptions, was self-consciously admitted. This distinction often but did not always correspond with differences between journalists who worked in a "mainstream" or alternative news venue; sometimes reporters and editors employed in the former also disagreed sharply among themselves in their conceptions of journalism.

This book suggests that journalistic relativism offers a paradoxically more "accurate" account of how reporters and editors actually operate as some cases, rather than others, mushroom to high-profile visibility. For example, though journalists often referred to the "Simpson" case as a unique event, chapter 5 contends that themes of three strands of previous highly profiled cases—gender, race, and celebrity cases—were reiterated in discussions cumulatively stimulated by the so-called trial of the century. Moreover, in 1989, criticisms of media coverage of the "Central Park jogger" case had made journalists more likely to cover the "Glen Ridge" case that emerged soon afterward than if "Central Park" had never occurred (and received extraordinary coverage). Likewise, it is hard to believe that in late 1990s New York City, the shooting of Amadou Diallo would have become quite as noteworthy had the apparently racial assault on Abner Louima not occurred beforehand.

As chapter 5 argues, then, journalistic precedents exist for the media as they do for the law. However, the media's particular brand of objectivity tends to obscure the active role played by editors and reporters in selecting and shaping events, while the notion of legal precedent unabashedly admits the importance of judges' decisions and lawyers' arguments. Moreover, journalistic precedents apparently unfold in a dialectical relationship to one another and to public reactions. For instance, during and after the "Central Park jogger" case, journalists knew they were criticized for ignoring other assaults on minority women as well as rapes committed by white men. Consequently, it may not have been coincidental—though also not simply intentional—that high among the next most publicized crimes in New York City were three, "Bensonhurst," "Glen Ridge," and the "St. John's" rape case,[3] involving white defendants. This interrelatedness is not necessarily negative; on the contrary, that the public and media can influence one another, at least to some extent, bodes well for both. Rather, my point is that the notion of "objectivity" as developed throughout the twentieth century may have discouraged journalists from acknowledging their own role—and their "subjective" reactions as well—relative to the social world within which they, too, are unavoidably entwined.

But chapter 5 also investigated another tenet of conventional media philosophy: the practice of presenting "two sides to every story." In virtually every case discussed in this book, media coverage echoed the structural organization of the law. Yet I would argue that, while the legal system has good reason to maintain a dualistic framework to adjudicate matters of guilt or innocence, the press has less analogous justification for doing so. In principle, nothing prevents journalists from covering stories in more complex ways. Thus, provoking assaults might in future play out differently indeed if the coverage of them by the media is less simplistic than in the past. For instance, journalists who are conscious of the problem of enmeshment between cases and causes might highlight this very issue through more analytically oriented news coverage of future crime cases. Indeed, by helping to better distinguish between two-sided legal cases and more multifaceted social problems—a task consonant with the turn to "public journalism" that New York University media professor Jay Rosen has advocated[4]—provoking assaults might be better understood by wider publics as both helpful, and not helpful, for redressing those problems themselves.

Of course, other observers might respond that this suggestion would make American journalism too "intellectual" and possibly boring. It might be further argued by some that two-sided and "partialized" news presentations are more likely to "sell"; on this interpretation, oversimplicity is not the media's fault but the American public's desire. Yet one of the most striking observations that emerged from the nearly two hundred interviews I conducted was that dislike of the media was frequently aired, often by those who had nothing more in common with other interviewees. Certainly such dislike may relate to substitutive (or displaced) social-psychic dynamics spurred by provoking assaults, as discussed in chapter 6: to some extent, the media can be unjustly blamed for problems in American society that journalists had nothing to do with creating, and which they have limited powers themselves to redress.

On the other hand, the tendency toward two-sidedness as analyzed in chapter 5—for which journalists do bear some responsibility, and which is not an inevitable component of goods news coverage—may have also engendered a great deal of cynicism. In this respect, partialization may "sell papers" while breeding distrust, even disgust, that might also discourage sales. More specifically, news coverage that explicitly sought to communicate the multifaceted character of provoking assaults might have avoided some of the resentment that many members of different communities ended up feeling about perceived racial and ethnic stereotyping by the media. For instance, resentment was expressed by some members of the Portuguese community about unnecessary references to "Portuguese rapists" in the "New Bedford" case that inspired this book (see chapter 1). Similarly, many members of New York City's African American and Latino communities expressed concerns about biased coverage, including "wolf pack" references, in the "Central Park" jogger case. Some members of Indianapolis's African American community resented racially prejudicial terms used to describe Mike Tyson. In "Bensonhurst," many working-class whites were enraged by media references—and by the very "naming" of a case—that conflated an entire community with some young people's racist acts, and which were perceived as reactivating prejudices against Italian Americans. Certainly this anger did not help residents of Bensonhurst to look candidly at racism surrounding the crime, and some people's reactions to it, in their neighborhood.

By contrast, media coverage that sought self-consciously to emphasize the complexity of a story might reveal the range of views that frequently unfold within and outside the dominant narratives that form around the prosecution and the defense. Moreover, by distinguishing carefully between cases and the causes they come to represent, news reports—both reportage and news analyses—would be able to indicate that, in cases like "Central Park" or "O.J. Simpson," several kinds of social discriminations, not one "or" the other, are symbolically relevant. Of course, this alternative scenario does not mean that, if crime news were presented more multisidedly and analytically, any and all resentment of the media would magically disappear. The "messenger" with unhappy tidings is likely to still be greeted, to some extent, resentfully. Substitutive social-psychic dynamics would still sometimes emerge, unfairly channeling resentment at the press for problems not of its own making. Nonetheless, overall, the goal of enriching—rather than oversimplifying—the quality and intellectual level of American journalism is an extremely worthwhile one.

SOCIAL MOVEMENT AND COMMUNITY ACTIVISTS

Regarding public reactions, I have already summarized this book's argument about the role of high-profile crimes of the provoking assault variety in American culture. As chapter 6 also explains, this role brings with it the advantages of providing a cultural vehicle for "talking politics" as well as disadvantages that include the social-psychic dynamics detailed above. Turning now to the ramifications of this analysis for social movements, we may find that how activists respond to analyses like the one in this book affects media and legal responses as well.

I already showed how one possible stance toward the relationship between social movement issues and provoking assaults is to engage the media directly, seeing symbolic high-profile crime cases as a way to change cultural "commonsense." This was obviously the attitude explicitly taken by Al Sharpton and others in the context of New York City cases, and by numerous activists involved with Los Angeles cases. A second position, explained by activist Joe Hicks (see chapter 6) in regard to the "O.J. Simpson" case, was to avoid engaging with the media in an instance that had already become sensationalized. In Hicks's view of "Simpson," though not necessarily high-profile crimes in general, efforts to insert a complex set of considerations into media discourse about the case were likely to become oversimplified. Aware, in effect, of the pitfalls of partialization, Hicks was careful not to contribute to its development.

Still another approach is for movement activists to consciously capitalize on both the symbolic aspects of high-profile crimes while insisting there are limits on what can be accomplished this way. Thus commentators representing an array of social movements might direct the media's attention to both symbolic ramifications of a given instance and to the limitations of crime cases themselves for accomplishing social movement goals. Interestingly, in this scenario, journalistic coverage could become a focus of analytic discussion and potential politicization. Such media critique might include the problems bequeathed by partialization, especially since "either/or" two-sided coverage has an obviously divisive tendency to juxtapose various social concerns—such as gender versus racial, or racial versus class discrimination—against one another.

Moreover, to the extent that social movements deliberately treat provoking assaults "with a grain of salt," less faith may be placed in the legal process and less burden on the outcome of individual instances. Although symbolically meaningful, the resolution of a given case cannot be taken as a substitute for larger and more systemic changes. For instance, from the standpoint of movements and organizations concerned about racial equality, the outcome in the federal "Rodney King" case (in which the police officers who apparently battered King were found guilty) remedied the unfairness of the Simi Valley jury's verdict of acquittal. On the other hand, from the perspective of such movements and organizations, also important is that neither verdict was likely to significantly alter conditions for the "class" of people who experienced ongoing police harassment due to the color of their skin. Moreover, attention to more systemic critique might alter resentful reactions that currently tend to volley back and forth only within the two-sided framework of a legal case *per se*. Again, to the extent such angered reactions can be redirected at social causes directly—whether by changing media responses themselves or by pushing for greater resources to mitigate, gender, class, and racial inequalities in American society—social movements have something to gain from acting on the the "pros" and "cons" of high-profile crimes.

Provoking assaults of the 1980s and 1990s, then, produced common effects at the same time they wrought varied ramifications, depending on whose perspective was entailed. In the first years of the twenty-first century, events involving terrorism necessitated greater public attention than has lately been paid to the kinds of crime cases—from the "Central Park jogger" to "O.J. Simpson"—I investigated. Yet it is hard to imagine that some of the same social and cultural dynamics analyzed here will not reappear in years to come. Future incidents will evoke arguments that combine passion and logic; likely, they will bode individual and specific as well as broad social effects. But perhaps people will also rebel, little by little, from two-sided frameworks that can limit—as high-profile crimes show, sometimes inappropriately—our ability to perceive and create a different world.

Dates and Descriptions of Provoking Assaults

THE "CENTRAL PARK JOGGER" CASE

April 19, 1989: In New York City, a twenty-eight-year old white investment banker was violently raped, beaten, and left for dead while jogging in Central Park. As a result of the assault, the rape victim had no recollection of what occurred. The crime was attributed to a group of five male African American and Latino teenagers, accused of going on a crime spree that night (the media referred to their alleged actions as "wilding"). However, DNA evidence that confirmed the confession of a serial rapist later suggested that the group of teenagers had been wrongfully charged.

April 21, 1989: Defendants Antron McCray, Kevin Richardson, Raymond Santana, Yusef Salaam, and Kharey Wise were arrested.

April 23, 1989: Defendants were arraigned after making videotaped statements to police about their guilt.

August 18, 1990: McCray, Salaam, and Richardson were convicted of rape, robbery, and assault.

September 1990: Richardson was convicted of attempted murder, rape, sodomy, robbery, assault, and riot. Wise was convicted of assault, sexual abuse, and riot.

January 2002: DNA samples showed that serial rapist Mathias Reyes was at the scene; Reyes claimed to have committed the crime alone.

August 12, 2002: Kharey Wise was the final defendant to be released from prison.

The defense lawyers in the first "Central Park jogger" trial included Michael Joseph, Howard Diller, Peter Rivera, Jesse Berman, and Robert Burns (on appeal, William Kunstler took the case of Yusef Salaam). The lawyers for the prosecution were Elizabeth Lederer and Timothy Clements.

THE "BENSONHURST/YUSEF HAWKINS" CASE

August 23, 1989: In Bensonhurst, Brooklyn, a sixteen-year-old male, Yusef Hawkins, was shot to death by one of a group of approximately thirty mostly Italian

American male youth who surrounded Hawkins and his friends. Hawkins was mistaken for someone dating Gina Feliciano, a young woman in the neighborhood. Instead, Hawkins and three friends had traveled by subway to this neighborhood to answer an ad for a car that was for sale.

August 28, 1989: Activist Reverend Al Sharpton led African American protestors in protest march through the streets of Bensonhurst. Twenty-eight more Saturday marches were conducted.

Sept. 6, 1989: Joseph ("Joey") Fama was indicted on two counts of second-degree murder. Six other young men from Bensonhurst had also been arrested, including Keith Mondello, who was also indicted on murder charges.

April 17, 1990: The trial of Fama and Mondello opened in Brooklyn.

May 18, 1990: Joseph Fama was found guilty of second-degree murder.

May 19, 1990: Keith Mondello was acquitted of murder and manslaughter charges, but was convicted of twelve lesser charges including riot and weapons possession.

January 12, 1991: During another march through Bensonhurst, Sharpton was attacked and stabbed in the chest by Michael Ricciardi, who breached a police-secured zone.

1991: African American film director Spike Lee dedicated his film *Jungle Fever*, which fictionalized the theme of an interracial relationship between a married black man and a blue-collar Italian American woman, to Yusef Hawkins.

In the "Bensonhurst" case, David DiChiara defended Joseph Fama, and Stephen Murphy was the attorney hired to defend Keith Mondello. On the state's side, the case was prosecuted by a team of lawyers that included James Kohler and Ed Boyar.

THE "RODNEY KING" CASE

March 3, 1991: In Los Angeles, California, after drinking at the home of friend Bryant Allen, thirty-four-year-old African American Rodney King drove down the Freeway 210 with Allen in the backseat. When signaled to pull over by police, King sped up—possibly, as some later reported, to one hundred miles per hour. After a seven-mile car chase, King finally was stopped; the police delivered fifty baton blows and six kicks to King within a period of two minutes, producing eleven skull fractures, brain damage, and kidney damage. George Halliday videotaped this incident from a nearby balcony. This tape was replayed on the national nightly news and, on March 10, a *Los Angeles Times* poll reported that 92 percent of respondents thought "excessive force" had been used.

March 15, 1991: Sergeant Stacey C. Koon, Officer Laurence M. Powell, Officer Theodore Briseno, and Officer Timothy Wind were arraigned. On March 26, the policemen pled not guilty.

March 5, 1992: Following a venue change, a state trial began in Simi Valley, California.

April 29, 1992: An acquittal of all four officers was delivered by the Simi Valley jury; immediately following this verdict, several days of rioting ensued in Los Angeles during which 2,383 people were known to have been injured and 13,212 people were arrested.

August 15, 1992: Arraignment of the officers takes place for a new federal trial that was held in downtown Los Angeles.

April 17, 1993: Verdicts were delivered in the federal trial. Koon and Powell were convicted of violating Rodney King's civil rights; Briseno and Wind were acquitted

Among the lawyers involved in the Simi Valley state trial were Terry White for the prosecution and Michael Stone, the attorney for Larry Powell on the defense side of the case.

THE "REGINALD DENNY" CASE

April 29, 1992: Rioting in Los Angeles broke out after the "Rodney King" verdict was handed down by an all-white jury in Simi Valley. That afternoon, at the corner of Florence and Normandy in downtown Los Angeles, Reginald Denny, a white truck driver, was pulled from his truck and beaten. More than ninety bones in his face were broken. The assault was videotaped from a helicopter by a cameraman.

May 12, 1992: "The LA Four" (Damian Williams, Antoine Miller, Keith Watson, and Gary Williams) were arrested in the incident.

October 18, 1993: Keith Watson and Damian Williams were convicted.

December 7, 1993: Damian Williams was sentenced to ten years for the beating of Reginald Denny; Gary Williams was sentenced to three years in prison and Antoine Miller received probation.

Among the attorneys involved in the "Reginald Denny" case were Johnnie Cochran, who advised Reginald Denny; on the defense side, Edi Faal was the defense attorney for Damian Williams.

THE "WILLIAM KENNEDY SMITH" CASE

March 30, 1991: In West Palm Beach, Florida, medical student William Kennedy Smith, nephew of the late President John F. Kennedy and Senator Ted Kennedy, went to the nightclub Au Bar accompanied by Senator Kennedy and his son Patrick. There Smith met a woman who was a local community college student. At 3:30 A.M., the woman drove Smith back to the Kennedy estate in West Palm Beach where he was staying. She agreed to go for a walk along the beach, but claimed that Smith had raped her. The woman reported the incident to the sheriff later that morning.

May 11, 1991: Kennedy Smith was arrested for misdemeanor battery and second degree sexual battery.

December 2, 1991: Kennedy Smith's trial began. The trial judge refused to allow testimony from three other women who claimed that Smith had attacked them as well.

December 23, 1991: Three weeks after the beginning of the trial in which both the woman and Smith testified, the jury deliberated for less than eighty minutes before returning a verdict of not guilty. Since then, several other women have come forward to say that Kennedy attacked them.

Kennedy Smith was represented at this trial by the nationally known, Miami-based criminal defense attorney Roy Black; the prosecutor in the case was Moira Lasch, an experienced attorney who had won the Florida Prosecutor of the Year Award in 1987.

THE "MIKE TYSON" CASE

July 18, 1991: In Indianapolis, Indiana, heavyweight champion boxer Mike Tyson and an eighteen-year-old beauty pageant contestant met at a pageant rehearsal, returning to his hotel room at 2:00 A.M.

July 22, 1991: A formal complaint of rape was filed against Mike Tyson.

September 9, 1991: Tyson was indicted on rape charges by a special grand jury.

January 27, 1992: Tyson's trial began in Indianapolis.

February 10, 1992: Tyson was found guilty on one count of rape and two counts of deviant sexual conduct.

July 1992: Tyson was sentenced to ten years, four of them suspended. Tyson hired high-profile attorney Alan Dershowitz to handle his case on appeal.

January 1993: Dershowitz filed an appeal brief with the Indiana Court of Appeals.

August 1993: By a 2–1 vote, the Indiana Court of Appeals upheld Tyson's conviction. Dershowitz filed an appeal with the Indiana Supreme Court.

September 1993: The Indiana Supreme Court denied Tyson's appeal without comment.

Among the lawyers involved in the "Mike Tyson" case, when originally tried in Indianapolis, were Greg Garrison on the side of the prosecution and James Voyles (as local counsel); Vincent Fuller and Kathleen Beggs were on the defense side of the case. Alan Dershowitz argued Tyson's case on appeal.

THE "O.J. SIMPSON" CASE

June 12, 1993: In Brentwood, California, Nicole Brown Simpson and her friend Ronald Goldman were murdered outside her condominium. On June 13, the bodies were discovered by neighbors and O.J. Simpson, who was in Chicago, flew back to Los Angeles where police detained him for questioning. No formal arrest was made.

June 17, 1993: Simpson was charged with two counts of murder; instead of surrendering, he led police on a low-speed, sixty-mile pursuit in a friend's white Ford Bronco.

January 24, 1995: The criminal trial opened in downtown Los Angeles.

March 15, 1995: LAPD officer Mark Fuhrman denied using racist remarks.

October 3, 1995: O.J. Simpson was found not guilty on two counts of murder.

October 23, 1995: The civil trial opened in Santa Monica, California.

February 4, 1997: In the civil case, a jury found Simpson liable and ordered him to pay $8.5 million in damages.

At the criminal trial, the case was prosecuted by Marcia Clarke and Christopher Dardens; on the defense side was a "dream team" of lawyers that included Johnnie Cochran, Barry Scheck, Alan Dershowitz, and Robert Shapiro.

Identifying the Top Twenty High-Profile Crimes, 1985–1996

The tables below are results of index studies I performed to identify the top twenty crimes as reported by the print media in New York City, Los Angeles, and nationwide from 1985 to 1996. I derived results by counting the number of articles that appeared under the categories of crimes (listed under tables 1 and 2) in indexes of the *New York Times* and the *Los Angeles Times*, respectively. I then used these results, and those obtained from a similar count using indexes of the *Chicago Tribune* and the "Allnews" category of Lexis-Nexis, as a basis for determining which crime cases were referred to most frequently in 135 small and large newspapers across the United States between 1985 and 1996.

TABLE 1. The *New York Times* Top Twenty Crime Cases, 1985–1996

1. O.J. Simpson	753
2. Howard Beach	306
3. Rodney King	252
4. John Gotti	257
5. Charles Keating	226
6. Michael Milken	211
7. Bensonhurst—Yusuf Hawkins	196
8. Central Park jogger	193
9. Tawana Brawley	176
10. Stanley Friedman	148
11. Joel Steinberg	155
12. Tonya Harding	134
13. Crown Heights	126

14. William Kennedy Smith	122
15. Glen Ridge	119
16. Tailhook	107
17. Bernhard Goetz	106
18. Leona Helmsley	105
19. Mike Tyson	100
20. Jeffrey Dahmer	<100

The numbers represent the total mentions of well-publicized individual crime cases as found in the *New York Times Index* for the years 1985–96, after scanning for the following categories: Assaults, Child Abuse, Burglary, Computer Crime, Corporate Crime, Crime and Criminals, Corruption, Ethics, Murders and Attempted Murders, Organized Crimes, Police (and Police Brutality where applicable), Political Corruption where found (which led to New York City Politics and Government), Rape, Sex Crimes, Sexual Harassment, and White Collar Crime. Not all of these categories were used in the index in a given year, but I checked each category for each year in case relevant information appeared. It is also important to note that certain kinds of crimes do not appear in the categories one might initially expect. This applies to organized crime cases, usually found under "Crime and Criminals" and "Murders and Attempted Murders," and to police brutality, which is listed under "Police." In addition, I searched for certain cases that seemed glaringly absent from the index study's initial results because they had been categorized elsewhere. For instance, the "Michael Milken" case, which featured in the savings and loan scandals of the late 1980s, appears under "Stocks and Bonds" and the "Charles Keating" case under "Banks and Banking," despite the huge amount of coverage they received. "Rodney King" appears under "Police."

TABLE 2. The *Los Angeles Times* Top Twenty Crime Cases, 1985–1996

1. O.J. Simpson	1,260
2. Rodney King	515
3. McMartin—child abuse	258
4. Menendez brothers	253
5. Michael Milken	185
6. Reginald Denny	142
7. Charles Keating	141
8. Night Stalker—Ramirez	70
9. Heidi Fleiss	70
10. Bernhard Goetz	66

11. Michael Jackson	64
12. Mayor Tom Bradley—corruption	62
13. Tonya Harding	61
14. William Kennedy Smith	59
15. Mike Tyson	43
16. Riverside, Cal.—videotaped beating of Mexican illegal immigrants	42
17. Tailhook	39
18. Nate Holden—sexual harassment (race)	32
19. Latasha Harlins	27
20. Billionaire Boys Club	26

As in table 1, the numbers represent the total mentions of high-profile crimes as found in the *Los Angeles Times Index* for the years 1985–96, after having scanned for the following categories: Assaults, Child Abuse, Commuter Crime, Corporate Crime, Corruption in Government, Crime, Domestic Violence, Gangs (a large category in the *Los Angeles Times Index*), Murders and Attempted Murders, Organized Crime, Police and Police Brutality, Rape, Sex Crimes, Sexual Harassment, White Collar Crime. Some of these categories appear some years and not others, but I have checked each category for each year to avoid missing major crime cases. Several crimes are listed under the name of the defendant, and may be cross-referenced in another category as well (this was true, for instance, for the "William Kennedy Smith," "Mike Tyson," and "Michael Jackson" cases). In certain instances, one only finds a given case listed under the defendant's name (this was true, for instance, of the "Michael Milken" and "Charles Keating" cases).

TABLE 3. Top Twenty Crime Cases as Reported Nationwide, 1985–1996

1. O.J. Simpson	103,589
2. Rodney King	25,190
3. Mike Tyson	9,864
4. Michael Milken	9,229
5. Tonya Harding	7,771
6. Charles Keating	7,679
7. Jeffrey Dahmer	7,295
8. William Kennedy Smith	7,178
9. Lorena Bobbitt	5,535
10. Reginald Denny	5,512

11. Tailhook	5,324
12. John Gotti	5,023
13. Howard Beach	5,004
14. Claus Von Bulow	4,386
15. Bernhard Goetz	4,319
16. Menendez brothers	3,677
17. Tawana Brawley	2,913
18. Michael Jackson	2,837
19. Bensonhurst	2,300
20. Central Park jogger	2,076

These findings were derived by running on the "Allnews" category of Lexis-Nexis the results obtained from the *New York Times*, *Los Angeles Times*, and *Chicago Tribune* index studies.

Acknowledging Intellectual Debts and Distinctions

To place this book in the larger intellectual context from which I drew inspiration, a number of other approaches to studying crime cases both sociologically and historically should be mentioned. As for sociological works, previous studies of high-profile crimes have tended to consider crime cases either somewhat more narrowly or more broadly than this work. For instance, commercial treatments have focused on the "Howard Beach," "Central Park jogger," "Bensonhurst," "Rodney King," and "O.J. Simpson" cases.[1] Other works have alluded to high-profile crime cases in the context of cultural criticism, but without giving particular incidents detailed scrutiny. For example, Murray Edelman's *Constructing the Spectacle* examined the role of media in creating symbolic cultural events; edited collections of shorter works have analyzed individual instances like the "Anita Hill," "William Kennedy Smith," and "Jeffrey Dahmer" cases, but under the broad rubric of "media spectacles."[2]

Other studies have approached highly profiled incidents by focusing on topics other than the cases themselves. For instance, sociologist Alphonse Pinckney targeted American racism as manifested through the "Howard Beach" and other late 1980s New York City cases.[3] Darnell Hunt thoroughly investigated media constructions of the social world, and diverse public reactions to "the media," in a superb study of the "O.J. Simpson" case.[4] A volume on media coverage of the "Simpson" case edited by Gregg Barak was also very useful for this project.[5] Legal scholar George Fletcher explored public outcries sympathetic to victims in the 1990s as expressed through a range of high-profile crime cases including "Rodney King," "Yankel Rosenbaum," "Mike Tyson," and "William Kennedy Smith."[6] In *A Woman Scorned: Acquaintance Rape on Trial*, anthropology professor Peggy Reeves Sanday focused on the 1991 "St. John's" case—highly publicized in New York City after the "Central Park jogger" and "Bensonhurst" cases, but also occurring around the same time as the "William Kennedy Smith," "Clarence Thomas," and "Mike Tyson" cases—to explore problems encountered by rape victims.[7] Journalism professor Helen Benedict used the "New Bedford," "Robert Chambers/Jennifer Levin," and "Central Park jogger" high-profile cases as examples of taken-for-granted sexism among reporters who covered "sex crimes" from the late 1970s through the 1980s.[8] However, it was not these authors' aim to explore how symbolic crime cases themselves emerge through the interactive participation of parties in the media, the public, and the legal system.

Specific works that explore the practices and mind-sets of each group of actors were extremely helpful for this work. Regarding the media, a rich "sociology of news" based on ethnographies of newspapers and television stations aided in assessing how journalists operate under short deadlines and competitive pressures. Studies by Herbert Gans, Gaye Tuchman, and Mark Fishman provided valuable insight into journalists' typical perspectives on the world.[9] In contrast to these works, though, this book also examines outside parties' views of the media, including the perspectives of social movement activists. Again, ensuing case studies suggest that journalists' practices are affected by such criticism in ways that may belie their professed commitment to objectivity and that appears to influence selection processes in future cases that become highly profiled. Consequently, this book attempts to provide a dynamic account of relationships between the media and the public as they unfold through ongoing controversies over crime cases.

This emphasis on ongoing, dialectic interaction also differentiates *Provoking Assaults* from studies that did focus on media relationships with other social actors. In *The Whole World Is Watching: Mass Media in the Making and Unmaking of the New Left*, Todd Gitlin argued that media coverage influenced the history of Students for a Democratic Society (SDS). According to Gitlin, a destructive combination of media attention and organizational in-fighting contributed to this New Left group's decline in the late 1960s.[10] Less well-known in the United States is a classic work of British criminology even more germane to studying American high-profile cases. Although Stuart Hall et al.'s *Policing the Crisis* relied on newspaper texts and theoretical analysis more than interview data, its authors thoroughly investigated the role of the judiciary and the state, not just the media, in generating a "moral panic" over crime in Great Britain.[11] Hall and his colleagues contended that collective anxieties about "mugging," a term imported from the United States, distracted attention from underlying and more implacable socioeconomic problems facing Britain in the early 1970s.[12] The concept of moral panics is one for which I am indebted, particularly insofar as it provides important insight into how an issue can suddenly become perceived as an urgent social problem through media coverage, even though that problem existed long beforehand. Moral panics also tend to be short-lived as moments during which public anxieties are at their height; their tendency to dissipate also helps explain why the effects of provoking assaults may not be long-lasting.

But the present study differs from these works, too, in that neither Gitlin nor Hall et al. investigated the possibility that media coverage might create unintended consequences not necessarily helpful for the press's own social image and power. The *Whole World is Watching* argued that SDS was virtually destroyed by journalistic intercession, and *Policing the Crisis* that the press succeeded in deflecting attention from deeper societal dilemmas. However, precisely because the present work stresses mutual interaction between media and publics, it implies tensions between actors that are likely to be ongoing for both. Provoking assaults conflate legal cases with social causes; they may bequeath "left over" dissatisfactions in the wake of only partially satisfying verdicts. Consequently, I argue that vestigial resentments underlay the public's efforts to keep high-profile crime cases alive. In studying crime cases of the 1980s and 1990s, the media's hold on American culture emerges as at once mighty and restricted; "the media" often evokes strong emotions from the public, sometimes being blamed for problems not entirely of its own creation.

Regarding public reactions, sociologists have demonstrated both these strengths and limitations of media effects; many studies have used focus groups to concretize cultural theories of reception. For instance, in *Talking Politics*, William Gamson conducted in-depth discussions to investigate public reactions to media coverage, particularly as these reactions revealed potential for collective change. One of three "collective action" frames viewers brought to news coverage was "injustice." Relevant to the present study is Gamson's conclusion, based on these focus groups, that Americans' views on a wide range of subjects are more socially oriented than many media characterizations suggest.[13]

Other sociological studies of reception focused on crime cases specifically. For example, in Britain, R. Emerson Dobash and Russell R. Dobash showed that women's fear of crime varied according to whether female television viewers had been victimized themselves[14]; among the popular cultural "texts" discussed by women in focus groups was the film adapted from the New Bedford case, *The Accused*. To study fear of crime in the United States, Esther Madriz conducted focus groups among African American, Latino, and white women in the early 1990s. She found that even though women faced greater chances of violent victimization from acquaintances, many feared assaults by strangers more; several women cited the "Central Park jogger" case as a symbolic marker that increased their fears.[15] Darnell Hunt studied African American, Latino, and white viewers' reactions to television coverage of the 1992 Los Angeles riots. This coverage depicted events in polarized terms of "black" and "white," and failed to report that more than half of those arrested in the aftermath of protests were Latino.[16] Each of these studies showed that even where media depictions of violent crimes were skewed, public reactions nevertheless displayed rich variety.

Like ethnographies of journalists, though, reception studies usually center only on one group—audiences—rather than on interaction between several sets of actors. (Hunt's study of reactions to the Los Angeles riots, though, did analyze interactions between viewing public and the media.) In general, little is heard from journalists themselves about why and how they came to construct crime stories simplistically or speciously. Moreover, while the work of Gitlin and Hall et al. did not take public criticisms of the media much into account, reception studies tend to veer in the opposite direction. Emphasis is placed on reacting publics' power to "resist" media influences, regardless of whether these reactions lead to changes in how the media actually works. By contrast, I document in this book how reacting publics, journalists, and representatives of the legal system become caught up in larger social, economic, and cultural processes only partly of their own makings; for example, partialization affects them all. This approach has the advantage of revealing how media and public actors tend to blame one another for problems they experience.

Regarding the role of the legal system, I was influenced by previous studies of popular and political trials. Among other writers, Hariman, Gewirtz, Minow, and Levinson imaginatively used rhetoric and literary criticism to analyze well-known court cases.[17] Several studies in this vein have explored the wide range of feelings, from anger to pleasure, which are expressed through narrative identifications in the courtroom;[18] others studies attest simply to growing interest in using narrative and storytelling to enrich the sociology of law.[19] Unlike many studies of news producers and audience reactions, this literature does emphasize interactive dynamics; it draws on trial transcripts and media texts to document diverse parties' "voices." While these studies were helpful, I rely heavily on the use of interviews, presuming that valuable insight can be gained from talking with those actually engaged with high-profile crime cases.

This book is linked to but different from other studies of crime cases in historical ways as well. Let me return to an important question raised earlier: What exactly distinguishes provoking assaults from other famous crime cases of other eras and places? One factor has to do with what provoking assaults are not: they are distinguishable from "political trials," which, according to Theodore Becker, occur when "members of a ruling elite believe a particular individual or group to be imminently hostile."[20] The trial of the Rosenbergs for treason in 1951 is a clear case on point. American political trials have also involved defendants' explicit use of courtrooms to publicize causes for which they claim to have been unjustly arrested. The 1968 trial of the "Chicago Seven" provides a good example, in which arrested activists proclaimed that the state was the criminal party at fault, and that they had acted in principled opposition against the Vietnam War.[21]

Yet political trials studied in this tradition diverge from provoking assaults in a number of ways. Whereas 1960s trials often involved explicit use of courtrooms for political purposes, provoking assaults of the 1980s and 1990s featured violence between individuals. Accused parties in provoking assaults did not explicitly challenge the state by committing crimes: perpetrators did not commit violent acts to make political points; nor were they using trials thereafter for the conscious goal of galvanizing social movements. Moreover, violent crimes alleged or committed were agreed, virtually universally, to be wrong; parties accused of rape, assault, or murder, and their sympathizers, found themselves squarely on the defensive in a way that "victims" of the state might not have.

Closest to provoking assaults, though, are what Lisa Cuklanz calls a new genre of "issue-oriented" trials. Cuklanz describes this genre as reflecting "specific issues that were brought to the fore by social movements"; moreover, some issue-oriented trials "involve issues of cultural politics that pit one subcultural group against another and are indirectly related to social change."[22] Even though Cuklanz herself focused on three cases that stimulated controversies about rape and rape reform laws between

1978 and 1985 — the "Rideout" case (involving marital rape), the "New Bedford" rape case, and the "Gary Dotson" case—she also alludes to the "Central Park jogger" and "Bensonhurst" cases in New York, and the "Rodney King" and "Latasha Harlins" cases in Los Angeles as examples of issue-oriented trials that did not involve gender *per se*. However, Cuklanz distinguishes between issue-oriented trials and celebrity cases like "William Kennedy Smith," "Mike Tyson," and (by extension of her analysis) "O.J. Simpson."[23] In this respect, her analytic framework is different than mine insofar as I treat celebrity cases as a subset of the larger category of provoking assaults. Cuklanz's contends that celebrity cases bring substantive issues to the fore only secondarily; fundamentally, she argues, these cases are about personality and the merging of news with entertainment. My sense, however, is that a cultural phenomenon was building through the 1980s and 1990s that blurred distinctions between celebrity and issue-oriented cases as vehicles of American political discourse. Certain common themes (for example, the playing of gender against race) eventually interconnected noncelebrity cases like "Central Park" with celebrity trials like "Mike Tyson" and "O.J. Simpson." Similarly, media and legal connections were drawn from "Rodney King" to "O.J. Simpson"; as these relationships unfolded, the former case influenced the latter's becoming interwoven with "serious" issues bequeathed through previous discussions of racial politics.

Despite their clearly agreed-upon differences from political trials, though, provoking assaults became social causes nevertheless. This suggests that, by the 1980s and 1990s, activists were making some of their claims relatively more indirectly than in the 1960s. They may have used violent crimes that were both hateful in character and universally agreed to be wrong, to crystallize points about ongoing forms of discrimination in American society.[24] Moreover, precisely because provoking assaults entail an indirectly politicized form, defense mechanisms may have come into play within group-based situations (see chapter 6). Here, my intention has been to appropriate Freudian defense mechanisms for specifically sociological usages. For an ongoing problem with the psychoanalytic tradition has been its application of such mechanisms in the effort to understand individuals'—rather than groups'—unconscious motivations.[25] In this respect, too, transcending the immediate topic of 1980s and 1990s high-profile crime cases *per se*, the present study is both influenced by and different from related works in the literatures just surveyed.

NOTES

PREFACE

1. See E. McLaughlin and K. Murji, "Ways of Seeing: Newmedia Reporting of Racist Violence," in M. May, ed., *Understanding Social Problems* (Oxford: Blackwell, 2000); B. Cathcart, *The Case of Stephen Laurence* (London: Viking, 1999).

1: WHEN CASES BECOME CAUSES

1. Interview, Roy Black, August 15, 1992, lawyer for William Kennedy Smith and William Lozano, two high-profile crime cases involving rape and police brutality, respectively.

2. Interview, Al Sharpton, September 1, 1993, activist and organizer of protests in the "Howard Beach," "Central Park jogger," and other high-profile crime cases.

3. See Richard Simon, "Anglo Vote Carried Riordan to Victory," *Los Angeles Times*, June 10, 1993, A25. The article mentions a poll at the time indicating that racial divisions affected Woo's defeat and Riordan's victory; it refers to reactions in a "city that went up in flames" when rioting broke out in Los Angeles following the 1992 acquittal of police officers in Simi Valley for assaulting Rodney King.

4. See in this tradition, for example, Joseph R. Grusfield, *The Culture of Social Problems* (Chicago: University of Chicago Press, 1981); Joel Best, *Images of Issues: Typifying Contemporary Social Problems* (New York: Aldine de Gruyter, 1995).

5. Spurious distinctions between the "theoretical" and the "empirical" have been carefully analyzed in the work of Pierre Bourdieu and, more recently, in that of sociologist Robert Alford. See, in particular, Pierre Bourdieu, *Outline of a Theory of Practice* (New York: Cambridge University Press, 1977), and *The Logic of Practice* (Cambridge: Polity Press, 1990); Robert Alford, *The Craft of Inquiry: Theory, Methods, Evidence* (New York: Oxford University Press, 1998).

6. Detailed descriptions of these cases are found in works devoted specifically to the topic of "political trials." See, e.g., *Political Trials*, ed. Theodore Becker (Indianapolis: Bobbs Merrill, 1971); Ron Christenson, *Political Trials: Gordian Knots in the Law*

(New Brunswick, N.J.: Transaction Publishers, 1989), and Andrew David, *Famous Political Trials* (Minneapolis: Lerner Publications, 1980). For a detailed account of the "Dreyfus" case in particular, see Robert L. Hoffman, *More Than a Trial: The Struggle Over Captain Dreyfus* (New York: Free Press, 1980). For chronicles of the other cases mentioned in the text, see Philip S. Foner, *The Case of Joe Hill* (New York: International Publishers, 1970); Dan T. Carter, *Scottsboro: A Tragedy of the American South* (New York: Vintage Books, 1994); Stephen J. Whitfield, *A Death in the Delta: The Story of Emmett Till* (Baltimore: Johns Hopkins University Press, 1988).

7. Kathleen Maguire and Ann L. Pastore, eds., *Sourcebook of Criminal Justice Statistics 2002*, available at www.albany.edu/sourcebook, table 2.1 (accessed June 9, 2004). With more specific regard to New York City, around the time that the "Central Park jogger" and "Bensonhurst" cases exploded into press coverage, see, e.g., Rex Smith, "Survey: Crime Fear High," *Newsweek*, January 6, 1989, 9, and "Living in Fear: 1 of 2 is a Victim of Crime," first in a *City on the Brink* series, *Newsday*, August 13, 1989.

8. As Kathleen Beckett writes in *Making Crime Pay: Law and Order in Contemporary American Politics* (New York: Oxford, 1997), "the most recent anticrime campaign (1993–1994) occurred as the reported crime rate plummeted and in the absence of widespread unrest" (p. 27).

9. See Stuart L. Hills's introduction to *Corporate Violence* (Lanham, Md.: Rowman and Littlefield, 1987).

10. An excellent description of this "toughening" criminal justice environment can be found in chapter 2 of Michael Tonry's *Thinking about Crime: Sense and Sensibility in American Penal Culture* (New York: Oxford University Press, 2004).

11. See Susan Faludi, *Backlash: The Undeclared War against American Women* (New York: Crown, 1991).

12. See Stephen Steinberg, *Turning Back: The Retreat from Racial Justice in American Thought and Policy* (Boston: Beacon Press, 1995).

13. See Michael Schudson, *The Power of News* (Cambridge: Harvard University Press, 1995).

14. See Lynn S. Chancer, "Playing Gender against Race through High Profile Crime Cases: The Tyson/Thomas/Simpson Patter of the 1990s," *Violence against Women* 4(1) (February 1998).

15. See Kimberle Crenshaw, "Whose Story Is It Anyway? Feminist and Antiracist Appropriations of Anita Hill, in Toni Morrison, ed., *Race-ing Justice, En-Gendering Power: Essays on Anita Hill, Clarence Thomas, and the Construction of Social Reality* (New York: Pantheon Books, 1992), 402–36.

16. Jessie Mangaliman and Jeremy Qittner, "Iron Mike's a No-Show," *New York Times*, June 20, 1955, A4.

17. For example, see the account of changes in rape laws that resulted from feminist intervention in Linda A. Fairstein, *Sexual Violence: Our War against Rape* (New York: William Morrow, 1993).

18. The two coasts were also linked, for example, by Sharpton's going to Los Angeles to lead a 1991 march protesting the beating of Rodney King.

19. Interview, Leo Wilensky, August 16, 1994.

20. See Lynn S. Chancer, "New Bedford, Massachusetts, March 6, 1983 –March 22, 1984: The 'Before' and 'After' of a Group Rape," *Gender and Society* 1 (1987): 239–60.

21. Ibid.

22. In September 1988, in the middle of the period of my research and soon before the "Central Park jogger" case, advertisers designated New York City the most important area of media influence in the nation with 7 million households (or 7.7% of the nation), annual gross income exceeding $266 billion, and gross media expenditures totaling over $114 billion. See Amy Alson, "Big Apple Ink," *Marketing and Media* 23(9) (September 1988): 74.

23. Although my interest had been piqued by highly profiled crimes in the major urban contexts of New York City and Los Angeles, I also decided to investigate cases that had achieved distinctly local as well as national notoriety. Because New York and Los Angeles are media centers, some overlap existed between the most well-known "local" cases and those accorded most national attention. A number of New York City and Los Angeles cases had attracted both local and national attention; other cases had become well-known subjects of national discussion apart from their relationship to distinctly local issues.

24. For exact dates, see openings to chapters 1 and 3, respectively.

25. Although I included the "Simpson" case as the seventh instance to which I devoted detailed attention, I did not presume at the time that it would amount to the "trial of the century." Another hypothesis is that the tremendous amount of attention given to the "Simpson" case may have manifested cultural interest in high-profile crime cases that had been brewing for over a decade. Years before the famous double murder's occurrence, high-profile crime cases had clearly generated comparisons of cases in a local and national contexts, and were already becoming established as a "larger" cultural phenomenon throughout the 1980s and 1990s.

26. Note that I omitted the "Michael Milken" and "Charles Keating" cases, evidently also accorded extraordinary national attention during the same period (again, see Appendix A). Though they involved savings and loan ("S&L") bank scandals these cases, too, were often interconnected in media-generated references. While detailed examination of these cases was prevented by their trials and publicity extending across nearly a decade, I also decided to exclude them because, unlike the other cases analyzed here, they were not violent crimes committed by individuals against other individuals. Nor did these instances generate organized protest by social movement activists, or produce the kind of debate about the implications of their class-based disparities as other cases had produced regarding racial and gender-based biases. However, while not fully investigated here, this book raises questions beyond its own purview about why class-related crimes like the Milken and Keating cases do not become "provocative" by the criteria already outlined.

27. At the time I was studying the New York City cases, the *Daily News* had the largest local circulation of any of the four dailies then in operation, including the *New York Times* (see Laurence Zuckerman, "The Last Stand of the Tabloids: As Newspaper

Competition Declines Nationwide, Three New York City Papers Slug it Out for Survival," *Time*, March 13, 1989). In Indianapolis and Palm Beach, the newspapers I selected were also the most well known and widely circulated in their vicinities.

28. I interviewed many of the same parties engaged through the media, the law and in public roles on three separate occasions. One set of interviews took place at the end of summer 1994, after the crime had first been committed; a second set of interviews took place during Simpson's 1995 criminal trial; and I conducted a third set of interviews with the same parties soon after this Simpson jury's verdict. For obvious reasons research into the Simpson case did not, at that time, include the judge, lawyers or jurors; here immediacy was a disadvantage since, in other cases, legal participants generously acceded to interviews in part because trials had concluded years before.

29. An important exception to this is found in the work of the Frankfurt School, especially Erich Fromm's discussion of specifically social defense mechanisms in *Escape from Freedom* (New York: Holt, Rinehart, and Winston, 1941). More recently, see also Wilfred Bion, *Experience in Groups and Other Papers* (New York: Basic Books, 1961).

2: THE RAPE OF THE CENTRAL PARK JOGGER

1. In December 2002, five convictions that resulted from the original prosecution of the "Central Park jogger" case in 1989 were vacated by a New York City judge on the basis of Mathias Reyes's confession that he had acted alone. Reyes's confession was confirmed by DNA evidence, which was not available in 1989 and 1990.

2. Helen Benedict, *Virgin or Vamp: How the Press Covers Sex Crimes* (New York: Oxford University Press, 1992), 191.

3. Ibid.

4. Ibid., 190.

5. That detectives knew the victim was white was confirmed in an off-the-record interview with a police official.

6. Timothy Sullivan, *Unequal Verdicts: The Central Park Jogger Trials* (New York: Simon and Schuster, 1992), 22.

7. Interview, Elizabeth Lederer, June 23, 1993.

8. Don Terry, "A Week of Rapes: The Jogger and 28 Not in the News," *New York Times*, May 29, 1989, 25.

9. Interview, Linda Fairstein, September 12, 1994.

10. Stuart Marques, "Park Marauders Call it Wilding," *Daily News*, April 22, 1989, 1–3.

11. Betty Liu Ebron, "No Repression of Rap after Rape-Case Singing," *Daily News*, April 22, 1989, 6.

12. Interview, Emily Sachar, June 28, 1993.

13. Interview, Lizette Alvarez, June 9, 1993.

14. See Lynn S. Chancer, "O.J. Simpson and the Trial of the Century? Uncovering Paradoxes in Media Coverage," in *Representing O.J.: Murder, Criminal Justice and Mass Culture*, ed. Gregg Barak (New York: Harrow and Heston, 1996).

15. Interview, reporter on the "Central Park jogger" case, September 26, 1994.

16. See the section later in chapter 3 concerning the media coverage of the "Bensonhurst" case for a discussion of the rape of an African American woman in Brooklyn. Also see Harold L. Jamison, "Another Woman Raped and Strangled to Death: Police Have No Suspects, Motive for Killing," Amsterdam News, May, 1989, regarding yet another violent crime against a woman of color that the New York Times did not initially cover.

17. See Herbert J. Gans, Deciding What's News (New York: Random House, 1979), 183.

18. Tuchman wrote two well-known articles in which she summarized her observations about journalists' everyday practices. See Gaye Tuchman, "Making News by Doing Work: Routinizing the Unexpected," American Journal of Sociology 79 (1973): 110–31, and "Objectivity as Strategic Ritual: An Examination of Newsmen's Notions of Objectivity," American Journal of Sociology 77 (1972): 660–79.

19. Stuart Hall, Chas Critcher, Tony Jefferson, John Clarke, and Brian Roberts, Policing the Crisis: Mugging, the State, and Law and Order (London: Macmillan, 1978), 106; see also the chapter titled "Balancing Accounts."

20. See Todd Gitlin, The Whole World Is Watching: Mass Media in the Making and Unmaking of the New Left (Berkeley: University of California Press, 1980), 27–28, where Gitlin discusses his overall observations about typical media processes.

21. The Edmund Perry case was less likely to generate outraged reactions since circumstances surrounding it were less clear-cut than in the consequent "Howard Beach" case. Whereas white youths had obviously assaulted Michael Griffith and chased him to his death, Perry's brother may have been engaged in a robbery. See Robert Ansen, Best Intentions: The Education and Killing of Edmund Perry (New York: Random House, 1987), 6.

22. This finding is based on an extensive search using the New York Times index for 1986 and 1987. See table 1 in appendix B for the number of articles written about this case between 1985 and 1996.

23. Media references to Sharpton, Maddox, and Mason were too extensive to list here. Note, though, the mention of their role in three books written from quite different perspectives: the introduction to Jim Sleeper, The Closest of Strangers: Liberalism and the Politics of Race in New York (New York: Norton, 1990); Charles J. Hynes and Bob Drury, Incident at Howard Beach: The Case for Murder (New York: Putnam, 1990), esp. ch. 6; and the chapter on "Contemporary Black Politics" in Charles Green and Basil Wilson, The Struggle for Black Empowerment in New York City: Beyond the Politics of Pigmentation (New York: McGraw Hill, 1992), 108–10.

24. See the description of the 1986 "Chambers" case, as it was popularly referred to in the media, in Helen Benedict, Virgin or Vamp (New York: Oxford, 1991): 147–48.

25. At the time, it was felt that Fairstein had lost the "Chambers" case. In Benedict's account (ibid.), she argues at least as strongly that Chambers's lawyer, Jack Litman, had won by successfully depicting Jennifer Levin as a "bad girl." See Benedict's

account of Linda Fairstein's role in the trial, ibid., 175–84, esp. 181, where she recounts anger over the "lightness" of Chamber's sentence.

26. It also sustained the pattern of continuous variation in another sense. Whereas anger was provoked by the "Tawana Brawley" case, insofar as proof that the rape had actually taken place was elusive (and, in the end, a grand jury pronounced that the rape had been a fraud), in the "Central Park" case the presence of a young woman's badly battered and sexually assaulted body left no doubt that a crime had actually occurred.

27. Within the brief history of high-profile cases already summarized, the "Central Park jogger" case was the only incident in which a group of minority youth had violently assaulted a white woman; other cases came close, but none were, strictly speaking, the same.

28. Lynn S. Chancer, "O.J. Simpson and the Trial of the Century? Uncovering Paradoxes in Media Coverage," in *Representing O.J.: Murder, Criminal Justice and Mass Culture*, ed. Gregg Barak (New York: Harrow and Heston, 1996), 86.

29. Some reporters and editors are willing to admit to this practice, however, without thinking it is controversial. This book overall argues that "objectivity" has become increasingly difficult to maintain, particularly when reporting the sorts of high-profile cases explored here.

30. Craig Wolff, "Youths Rape and Beat Central Park Jogger," *New York Times*, April 21, 1989, B1.

31. E.g.,"Wolf Pack's Prey," *Daily News*, April 21, 1989, 1–3, 29.

32. Ibid. See also Denis Hamili, "Like Bambi, in Hunting Season," *Newsday*, April 21, 1989, 4; Jimmy Breslin, "Violence in the Night Grabs Lone Jogger," *Newsday*, April 21, 1989, 4.

33. Editorial, "Juvenile Delinquency Does Not Apply," *Daily News*, April 22, 1989, 11.

34. Mike McAlary, "A Song That Didn't Make Hearts Sing," *Daily News*, April 30, 1989, 2.

35. Mark Kriegel, "Lived a Dream Life," *Daily News*, April 21, 1989, 2.

36. Interview, reporter, June 28, 1993.

37. Interview, *Daily News* reporter, June 28, 1993. But note that such language was not being used to describe the acts of white youths; in looking back over the coverage of "Howard Beach," for example, this language does not appear in any of the papers, even though the case involved a murder of a black by a group of whites.

38. Interview, Lizette Alvarez, June 9, 1993.

39. I make the same point with respect to all the "provoking assaults" considered in this book—namely, that indignant public reactions are a key contributing factor to the evolution of high-profile cases into provoking assaults.

40. See Jurgen Habermas, *The Structural Transformations of the Public Sphere: An Inquiry into a Category of Bourgeois Society* (Cambridge: MIT Press, 1994), esp. 158–75, 181–235. Habermas does not see this transformation as a positive development, but rather one that "administers" debates in a process of breaking down previous separations be-

tween "private" and "public" spheres. Whether viewed negatively or positively, however, Habermas documents a change that significantly altered where and how discussion of broad social issues take place.

41. Interview, William Perkins, August 25, 1993.

42. Interview, Nomsa Brath, June 24, 1993.

43. Interview, November 1, 1994.

44. Nadine Brozan, "3 Prayer Vigils Held as Victim of Attack Remains in Coma," *New York Times*, April 26, 1989, B4.

45. Susan Chira, "Rape Suspects' Neighbors Feel Accused," *New York Times*, May 1, 1989, A1, B6.

46. Adam Nagourney, "Park Crime Divides City," *Daily News*, April 26, 1989, 5.

47. Charles J. Hynes and Bob Drury, *Incident at Howard Beach: The Case for Murder* (New York: Putnam, 1990), 99–106; also see Al Sharpton's *And Tell Pharoah: The Autobiography of the Reverend Al Sharpton* (New York: Doubleday, 1996), 103.

48. Interview, Al Sharpton, September 1, 1993.

49. See discussion of journalists' concern with not taking political stances in Herbert J. Gans, *Deciding What's News* (New York: Vintage, 1979), 184.

50. Michel Marriott, "Harlem Residents Fear Backlash from Park Rape," *New York Times*, April 24, 1989, B2.

51. Earl Caldwell, Op-Editorial, *Daily News*, April 24, 1989, 29.

52. Ibid.

53. Paul La Rosa, "Ed: Don't Put Blame on Society," *Daily News*, April 25, 1989, 4.

54. Quotes from Barry Grey taken from Celestine Bohlen, "The Park Attack, Weeks Later: An Anger that Will Not Let Go," *New York Times*, May 12, 1989, B1–B2.

55. Bill Reel, "Wanted: Punishment That Fits Crime," *Daily News*, April 25, 1989, 29.

56. Letter to the Editor, from John H. Gutfreund, *New York Times*, April 27, 1989, 30.

57. Full-page ad signed by Donald Trump, *New York Times*, May 1, 1989, A3.

58. Celestine Bohlen, "The Park Attack, Weeks Later: An Anger That Will Not Let Go," *New York Times*, May 12, 1989, B1–B2.

59. Ibid.

60. J. Zamgba Browne, "Trump's 'Kill Them' Ad Condemned," *Amsterdam News*, May 6, 1989, 1, 33.

61. See James Goodman, *Stories of Scottsboro* (New York: Vintage Books, 1995).

62. See Harold L. Jamison, "Another Woman Raped and Strangled to Death: Police Have No Suspects, Motive for Brutal Killing," *Amsterdam News*, May 6, 1989, 1.

63. "The Central Park Rape: Naming Names," Editorial, *Amsterdam News*, May 13, 1989.

64. Interview, Emma Jones, November 3, 1994.

65. Lisa Kennedy, "Body Double: The Anatomy of a Crime," *Village Voice*, May 9, 1989, 31.

66. Greg Tate, "Leadership Follies: From Mau Maus to Mr. Charlie," *Village Voice*, May 9, 1989, 33.

67. Wilbert Tatum, "The Central Park Rape Case: Naming Names," *Amsterdam News*, May 13, 1989, 14.

68. Greg Tate, "Leadership Follies: From Mau Maus to Mr. Charlie," *Village Voice*, May 9, 1989, 33.

69. Helen Benedict, *Virgin or Vamp: How the Press Covers Sex Crimes* (New York: Oxford University Press, 1992), 208.

70. See the following two editorials: Ronnie Eldridge, "Central Park Can Be Ours," *New York Times*, May 4, 1989; Elizabeth Holtzman, "Rape—The Silence Is Criminal," *New York Times*, May 5, 1989.

71. Benedict failed to mention either of the two editorials cited in the previous note, and an opinion piece written by Susan Brownmiller (*Daily News*, May 7, 1989, 45) in her chapter on the "Central Park" case in *Virgin or Vamp*.

72. Elizabeth Holtzman, "Rape—The Silence Is Criminal," *New York Times*, May 5, 1989.

73. See Ellis Cose, "Rape in the News: Mostly about Whites," *New York Times*, May 7, 1989, 27.

74. Susan Brownmiller, *Daily News*, May 7, 1989, 45.

75. Ibid.

76. Ibid.

77. See the discussions of sociologically diverse masculinities in relation to crime in James W. Messerschmidt, *Capitalism, Patriarchy, and Crime: Toward a Socialist Feminist Criminology* (Totowa, N.J.: Rowman and Littlefield, 1986), 132–33, and in Messerschmidt's *Masculinities and Crime: Critique and Reconceptualization of Theory* (Lanham, Md.: Rowman and Littlefield, 1993), 15.

78. This term, and the debates over gender, race, and class to which it refers, is taken from the title of Judith Rollins's book *Between Women: Domestics and Their Employers* (Philadelphia: Temple University Press, 1985).

79. See bell hooks, *Feminist Theory: From Margin to Center* (Boston: South End Press, 1984). But it should also be noted that Brownmiller herself had been criticized before for failing to differentiate variations in gendered experiences of both women and men according to race. Brownmiller's discussion of the "Emmett Till" case in *Against Our Will: Men, Women and Rape* (New York: Bantam Books, 1976) was roundly criticized by criminologists Julia R. and Herman Schwendinger in *Rape and Inequality* (Beverly Hills: Sage, 1983).

80. See hooks's discussion of "invisibility," *Feminist Theory*, 11.

81. See, for example, the conclusion to Gans's *Deciding What's News*, 279–99. A good discussion of this problem is also found in Mark Fishman's ethnographic newspaper study *Manufacturing the News* (Austin: University of Texas Press, 1980).

3: THE MURDER OF YUSEF HAWKINS

1. This account has been pieced together using media materials and, more importantly, interviews with community residents, social movement activists, and legal parties involved with the case. Original media accounts did not mention the fact that a

black youth, Russell Gibbons, was also present among the white youths who attacked Yusef Hawkins and his friends. Obviously, Gibbons's presence does not negate the clearly racial differences separating those attacked from their attackers, but it does suggest the presence of complexities not immediately acknowledged in highly publicized social constructions of the case.

2. John DeSantis, For the Color of His Skin: The Murder of Yusef Hawkins and the Trial of Bensonhurst (New York: Pharos Books, 1991), 76.

3. Ibid., 8.

4. Ralph Blumenthal. "Black Youth Is Killed by Whites; Brooklyn Attack Is Called Racial," New York Times, August 25, 1989, A1 and B2.

5. Ibid.

6. Interview, James Kohler, September 8, 1993.

7. Blumenthal, "Black Youth Is Killed by Whites," A1.

8. The Democratic primary pitting Mayor Koch against David Dinkins would be held on September 12, 1989; because New York City was still seen as largely Democratic, the winner of the primary was thought likely to win the mayoral election itself in November.

9. Clifford D. May. "Youth's Killing Deplored by Mayoral Candidates," New York Times, August 25, 1989, B2.

10. Interview, Pat Hurtado, November 20, 1994.

11. In chapter 2 I defined "journalistic individualism" the belief on the part of editors and reporters that media attention given to a particular case stems from the unique aspects of a story rather than from its general or patterned characteristics when placed in social context.

12. Interview, William Glaberson, June 23, 1993.

13. Stuart Marques, "30 Teens Chase, Shoot Youth, 16," Daily News, August 25, 1989, 1–3.

14. Don Terry, "On Slain Youth's Block, Sorrow and Bitterness," New York Times, Friday, August 25, 1989, B2.

15. Ibid.

16. Jared McCallister and Geoffrey Tomb, "Why Did Son Die, Asks Grieving Dad?" Daily News, August 25, 1989.

17. Michael T. Kaufman, "Despair Comes Twice to a Brooklyn Family," New York Times, August 26, 1989, 26; Claire Seront, "1 in Attack Is Beach Victim Kin," Daily News, August 25, 1989, 22.

18. Blumenthal, "Black Youth Is Killed by Whites," B2.

19. Hall et al., Policing the Crisis: Mugging, the State, and Law and Order (London: Macmillan, 1978); Todd Gitlin, The Whole World Is Watching: Mass Media in the Making and Unmaking of the New Left (Berkeley: University of California Press, 1980.

20. Ibid.

21. In fairness to Kaufman, though, this April 25, 1989 New York Times feature ("Park Suspects: Children of Discipline," A1) represents a reporter's gambit of going against stereotypical expectations. In the very next sentence, Kaufman proceeds to

say, "But four lived in a building with a doorman, and one went to parochial school. One received an allowance of $4 a day from his father, while another had just received an 'A' on a report he had written about John Steinbeck's 'Of Mice and Men.'" Yet defensive reactions were likely to arise in response even to this coverage, both because it focused scrutiny on an entire neighborhood to understand the acts of a few and insofar as Kaufman's amazement at learning about the allowance and the "A" reinforces stereotypical presumptions.

22. See the discussion of "public reactions" in chapter 2 for a more in-depth account of such reactions' occurrence on this "side" of the "Central Park jogger" case.

23. Interview, Al Sharpton, September 1, 1993.

24. Don Singleton, "Local Chorus: It Wasn't Race," *Daily News*, August 25, 1989, 2.

25. Ibid.

26. Michael T. Kaufman. "Despair Comes Twice to a Brooklyn Family," *New York Times*, August 26, 1989, 26–27.

27. Mike McAlary, "A Song That Didn't Make Hears Sing," *Daily News*, April 30, 1989, 19.

28. Mike McAlary, "Hate Street, in Brooklyn," *Daily News*, August 25, 1989, 3, 26.

29. Kaufman. "Despair Comes Twice to a Brooklyn Family," 27.

30. See Nadine Brozan, "3 Prayer Vigils Held as Victim of Attack Remains in Coma," *New York Times*, April 26, 1989, B4.

31. See the interviews with Lizette Alvarez and other reporters in chapter 2.

32. Interview, Pat Hurtado, November 20, 1994.

33. See chapter 2 note 36.

34. In *Deciding What's News* (New York: Random House, 1979), Gans writes that "[j]ournalists generally describe themselves as liberals" (211), though he goes on to discuss the vagueness of the usage of this term.

35. Sam Roberts, "When Crimes Become Symbols," *New York Times*, May 7, 1989, IV, 1, 28.

36. Interview, Pat Hurtado, November 20, 1994.

37. This conclusion is based on the index survey of the *New York Times* coverage I conducted.

38. Special to *New York Times*, "5 Youths Held in Sex Assault on Mentally Impaired Girl, 17," *New York Times*, May 25, 1989, A1.

39. Bill Turque and Sue Huchison, "Gang Rape in the Suburbs," *Newsweek* 113(89) (1989): 26.

40. What's more, coverage of "Bensonhurst" provided both a variation on as well as continuity with the prior themes of "Glen Ridge": whereas the "Glen Ridge" case focused attention on a crime alleged to have been committed by youths who were white and well-to-do, now the Brooklyn murder highlighted violence of which white working-class youths were also apparently capable.

41. Stuart Marques, "30 Teens Chase, Shoot Youth," *Daily News*, August 25, 1989, 3 (emphasis added).

42. That which is statistically unusual here is not racially motivated assaults—

indeed, there is good evidence that these occurred with frequency—but, relatively speaking, racially motivated assaults in Brooklyn that resulted in murder.

43. See Tuchman, chapter 2 note 17; Gans, note 34; and Mark Fishman, *Manufacturing the News* (Austin: University of Texas Press, 1980).

44. Of all people, reporters understand the potential harms that can come from being quoted "on the record." Thus, the point made in the text regarding the role of reporters in creating high-profile cases is based on the data of media texts themselves, sometimes through "off the record" admissions and at other times through revealing bits of conversation.

45. Nick Ravo, "250 Whites Jeer Marchers in Brooklyn Youth's Death," *New York Times*, August 28, 1989, B3.

46. Interview, Mary Wright, August 12, 1999.

47. Interview, Al Sharpton, September 1, 1993.

48. James Harney with Alfred Lubrano, "Tension Up as Marchers, Residents, Trade Taunts," *Daily News*, August 28, 1989, 5.

49. Nick Ravo. "250 Whites Jeer Marchers in Brooklyn Youth's Death," *New York Times*, August 28, 1989, B3.

50. Ibid.

51. See chapter 2, note 52.

52. Celestine Bohlen, "Racial Link in Brooklyn Killing Divides Mayoral Candidates," *New York Times*, August 29, 1989, A1.

53. Ibid.

54. Ibid.

55. Bob Herbert, "Back to Mississippi, 1955," *Daily News*, August 27, 1989, 4 and 32.

56. Bob Herbert, "Ed's Gotten Wider, and His Principles Are A Lot Thinner," *Daily News*, August 29, 1989, 4.

57. Howard Pinderhughes, *Race in the Hood: Conflict and Violence among Urban Youth* (Minneapolis: University of Minnesota Press, 1997), 92.

58. Ibid., 91.

59. Ibid., 46.

60. Other sociological treatments of this same problem are found in William Julius Wilson's *The Truly Disadvantaged* (Chicago: University of Chicago Press, 1987), and more recently in Wilson's *When Work Disappears* (Cambridge: Harvard University Press, 1996). See also, Stanley Aronowitz and William DiFazio, *The Jobless Future: Sci-Tech and the Dogma of Work* (Minneapolis: University of Minnesota Press, 1994).

61. Pinderhughes, *Race in the Hood*, 47.

62. Ibid., 88.

63. Ibid., 93.

64. Recall Sharpton's objection to characterizations of the murder as resulting from "some romance issue."

65. Interview, Donna Marconi, July 15, 1993.

66. Interview, Father Arthur Minicello, July 15, 1993.

67. Interview, John Carmine, September 8, 1993.

68. Interview, James DiPietro, June 22, 1993.

69. Interview, local resident who preferred to remain anonymous, July 15, 1993.

70. Anonymous interview, November 22, 1993.

71. See chapter 2's section on public reactions to the "Central Park jogger" case, especially that of Colin Moore, who later defended one of the arrested youth and was quoted as believing the young men were being "railroaded."

72. Phillippe Bourgois, *In Search of Respect: Selling Crack in El Barrio* (Cambridge: Cambridge University Press, 1996), 2–8, 12, 16–18.

73. Pinderhughes, *Race in the Hood*, 89.

74. Ibid., 98–99.

75. Ibid., 85–128.

76. See Laurie Silberg, "Town Still Struggling in Wake of Alleged Gang-Sex Assault," and the editorial in *Glen Ridge Paper*, June 1, 1989, 1, 10.

77. Interview, Edward Callahan.

78. During an interview, Judge Cohen explained that the Rape Shield law did not apply to the "Glen Ridge" case (and therefore did not protect the young woman from victim-blaming questions) because of the complicating issue of mental retardation. That is to say, exploring questions of prior sexual activity was relevant to the question of ability to consent. See also Bernard Lefkowitz, *Our Guys: The Glen Ridge Rape and the Secret Life of the Perfect Suburb* (Berkeley: University of California Press, 1997), 306.

79. Ibid., 312.

80. Interview, Jack Spatola, September 8, 1993.

81. Elizabeth Kolbert, "Youth's Funeral Focuses on Racial Divisions," *New York Times*, August 31, 1989, A1 and B2.

82. James C. McKinley Jr. "Protestors and Police Trade Blame for Violence," *New York Times*, September 2, 1989, A25, B2. See also Dennis Hevesi, "No Violence as 300 March into Bensonhurst Again," *New York Times*, September 3, 1989, 40.

83. "The Blood on the Brooklyn Bridge," *New York Times*, Editorial, September 2, 1989, 22.

84. Don Terry, "Black Voters Say It's Time for Dinkins," *New York Times*, September 10, 1989, 42.

4: *IN RE* THE LEGAL SYSTEM

1. Paul Gewirtz, "Visions and Voyeurs: Two Narrative Problems of the Criminal Trial." In *Law's Stories: Narrative and Rhetoric in the Law*, ed. Paul Gewirtz, Martha Minow, and Sanford Levinson (New Haven: Yale University Press, 1996), 135.

2. See Gary Minda, *Postmodern Legal Movements: Law and Jurisprudence at Century's End* (New York: New York University Press, 1995), esp. ch. 4.

3. Ibid., 62, 78–79.

4. Ronald Sullivan, "Critics Fault Selection of Judge in Jogger Case," *New York Times*, August 7, 1989, B4.

5. Marvine Howe, "4th Suspect Faces Murder Charge in Death of Youth in Bensonhurst," *New York Times*, September 9, 1989.

6. Interview, Jesse Berman, September 12, 1992.

7. Interview, Jeffrey Modisett, May 6, 1993.

8. Interview, Judge Thomas Galligan, September 12, 1994.

9. Ibid.

10. Interview, Judge Patricia Gifford, November 13, 1992.

11. Ibid.

12. Ibid.

13. Interview, Judge Bernard Cohen, September 15, 1993.

14. Ibid.

15. Interview, Judge Galligan.

16. Ronald Sullivan, " 'Participants' May Testify in Jogger Case," *New York Times*, June 14, 1990.

17. William Glaberson, "Racial Tensions from Slaying Seen at Trial," *New York Times*, April 3, 1990.

18. Interview, Judge Galligan.

19. Glaberson, "Racial Tensions from Slaying Seen at Trial."

20. Interview, Judge Gifford.

21. Interview, Judge Cohen.

22. Ibid.

23. Interview, Sharonne Salaam, September 21, 1994.

24. Interview, Roy Black, June 7, 1993.

25. Ibid.

26. Interview, Vincent Fuller and Kathleen Beggs, January 11, 1993.

27. Interview, James Voyles, November 1992.

28. Ibid.

29. Ibid.

30. Interview, Alan Dershowitz, January 4 and 5, 1993; these views were also elaborated on in a telephone interview on April 30, 1993.

31. Ibid.

32. Notes from Dershowitz's appearance on the *Maury Povich* show, January 4, 1993.

33. Interview, Roy Black.

34. Interview, Christine Stapleton, November 19, 1992.

35. Ibid.

36. Interview, Gregory Garrison, November 16, 1992.

37. Interview, Robert Burns, June 15, 1993.

38. Interview, William Kunstler, September 21, 1994.

39. Interview, Michael Joseph, August 7, 1992.

40. William Glaberson, "Jogger Defense Case: Scattershot Approach," *New York Times*, July 13, 1990.

41. Ronald Sullivan, "Brutality of Rape Detailed as Jogger Trial Opens," *New York Times*, June 26, 1990; see also, for a description of Lederer's calm but intense account of brutality the jogger suffered, Ronald Sullivan, "Keeping Emotions under Control at Jogger Trial," *New York Times*, July 2, 1990.

42. Telephone interview, juror, September 1994.

43. Interview, juror, September 20, 1994.

44. Interview, Elizabeth Lederer, June 23, 1993.

45. Ibid.

46. Telephone interview, Timothy Clements, June 1993.

47. Interview, juror, September 20.

48. Ibid.

49. Spike Lee, "The Right Thing: Self-Defense, Vote," *Daily News*, August 31, 1989; and interview James Kohler, September 26, 1994.

50. Interview, Ed Boyar, September 26, 1994.

51. See John Kifner, "Bensonhurst: A Tough Code in Defense of a Closed World," *New York Times*, September 1, 1989; see also the discussion in chapter 3 of resentment at Gina Feliciano felt by some people living in Bensonhurst at the time of Yusef Hawkins's murder.

52. William Glaberson, "Murder Trial Is Told of Boast in Bensonhurst," *New York Times*, April 17, 1990.

53. Interview, Stephen Murphy, November 10, 1999.

54. Interview, Terry White, August 17, 1994.

55. Ibid.

56. Interview, Ira Reiner, September 30, 1994 (also re-interviewed on October 3, 1994).

57. Interview, Michael Stone, August 24, 1994.

58. Ibid.

59. Ibid.

60. Ibid.

61. Interview, Edi Faal, December 8, 1994.

62. Ibid.

63. Ibid.

64. Telephone interview, Edi Faal, August 10, 2001.

65. Interview, juror, September 20, 1994.

66. Interview with juror on the "Bensonhurst" trial of Joseph Fama, September 25, 1994.

67. Ibid.

68. Interview, juror, January 1995.

69. Interview, Tonya Bailey, November 20, 1994.

70. Interview, juror, November 20, 1994.

71. Interview, juror, October, 1994.

72. Ibid.

1. Jay Rosen, *What Are Journalists For?* (New Haven: Yale University Press, 1999), 69–70.

2. See Michael Schudson, *Discovering the News: A Social History of American Newspapers* (New York: Basic Books, 1978), and *The Power of News* (Cambridge: Harvard University Press, 1995).

3. Interview, Christine Stapleton, November 19, 1992.

4. Interview, Frank Cerobin, November 19, 1992.

5. Interview, Robin Kish, November 20, 1992.

6. Interview, Joe Gelarden, May 5, 1993.

7. Interview, Barb Berggoetz, May 5, 1993.

8. Interview, Neal Moore, May 5, 1993.

9. Interview, Leo Wilensky, August 16, 1994.

10. Interview, Jim Newton, August 12, 1994.

11. Interview, Michael Janofsky, August 12, 1994.

12. Joshua Gamson, *Claims to Fame: Celebrity in Contemporary America* (Berkeley: University of California Press, 1994), 186.

13. See my discussion of this media propensity in chapter 2.

14. Interview, Andrea Ford, August 12, 1994.

15. Deirdre Carmody, "News Media's Use of Accuser's Name Is Debated," *New York Times*, April 18, 1991.

16. William Glaberson, "Times Article Naming Rape Accuser Ignites Debate on Journalistic Values," *New York Times*, April 26, 1991, A14.

17. Interview, Janofsky.

18. Rosen, *What Are Journalists For?*

19. Phil Berger, "A Drama That Will Rival the Ring When Tyson Faces His Accuser," *New York Times*, January 22, 1992, 1–2.

20. Larry Hackett, "The Main Event: Rape Trial Tyson's Biggest Fight," *Daily News*, January 26, 1992, 1, 21.

21. Berger, "A Drama That Will rival the Ring," 1.

22. Linda Yglesias, "Spotlight on the Accuser" (including box on "The Life and Times of Iron Mike"), *Daily News*, January 26, 1992.

23. Charles M. Sennoti, "Tyson and Smith: Same, Different," *Daily News*, September 20, 1991, 1, 2.

24. Larry Hackett, "Quick Jabs at Jury: Tyson Panel-Selection Process Assailed," *Daily News*, January 28, 1992.

25. Phil Berger, "Tyson Stays Silent; His Supporters Don't," *New York Times*, January 28, 1992.

26. Linda Yglesias, "Still A Gem in Gym: Young Fighters on the Way Up Support Mike," *Daily News*, September 12, 1991, 3.

27. In chapters 2 and 3, I described an analogous interplay between media coverage and public reactions when discussing the "Central Park" and "Bensonhurst" cases.

28. Phil Berger, "Tyson, Women and Trouble: Views Differ on Who Is Victim," *New York Times*, October 21, 1991, A1, C1.

29. See Lynn S. Chancer, "Playing Gender against Race through High-Profile Crime Cases: The Tyson/Thomas/Simpson Pattern of the 1990s," *Violence against Women* 4:1 (1998).

30. Interview, Wilensky.

31. Interview, Dennis Schatzman, August 23, 1994.

32. Interview, Dennis Schatzman, February 10, 1997.

33. Interview, Ed Boyer, August 15, 1994.

34. Interview, *Los Angeles Sentinel* reporter, August 15, 1994.

35. Ibid.

36. Interview, Boyer.

37. Darnell M. Hunt, *O.J. Simpson Facts and Fictions: News Rituals in the Construction of Reality* (Cambridge: Cambridge University Press, 1999), 96.

38. Interview, Boyer.

39. Interview, *Los Angeles Sentinel* reporter.

40. Interview, Schatzman, February 10, 1997.

41. See Hunt's description of this process in *O.J. Simpson Facts and Fictions.*

42. Interview, Wilensky.

43. Interview, David Margolick, August 13, 1994.

44. Interview, Seth Mydans, August 13, 1994.

45. Ibid.

6: TAKING SIDES: DIVERSE PUBLIC REACTIONS

1. Some interviews were also conducted in New York City, though I concentrated mostly on Los Angeles where people felt even more connected to the crime because of its having occurred locally. It should also be noted that the "O.J. Simpson" case received more media attention in Los Angeles than in New York precisely because it was taken to be a "local story."

2. It should be added, however, that many television crime shows like *Law and Order* are based on actual incidents. Moreover, "reality" shows like *Cops* and *America's Most Wanted* draw explicitly on public interest in solving "real" incidents. That such genres play upon the "real" confirms the greater participatory interest, even excitement, that emanates from knowing that crimes actually happened.

3. Patricia Ewick and Susan S. Silbey, *The Common Place of Law: Stories from Everyday Life* (Chicago: University of Chicago Press, 1998), 16.

4. See William Gamson, *Talking Politics* (New York: Cambridge University Press, 1992).

5. Interview, hospital worker, Los Angeles, October 7, 1994.

6. Interview, UCLA student, Westwood Starbucks, October 7, 1994.

7. Interview, group of largely Latino and African American high school students, Fairfax High School, November 3, 1994.

8. Random interviews, Merchant Plaza, Indianapolis, Indiana, November 14, 1992.

9. These were discussed both in the context of the "Central Park" and "Bensonhurst" cases, and also in chapter 4's discussion of the legal system law (since attorneys later build their own dominant narratives, borrowing in part on public reactions).

10. Random interview, November 14, 1992.

11. Random interviews, Merchant Plaza.

12. Interview, Debra Dayton, November 1992.

13. Interview, Billie Breaux.

14. Interview, local activist who preferred to remain anonymous.

15. Interview, Reverend Stacy Shields, November 14, 1992.

16. Tropp ran a human services agency that mainly sought to prevent violence against women and to help those who were victims of it.

17. Interview, Naomi Tropp, November 15, 1992.

18. Interview, Black Family Forum members, May 7, 1993.

19. Ibid.

20. Random interviews, Merchant Plaza.

21. Interview, Reverend Charles Williams, November 14, 1992.

22. Denny Abbott, "Haven't Rape Victims Been Through Enough Already?" *Palm Beach Post*, December 22, 1991, E1–5.

23. Anonymous interview.

24. Ibid.

25. Interview, Reverend Cecil Murray, September 27, 1995.

26. Interview, Linda Johnson, Los Angeles, September 15, 1995.

27. Interview, Edwin, a student at UCLA, October 7, 1994.

28. Interview, American history class, Fairfax High School, Los Angeles, California, November 3, 1994.

29. Ibid.

30. These stages were soon after the double homicides were first reported, when the verdict was expected in the Simpson criminal trial (but had not yet been delivered), and soon after the verdict was announced.

31. Until that point, gender (i.e., domestic violence as a social problem) appeared in media and public discussions more than discussions of racial prejudices.

32. Interview, activist in the Women's Action Coalition, September 20, 1995.

33. Ibid.

34. Interview, October 7, 1994.

35. Interview with a group of a man and two women, October 7, 1994.

36. Interview with group of two men, October 7, 1994.

37. Interview, September 19, 1995.

38. Interview with administrative assistant., September 20, 1995.

39. Anonymous interview, September 15, 1995.

40. More specifically, this young woman described her sense that people would be

angry if Simpson was convicted: "But like I say, when 'Rodney King' happened, the world didn't know how the LAPD was but we knew, black people in the community, we knew. We thought we got you now, so justice can be served. Justice at last. Then, when the tapes were heard, you still did nothing. The verdict was in, everybody not guilty, and everyone's tempers were rising. . . . It's built up anger . . . now it [the "O.J. Simpson" case] just brings back old wounds when you see this. And people are just so mad because you're disrespecting the whole community, disrespecting the people as a whole, no matter what."

41. Interview, Edwin.

42. Interview, young woman outside courtroom, September 15, 1995.

43. Interview, Candace Kim, August 14, 1994.

44. Interview, Angela Oh, August 14, 1994.

45. Interview with administrative assistant.

46. More specifically, this viewpoint intimated that indictments in the "Glen Ridge" case were used to compensate for media and criminal justice biases toward minority and lower-class young defendants about which many people had protested in the April 1989 "Central Park" case. Coming as attention did to "Glen Ridge" soon thereafter in May 1989, these parties felt the media, as well as prosecutors, were "picking on" rich white kids to show that the system was not prejudiced after all.

47. These social-psychic dynamics often, but did not necessarily, appear together in interviews I conducted: some parties concentrated more on one than the other. For instance, some people in the "Simpson" case were concerned that the defendant had been framed (therefore seeing Simpson as a sympathetic figure) but drew back from in any way blaming Nicole Brown Simpson and Ronald Gold for the brutal murders they suffered. Similarly, some people who emphasized that Nicole Brown Simpson was not as "pure" as her media image suggested also said that, still, perhaps Simpson was guilty. Clearly, this emphasis on one dynamic and not the other can (and did sometimes) happen in other cases as well.

48. *Our Guys* is the title of a book (Berkeley: University of California Press, 1998) written about this case by Columbia journalism professor Bernard Lefkowitz, obviously alluding to the fondness with which some community members viewed a group of star high school football players in their town.

7: HIGH-PROFILE CRIMES AND AMERICAN CULTURE

1. This quote is taken from an Internet story on *Talk Left: The Politics of Crime*, August 31, 2003.

2. See the conclusion of Gary Minda, *Postmodern Legal Movements: Law and Jurisprudence at Century's End* (New York: New York University Press, 1997), especially pp. 256–57.

3. The "St. John's rape" case, as it was called in media and public accounts at the time, involved a young Jamaican woman who was allegedly assaulted by a group of lacrosse players at St. John's University in Queens, New York in March 1990. An incisive account of this case, and how it surprisingly resulted in acquittal for the defen-

dants, is found in noted anthropologist Peggy Reeves Sanday's study *A Woman Scorned* (New York: Doubleday, 1996).

4. See Jay Rosen, *What Are Journalists For?* (New Haven: Yale University Press, 2001).

APPENDIX C:
ACKNOWLEDGING INTELLECTUAL DEBTS AND DISTINCTIONS

1. More popular accounts have been written about the "O.J. Simpson" and "Rodney King" cases than are easily listed here. Regarding "Howard Beach," one book has appeared by the prosecutor of that case. See Charles J. Hynes and Bob Drury, *Incident at Howard Beach: The Case for Murder* (New York: Putnam, 1990). One popular chronicle was written of the "Bensonhurst" case. See John DeSantis, *For the Color of His Skin: The Murder of Yusef Hawkins and the Trial of Bensonhurst* (New York: Pharos Books, 1991). Another was written about the "Central Park jogger" case. See Timothy Sullivan, *Unequal Verdicts: The Central Park Jogger Trials* (New York: American Lawyer Books/Simon and Schuster, 1992). Regarding the "Mike Tyson" case, see Mark Shaw, *Down for the Count: The Shocking Truth behind the Mike Tyson Rape Trial* (Champaigne, Ill: Sagamore Publishing, 1993).

2. See Murray Edelman, *Constructing the Political Spectacle* (Chicago: University of Chicago Press, 1988); and Marjorie Garber, Jann Matlock, and Rebecca L. Walkowitz, eds., *Media Spectacles* (New York: Routledge, 1993).

3. See Alphonse Pinckney, *Lest We Forget White Hate Crimes: Howard Beach and Other Racial Atrocities* (Chicago: Third World Press, 1984).

4. See Darnell M. Hunt, *O.J. Simpson Facts and Fictions: News Rituals in the Construction of Reality* (Cambridge: Cambridge University Press, 1999).

5. See Gregg Barak, ed., *Representing O.J.: Murder, Criminal Justice, and Mass Culture* (New York: Harrow and Heston, 1999).

6. See George B. Fletcher, *With Justice for Some: Victims' Rights in Criminal Trials* (Reading, Mass.: Addison-Wesley, 1990).

7. See Peggy Reeves Sanday, *A Woman Scorned: Acquaintance Rape on Trial* (New York: Doubleday, 1996).

8. See Helen Benedict, *Virgin or Vamp: How the Press Covers Sex Crimes* (New York: Oxford University Press, 1992).

9. See, because important among these works, Herbert J. Gans, *Deciding What's News* (New York: Vintage Books, 1980); Gaye Tuchman, *Making News: A Study in the Construction of Reality* (New York: Free Press, 1978); and Mark Fishman, *Manufacturing the News* (Austin: University of Texas Press, 1980).

10. Todd Gitlin, *The Whole World Is Watching: Mass Media: Mass Media in the Making and Unmaking of the New Left* (Berkeley: University of California Press, 1980). See especially pp. 283–92, concerning implications for social movements of media practices.

11. Hall *et al.* drew on the idea of a moral panic as formulated by Stan Cohen in *Folk Devils and Moral Panics: The Creation of the Mods and Rockers* (London: MacGibbon and Kee, 1972): "Societies appear to be subject, every now and then, to periods of moral panic. A condition, episode, person or group of persons emerges to become defined

as a threat to societal values and interests; its nature is presented in a styled and stereotypical fashion by the mass media; the moral barricades are manned by editors, bishops, and other right-thinking people; socially accredited experts pronounce their diagnoses and solutions; ways of coping are evolved or (more often) resorted to; the condition then disappears, submerges or deteriorates and becomes more visible. Sometimes the object of the panic is quite novel and at other times it is something which has been in existence long enough, but suddenly appears in the limelight. Sometimes the panic is passed over and is forgotten, except in folklore and collective memory; at other times it has more serious and long lasting repercussions and might produce such changes as those in legal and social policy or even in the way society conceives itself" (28).

12. See Stuart Hall, Chas Critcher, Tony Jefferson, John Clarke, and Brian Roberts, *Policing the Crisis: Mugging, the State, and Law and Order* (New York: Holmes and Meier Publications, Inc., 1978).

13. William Gamson, *Talking Politics* (New York: Cambridge University Press, 1991), xi, 54–58, 83.

14. R. Emerson Dobash and Russell R. Dobash, *Women Viewing Violence*, ed. Philip Schlesinger (London: British Film Institute, 1992).

15. See Esther Madriz, *Nothing Bad Happens to Good Girls: Fear of Crime in Women's Lives* (Berkeley: University of California Press, 1997).

16. See Darnell Hunt, *Screening the Los Angeles "Riots": Race, Seeing, and Resistance* (Cambridge: Cambridge University Press, 1996).

17. See, for example, the studies of popular trials presented in Robert Hariman, ed., *Popular Trials: Rhetoric, Mass Media, and the Law* (Tuscaloosa: University of Alabama Press, 1990). Regarding the use of narrative to analyze both legal and social events, see contributions by Gewirtz, Minow, and Levinson in *Law's Stories: Narrative and Rhetoric in the Law* (New Haven: Yale University Press, 1996).

18. See, for example, Kristin Bumiller's interesting discussion of the "Central Park jogger" case in *Feminism, Media and the Law*, ed. Martha A. Fineman and Martha T. McCluskey (New York: Oxford University Press, 1997).

19. A good summary of growing interest in using narrative to illuminate specifically sociological questions is found in Margaret R. Somers and Gloria D. Gibson, "Reclaiming the Epistemological 'Other': Narrative and the Social Construction of Identity," in *Social Theory and the Politics of Identity*, ed. Craig Calhoun (Oxford: Blackwell, 1994).

20. Regarding the literature on political trials, see Theodore Becker, "Introduction," in Becker, ed., *Political Trials* (Indianapolis: Bobbs Merrill, 1971), xii. See also Ron Christenson, *Political Trials: Gordian Knots in the Law* (New Brunswick, N.J.: Transaction Publishers, 1989; and Andrew David, *Famous Political Trials* (Minneapolis: Lerner Publications, 1980). Probably the classic work on political trials, however, is Otto Kirchheimer's *Political Justice: The Use of Legal Procedures for Political Ends* (Princeton: Princeton University Press, 1961).

21. Regarding the case of the "Chicago Seven," see David R. Farber, *Chicago '68* (Chicago: University of Chicago Press, 1988); John Schultz, *The Chicago Conspiracy Trial* (New York: Da Capo Press, 1993).

22. Lisa M. Cuklanz, *Rape on Trial: How the Mass Media Construct Legal Reform and Social Change* (Philadelphia: University of Pennsylvania Press, 1996), 38.

23. Ibid., 37.

24. This is not to suggest that there have not been other decades when violent crimes were later politicized through social movement protests. However, what I believe to be distinctive about provoking assaults of the 1980s and 1990s is that they produce ongoing sequences of substantively interconnected cases.

25. An important exception to this is found in the work of the Frankfurt School, especially Erich Fromm's discussion of specifically social defense mechanisms in *Escape from Freedom* (New York: Holt, Rinehart, and Winston, 1941). More recently, see Wilfred Bion, *Experience in Groups and Other Papers* (New York: Basic Books, 1961).

Alford, Robert. 1998. *The Craft of Inquiry: Theory, Methods, Evidence*. New York: Oxford University Press.

Ansen, Robert. 1987. *Best Intentions: The Education and Killing of Edmund Perry*. New York: Random House.

Aronowitz, Stanley, and William DiFazio. 1994. *The Jobless Future: Sci-Tech and the Dogma of Work*. Minneapolis: University of Minnesota Press.

Barak, Gregg, ed. 1999. *Representing O.J.: Murder, Criminal Justice, and Mass Culture*. New York: Harrow and Heston.

Becker, Theodore, ed. 1971. *Political Trials*. Indianapolis: Bobbs Merrill.

Benedict, Helen. 1992. *Virgin or Vamp: How the Press Covers Sex Crimes*. New York: Oxford University Press.

Bion, Wilfred. 1961. *Experience in Groups and Other Papers*. New York: Basic Books.

Bourdieu, Pierre. 1990. *The Logic of Practice*. Cambridge: Polity Press.

———. 1977. *Outline of a Theory of Practice*. New York: Cambridge University Press.

Bourgois, Phillippe. 1996. *In Search of Respect: Selling Crack in El Barrio*. Cambridge: Cambridge University Press.

Brownmiller, Susan. 1976. *Against Our Will: Men, Women and Rape*. New York: Bantam Books.

Carter, Dan T. 1994. *Scottsboro: A Tragedy of the American South*. New York: Vintage Books.

Chancer, Lynn S. 1987. "New Bedford, Massachusetts, March 6, 1983–March 22, 1984: The 'Before' and 'After' of a Group Rape." *Gender and Society* 1, 239–60.

———. 1996. "O.J. Simpson and the Trial of the Century? Uncovering Paradoxes in Media Coverage." In *Representing O.J.: Murder, Criminal Justice, and Mass Culture*, ed. Gregg Barak. New York: Harrow and Heston.

Christenson, Ron. 1989. *Political Trials: Gordian Knots in the Law*. New Brunswick, N.J.: Transaction Publishers.

Cohen, Stan. 1972. *Folk Devils and Moral Panics: The Creation of the Mods and Rockers.* London: MacGibbon and Kee.

Crenshaw, Kimberle. In *Race-ing Justice, En-Gendering Power: Essays on Anita Hill, Clarence Thomas, and the Construction of Social Reality,* ed. Toni Morrison. (New York: Pantheon Books, 1992).

Cuklanz, Lisa M. 2000. *Rape on Prime Time: Television, Masculinity, and Sexual Violence.* Philadelphia: University of Pennsylvania Press.

———. 1996. *Rape on Trial: How the Mass Media Construct Legal Reform and Social Change.* Philadelphia: University of Pennsylvania Press.

David, Andrew. 1980. *Famous Political Trials.* Minneapolis: Lerner Publications.

DeSantis, John. 1991. *For the Color of His Skin: The Murder of Yusef Hawkins and the Trial of Bensonhurst.* New York: Pharos Books.

Edelman, Murray. 1988. *Constructing the Political Spectacle.* Chicago: University of Chicago Press.

Ewick, Patricia, and Susan S. Silbey. 1998. *The Common Place of Law: Stories from Everyday Life.* Chicago: University of Chicago Press.

Fairstein, Linda. 1993. *Sexual Violence: Our War against Rape.* New York: William Morrow.

Faludi, Susan. 1991. *Backlash: The Undeclared War against American Women.* New York: Crown.

Farber, David R. 1988. *Chicago '68.* Chicago: University of Chicago Press.

Fineman, Martha, and Martha T. McCluskey, eds. 1997. *Feminism, Media and the Law.* New York: Oxford University Press.

Fishman, Mark. 1980. *Manufacting the News.* Austin: University of Texas Press.

Fletcher, George B. 1990. *With Justice for Some: Victims' Rights in Criminal Trials.* Reading, Mass.: Addison Wesley.

Foner, Philips S. 1970. *The Case of Joe Hill.* New York: International Publishers.

Fromm, Erich. 1941. *Escape from Freedom.* New York: Holt, Rinehart and Winston.

Gamson, William. 1991. *Talking Politics.* New York: Cambridge University Press.

Gans, Herbert J. 1979. *Deciding What's News.* New York: Vintage.

Garber, Marjorie, Jann Matlock, and Rebecca L. Walkowitz, eds. 1993. *Media Spectacles.* New York: Routledge.

Gewirtz, Paul, Martha Minow, and Sanford Levinson. 1996. *Law's Stories: Narrative and Rhetoric in the Law.* New Haven: Yale University Press.

Gitlin, Todd. 1980. *The Whole World is Watching: Mass Media in the Making and Unmaking of the New Left.* Berkeley: University of California Press.

Green, Charles, and Basil Wilson. 1992. *The Struggle for Black Empowerment in New York City: Beyond the Politics of Pigmentation.* New York: McGraw Hill.

Habermas, Jurgen. 1994. *The Structural Transformation of the Public Sphere: An Inquiry into a Category of Bourgeois Society.* Cambridge: MIT Press.

Hall, Stuart, Chas Critcher, Tony Jefferson, John Clarke, and Brian Roberts. 1978. *Policing the Crisis: Mugging, the State, and Law and Order.* London: Macmillan.

Hariman, Robert, ed. 1990. *Popular Trials: Rhetoric, Mass Media and the Law.* Tuscaloosa: University of Alabama Press.

Hoffman, Robert L. 1980. *More Than a Trial: The Struggle Over Captain Dreyfus*. New York: Free Press.

hooks, bell. 1984. *Feminist Theory: From Margin to Center*. Boston: South End Press.

Hunt, Darnell M. 1999. *O.J. Simpson Facts and Fictions: News Rituals in the Construction of Reality*. Cambridge: Cambridge University Press.

———. 1997. *Screening the Los Angeles "Riots": Race, Seeing, and Resistance*. Cambridge: Cambridge University Press.

Hynes, Charles J., and Bob Drury. 1990. *Incident at Howard Beach: The Case for Murder*. New York: Putnam.

Lefkowitz, Bernard. 1997. *Our Guys: The Glen Ridge Rape and the Secret Life of the Perfect Suburb*. Berkeley: University of California Press.

Madriz, Esther. 1997. *Nothing Bad Happens to Good Girls: Fear of Crime in Women's Lives*. Berkeley: University of California Press.

Messerschmidt, James W. 1986. *Capitalism, Patriarchy, and Crime: Toward a Socialist Feminist Criminology*. Lanham, Md.: Rowman and Littlefield.

———. 1993. *Masculinities and Crime: Critique and Reconceptualization of Theory*. Lanham, Md.: Rowman and Littlefield.

Minda, Gary. 1995. *Postmodern Legal Movements: Law and Jurisprudence at Century's End*. New York: New York University Press.

Moorti, Sujata. 2002. *Color of Rape: Gender and Race in Television's Public Spheres*. Albany: State University of New York Press.

Pinderhughes, Howard. 1997. *Race in the Hood: Conflict and Violence among Urban Youth*. Minneapolis: University of Minnesota Press.

Pinkney, Alphonse. 1984. *Lest We Forget White Hate Crimes: Howard Beach and Other Racial Atrocities*. Chicago: Third World Press.

Projansky, Sarah. 2001. *Watching Rape: Film and Television in Postfeminist Culture*. New York: New York University Press.

Rollins, Judith. 1985. *Between Women: Domestics and Their Employers*. Philadelphia: Temple University Press.

Sanday, Peggy Reeves. 1996. *A Woman Scorned: Acquaintance Rape on Trial*. New York: Doubleday.

Schlesinger, Philip, R. Emerson Dobash, and Russell R. Dobash, eds. 1992. *Women Viewing Violence*. London: British Film Institute, 1992.

Schudson, Michael. 1995. *The Power of News*. Cambridge: Harvard University Press.

Schultz, John. 1993. *The Chicago Conspiracy Trial*. New York: Da Capo Press.

Schwendinger, Julia, and Herman Schwendinger. 1983. *Rape and Inequality*. Sage: Beverly Hills.

Shaw, Mark. 1993. *Down for the Count: The Shocking Truth behind the Mike Tyson Rape Trial*. Champagne, Ill.: Sagamore Publishing.

Sennett, Richard, and Jonathan Cobb. 1972. *The Hidden Injuries of Class*. New York: Knopf.

Sharpton, Al. 1996. *And Tell Pharaoh: The Autobiography of the Reverend Al Sharpton*. New York: Doubleday.

Sleeper, Jim. 1990. *The Closest of Strangers: Liberalism and the Politics of Race in New York.* New York: Norton.

Somers, Margaret R., and Gloria D. Gibson. 1994. "Reclaiming the Epistemological 'Other': Narrative and the Social Construction of Identity." In *Social Theory and the Politics of Identity*, ed. Craig Calhoun. Oxford: Blackwell.

Steinberg, Stephen. 1995. *Turning Back: The Retreat from Racial Justice in American Thought and Policy.* Boston: Beacon Press.

Sullivan, Timothy. 1992. *Unequal Verdicts: The Central Park Jogger Trials.* New York: Simon and Schuster.

Surette, Ray. 1998. *Media, Crime and Criminal Justice: Images and Realities.* Belmont, Cal.: Wadsworth.

Tuchman, Gaye. 1978. *Making News: A Study in the Construction of Reality.* New York: Free Press.

———. 1973. "Making News by Doing Work: Routinizing the Unexpected." *American Journal of Sociology* 79, 110–31.

———. 1972. "Objectivity as Strategic Ritual: An Examination of Newsmen's Notions of Objectivity." *American Journal of Sociology* 77, 666–79.

Whitfield, Stephen J. 1988. *A Death in the Delta: The Story of Emmett Till.* Baltimore: John Hopkins University Press.

Wilson, William Julius. 1996. *When Work Disappears.* Cambridge: Harvard University Press.

———. 1987. *The Truly Disadvantaged.* Chicago: University of Chicago Press.

Faal, Edi, 158–61, 170, 260, 269
Fairstein, Linda: and "Central Park jogger" case, 30–31; and Chambers case, 36, 128
Faludi, Susan, 10–11
Fama, Joseph, 61, 146–47, 150, 162, 167, 268
Feliciano, Gina, and "Bensonhurst" case, 65–67, 72–73, 92, 103, 147–50, 239, 268
feminism: and backlash, 10–11; and Smith case, 227–28. *See also* gender; women
Fishman, Mark, 182, 277
Fletcher, George, 276
Ford, Andrea, 183, 188
Freud, Sigmund, 238
Fuhrman, Mark, 117, 183, 232–33, 236, 270
Fuller, Vincent, 131–32, 190–91, 270

Galligan, Thomas, 120–22, 125–28
Gamson, William, 180, 278
Gans, Herbert, 33, 182, 277
Garrison, Gregory, 137, 190–91, 270
gay rights, 10–11
Gelarden, Joe, 177
gender: and "Bensonhurst" case, 65–66, 80; and "Central Park jogger" case, 9, 47–52, 55–58, 141–43; and "Glen Ridge" case, 101–2; and high-profile crimes, 5; and race, 14, 37, 187, 196, 254; and Tyson case, 217–23; and violence, in New York City, 36–37. *See also* women
Gewirtz, Paul, 116, 172
Gibbons, Russell, 289n1
Gifford, Patricia, 121–23, 126, 128, 223
Gitlin, Todd, 26, 34–35, 38, 59, 68, 277
Giuliani, Rudolph: and "Bensonhurst" case, 62, 211; and Diallo case, 4
Givens, Robin, 191

Glaberson, William, 18, 65–66, 125, 141, 148, 161, 188
"Glen Ridge" case: and blame, 239, 241; and community, 19, 99–102, 243; juror selection in, 126–27; media coverage of, 77–79, 110, 123–24, 261, 298n46; and violence against women, 245–46
Goetz, Bernhard, 35
Goldin, Harrison, 89
Goldman, Ronald, 117–18, 178, 270
Gray, Barry, 47
Griffith, Michael, murder of, 36, 45, 67, 107. *See also* "Howard Beach" case
Gutfreund, John H., 48

Habermas, Jurgen, 43, 286–87n40
Hall, Stuart, 34–35, 38, 68, 277
Halliday, George, 151, 154, 180, 268
Harlins, Latasha, 4–5, 183, 231
Harris, Dylan, 12
hate crimes, 11
Hawkins, Diane, 88
Hawkins, Fred, 66–67
Hawkins, Yusef: funeral of, 106–7; murder of, 4, 7, 61, 104, 146, 267–68. *See also* "Bensonhurst" case
Herbert, Bob, 89–90
Hicks, Joe, 248, 264
high-profile crimes: and blame, 15–17, 100; and celebrity, 177–80; and civil rights, 83–88; and class, 10, 100–101, 184; and diversity of participants, 8–9, 25–26; evidence in, 169; and exceptionalizing, 25; as hate crimes, 11; judges in, 120–24, 170–71; jurors in, 161–64, 171–72; lawyers in, 127–29, 169–71; as legal cases, 12–15, 18, 100–101, 115–20, 172, 242, 258–60; links among, 17–19, 68, 187, 196, 229–30; media coverage of, 11–12, 18, 23, 25–26, 68–69, 99, 102–3, 255–56, 274–75 (*see also* journalists;

high-profile crimes (*continued*)
   and names of individual newspapers);
   methodology in study of, 19–26,
   186–87, 251–52, 284n28; and moral
   panic, 299–300n11; naming of, 7,
   100, 263; in 1980s and 1990s, 9–10;
   and objectivity, 25, 116, 172, 185–89,
   260–64; partialization of, 12–15, 25,
   117–18, 143–46, 214–15, 246–48,
   256–57; as politics, 251–52; as "provoking assaults," 6–7, 108–9; public
   reaction to, 9–10, 68–69, 210–15,
   243–44; and race, 4–5, 182–83; and
   social issues, 5–6, 68, 118, 170–71,
   226–27, 242–43, 247, 252, 254–55;
   social-psychic dynamics of, 213–14,
   238–48, 257–58; televising of trials
   of, 120–24; in urban areas, 283n23;
   victims of, 15–17, 187, 241–42. *See
   also names of individual cases*
Hill, Anita, 181–83, 228
Hills, Stuart, 9
Holtzman, Elizabeth, 56, 62, 83
"Howard Beach" case, 18, 59; compared
   to "Bensonhurst" case, 62–66;
   lawyers in, 128, 147; media coverage
   of, 35–36; and race, 45–46
Hunt, Darnell, 202, 276, 278
Hurtado, Pat, 64, 74, 76, 81
Hynes, Charles, 18, 128

Ja Du, Soon, 183
Janofsky, Michael, 179, 189
Johnson, Linda, 229–30
Johnson, Rose, 229
Jones, Emma, 53–54
Joseph, Michael, 141, 267
journalists: individualism of, 180–81;
   objectivity of, 174–75, 195, 260–61;
   race of, 201–4; relativism of, 37–38,
   64, 80, 160–61, 185–89, 261–64;
   and social issues, 174–76. *See also*
   media

judges, appointment of, to high-profile
   cases, 120–24, 259
Jungle Fever, 268
jurors: in high-profile cases, 161–64,
   259; influence of media on, 124–25;
   selection of, 125–27, 130, 151–52

Kaufman, Michael, 69, 71–72, 81, 97
Keating, Charles, 9, 254, 283n26
Kennedy, Lisa, 53
Kennedy Smith, William. *See* Smith,
   William Kennedy, case of
Kim, Candace, 239
King, Rodney, case of, 5, 268–69; and
   blame, 15, 156, 241; compared to
   Simpson case, 234–35, 238; and
   Denny case, 158–60, 260; jury in,
   151–54, 234–35; and legal appeals,
   17, 257, 265; media coverage of, 21–
   22, 153–57, 180–81, 186; and police
   brutality, 117, 152, 155, 230, 232, 244,
   255; and protest, 211; and race, 153–
   54, 183–84, 188, 231–32
Kish, Robin, 177
Klein, Melanie, 246
Kliebold, Eric, 12
"Kobe Bryant" case. *See* Bryant, Kobe,
   case of
Koch, Edward: and "Bensonhurst" case,
   4, 62, 88–90, 107–8; and "Central
   Park jogger" case, 47, 59, 83, 210–11
Kohler, James, 62, 80, 146–47, 268
Koon, Stacey C., 268
Kunstler, William, 128, 138–39, 267

Lasch, Moira, 136, 270
lawyers: in high-profile crimes, 127–29,
   259–60; in media, 131–37; and social
   issues, 139–40
Lederer, Elizabeth, 30–31, 42, 128, 141–
   43, 267
Lee, Spike, 108, 146, 268
Lefkowitz, Bernard, 101, 298n48

legal cases: high-profile crimes as, 12–15, 18, 100–101, 115–20, 258–60; judge appointment in, 120–24; and objectivity, 119–20, 160–61; partialization in, 117–18, 190; public audiences of, 229–30; and social issues, 118–19, 139–40, 213. *See also* judges; jurors; lawyers

Levin, Jennifer, 36, 128

Lopez, Steve, 120

Los Angeles Multi-Cultural Coalition, 248

Los Angeles Police Department: and King case, 151; and Simpson case, 13, 129, 183, 200, 244–45

Los Angeles riots (1992), 5, 19, 151, 153, 156–61. *See also* Denny, Reginald; King, Rodney

Los Angeles Sentinel, coverage of high-profile crimes in, 23, 199, 203

Los Angeles Times, coverage of high-profile crimes in, 11, 18, 21, 273–74; coverage of King case in, 183; coverage of Simpson case in, 178–79, 188, 202–4

Louima, Abner, case of: and blame, 15–16; and lawyers, 18–19, 129; media coverage of, 186, 261

Lozano, William, case of, 128–29, 171

Maddox, Alton, 36, 59

Madriz, Esther, 278

Marconi, Donna, 92–93, 97

Margolick, David, 18, 188, 205–6

Marques, Stuart, 65, 79, 81

Mason, C. Vernon, 36, 59

May, Clifford, 63

McAlary, Mike, 40, 72, 81

McAllister, Jared, 66

McCray, Antron, 141, 267

media: coverage of high-profile crimes in, 11–12, 18, 23, 25–26; influence on jurors of, 124–27; and lawyers, 127;

and "newsworthiness," 32–33, 37–39, 175, 180, 198–99, 207–8; objectivity of, 37–38, 64, 80, 174–75, 185–89, 260–62; partialization by, 189–96; as public sphere, 43; sociology of, 34–35, 43; and televising of trials, 122–24. *See also* journalists; *and names of individual newspapers*

Menendez brothers, case of, 184

"Mike Tyson" case. *See* Tyson, Mike, case of

Milken, Michael, 9, 254, 283n26

Miller, Antoine, 269

Minda, Gary, 119–20, 260

Minichello, Arthur, 93

Modisett, Jeffrey, 121

Mondello, Keith, 67, 128, 147, 150, 268

Moore, Colin, 50

Moor, Neal, 178

Morrison, Toni, 14

Murphy, Stephen, 67–68, 80, 92, 109, 128, 147–50, 268

Murray, Cecil, 229

Mydans, Seth, 188, 206–7

National Organization of Women, 211

Nelson, Jill, 14

"New Bedford" case, 19–21, 263

New York Police Department: and Diallo case, 4, 15; and Louima case, 129

New York Post: coverage of "Central Park jogger" case in, 39; coverage of high-profile crimes in, 11

New York Times: coverage of "Bensonhurst" case in, 62–63, 65–67, 71, 82, 88–89, 148; coverage of "Central Park jogger" case in, 39, 45, 55–56, 69, 76, 125, 141; coverage of high-profile crimes in, 11, 18, 21, 23, 110, 272–73; coverage of rape cases in, 31–32; coverage of Simpson case in, 179, 205–7; coverage of Smith case in, 188; coverage of Tyson case in, 190

Newsday (New York): coverage of "Bensonhurst" case in, 64, 95; coverage of "Central Park jogger" case in, 39
Newton, Jim, 179, 188

objectivity: and high-profile crimes, 25, 116, 160–61, 185–89; of the media, 37–38, 64, 80, 174–75, 189, 195, 260–64
Oh, Angela, 239–40
"O. J. Simpson" case. *See* Simpson, O. J., case of
Omnibus Crime Bill, 10
Owens, Thaddeus, 120, 148

Palm Beach Post (Florida): coverage of high-profile crimes in, 23
partialization: in "Central Park jogger" case, 143–46; of high-profile crimes, 12–15, 25, 214–15; in legal cases, 13–15; in the media, 189–96, 262–64; in Simpson case, 246–47
Perkins, William, 43–45, 53, 59
Perry, Edmund, 35
Pinckney, Alphonse, 276
Pinderhughes, Howard, 90–92, 98
police brutality: and blame, 15–16; in King case, 117, 152, 155, 230, 232; and protest, 211
Powell, Laurence M., 153, 268
protests: and police brutality, 211; and social issues, 213–14, 244
provoking assaults. *See* high-profile crimes
public reactions: to high-profile crimes, 9–10, 68–69, 210–15; to Simpson case, 212, 215–16, 232–39; to Tyson case, 217–27

race: and "Bensonhurst" case, 62–66; and Bryant case, 253; and "Central Park jogger" case, 33–34, 46–48, 76–77; and crime, in New York City, 35–36, 45; and gender, 14, 187, 196, 254; and high-profile crimes, 4–5, 182–83, 229, 263; of journalists, 202–4; and Simpson case, 13, 183, 229, 242–43; and Tyson case, 193–94, 219–25, 227, 230–31
rape: and blame, 16, 19–20, 101–2; in "Central Park jogger" case, 47–52; media coverage of, 31–34, 187–88, 262; and race, 182–83; and Smith case, 227–28. *See also* date rape; women, violence against
Ravo, Nick, 82, 88
Reel, Bill, 48
"Reginald Denny" case. *See* Denny, Reginald, case of
Reiner, Ira, 152–53
relativism: in journalism, 37–38, 64, 80, 160–61, 185–89
Reyes, Mathias, 29, 241, 284n1
Ricciardi, Michael, 268
Richardson, Kevin, 267
Riordan, Richard, 5
riots: and "Bensonhurst" case, 105–6, 108; in Crown Heights (1991), 4; in Los Angeles (1992), 5, 151, 153
Rivera, Peter, 141, 267
Roberts, Sam, 76
"Rodney King" case. *See* King, Rodney, case of
Rosen, Jay, 174–75, 189–90, 262
Rosenbaum, Yankel, 4

Sachar, Emily, 32
Salaam, Sharone, 128
Salaam, Yusef, 137–38, 267
Sanday, Peggy Reeves, 276
Santana, Raymond, 141, 267
Schatzman, Dennis, 199–200, 203–4
Scheck, Barry, 18, 271
Schoenfeld, David, 253
Schudson, Michael, 175
"Scottsboro Boys" case, 50–51